Signing the Body

The first major scholarly investigation into the rich history of the marked body in the early modern period, this interdisciplinary study examines multiple forms, uses, and meanings of corporeal inscription and impression in France and the French Atlantic colonies from the late sixteenth through early eighteenth centuries. Placing into dialogue a broad range of textual and visual sources drawn from areas as diverse as demonology, jurisprudence, mysticism, medicine, pilgrimage, commerce, travel, and colonial conquest that have formerly been examined largely in isolation, Katherine Dauge-Roth demonstrates that emerging theories and practices of signing the body must be understood in relationship to each other and to the development of other material marking practices that rose to prominence in the early modern period. While each chapter brings to light the particular histories and meanings of a distinct set of cutaneous marks—devil's marks on witches, demon's marks upon the possessed, devotional wounds, Amerindian and Holy Land pilgrim tattoos, and criminal brands—each also reveals connections between these various types of stigmata, links that were obvious to the early modern thinkers who theorized and deployed them. Moreover, the five chapters bring to the fore ways in which corporeal marking of all kinds interacted dynamically with practices of writing on, imprinting, and engraving paper, parchment, fabric, and metal that flourished in the period, together signaling important changes taking place in early modern society. Examining the marked body as a material object replete with varied meanings and uses, *Signing the Body: Marks on Skin in Early Modern France* shows how the skin itself became the register of the profound cultural and social transformations that characterized this era.

Katherine Dauge-Roth is Associate Professor of Romance Languages and Literatures at Bowdoin College.

This brilliant and gracefully written study weaves an eclectic and original corpus of primary sources into a compelling argument about the cultural implications of body marking in France and its colonies during the early modern period. In addition to being understood as magical signs, devotional gestures or material by-products of the power of the imagination, body marks also served as a powerful means of self-fashioning, and as signs of identification and authoritative control. The book is a must read for anyone interested in how the ancient practice of body marking became transformed into a product of the modern state.

—Allison Stedman, Professor of French,
University of North Carolina, Charlotte

Whole worlds of meaning were legible in the marks written by God and man, nature and the cosmos, on the delicate surface that clothed, however porously, the bodies of Renaissance men and women. Wounds of many different provenances; tattoos on pilgrims from the holy land, on prisoners and on the native peoples across the globe; birthmarks of various colors and shapes spoke to matters of deep cultural exigency. In this book Katherine Dauge-Roth constitutes, explores and interprets beautifully a whole lost archive of writing on the body.

—Thomas W. Laqueur, Helen Fawcett Distinguished Professor
Emeritus of History, University of California, Berkeley

Signing the Body reveals how cutaneous marks were deeply embedded in early modern European culture. In this abundantly researched work, Dauge-Roth examines demonic marks and sacred stigmata, the branding of criminals, Amerindian tattooing, and the Jerusalem tattoos traditionally received by Christian pilgrims. These diverse dermal practices are united, Dauge-Roth argues, by the desire to make the human body a stable site of signification in an age of cultural upheaval and physical mobility. *Signing the Body* reveals the ubiquity of body marking in early modern Europe, confirming the relatively familiar status of European tattooing practices once thought extraordinary.

—Craig Koslofsky, Professor of History and Germanic Languages
and Literatures, University of Illinois at Urbana-Champaign

Signing the Body

Marks on Skin in Early Modern France

Katherine Dauge-Roth

Routledge
Taylor & Francis Group

LONDON AND NEW YORK

First published 2020
by Routledge
2 Park Square, Milton Park, Abingdon, Oxon OX14 4RN

and by Routledge
52 Vanderbilt Avenue, New York, NY 10017

Routledge is an imprint of the Taylor & Francis Group, an informa business

British Library Cataloguing-in-Publication Data
A catalogue record for this book is available from the British Library

Library of Congress Cataloging-in-Publication Data
A catalog record has been requested for this book

ISBN: 978-0-754-65772-9 (hbk)
ISBN: 978-0-429-46603-8 (ebk)

Typeset in Sabon
by Integra Software Services Pvt. Ltd.

Contents

Figures

Acknowledgments

This book has been a long time in the making. My scholarly self has been nourished and sustained over the many years of this project by the support and guidance of many wonderful colleagues whom I am fortunate to call friends. Catherine Brown and Domna Stanton first cultivated my love of early literature and culture and my interest in the premodern body. As this book took shape, I benefitted immensely from the warm collegiality and dynamic spirit of scholarly exchange that characterize the Society for Interdisciplinary French Seventeenth-Century Studies. I thank my fellow *dix-septièmistes* for their engaged and insightful responses to my work, which have enriched it in important ways. Among many cherished colleagues, I am especially grateful to Francis Assaf, Faith Beasley, Jean-Vincent Blanchard, Juliette Cherbuliez, Ana Conboy, Didier Course, Mark DeVitis, Perry Gethner, Claire Goldstein, Bernadette Höfer, Katharine Ibbett, Ellen McClure, Sara Melzer, Jeffrey Peters, Christophe Schuwey, Allison Stedman, Deborah Steinberger, Micah True, Holly Tucker, and Rebecca Wilkin for their encouragements and suggestions. Craig Koslofsky, whose current work on early modern skin I encountered as I was finishing this book, has already become a precious interlocutor and treasured collaborator. Closer to home, fellow early modernists and dear friends Kirk Read and Rose Pruiksma generously read and discussed early versions of several pieces of this manuscript with great intelligence and benevolence. I am deeply grateful to Abby Zanger, whose enthusiasm for the project from its early days, careful reading of the entire manuscript in its final stages, and brilliant advice throughout the revision process have been vital to the completion of this book.

I am incredibly fortunate at Bowdoin to be surrounded by generous and inspiring colleagues from across the disciplines, too many to name, whose interest in my work and encouragement have been invaluable. I extend special thanks to my colleagues in Sills Hall and in the Department of Romance Languages and Literatures, and to the marvelous members of the Bowdoin Medieval and Early Modern Studies Colloquium for their helpful suggestions, good humor, and intellectual complicity. For their support and friendship over the many years of researching and writing this book,

I thank Mark Battle, Thomas Baumgarte, Meryem Belkaïd, Charlotte Daniels, Chuck Dorn, Davida Gavioli, Jennifer Clarke Kosak, Arielle Saiber, Karen Topp, Bill VanderWolk, Krista Van Vleet, and Tricia Welsch. Many thanks go as well to my talented students whose terrific intelligence, curiosity, and enthusiasm fuel my own.

To the friends and family near and far who have contributed to this book's completion in more ways than they know, and kept me laughing along the way, I owe endless gratitude. In addition to those already named above, beloved friends Sylvia Babey, Sylvain Babey, Rachel Bennett, Mark Benson, Tim Blair, Olivier Blanc, Renée Blanchard Culbertson, Ruth Bouchard Klein, Marta Caraion, Kate Dempsey, Susie Dorn, Melissa Hayes Albert, Artie Greenspan, Christiane Guillois, Mike Henning, Katie Jewett, Lawrence Kovacs, Kathy Lauten, Michele Lettiere, Sarah Lombardi, Camille Parrish, Laurent Schlittler, Kristin Seymour, and Kathy Thorson have sustained me and graced my life with their presence. Many thanks go too to friends from the Center for Teaching and Learning and the Unitarian Universalist Church of Brunswick for their warmth and community. I give heartfelt thanks to my loving family on both sides of the Atlantic, who has accompanied me in this project for so long with interest, compassion, and encouragement. Special thanks for their love and support go to my brothers Andrew and George Roth, their partners Francesca Basilico and Tamar Halpern, my uncle Franklin Roth, my sister and brother-in-law Béatrice Dauge Kaufmann and Daniel Kaufmann, and my second parents, Marion and Michel Dauge. I am forever grateful to my parents, George and Shirley Roth, whose constant support and unfailing love have carried me always.

Finally, my deepest gratitude goes to the three amazing people with whom I am blessed to share my life. My son Aymeric, whose love, caring, and joy brighten each and every day, has never known a time when I have not been researching and writing this book. I will never forget his observation made at an early age to his good friend Chloe: "Mamas work more than Papas," he said to her earnestly, and surely he felt that was true. My daughter Claire, whose extraordinary spirit, intelligence, and all out engagement with life inspire me always, grew into an adult as this book took shape. Her faith in me, advice, and encouragement have mattered more than she could ever know. She will be pleased that her often-repeated proclamation of "just finish it!" has finally been heeded. My husband, Alexandre, patient listener and confidant, steadfast companion, and cherished accomplice in all things, has tirelessly supported me in countless ways throughout the many years of this project. To him I give my immense thanks, deep admiration, and enduring love. This book is dedicated to them.

* * *

Bowdoin College has generously supported my research at home and abroad toward the completion of this project with several research and publication grants, for which I am deeply grateful.

The task of locating the images and obtaining the many photographic reproductions that fill the pages of this book was no small undertaking, and I am indebted to many for their help. Regarding the portrait of the unknown pilgrim that graces this book's cover and many of its pages, I have many people to thank. I am grateful to Betsy Wieseman, Curator of Dutch Painting at the National Gallery in London, who first brought the portrait's existence to my attention, and to Susan Blakney, Chief Conservator at West Lake Conservators, Ltd., who beautifully restored the painting, for generously sharing her own research on the portrait and for her invaluable help contacting the portrait's owner and securing photographs. I am deeply indebted to the painting's owner, who wishes to remain anonymous, for allowing me to have the portrait photographed by the talented Andy Olenick and to both of them for their kind permission to publish his photographs. I am also grateful to Jessica Marten, Curator at the Memorial Art Gallery of the University of Rochester, for her generous assistance locating a photographer up to the task. For his insightful counsel and extensive research regarding the composition and possible provenance of the painting, I thank art historian Mark DeVitis. Thanks go too to Cécile Bosman, Curator of Maritime Art at the Het Scheepvaartmuseum in Amsterdam, for her opinion regarding the ship in the background. Finally, I thank Denis Augier, Cécile Barrois, Lisa DeBoer, Rose Pruiksma, and Susan Wegner who also provided helpful suggestions for the portrait's identification and interpretation.

For alerting me to the existence of the extant fleur-de-lis branding iron in his collection (now housed at the Acadian Museum of the University of Moncton, New Brunswick, Canada) and for generously sharing his photographs and research regarding the iron, I thank Ghislain Savoie. I am also grateful to Jean-Pierre Hardy, former director of New France History and Archaeology at the Canadian Museum of Civilizations, for his expert opinion on this extraordinary artifact.

Photographer Denis Griggs provided his artistic skill in photographing the 1616 coin that appears here. Yu Watanabe generously provided a high resolution scan of a rare portrait of Jeanne des Anges from his private collection. For help locating or reproducing several other images throughout this book, my gratitude also goes to Jennifer Edwards, James Goodfriend, Carmen Greenlee, Juli Haugen, Joachim Homann, Bernard LeBlanc, Jessica Marten, as well as to the many photographers and librarians at academic institutions both in the United States and in Europe whose attention and efficiency helped me bring these images to light.

For their kind assistance with translations, I thank Barbara Weiden Boyd, Marion Dauge, Jennifer Clarke Kosak, Erika Nickerson, Arielle Saiber, Bryn Savage, and Samatha Waxman.

Finally, many thanks go to Erika Gaffney, who first believed in this project, and to Michelle Salyga, Tim Swenarton, Bryony Reece, Sasikumar Selvaraj, and the rest of the editorial team who saw it through to publication.

Earlier versions of Chapter 5 appeared as "Textual Performance: Imprinting the Criminal Body," in *Intersections*, edited by Faith Beasley and Kathryn Wine (Tubingen: Gunter Narr, 2005), 126–42 and "Marquage du corps et modernité: La flétrissure des condamnés aux XVIIe et XVIIIe siècles en France," in *Écritures du corps. Nouvelles perspectives*, edited by Pierre Zoberman, Anne Tomiche, and William J. Spurlin (Paris: Classiques Garnier, 2013), 17–30. Material from these essays is used here with kind permission.

Introduction

The impressionable body

In 1647, French Jesuit Théophile Raynaud (1583–1663) published a voluminous four hundred and fifty-three-page treatise entirely devoted to marks on skin.[1] Raynaud investigated Old and New Testament references to corporeal marking, discussing the mark of Cain, the Hebrew tradition of circumcision, and the marks of Christ claimed by Saint Paul. He devoted extensive treatment to the sacred stigmata of Christian martyrs and saints across time. Examining human-made marks, he discussed physical signs of nobility, brands, and tattoos on slaves and criminals; false birthmarks worn by con men; and marks made on the body in healing and in mourning. He critiqued what he referred to wholesale as the "superstitious stigmata of Jews, pagans, heretics, and the Antichrist," investigating cutaneous marks ranging from magical characters drawn upon the skin to the infamous mark of the beast.[2] Intervening in contemporary debates over marks made by the devil and his demons upon their followers, he analyzed such supernatural signs at length. Indeed, as highlighted by Raynaud's descriptive title, *De Stigmatismo, Sacro et Profano, Divino, Humano, Dæmoniaco*, his work set out to examine diverse signs "imprinted on the human body from the outside with force" by powers both natural and supernatural, documenting a wide range of marks inscribed, impressed, tattooed, branded, and cut into the skin.[3] Raynaud's text, the first of its kind, brought together a myriad of cutaneous marks and their meanings, creating a vast catalogue of signs on skin.

The appearance in the mid-seventeenth century of this major treatise on *stigmata*, defined by Raynaud as all "visible and truly physical marks" made upon the body, attests to the importance early modern thinkers attributed to corporeal marks and their theorization.[4] Raynaud's history of *stigmata* was by no means an isolated scholarly endeavor. It reflected a wide interest in cutaneous marks and their meanings both among his learned contemporaries and in popular belief and practice. Medical, astrological, theological, demonological, literary, and judicial texts of the early modern period all attest to the proliferation of marks on skin, created, theorized, and deployed in realms as diverse as occult magic, criminal jurisprudence, devotional practice, and colonial conquest. The same period that witnessed the rise of the pilgrim tattoo also experienced an unprecedented increase in the appearance of divinely inspired stigmatic wounds. The same judicial system that, at the height of the witch trials, theorized and gave credence to the devil's mark upon witches as a sign of proof also restored and reconfigured the ancient Roman rite of marking slaves, soldiers, and criminals. Cutaneous signs not only adorned the bodies of the native peoples whom early modern European colonists encountered in the Americas but also circulated back home on the bodies of pilgrims, witches, lovers, convicts, magicians, and nuns. From devil's marks, divine stigmata, and criminal brands, to the tattoos and scarifications of pilgrims, soldiers, and women religious, early modern Europe witnessed a remarkable multiplication and convergence of signs impressed upon the skin. It is this extraordinary profusion of cutaneous signs and the careful attention early moderns paid to them that have inspired this study.

While scholars of early modern Europe have long referred to discourses of authority as being metaphorically "inscribed" or "imprinted" upon the body, until recently, little notice had been paid to the literal, material marking of the body in this period.[5] Over the last three decades, historians, art historians, folklorists, anthropologists, and literary scholars have begun to document past practices of corporeal marking in Europe and the Atlantic world, questioning long-standing assumptions about the history and meanings of the cutaneous sign.[6] The skin itself has come to the fore as a meaningful object of study across time and disciplines, inspiring scholarship, conferences, exhibitions, and collective projects.[7] Together, these investigations have begun to build a more sophisticated understanding of the cultural history of skin and of various body marking practices and their particular meanings in the West. *Signing the Body: Marks on Skin in Early Modern France* draws on and extends this body of exciting work by bringing together in a single study diverse practices and beliefs about the cutaneous mark in the early modern period as attested in a number of discourses and contexts. In so doing, it follows the lead of early modern theoreticians of the corporeal mark, who saw intimate connections between the many types of body marking so prevalent in their time. As Raynaud's wide-ranging treatment of *stigmata* suggests, sixteenth- and seventeenth-century writers who set out to examine one kind of corporeal mark consistently made comparisons with several other types of cutaneous signs. Early modern demonologists could not write about the devil's mark without evoking its opposites and models, God's mark of baptism on Christians and divine stigmata. Nor could they avoid raising the question of the birthmark, with which the devil's mark was often confused, or refrain from comparing the devil's impression of a sign upon his followers to the ancient branding of slaves.[8] Skeptics who criticized the supernatural scars worn by Loudun prioress Jeanne des Anges (1605–1665) compared them to alchemical inscriptions made on the skin as well as to Amerindian, pilgrim, and lovers' tattoos.[9] Recollet missionary Gabriel Sagard-Théodat (†1636) referenced Holy Land pilgrim tattooing in his treatment of body ornamentation among the indigenous peoples he encountered in the territories that the French would call New France.[10] As will become obvious throughout the readings offered in this book, writers frequently digressed from one form of marking to another or used the discussion of one kind of marking to support their arguments about another, making links across genres, across time, and across continents. These have been the threads that I have followed throughout my work and that I weave together here.

Stigmata, marks, characters, and signs

Diverse forms of corporeal marking shared a common vocabulary in the early modern period, a semantic intimacy that further testifies to the close relationships early moderns saw between different types of marks on skin. These versatile terms both point to inheritances from the past and bear witness to sixteenth- and seventeenth-century innovations. They touch at once the supernatural and the natural, emanating from domains as diverse as medicine, magic, jurisprudence, astrology, theology, politics, physiognomy, literature, demonology, history, and commerce. Raynaud's chosen word, *stigmata*, carried multiple meanings. Today we know *stigmata* as denoting the five corporeal marks made on God's elect in imitation of Christ's crucifixion wounds. While period dictionaries foreground this usage for *stigmates* introduced by the Franciscans whose thirteenth-century founder had famously born such marks, for Raynaud and his contemporaries the term had far greater semantic reach.[11] Early modern thinkers who wrote about *stigmata* gave this Latin name to all discernable traces upon the skin, whether supernatural or natural, distinctive or punitive, chosen or imposed. *Stigmata* is the plural of *stigma*, a word etymologically and historically linked to acts of impression and puncturing, as Raynaud underlines: "There is a Greek name for stigma [*stigmatis*], denoting an impressed mark [*notam*], or indeed a puncture [*punctus*]."[12] *Stigma*, a transliteration from the Greek word στίγμα meaning a "mark made by a pointed instrument, brand," in turn derives from the Greek στίζειν [stizein], meaning to prick or to puncture.[13] *Stigmata*, then, which referred in the early modern period to marking practices and phenomena both ancient and modern, had its origins in the penetration of the skin. It signified as much marks of circumcision, scars, brands, and tattoos as it did the bleeding wounds that appeared on the bodies of saints, as much marks left by disease, the knife, the iron, or the planets as it did God- or devil-made signs upon the skin.[14]

Other key words used widely in the period to reference cutaneous impressions—"marks," "characters," and "signs"—earned equally extensive and multivalent definitions in period dictionaries.[15] Contemporary usage of these terms exposes the rich associations early moderns made between various kinds of corporeal marking as well as between marks on skin and other prevalent types of impression and engraving performed on paper, metal, clothing, and commercial goods. As Antoine Furetière's

(1619–1688) lengthy entries for the noun *marque* and the verb *marquer* in his 1690 *Dictionnaire universel* confirm, a "mark" could refer just as easily to the devil's impression upon a witch's skin, God's sign upon his faithful, the brand upon the skin of a fugitive, or a soldier's battle scar as it could to a nobleman's coat of arms, the insignia with which artisans identified their work or merchants their cargo.[16] Furetière defined a *caractère* not only as a "certain figure traced on paper, on bronze, on marble, or on other materials with the quill, burin, scissors, or other instruments, to signify or to indicate something" but also as a birthmark, a sign God or the devil made upon his faithful, and a mark inscribed on the foreheads of slaves among the ancients.[17] The other major dictionary of the period, the *Dictionnaire de l'Académie française* (1694), noted that while printers and metal smiths had their "characters," so too did magicians, astrologers, Christians, noblemen, priests, countries, and criminals. All wore distinctive marks that identified them and their unique characteristics: "that distinguish so much one thing from another that it can be easily recognized."[18] Similarly, for the dictionary authors of the seventeenth century, a *signe* meant as much a birthmark —"certain marks or natural blemishes one has on the body. *He has a sign on the face, a sign on the hand*"—as it did an authenticating seal or signature, or a symbol displayed to identify a shop—"ivy, or a cabbage on the door of a house, is the *sign* of a cabaret."[19] "A child that had been lost for a long time was recognized by a *sign* that he had on his thigh," just as God's chosen would be recognized at the Apocalypse by "the *signs* on their foreheads."[20]

As Karl Jaberg notes in his examination of the birthmark, such prolific words, whose semantic reach allows for easy navigation between worlds and systems, may even have provided inspiration through association, generating new beliefs and practices thanks to their linguistic proximity:

> Words endowed with a rich gamut of overtones like SIGNUM and some of its synonyms are particularly apt to mediate between the linguistic correlatives of physique and psyche, the rational and the irrational, the earthly and the otherworldly, since their own semantic ambit extends from the brand to the divine miracle. This heavy semantic load, in turn, tends to stir the imagination and to foster a zest for associations and thus contributes to the rise of novel forms of belief, exemplifying the incessant give-and-take that prevails in the relations between word and meaning.[21]

Not only, then, do the many meanings for these terms offered in the pages of seventeenth-century dictionaries testify to the diversity and interconnectedness of the marking practices they unite, but they may even have contributed to the development of new signs on skin or ways of conceiving of them, as thinkers drew inspiration from this rich network of intertwined associations.[22]

An impressionable surface

The skin, as the physical boundary between inside and outside, private and public, self and other, serves as a privileged surface for expressing identity and claiming control over one's body.[23] As the prevalence of skin as a trope in the work of many contemporary French theorists attests, the skin's liminal, in-between role makes it a highly charged space, fraught with meaning.[24] The act of marking the skin becomes, therefore, a powerful means for defining the body's interior, making identity visible, performing belonging, and asserting control. Early modern understandings of cutaneous signs were grounded in common notions of the human body as impressionable and of the skin as a ready surface for the literal inscription of signs by forces both natural and supernatural, signs that could speak truths about the body that bore them. Multiple inheritances fed this vision of the impressionable body. As Raynaud's treatment of both Hebrew and Christian sources testifies, religious traditions invested enormous power in the cutaneous mark to express devotion, to identify the faithful, and to condemn the damned. The "character" impressed by God through circumcision in Jewish tradition, on the body of Cain for protection during his wanderings, in baptism on the bodies of Christians claimed as God's own, or on the foreheads of the elect at the end of time, proved a powerful metaphor in the writings of the early Christian Church, frequently referenced by early modern theologians across Catholic and Protestant confessional lines.[25] French Jansenist Nicolas Fontaine (1625–1709) asserts in his 1691 *Dictionnaire chrétien*, citing Bishop Basil of Caesarea (329–379), that Christians should "always carry the idea of God imprinted like an indelible seal upon our heart," a seal that, according to the Church Fathers, "must be imprinted as on diamond, . . . so that it will always retain that which has been imprinted."[26] God protects (present tense): protects his faithful with the impression of his "seal," affirms Fontaine, referencing Pope Gregory I (ca. 540–604), just as

> [w]e place a seal on a letter so that it stays closed, and so that no one may be so bold as to open it. This is how . . . when the demon sees our hearts closed with a seal, he backs away, and doesn't have the courage to attempt entry.[27]

Indeed, early theologians conceived of the battle between the devil and God for each human life in terms of cutaneous marks. In the words of John Chrysostom (ca. 349–407), Christians were always "fearing that after tracing on their hearts these characters of life, [the demon] might come back to erase them, and engrave there other barbarous and deformed signs, that are nothing other than the characters of death."[28] In the spiritual realm, devotion, election, and damnation were made visible through metaphorical or material marking of the skin.

Medicine, too, saw the skin as a surface replete with signs, upon which disease or health was made manifest and through whose interpretation diagnosis could be reached. While Renaissance anatomists seem to have had little regard for the importance of the human skin, casting it as a surface that had to be gotten beyond to reveal more vital organs within, doctors examining the body from a physiological standpoint clearly placed faith in its signs in making determinations about their patients' well-being.[29] Complexion—an idea born of humoral theory but used more often in the later sixteenth century to mean the color, texture, condition, and temperature of the skin, as well as the marks upon it—was interpreted by the diagnosing physician as an indicator of physical and mental health or illness.[30] As Furetière explains in his definition of *signe*, in the case of sickness, the doctor read exterior signs to determine its nature and probable course: "In medicine we call symptoms the signs that make known the quality and the duration of an illness; diagnostic and prognostic signs."[31] Signs on the body's surface revealed hidden truths beneath, as French royal surgeon Ambroise Paré (ca. 1509–1590) underlines: "the sign is nothing more than a visible and manifest mark, which leads us to the knowledge of something obscure and hidden."[32] A surface of no small significance, the skin emitted signs that revealed otherwise unknowable bodily depths. At the same time, as the point of contact between the individual and the world, the skin became a privileged medium that betrayed the workings of forces both natural and supernatural.

Nowhere was the Renaissance vision of the body as impressionable and saturated with readable signs more apparent than in theories offered by the widely practiced divinatory sciences of physiognomy, chiromancy, metoposcopy, and moleoscopy.[33] While physiognomy was founded on analysis of physical features to determine character traits, chiromancy and metoposcopy examined the skin's markings on the hand and face respectively, and moleoscopy, as the name suggests, drew conclusions according to the placement of moles upon the body. Prevalent from the early sixteenth century but popularized by the 1586 publication of *De Humana Physiognonomia* by Italian natural philosopher Giambattista della Porta (1535–1615), physiognomy and its companion sciences were grounded in an astrological understanding of the human body as inscribed from birth with the signatures of the universe, as French cleric and occult philosopher Jean Belot explains in his 1640 treatise on chiromancy:

> It is a very certain thing that every human creature when born keeps imprinted in some part of the body the mark of the sign and planet governing the hour and moment that they were conceived and born; these marks are found in the parts of the body that correspond to the signs and the planets.[34]

Like medicine, whose astrological leanings were still strong in this period, physiognomy's interpretive systems saw the human body in intimate relationship to the cosmos, the microcosmic version of the vast macrocosm of the heavens. Belot writes,

There is such a great correspondence between celestial and elementary bodies that we could not emphasize it more. There is ... such an analogy between each of our human members and superior bodies, that there is not a member that is not ruled over by their influences.[35]

Given this understanding, in the words of German physician, theologian, and occult philosopher Heinrich Cornelius Agrippa von Nettesheim (1486–1583), "[e]verything therefore hath its character pressed upon it by its star for some peculiar effect, ... and these characters contain, and retain in them the peculiar natures, virtues, and roots of their stars."[36]

Signs inscribed on the body's surface thus formed a veritable constellation of meaning, as poignantly suggested by the engraving of moles on a woman's body published in English physiognomist Richard Saunders's (1613–1675) 1653 *Treatise of the Moles of the Body of Man and Woman*, whose presentation reminds the viewer of the starry heavens they reference (see Figure I.1).[37] Physiognomists provided detailed diagrams and explanations linking particular signs on the body to planetary influences, as Belot's famous chiromantic hand, teeming with text, shapes, and symbols, illustrates (see Figure I.2). For Belot, signs on skin formed a decipherable language: "We find in our hands in diverse places well-formed and very apparent letters which, according to the place where they are found are of great and admirable meanings."[38] Metoposcopy's founder, Italian mathematician-physician-astrologer Gerolamo Cardano (1501–1576) likewise considered a whole geometry of cutaneous signs in his analysis of the lines and marks of the human face, specifying that "[b]y lines we do not only mean long cuts, but also all kinds of marks, and different characters, like crosses, little circles, little bumps, raised discolorations, little stars, squares, triangles, capillary lines, and others of this nature," for which he provided visual examples, giving his readers a new figurative language with which to identify and interpret them (see Figure I.3).[39] Cardano filled over two hundred pages with model heads, differentiated by gender, mapping a diversity of lines and marks upon the forehead and providing a precise key to their interpretation according to planetary zones drawn on the face (see Figure I.4).[40] Lines in the forehead signified everything from courage to homicidal tendencies, from happiness in love to death by drowning. Similarly, birthmarks, or *naevi*, bode favorably or unfavorably for their bearers according to their perceived rarity, color, form, and placement on the skin: bad signs were generally irregular, while well-formed marks signaled good; marks appearing on the right side of the face were generally positive—signifying, among other things, intelligence, health, wealth, or successful marriages and births—while those on the left were negative—warning, for example, of sexual depravity, aggressive behavior, sickness, or calamitous events.[41] The parade of heads and hands typical of these popular metoposcopic and chiromantic treatises provided the reader with an extensive catalogue of body marks against which the outer traits of any

Figure I.1 Map of moles on a woman's body, Richard Saunders, *Treatise of the Moles of the Body of Man and Woman*, in *Physiognomie and Chiromancie, Metoposcopie*, 2nd ed. (London: Nathaniel Brook, 1671), following p. 330. Princeton University Library.

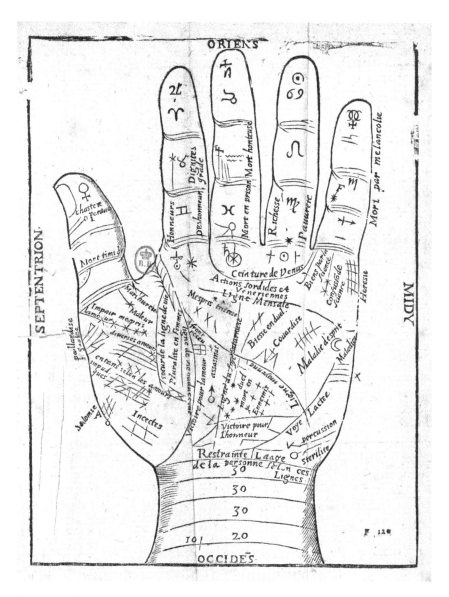

Figure I.2 Chiromantic hand, Jean Belot, *Traité de Physionomie*, in *Œuvres* (Rouen: Jacques Cailloüé, 1640), folded plate following p. 110. Bibliothèque Nationale de France.

Ceux qui font *Malins* par leur propre nature , denoncent toufiours du mal , comme font les *Charaɛteres de Saturne* , la *Lettre X* , les *petites Grilles* , & tout *Signe irregulier* , mal formé , & confus : fçavoir les *Cercles diuifez* , les *Signes Rompus* , *Non continus* , & *Empefchés* ; tous lefquels ne predifent iamais rien de bon , mais toufiours du mal : tels font les fuivants ;

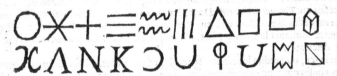

Mais ces Charaɛteres font *Bons* , lefquels gardent vne certaine efgalité , ainfi que font les *Cercles* , les *Eſtoilles* , les *Croix* , les *Lignes Paralleles* , les *Triangles* , les *Quadrangles* , les *Cubes* , & autres femblables.

Figure I.3 Cutaneous marks and their interpretation, Gerolamo Cardano, *La Metoposcopie* (Paris: Thomas Jolly, 1658), vii. Princeton University Library.

person could be compared and their inner moral character and destiny known.[42]

Casting the human body as imprinted by the forces of the universe, these influential divinatory sciences powerfully informed an early modern vision of the body as an impressionable entity whose exterior markings told stories about the person who bore them and about that individual's relationship to the universe. They contributed substantially to an understanding of marks on skin as powerful signifiers of identity, destiny, and authority, therein challenging the hierarchy established by period anatomists for whom the inside mattered most. Saunders argues this point in his treatise:

> Science, which is conversant about the knowledge of the humane body, ought not onely to be imployed about the intrinsecal parts, but rather to scrutinize the exteriour. From and by the extrinsecal parts of the body, we may know the natural fortitudes and debilities of the same; as also from thence we discern the substantial form and qualities thereof.[43]

As the chapters of this book reveal, Saunders's conviction regarding the importance of the body's exterior and the signs it carried was shared in the early modern period not only by physiognomists but also by ecclesiastics, physicians, demonologists, jurists, and laypeople, who saw the skin as a medium for inscription by various scribes, be they God, the devil, the

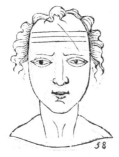

Cette conftitution denote vn homme de mœurs deprauées, foupçonneux, impudique, & qui pourra mourir fubitement.

Mais vne femme non apprehenfiue, toute-fois legere, & portée à la paillardife.

Il fera vaillant, & vindicatif, qui offenfera li-brement les autres, & qui fera luy-mefme blef-fé par le fer, ou par le feu.

Et la femme receura des playes de fon pro-pre mary, ou de fes parens.

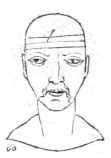

Ces lignes trauaillent l'homme de fievres ai-guës, lefquelles recidiueront autant de fois que ces lignes feront entrecoupées : toutefois il en échapera à caufe de la plus grande force des lignes droites.

Elles marquent auffi vne femme laborieufe, & prudente : mais fujette à maladies, & au flux de fang.

Ces lignes menacent l'homme de bleffures en la tefte, & s'il y a plufieurs petites lignes, il au-ra auffi plufieurs bleffures.

Et la femme receura vn coup en la tefte, où il y tombera deffus quelque chofe, dont elle fera bleffée.

C

Figure I.4 Metoposcopic heads, Gerolamo Cardano, *La Metoposcopie* (Paris: Thomas Jolly, 1658), 17. Princeton University Library.

tattoo artist, or the executioner. These forces left discernable traces of their passage that indicated something about their bearer's life, identifying them with a distinctive material sign. The so-called character—the legible mark imprinted upon the skin—thus revealed a great deal about the character, as we most often use the term today, of its bearer, an idea that traverses the diverse contexts examined across the pages of this study.

Any discussion of early modern ideas of the human body's "impressionability" would not be complete without considering further a question that occupied scientific discussion and debate well into the eighteenth century and beyond, crossing physiognomic, medical, philosophical, and religious discourses: the origins of the birthmark. Much discussed theories about the birthmark's etiology reinforced a vision of the fetal body as soft, highly impressionable, and intensely vulnerable to outside forces, influencing in important ways how early moderns understood and theorized corporeal marking more generally.[44] In addition to the planets and the stars, God and the devil did their handiwork on this soft body, shaping the fruit of a woman's womb to convey messages about sinful acts perpetrated and to provide signs predicting events to come. In his immensely popular *Histoires Prodigieuses* (1560), French writer, editor, and translator Pierre Boaistuau (ca. 1517–1566) delighted his readers with stories of countless so-called monsters, their births resulting from the deeds and dramas of the parents or communities to whom they belonged.[45] The famous, oft-reproduced "monster of Ravenna," with its bird's wings and talon, fish tail, and hermaphroditic sexual organs, sported textual and figurative markings as well: an epsilon and a cross on its chest and the figure of an eye on its knee (see Figure I.5).[46] God thus conveyed messages—in this case his displeasure with religious conflict—through a language of corporeal inscription.

While supernatural forces could imprint the fetus with signs, the centerpiece for the debate about corporeal impressionability was the pregnant woman's powerful imagination. Itself thought to be extraordinarily receptive to impression by outside images, a woman's imagination was believed capable of imprinting those images in turn upon the fetal body.[47] Early modern theoreticians of the birthmark conceived of the pregnant woman's body as a sort of print shop, where the imaginative faculty impressed particularly potent images collected in the expectant mother's mind upon the soft flesh of the fetus within her. As Benedictine monk and theologian Leonard Vair (ca. 1540–1603) explains,

> [If] a woman conceives of something in her mind, or if by setting her sights on all that she meets she puts something into her imagination, the exterior parts of the body of the child will most often represent and be marked by the thing in question. . . . Because the power and the nature of the imagination is so strong that as soon as the woman . . . contemplates a thing intensely, immediately it forges and constructs in her mind the resemblance of what she saw. It results that the child very often receives the shape of diverse things, and is in some places covered with marks, blemishes and warts that cannot be easily removed.[48]

Figure I.5 The Monster of Ravenna, Pierre Boaistuau, *Histoires Prodigieuses* (Paris: Vincent Sertenas, Jean Longis, and Robert Le Mangnier, 1560), fol. 172. Bayerische Staatsbibliotek, München, S nv/So (b) 417, urn:nbn:de:bvb:12-bsb11347300-8.

Popular belief that birthmarks were the product of unsatisfied maternal cravings, or *envies*, and thus the outward sign of the mother's inward longings, was widespread.[49] Though, as Paré describes, birthmarks took on "diverse forms," most were "named according to the figures they represent[ed], like cherries, strawberries, blackberries, figs, grapes, melons, apricots, and others," fruits pregnant women apparently craved.[50] During the 1609-1611 Aix-en-Provence witch trial of priest Louys Gaufridy, a miller examined by doctor Jacques Fontaine (†1621?) invoked this commonly accepted idea to explain his unusual birthmark and thus avoid prosecution as a witch:

> It happened while pursuing the trial of Gaufridy that we examined a miller from Saint Maximin named Germanon, on whose body, on the left shoulder, we found a large black mark. . . . He . . . told us that it was the image of a pig's liver that his mother had desired to eat while she was carrying him in her womb.[51]

French physician-poet Claude Quillet (1602–1661) warns pregnant women to exercise caution so as not to allow such "hideous and deformed objects" imprint their minds and be engraved upon their unborn children, explaining: "as nature's work advances, the spirits, descending from the brain, mix with the prolific essence in the uterus and penetrate it in all its parts. They engrave there through an invincible strength the same images with which they were struck."[52] Popular lore even recommended that a pregnant woman startled by an object or taken with a sudden craving touch herself in a hidden place so that any resulting birthmark would appear there on her child, rather than on the face or another more visible place.[53]

The extraordinary power of the feminine imagination and the impressionability of the soft fetal body served as touchstones in the early modern period for discussion of the vulnerability of all human bodies to imprinting and engraving by exterior forces. When doctors, theologians, and demonologists discussed other kinds of corporeal marking, they frequently referenced the potency of a woman's imagination to mark the fetus. For example, in debates about both devil's marks on witches and divine stigmata on saints, supporters as well as skeptics consistently cited the feminine imagination's natural ability to produce marks either to refute or to bolster belief in those signs' validity as supernatural. French demonologist and judge Pierre de Lancre (1553–1631) opened his discussion of devil's marks by denouncing detractors who, citing medical authorities, likened the marks found on witches to the natural marks imprinted during pregnancy.[54] Italian philosopher Pietro Pomponazzi (1462–1525) cited the power of the pregnant woman's imagination to argue that natural causes were behind Saint Francis of Assisi's thirteenth-century stigmata, a product of the imagination:

> Because if a woman at the moment of conception can, through the application of her imagination, engender a fetus truly marked by the image that she

conceives of, if a pregnant woman can, by imagining for example a pomegranate, give her child the marks of a pomegranate, if the image of leprosy brings on leprosy, why then could not the heart and the other members not receive similar marks? Certainly, this does not seem any less reasonable.[55]

When writers call upon the notion of fetal marking by the maternal imagination to theorize other types of corporeal marking upon the skin of adults, they reveal that impressionability was not unique to that still developing body but was shared by the skin of fully formed adults, seen as vulnerable to impression by powerful forces both within and without.

From the devil's mark to the judicial brand

This book begins with an examination of the devil's mark, the material sign purportedly impressed upon a witch's skin by Satan himself, which came to light during the witch trials that raged throughout Europe from the late fifteenth through seventeenth centuries. Chapter 1, "Seals of Satan: demonologists and the devil's mark," investigates the diverse models that spurred the invention and theoretical elaboration of this physical mark upon the witch's body in the late sixteenth century. Cast as an imitation and inversion of the divine mark placed on Christians in baptism, the devil's mark earned judicial value in France as material proof of its bearer's guilty relationship with the devil. My investigation exposes the origins and theoretical underpinnings of the devil's mark and recasts it as part of a wider culture of marking as well as a response to modern jurisprudence that placed increasing value on material proof and empirical authentication.

My reading of the devil's mark lays the groundwork for the analysis of another new kind of corporeal mark created in the highly gendered context of the infamous demonic possession cases of the seventeenth century that took place in convents at Loudun (1632–1637), Louviers (1643–1647), and Auxonne (1658–1663). Here, possessing demons engraved figurative and epigraphic signs on the skin of demoniacs or wrote them in blood on cloths that issued forth from the women's mouths. In Chapter 2, "Demonic marks, divine stigmata: the female body inscribed," I argue that the innovative replacement of demons' transient "signs of departure" by corporeal marks relied on accepted notions of female impressionability, the theorization of the devil's mark, and the rising incidence of stigmatic phenomena in the period. More importantly, I show that not only did the nuns' marked bodies, literally construed as texts, serve purposes of Catholic propaganda, but that these women's epigraphic wounds must also be understood as an enterprise of self-fashioning undertaken by demoniacs who wished to recast themselves as *dévotes*. Highly conscious of the signifying potential of their corporeal marks, these nuns used self-inscription both during and following their possession experiences to reclaim some degree of control over their bodies and perform their reinscription into the realm of the sacred.

Having explored corporeal marking practices belonging to demonological and spiritual realms that are rather foreign to our modern sensibilities, I turn in Chapters 3 and 4 to a mark with which we more closely identify today, the tattoo. These two chapters pair the narratives of Western-going explorers, missionaries, and colonists with those of Eastern-going Holy Land pilgrims to uncover the methods and meanings behind the early modern tattoo. In Chapter 3, "The Amerindian tattoo: signs of identity in New France," I examine the textual and visual representations made by the French of the body marking practices they witnessed among the indigenous peoples of the Americas, exposing a range of responses characteristic of a nation that, at least to a greater degree than other European colonizing powers, sought to understand and assimilate the people among whom they lived. Next, I reveal that though seventeenth-century writers often cast tattooing as a "savage" art and associated it with their New World others, when they sought to explain Amerindian practices to their French reader they compared them to both ancient and contemporary European marking practices, emphasizing similarity rather than difference. Finally, I examine how some colonists chose to adopt Amerindian tattooing techniques to express new hybrid identities for themselves as inhabitants of New France. In Chapter 4, "Arms of Jerusalem: the European pilgrim tattoo," I return to the Old World and follow the trail of the Holy Land tattoo, which circulated on the bodies of European pilgrims from the last years of the sixteenth century forward. I show how these tattoos served as a memorial to their pilgrimage, a safeguard for their passage home, a devotional gesture, and a powerful means of self-fashioning.

The criminal body is the focus of Chapter 5, "Stigma and state control: branding the deviant body." In this final chapter I consider how, in an age before fingerprinting, photographs, and computerized records, early modern French authorities solved the problem of identifying repeat criminal offenders by branding them on the shoulder with a hot iron. I examine how state officials reinvented the brand in the sixteenth century, which first took the form of the fleur-de-lis—the symbol *par excellence* of royal authority—and later that of crime- or sentence-specific letters, casting it as a useful administrative imprint rather than a punishment in and of itself. Circulating on the convict's body like a printed text, the mark declared his past transgression and rendered his social reinsertion difficult. Like the brands, seals, and marks placed on texts and goods during the period, the brands imprinted on the bodies of convicts served as signs of identification and authoritative control, declaring the King's hold over all members of the social body. In this chapter, I argue that rather than representing a practice of unenlightened times, judicial branding must be understood as a product of the modern state, closely related to the proliferation of marking practices in the print and commercial realms and of new mechanisms of state control.

The criminal brand—alongside magical signs, devil's marks, demonic scars, stigmata, and tattoos—participated in a culture where marks proliferated and, like them, signs made upon the body communicated identity, belonging, authority, and truth.

Final notes

As its title and these chapter summaries suggest, this book adopts as its center early modern France and its Atlantic colonies, the areas from which I have drawn the majority of my sources and in which I am most at home as a scholar. Nonetheless, while my study remains mindful of specificities unique to the French context, the conclusions I draw about acts of signing the body in France are in most cases translatable to other geographical areas of Europe and even across Catholic-Protestant confessional lines. How particular or widespread a theory or practice was varies among the different kinds of body marking I examine. Texts and ideas circulated widely during the early modern period, and in many cases, it is possible to trace the progression of a concept from one area or writer to another; such was the rich cross-fertilization and exchange characteristic of this print-filled time. In theorizing body marking, early modern intellectuals themselves systematically reached beyond ever-shifting frontiers, relying on the work of scholars from across disciplines, nations, and confessions. Moreover, common popular beliefs and marking practices prevalent in France frequently found their echoes in other countries, and vice-versa, across Europe. French artists and writers who documented their travels in the Americas shared numerous observations and experiences in common with Englishmen who testified to their own, as did pilgrims of diverse European origins, both Catholic and Protestant, who traveled to Jerusalem. State-sanctioned criminal branding was practiced widely across Europe, the brand taking on diverse shapes according to the political power that made it. So, while this book focuses primarily on early modern France, I consider throughout pertinent works and images produced both inside and outside of its territories and draw on scholarship whose interests traverse early modern Europe and the Atlantic World. It is my hope that the resonances and implications of my investigations here extend quite naturally beyond France's frontiers, just as the theorization and development of corporeal marking in early modern France participated in much wider discussions and phenomena happening across Europe and in its colonies.

No treatment of body marking in the early modern period could ever cast its net wide enough to capture all the varied contexts, uses, and meanings of marks on skin in their full nuanced complexity. As with any project, I have had to limit the scope of my investigation. Following the seventeenth-century example of Théophile Raynaud, I have focused on instances of signing the body that were generally not considered to be the product of natural forces within the body but instead were imposed—or believed to be—from without, made either through supernatural influence or by human hands. Several kinds of marks on skin have not found their place within the covers of this book, though they resonate in highly interesting ways with the types of marking I do examine. While I have given brief consideration in this introduction to birthmarks because their theorization provides useful background for the ways in which early moderns thought about body marking more generally, I have not devoted an entire chapter to their study. Nor have I discussed medical conditions such as leprosy or syphilis, whose cutaneous manifestations were highly prevalent and widely represented in the literature of the period. Ceremonial inscriptions on the skin, practiced by learned adepts of natural magic, as well as more popular magical rites of signing the body, do not receive full treatment here, nor do popular healing techniques that involved incision or the drawing of signs upon the skin. I have not dealt with scars that serve as memorials to past disease, accident, or combat and tell stories about the individuals who bear them. My analysis of branding does not include full examination of corporeal marking in the context of the Atlantic slave trade, as historians Katrina Keefer and Craig Koslofsky are currently exploring this important question in depth.[56] Cosmetic markings such as *mouches*—imitation birthmarks fashioned of black taffeta, placed upon the face and upper body to hide blemishes or to enhance the whiteness of the complexion—also exceed the scope of this book.[57] All of these signs on skin would prove important and fascinating extensions of my work here, and it is my hope that others, whose interest I may have "piqued," will close the gaps and enrich scholarship on the marked body further in the years to come.

In the "Argumentum" of his lengthy treatise on stigmata, Raynaud says about his own ambitious choice of topic that "the variety of these corporeal and visible stigmata, which we have undertaken to explain in this treatise, is altogether huge."[58] Raynaud's words remain true for the present study. My own research has led me to examine a vast and varied corpus and to assemble for analysis primary sources and scholarly work on corporeal marking from highly diverse areas. The breadth of my topic and its interdisciplinary nature has made my work both wonderfully exciting and intensely challenging. Yet, by placing these seemingly disparate practices of corporeal inscription and impression back into dialogue with each other, *Signing the Body* reveals the importance of the human body as a privileged surface for making identity, belonging, authority, and belief powerfully legible in an era marked by profound transformation. Moreover, the examination of the signed body as a product of and participant in the rapidly expanding culture of marking in the theological, judicial, political, and commercial realms that characterized the mid-sixteenth through mid-eighteenth centuries reveals that marks on skin, while informed by long-standing traditions, were also distinctly signs of modernity. Finally, the instances of self-elected inscription that I explore here, namely tattooing and scarification, point to an early modern understanding of corporeal marking as a tool for self-fashioning, a vision that we cannot help but see reflected in our own tattoo renaissance today.[59]

Notes

1 Théophile Raynaud, *De stigmatismo, sacro et profano, divino, humano, daemo-niaco* [1647], 2nd ed. (Lyon: Antoine Cellier, 1654). A prolific writer, Raynaud produced ninety-two works that spanned the field of theology. He compiled his collected works in nineteen volumes prior to his death, published by fellow Jesuit Jean Bertet, *Theophili Raynaudi Societatis Jesu theologi opera omnia: tam hactenus inedita, quam alias excusa, longo authoris labore aucta et emendata* (Lyons: Horace Boissat, Georges Réméus and Camille de Neufville, 1665). Edward Phillips, "Théo-phile Raynaud," *The Catholic Encyclopedia*, vol. 12 (New York: Robert Appleton Company, 1911), accessed July 30, 2012, www.newadvent.org/cathen/12672c. htm. I have maintained original spelling and capitalization in titles of works and quotations from source texts throughout the book.

2 Raynaud, *De Stigmatismo*, 331. All translations from the original Latin text are by Erika Nickerson and Samantha Waxman, and verified by Barbara Weiden Boyd. All other translations in this book are my own unless otherwise noted.

3 Ibid., 17. Raynaud lays out his project in his "Argumentum," *De Stigmatismo*, 11–22.

4 Ibid., 10. Raynaud excludes from his investigation marks made on animals, as well as marks he believes to be innate or produced by illness, which he none-theless considers "stigmata" and discusses briefly; ibid., 14–17.

5 The idea of the body as inscribed by discourses of power—political, scientific, judicial, religious—is most often attributed to Michel Foucault. See, for example, his *Discipline and Punish: The Birth of the Prison*, trans. A. Sheridan (New York: Vintage Books, 1979), 25.

6 I provide here only a sample of relevant work that has been particularly useful for my project, referencing further sources throughout the book. Jane Caplan's collected volume, *Written on the Body: The Tattoo in European and American History* (Princeton, NJ: Princeton University Press, 2000), includes, for the early modern period, Jennipher A. Rosecrans, "Wearing the Universe: Symbolic Markings in Early Modern England," 46–60 and Juliet Fleming, "The Renais-sance Tattoo," 61–82, that first appeared in *Res: Anthropology and Aesthetics* 31 (1997): 34–52 and also appears in Fleming's *Graffiti and the Writing Arts of Early Modern England* (Philadelphia, PA: University of Pennsylvania Press, 2001), 79–112; all references here are to the Caplan edition. On earlier tradi-tions that informed early modern practices and understandings, see contribu-tions to Caplan's volume by C.P. Jones, "Stigma and Tattoo," 1–16, Mark Gustafson, "The Tattoo in the Later Roman Empire and Beyond," 17–30, and Charles W. MacQuarrie, "Insular Celtic Tattooing: History, Myth and Meta-phor," 32–45. Dominique de Courcelles's edited volume, *Stigmates, Les Cahiers de l'Herne* 75 (Paris: Éditions de l'Herne, 2001) assembles key primary texts and scholarship on stigmata. See also important work by François Delpech, "Les Marques de naissance: Physiognomonie, signature magique et charisme souver-ain," in *Le Corps dans la société espagnole des XVIe et XVIIe siècles*, ed. Augustin Redondo (Paris: Publications de la Sorbonne, 1990), 27–49 and "La 'marque' des sorcières: logique(s) de la stigmatisation diabolique," in *Le Sabbat des sorciers. XVe-XVIIIe siècles*, ed. Nicole Jacques-Chaquin and Maxime Préaud (Grenoble: Jérôme Millon 1993), 347–68; Marie-Luce Demonet, "Les marques insensibles, ou les nuages de la certitude," *Littératures Classiques* 25 (Fall 1995): 97–134; Nicole Pellegrin, "L'écriture des stigmates. (XVIe-XVIIIe siècles)," in *La Blessure corporelle. Violences et souffrances, symboles et repré-sentations*, ed. Pierre Cordier and Sébastien Jahan, *Les Cahiers du Gerhico* 4 (2003): 41–62, republished as "Fleurs saintes. L'écriture des stigmates (XVIe-XVIIIe siècles)," in *Femmes en fleurs, femmes en corps. Sang, Santé, Sexualités du*

Moyen Âge aux Lumières, ed. Cathy McClive and Nicole Pellegrin (Saint-Étienne: Publications de l'Université de Saint-Étienne, 2010), 101–22; Mordechay Lewy, "Jerusalem unter der Haut. Zur Geschichte der Jerusalemer Pilgertätowierung," trans. Esther Kontarsky, *Zeitschrift für Religions und Geistesgeschichte 55*.1 (2003): 1–39, first published in Hebrew under the English title "Towards a History of Jerusalem Tattoo Marks among Western Pilgrims," *Cathedra 95* (2000): 37–66; Valentin Groebner, *Who Are You? Identification, Deception, and Surveillance in Early Modern Europe*, trans. Mark Kyburz and John Peck (New York: Zone Books, 2007), ch. 4, 95–116; Craig Koslofsky, "Knowing Skin in Early Modern Europe, c. 1450–1750," *History Compass* 12/10 (2014): 794–806, and work in progress presented in several conference papers, "Branding on the Face in England, 1600–1800," American Comparative Literature Association, Harvard University, Cambridge, MA, March 17–20, 2016, "A Deep Surface? Taking Stock of the History of Skin in Early American Studies," 23rd Annual Conference of the Omohundro Institute of Early American History and Culture, Ann Arbor, MI, June 15–17, 2017, and "Tattooed Servants: The Jerusalem Arms in the Atlantic World," Renaissance Society of America Annual Conference, New Orleans, LA, March 22–24, 2018.

7 Recent work on the skin includes: Claudia Benthien, *Skin: On the Cultural Border Between Self and Other*, trans. Thomas Dunlap (New York: Columbia University Press, 2002 [original German ed. 1999]); Steven Connor, *The Book of Skin* (London: Reaktion Books, 2004); Nina Jablonski, *Skin: A Natural History* (Berkeley: University of California Press, 2006) and *Living Color: The Biological and Social Meaning of Skin Color* (Berkeley: University of California Press, 2012). For work on skin specific to the early modern period, see: Mieneke te Hennepe, "Of the Fisherman's Net and Skin Pores. Reframing Conceptions of the Skin in Medicine, 1572–1714," in *Blood, Sweat and Tears: The Changing Concepts of Physiology from Antiquity into Early Modern Europe*, ed. Manfred Horstmanshoff, Helen King, and Claus Zittel (Leiden: Brill, 2012), 523–48; Christina Malcolmson, *Studies of Skin Color in the Early Royal Society: Boyle, Cavendish, Swift* (Burlington, VT: Ashgate Press, 2002); and Koslofsky, "Knowing Skin" and work in progress referenced above. On the medieval period, see the essays collected in *Writing on Skin in the Age of Chaucer*, ed. Nicole Nyffenegger and Katrin Rupp (Berlin: De Gruyter, 2018) and Peter Biller et al., *Black Skin the Middle Ages/La Peau noire au Moyen Âge* (Sismel-Edizioni del Galluzzo, 2014). Didier Anzieu's early *The Skin Ego: A Psychoanalytic Approach to the Self* (New Haven, CT: Yale University Press, 1989 [original French ed. 1985]) remains an important theoretical source; on Anzieu's model, see Alfred Gell, "Theoretical Introduction" to *Wrapping in Images: Tattooing in Polynesia* (Oxford: Clarendon Press, 1993), 28–31. Several conferences have addressed the history of skin and/or body marking: *La Peau humaine. La pelle humana. The human skin*, special issue of *Micrologus. Natura, Scienze e Società Medievali* 13 (2005) collects papers presented at a 2002 conference at the universities of Lausanne and Geneva, Switzerland; "Nella Pelle/Into the Skin: First International Conference on the Identity, Symbolism, and History of Permanent Body Marks," Universitario Pontifica Università Ubaniana, Vatican City, Rome, Italy, December 5–6, 2011; and "The Porous Body in Early Modern Europe," King's College, London, England, November 30–December 1, 2017, organized by the "Renaissance Skin Project" at King's College, London, a research initiative led by historian Evelyn Welch and funded by the Wellcome Trust. Exhibitions include: "My Skin," curated by Mieneke te Hennepe, Boerhaave Museum, the National Museum of the History of Science and Medicine, Leiden, Netherlands, 2007; "Skin," curated by Javier Moscoso, Wellcome

Collection, London, June 10–September 26, 2010; "Skin/Peau," Musée de la Main, Fondation Claude Verdun, Lausanne, Switzerland, June 16, 2011–April 29, 2012; "Tatoueurs, tatoués," Musée du quai Branly, May 6, 2014–October 18, 2015, see Musée du Quai Branly, *Tatoueurs, Tatoués* (Arles: Actes Sud, 2014); and "Les signes du corps," The Musée Dapper, September 23, 2004–April 3, 2005, see Falgayrettes-Leveau, *Signes du corps*. Web-based work such as the Renaissance Skin Project's site, www.renaissanceskin.ac.uk/, and historian Anna Felicity Friedman's tattoohistorian.com bridge the gap between popular interest in marks on skin and ongoing scholarship in these areas.

8 See, for example, Pierre de Lancre, *Tableau de l'inconstance des mauvais anges et démons* (Paris: Jean Berjon, 1612), "De la marque des Sorciers," Discours II, 181–84 and 190–91, who cites the mark of baptism, circumcision, divine stigmata, birthmarks, and brands, and Jacques Fontaine, *Discours des marques des sorciers* (Paris: Denis Langlois, 1611), 6, 8 and 13–14, who also compares them to the mark of a master upon the clothing of servants or soldiers. Raynaud devotes the entire section III of his *De stigmatismo* to "Stigmatismus Dæmoniacus," 349–453, making comparisons with divine marks, brands on slaves, and birthmarks, 352–53. The sixteenth-century theorization of the devil's mark depends deeply on these other kinds of marking as models, as discussed in Chapter 1 and Delpech, "La 'marque' des sorcières."

9 François Gayot de Pitaval (1673–1743), *Causes célèbres et intéressantes, avec les jugemens qui les ont décidées*, 20 vols. (Paris: Theodore Legras et al., 1734–1748), vol. 2, 520–21 and 533 and Abbé d'Aubignac, *Relation de M. Hédelin, Abbé d'Aubignac, touchant les possédés de Loudun au mois de septembre 1637*; rpt. in Robert Mandrou, *Possession et sorcellerie au XVIIe siècle. Textes inédits* (Paris: Fayard, 1979), 153. See the Conclusion for examples.

10 Gabriel Sagard-Théodat, *Le Grand voyage du pays des Hurons suivi du dictionnaire de la langue huronne* [1632], ed. Jack Warwick (Montréal: Presses de l'Université de Montréal, 1998), 229 and *Histoire du Canada* (Paris: Claude Sonnius, 1636), 374.

11 "Stigmates," Antoine Furetière, *Dictionnaire universel, Contenant generalement tous les Mots François, tant vieux que modernes, & les Termes de toutes les Sciences et des Arts*, 3 vols. (La Haye and Rotterdam: Arnout & Reinier Leers, 1690) and the *Dictionnaire de l'Académie françoise* (Paris: Jean-Baptiste Coignard, 1694). Furetière's groundbreaking dictionary, which he began compiling in the 1670s when he became frustrated with the Académie française's approach to their dictionary project, was first published posthumously in the Netherlands in 1690.

12 Raynaud, *De Stigmatismo*, "Proloquium," 9.

13 "Stigma," *Oxford English Dictionary*, 2nd ed., 1989, online version June 2012, accessed June 24, 2012, www.oed.com/view/Entry/190242, and "Stigmate," Alain Rey, *Dictionnaire historique de la langue française* (Paris: Le Robert, 1992), vol. 2, 2020. See also Pierre Adnès, "Stigmates," in *Dictionnaire de spiritualité ascétique et mystique*, ed. Marcel Viller, F. Cavallera, and J. de Guibert, 17 vols. (Paris: G. Beauchesne, 1932-95), vol. 14, 1211–43.

14 See, for example, "Stigma," Robert Estienne, *Dictionnaire Latinogallicum* (London: Carolum Stephanum, 1552); "stigmatiser, stigmatisée," Randle Cotgrave, *A Dictionarie of the French and English Tongues* ([London: A. Islip, 1611] Hildesheim: Georg Olms Verlag, 1970); and "Stigmates," Furetière, *Dictionnaire universel*. See also Pellegin's treatment of the eighteenth-century *Encyclopédie*'s definitions of *stigmates*; "L'écriture des stigmates," 41–42. Early French equivalents *stigmac* (1495) and *estigmate* (ca. 1549) designate a mark revealing dishonor or shame. The term *stigmat* also designated "a mark left on the skin by an illness" at the beginning of the sixteenth century. *Stigmate* refers as well to the brand in

sixteenth-century discussions of ancient practices, but by 1669 it could designate the contemporary criminal brand. According to Rey, 1680 marks the first use in French of *stigmates* to designate the replication of the wounds of Christ on the bodies of mystics, though this seems late, given their currency; "Stigmate," Rey, *Dictionnaire historique*, vol. 2, 2020.

15 See definitions of the French terms *signe, caractère*, and *marque* in Furetière, *Dictionnaire universel*, the *Dictionnaire de l'Académie françoise*, and Cotgrave, *A Dictionarie*. See also Pierre Richelet, *Le Nouveau dictionnaire françois* (Lyon: Jean-Baptiste Girin, 1719), quoted by Alain Faudemay, *Le Clair et l'obscur à l'âge classique* (Geneva: Slatkine, 2001), 74.

16 "Marque" and "marquer," Furetière, *Dictionnaire universel*.

17 "Caractere," Furetière, *Dictionnaire universel*.

18 "Caractere," *Dictionnaire de l'Académie françoise*.

19 "Signe," *Dictionnaire de l'Académie françoise*, emphasis in original, and "signe," Furetière, *Dictionnaire universel*.

20 "Signe," Furetière, *Dictionnaire universel*. Emphasis in original.

21 Karl Jaberg, "The Birthmark in Folk Belief, Language, Literature, and Fashion," *Romance Philology* 10 (1956–57): 307–42; 316–17.

22 The rise of the devil's mark in the sixteenth century, which grew out of ideas borrowed from a variety of domains within the semantic realm of the word *marque*, is a case in point. See Chapter 1 and Delpech, "La 'marque' des sorcières."

23 On the skin's role in identity and socialization, see Terrence Turner, "The Social Skin," in *Not Work Alone: A Cross-Cultural View of Activities Superfluous to Survival*, ed. Jeremy Cherfas and Robert Lewin (London: Temple Smith, 1980), 112–40, rpt. in the *Journal of Ethnographic Theory* 2.2 (2012): 486–504; Anzieu, *The Skin Ego*; Gell, *Wrapping in Images*; David Le Breton, *Signes d'identité. Tatouages, piercings et autres marques corporelles* (Paris: Métailié, 2002) and "Anthropologie des marques corporelles," in *Signes du corps*, ed. Christiane Falgayrettes-Leveau (Paris: Musée Dapper, 2004), 73–119; Benthien, *Skin: On the Cultural Border Between Self and Other*; and Connor, *The Book of Skin*. See further work on skin cited above.

24 These include Roland Barthes, Jacques Derrida, Gilles Deleuze, Jean-François Lyotard, Jacques Lacan, Julia Kristeva, and Didier Anzieu. See Fleming's discussion in "The Renaissance Tattoo," esp. 61–67.

25 According to Genesis 4:15, God set a mark upon Cain to protect him even as he cursed him for killing his brother. In Revelations 7:2–8, the faithful receive the seal of God on their foreheads prior to the earth's destruction. Furetière's citation of both of these examples indicates their prevalence as references; "Signe," *Dictionnaire universel*.

26 "Cachet," Nicolas Fontaine, *Dictionnaire chrétien* (Paris: Chez Elie Josset, 1691), 89–90.

27 Ibid., 89.

28 "Caracteres," Fontaine, *Dictionnaire chrétien*, 92–93.

29 Connor, *The Book of Skin*, 12–15.

30 Ibid., 19–23, Groebner, *Who Are You?*, 117–48, Nancy G. Siraisi, *Medieval and Early Renaissance Medicine. An Introduction to Knowledge and Practice* (Chicago: University of Chicago Press, 1990), esp. 104–6 and 120–25, and Laurence Brockliss and Colin Jones, *The Medical World of Early Modern France* (Oxford: Oxford University Press, 2004), 110–15.

31 "Signe," Furetière, *Dictionnaire universel*.

32 Ambroise Paré, *Œuvres complètes d'Ambroise Paré*, ed. J.-F. Malgaigne, vol. 3 (Paris: J.-B. Baillière, 1841), bk. 20, ch. 3, 79.

33 See Jean-Jacques Courtine and Claudine Haroche, *Histoire du visage. Exprimer et taire ses émotions (du XVIe siècle au début du XIXe siècle)* (Paris: Payot et Rivages, 1988), esp. 58–67. Among the better-known treatises from this tradition are: Bartolommeo della Rocca Cocles, *Chyromantie ac Physionomie Anatasis* (Bologna: Joannem Antonium, 1504), published in French as *Le compendion & brief enseignement de physiognomie & chiromancie* (Paris: Pierre Regnault, 1546); Giambattista della Porta, *De Humana Physiognomonia* (Vici Aequensis: Cacchius,1586), published in French as *La Physiognomie humaine* (Rouen: J. et D. Berthelin, 1655); Jérôme Cardan [Girolamo Cardano], *La Metoposcopie*, trans. C.M. de Lavrendiere (Paris: Thomas Jolly, 1658); and Richard Saunders, *Physiognomonie and Chiromancie, Metoposcopie* (London: Nathaniel Brook, 1653, 2nd ed. 1671), all references here to 2nd edition; Marin Cureau de la Chambre, *L'art de connaître les hommes*, 2nd ed. (Paris: J. D. Allin, 1653); Jean Belot, *Œuvres de M. Jean Belot* (Rouen: Jean Berthelin, 1669). See also Delpech, "Les marques de naissance," 30, n. 15. Groebner discusses their late-medieval predecessors, *Who Are You?*, 125–29.

34 Belot, *Œuvres*, bk. 2, ch. 3, 228.

35 Ibid., bk. 2, ch. 9, 281. Swiss physician-astrologer Paracelsus (1493–1541) and, later, German philosopher and Lutherian theologian Jakob Böhme (1574–1624) made the "doctrine of signatures," which argued for correspondences between heavenly bodies and all living things, famous in the West. Herbal remedies could thus be prescribed in accordance with a given plant's astrological correspondence to certain parts of the body.

36 Heinrich Cornelius Agrippa von Nettesheim, *Three Books of Occult Philosophy*, ed. Donald Tyson and trans. James Freake (St. Paul, MN: Llewellyn, 1993), 102.

37 Saunders, *Treatise of the Moles of the Body of Man and Woman*, in *Physiognomie*, 307–69. Apart from his original treatise on moles, Saunders replicates in English translation the entirety of Belot's *Œuvres* in his *Physiognomie* without crediting him, making only minor textual additions and innovations, though his text does include many new diagrams, some based on Cardano. He reprints Belot's chiromantic hand, translating its labels; ibid., 51.

38 Belot, *Œuvres*, bk. 1, ch. 2, 30.

39 Cardan, *La Metoposcopie*, "Règles générales," iv and vii.

40 See also Saunders, *Physiognomonie*, 212–20, and for similar sets of hands, 105–60. Belot provides similar readings for the marks of the hand in his *Traité de la chiromance*, which first appeared in his *Instruction Familiere* (Paris: Nicolas Rousset and Nicolas Bourdin, 1619), 1–53.

41 Cardan, *La Metoposcopie*, "Règles générales," vi-vii, 181, and 184–221.

42 Groebner points out that physiognomic readings ultimately remain, however, profoundly anti-individualist, since each mark on the skin must be read the same way for all human beings, a specific "character" or "note" always signifying the same set of attributes; Groebner, *Who Are You?*, 126.

43 Saunders, *Physiognomonie*, 24. Sanders replicates in English translation the entirety of Belot's *Œuvres* in his 1653 work without crediting him. Besides his original treatise on moles, he makes only minor textual additions and innovations, though his text does include many new diagrams, some based on Cardano. He reprints Belot's chiromantic hand, translating its labels; ibid., 51.

44 For in-depth treatment of the birthmark, see Delpech, "Les Marques de naissance," 27–49 and Jaberg, "The Birthmark." Jacques Gélis cites nineteenth-century discussion of the birthmark in *History of Childbirth: Fertility, Pregnancy and Birth in Early Modern Europe*, trans. Rosemary Morris (Boston: Northeastern University Press, 1991), 53–8 and 203.

45 Pierre Boaistuau, *Histoires Prodigieuses* (Paris: Vincent Sertenas, Jean Longis, and Robert Le Mangnier, 1560). Ambroise Paré reproduces this image in *Des monstres et prodiges* [1573], ed. Jean Céard (Geneva: Droz, 1971). On monster narratives, see Marie-Hélène Huet, *Monstrous Imagination* (Cambridge, MA: Harvard University Press, 1993), esp. ch. 1, 13–35 and Jean Céard, *La nature et les prodiges* (Geneva: Droz, 1977).

46 Pierre Boaistuau, *Histoires Prodigieuses*, fols. 172–73. Boaistuau interprets the epsilon as signifying virtue, coupled with the sign of the cross to convey a clear message that the people should turn back to Christ. The eye on the knee signifies their affection for terrestrial things.

47 Huet, *Monstrous Imagination*; Rebecca M. Wilkin, "Feminizing the Imagination in France, 1563–1678," (PhD diss., University of Michigan, 2000) and "Essaying the Mechanical Hypothesis: Descartes, La Forge, and Malebranche on the Formation of Birthmarks" in *Observation and Experiment in Seventeenth-Century Anatomy, Early Science and Medicine* 13.6 (2008): 533–67. On the eighteenth-century endurance of the idea, see Gélis, *History of Childbirth*, 54, Huet, *Monstrous Imagination*, 18–19, 35, and 56–78, and Philip K. Wilson, *"Out of Sight, Out of Mind?": The Daniel Turner-James Blondel Debate over Maternal Impressions* (Baltimore, MD: Johns Hopkins, 1987). In addition to period authors cited here, see also Nicolas Rémy, *Demonolatriæ libri tres* [Lyon: Vincentii, 1595], trans. E.A. Ashwin, *Demonolatry*, ed. Montague Summers (Secaucus, NJ: University Books, 1974), bk. 1, ch. 6, 23–26; Michel de Montaigne, *Essais* [1580] bk. 1, ch. 20; Nicolas de Malebranche, *De la recherche de la vérité* [1674–1675], ed. Geneviève Rodis-Lewis (Paris: J. Vrin, 1945), 1:234–43; Jacques Blondel, *The Strength of Imagination in Pregnant Women examin'd* (London: J. Peele, 1727), which appeared in French as *Dissertation physique sur la Force de l'imagination Des Femmes enceintes sur le Fetus*, trans. Albert Brun (Leiden: Gilbert Langerak and Theodore Luct, 1737); and Daniel Turner, *The Force of the Mother's Imagination Upon Her Foetus in Utero* (London: J. Walthoe et al., 1730).

48 Leonard Vair, *Trois livres des charmes, sorcelages, ou enchantemens*, trans. Julian Baudon (Paris: Nicolas Chesneau, 1583), bk. 1, ch. 2, 19–20; full discussion, 14–24.

49 See also Gélis, "Cravings and Imaginings," *History of Childbirth*, 53–58 and Jaberg, "The Birthmark," 311–15.

50 Ambroise Paré, *Œuvres complètes*, vol. 2, 679. We still speak of red birthmarks today as "strawberries." Paré, however, rejects maternal desire as a source and sees instead a role for menstrual blood, 679–80, an idea that physician Lauren Joubert (1529–1582) refutes in his *Erreurs populaires* (Bordeaux: S. Millanges, 1578), bk. 2, ch. 3, 159–60; full discussion, 156–60.

51 Fontaine, *Discours des marques*, 13–14. On desire for meat, see Vair, *Trois livres des charmes*, bk. 1, ch. 2, 21.

52 Claude Quillet, *La Callipédie*, trans. J.M. Caillau [1665, 1st Latin ed. 1655] (Paris: Durand and Pissot, 1749), bk. 3, 92.

53 Jaberg, "The Birthmark," 313. This idea continues to have currency in many cultures today.

54 De Lancre, *Tableau de l'inconstance*, 181. See also Fontaine, *Discours des marques*, 13–14.

55 Pietro Pomponazzi, *De naturalium effectuum causis, sive de incantationibus* [composed 1520]; *Les Causes des merveilles de la nature ou Les Enchantements* [1567], ed. and trans. Henri Busson (Paris: Les Éditions Rieder, 1930), 149. For the opposing argument, see François de Sales, *Traité de l'Amour de*

Dieu [1616] in *Œuvres de saint François de Sales*, ed. André Ravier and Roger Devos (Paris: Gallimard, La Pléiade, 1969), 657–59.

56 Marks on African captives brought as slaves to the Atlantic colonies included so-called country marks and brands made on the skin of captives by slave owners, traders, and companies. Both kinds of marks were used by plantation owners and colonial authorities for identification of enslaved persons, in particular in the case of runaway slaves. See Katrina H.B. Keefer, "Marked by Fire: Brands, Slavery, and Identity," *Slavery & Abolition* (2019), DOI: 10.1080/0144039X.2019.1606521, and Koslofsky, "Knowing Skin" and "A Deep Surface?" On "country marks," see also Michael A. Gomez, *Exchanging our Country Marks: The Transformation of African Identities in the Colonial and Antebellum South* (Chapel Hill, NC: University of North Carolina Press, 1998).

57 On *mouches*, see Jaberg, "The Birthmark," 332–38 and Claire Goldstein, "*Mouches Volantes*: The Enigma of Paste-On Beauty Marks in 17th-Century France" (unpublished manuscript, last modified May 2019), Microsoft Word file.

58 Raynaud, *De Stigmatismo*, 18.

59 This term was popularized by Arnold Rubin in *Marks of Civilization: Artistic Transformations of the Human Body* (Los Angeles: Museum of Cultural History, University of California, 1988). Among treatments of body modification today, see: Clinton Sanders, *Customizing the Body: The Art and Culture of Tattooing* (Philadelphia, PA: Temple University Press, 1989, rev. ed. 2008); Le Breton, *Signes d'identité* and "Anthropologie des marques corporelles"; Terrence Margo DeMello, *Bodies of Inscription: A Cultural History of the Modern Tattoo Community* (Durham, NC: Duke University Press, 2000); and Victoria Pitts, *In the Flesh: The Cultural Politics of Body Modification* (New York: Palgrave Macmillan, 2003).

1 Seals of Satan
Demonologists and the devil's mark

In 1581, Doctor Claude Caron (†1609) of Annonay, known throughout the region for his extraordinary medical skill, began hearing stories of a number of young women from the surrounding villages and countryside who were showing signs of demonic possession.[1] The women were brought to the priests in Annonay, who searched for the cause of their trouble through exorcism. Their demons, notably one named Miron, who spoke through the mouth of twenty-two-year-old Magdaleine, accused Katherine Boyraionne, a woman in her fifties from the neighboring village of Saint Safforin, of enchanting the girls and causing their possession.[2] Boyraionne was brought in for questioning and challenged by the young women and their demons, but she denied any involvement in their possession. Unable to substantiate their suspicions about Boyraionne, the priests interrogated her daughter, who testified that her mother had brought her to the sabbat—the regular nocturnal gathering of witches and demons, filled with heretical debauchery—and instructed her in witchcraft.[3] Though her daughter pleaded that she confess, Boyraionne persisted in denying any wrongdoing and was handed over to the secular authorities. According to the young women's possessing demons, the key to proving her identity as a witch—"the way to reveal her witchdom"—lay in examining Boyraionne closely for a "character" made by the devil himself on her left shoulder.[4] Caron's suspenseful narrative of her examination—the surgeon's hand guided in its search by none other than the demon Miron himself—invites his readers to witness the mark's discovery alongside the assembled doctors and local authorities:

> This was ordered, the doctors and surgeons were called in, her eyes were tightly covered, her shoulders exposed, and the search was conducted for this character. At first we could only see a polished and uniform expanse of skin, but when the devil Miron noticed our slowness to discover where the hare lay, mocking us he showed us the place with a great burst of laughter. Now, given our ignorance, [Miron], without saying anything, directed the hand of the surgeon to prick the place where we thought the character was. He [the surgeon] sometimes

pricked in one part of the shoulder, and when the witch moved because of the pain, sometimes on the other side, then on the other without stopping, according to where we thought we would find the mark, the witch always feeling the probe. But finally having arrived by chance at the very spot where the character was, and by looking closely, we observed in this place a shape about the size of a small coin, from whose center emanated several filaments branching out toward its circumference, and not very apparent. So the surgeon who was holding the probe, which was as long as a finger, inserted it into that center on our command and in the presence of many trustworthy people. He pushed it in so far that he put more than half of it into her shoulder without the witch moving in the least. Nor did she make any sign of having been hurt, though before she had become strangely ferocious at the least prick that he had given her. When the probe was pulled out of the witch's shoulder, no blood appeared. She was condemned to torture to reveal the truth of this matter.[5]

This judicial scene of the search for the devil's mark, recounted here in vivid detail by Caron, played itself out again and again in courts across early modern Europe at the height of the witch trials, which in France knew their greatest frequency and ferocity from about 1560 to 1640.[6] As Caron's description illustrates, in their quest to locate this physical mark, court examiners stripped and blindfolded the accused, examined her skin closely for any visible marks, and probed her flesh extensively with a needle or awl to locate any spots of insensitivity—a defining characteristic of the devil's mark.[7] The belief that the devil often left multiple marks upon a witch's body and that his marks were usually hidden—even invisible to the naked eye—left the entire expanse of the accused's skin vulnerable to the surgeon's needle.[8]

The search to uncover the devil's mark was informed by a conviction shared by period demonologists—the learned elite theologians, judges, and doctors who examined questions surrounding the devil, demons, and their relationships with humans—that witches had intimate commerce with the devil during the sabbat. The ritual culminated in the devil placing a physical mark upon the bodies of his new initiates, as pictured in Italian Franciscan demonologist Francesco Maria Guazzo's 1608 *Compendium Maleficarum* (see Figure 1.1), and signing a mutual pact.[9] The cutaneous mark thus declared its bearer's sworn identity as a guilty member of Satan's fraternity of followers, its manifest presence representing sufficient evidence for most judges to justify the passage to judicial torture in view of obtaining a confession, while for others the discovery of devil's marks alone served as sufficient proof for a capital conviction.[10] As historian William Monter has noted, the widespread use of the mark across Protestant and Catholic lines in a time otherwise deeply divided by confession is testament to its conceptual power as well

Figure 1.1 The devil marking his faithful at the sabbat, Francesco Maria Guazzo, *Compendium Maleficarum* (Milan: Apud Haeredes August. Tradati, 1608), 17. Beinecke Library, Yale University.

as to its usefulness.[11] Even judge Henry Boguet (1550–1619), who presided over trials in the Jura region from 1598 to 1612 and believes—because he cannot always find them—that not all witches necessarily bear marks, concludes that "these marks have such an importance in matters of witchcraft that they serve as a very strong presumption of guilt against the accused so that, if they are joined by other evidence, it is permissible to condemn them."[12] For Pierre de Lancre (1553–1631), Bordeaux judge and crown-appointed leader of the Basque region trials of 1609, the reliability of the mark is simply obvious to any experienced modern judge:

> The mark that Satan imprints on his faithful is of great consideration for the judgment of the crime of witchcraft, as also testified by all the moderns who have been judges like myself, who believe that the marks are such strong pieces of evidence, and lead to such strong presumptions of guilt against witches, that being joined . . . with other evidence it is admissible to proceed with their condemnation.[13]

Demonologists recorded numerous shapes, sizes, and locations for the marks they found upon the skin of the accused. While they often saw the depraved nature of the devil reflected in cutaneous signs made in the shape of an animal—a hare, toad, bat, owl, spider, mouse, dog—or its footprint, they also frequently found more conventional marks in the form of warts, moles, excrescences of skin, and birthmarks, like the one found on Katherine Boyraionne, in the "shape of a small coin, from whose center emanated several filaments."[14] The devil's mark also varied in size among reports, as De Lancre affirms, "sometimes big, and sometimes as small as the head of a pin."[15] The mark's diversity of shape and size was equaled only by the multiplicity of its possible locations on the body. It traveled the whole surface of the witch's skin, as Boguet attests:

> [W]itches are marked, as they say, some on the shoulder, others underneath the tongue, or sometimes under the lip, others on the shameful parts. In short, there is not a witch who is not marked in some part of his body.[16]

Though Jacques Fontaine (†1621?), doctor to the young King Louis XIII and medical expert in the 1609–1611 trial for witchcraft of priest Louys Gaufridy in Aix-en-Provence, asserts that "for the most part one finds them marked very apparently," most demonologists argue the contrary.[17] While they suggest that the mark could be imprinted anywhere on the skin, they also agree that the devil generally favors more hidden spots to avoid detection, as De Lancre deplores:

> [H]e often imprints them, either in parts so dirty that one is horrified to go look for them there, like in a man's anus, or in a woman's genitals, or, since he is extreme and unnatural, in the most noble and precious place that exists in a person, where it seems impossible to imprint them, like in the eyes, or in the mouth.[18]

The devil thus proves himself to be a prolific and prodigious marker of bodies, able to imprint a variety of marks, even in seemingly "impossible" places. The multiplicity of forms and locations he employs does not trouble most of the mark's interpreters, who argue that he maintains flexibility in his choices so as to better thwart the efforts of those who would seek to control him. Indeed, he often buries his mark so well, De Lancre writes tellingly, "that you would have to tear the body in question to pieces to find it."[19]

As the devil's mark became commonplace through judicial repetition, the faith many judges placed in it as an objective sign of guilt also came to be shared by the wider population. While popular belief in supernatural signs on skin, as attested in common beliefs about birthmarks, undoubtedly contributed to the acceptance of the devil's mark, people of the lower classes became well acquainted with the mark as an authenticating sign through what they witnessed at trials and executions.[20] There they heard accusations and confessions that included marking by the devil or watched, in the case of public prickings, the mark be revealed upon the witch's skin.[21] In Aix, the local population reportedly saw in the revelation of the accused Gaufridy's marks absolute confirmation of his identity as a witch: "The news about this spread quickly among all the common people, that he was truly a witch, and that it could not be otherwise because he was marked."[22] During trials, lay plaintiffs and witnesses regularly called upon the mark as a sign of proof. Jurist and political philosopher Jean Bodin (1530–1596) cites, for example, the 1571 case of a man who, offered amnesty in exchange for naming his accomplices, called on the authority of the mark to support his accusations: "And to prove the veracity of his testimony, he said that they were marked, and that they would find the mark by stripping them."[23] Those accused of witchcraft were themselves all too well aware of the mark's power to convict. Some even voluntarily submitted to pricking, believing the absence of a mark would definitively prove their innocence, while others attempted to obliterate any potentially suspicious spots on their own skin prior to their examination, as De Lancre relates:

> Being twenty or thirty [accused women] in the same prison, they examined each other. And if they found the mark, the devil had taught them to scratch themselves and tear the skin so excessively that some-times their shoulders resembled tortured shoulders, which had just suffered the whip or violent flagellations.[24]

Given the importance attributed to the devil's mark in the late sixteenth and early seventeenth centuries, we might assume that this sign on skin, so common in the trials of that period, was part of a long-standing demono-logical tradition. We would be wrong. The devil's mark played no role in the witch persecutions of the later Middle Ages. The infamous 1486 *Malleus Maleficarum*, or *Hammer of Witches*, by Dominican inquisitors Heinrich Kramer and Jacob Sprenger, well known as the bible of witchcraft persecution, did not mention the devil's mark, nor can that work be credited with the invention of the witches' sabbat, the gathering so closely tied to it.[25] Yet during the years between the publication of that compen-dium and the trials of the late sixteenth century, the *stigmata* or *sigillum diaboli* appeared and took a prominent place in theological and medical treatises, trial records, and the popular imagination. As Martine Ostorero has shown, the earliest sightings of anything resembling the devil's mark emanate from the Vaud region of Switzerland in the early fifteenth century, leading to a "profusion of diabolical marks and signs" of varying sorts in trial records from Vaud and Geneva by the beginning of the sixteenth.[26] Body parts promised to the devil as a sign of allegiance—a finger, a nail— and wounds left on the body where the devil had taken blood as ink for signing his pact with the witch represented early forms of what would later become the devil's mark. But it was not until the later sixteenth century that the mark became an authoritative sign of proof, locatable and verifiable upon the witch's skin, a status it would enjoy in many jurisdictions through much of the seventeenth century, despite hesitations, inconsistencies, and disagreements among demonologists and courts over the mark's judicial value, constancy, and even existence.[27] Caron's 1581 eye-witness account of the unveiling of the diabolical sign upon the accused Boyraionne's body—a mark at first imperceptible, then slowly coming into view and finally fully apparent to all—thus provides an apt metaphor for the mark's historical emergence. Boyraionne's examiners at first display little confidence, their own apparent blindness to the mark mirroring that of the accused witch who wears the blindfold. Not only do they need a demon to guide them, but their "ignorance" causes them to prick at random until they hit "by chance" the spot of insensitivity. From invisibility, the mark then appears before their eyes in seemingly miraculous fashion: where "at first [they] could only see a polished and uniform expanse of skin," by "looking closely," they discover a unique and recognizable mark.

We are tempted to dismiss early modern belief in the devil's mark and the practice of pricking for it as a sign of backwardness and perversion, part and parcel of far-fetched stories of horrific sabbat rituals, the product of the overactive imaginations and sadistic leanings of early modern demonologists, an analysis that would not be entirely inaccurate. However, before we make such a claim, we must also recall that the writers who so earnestly conceived and described the devil's mark were among the most well-educated minds of their time. Far from being removed from or opposed to other systems of inquiry, the science of demonology—and the learned thinkers who pursued its questions—was fully integrated into the intellectual life of the period.[28] Moreover, no respected intellectual of this era could refuse to acknowledge the reality of the devil as a force to be reckoned with and an active influence in the daily lives of human beings. While period demonologists struggled with several theoretical problems posed by the devil's mark and their experience of it during witch trials, they firmly believed the reality of what they described. How, then, can we explain the invention and rise to prominence of this new cutaneous sign at the end of the sixteenth century? What inspired the creation of the devil's mark and gave it viability as a sign of proof in the early modern era? The answers to this question are many. In what follows, I will examine some of the key models and forces that contributed to the mark's creation, theorization, and valorization from the mid-sixteenth through mid-seventeenth centuries.

Marks of identity and authority

Early modern demonologists and the elite who read them gave credence to the devil's mark because it made sense within the popular and learned traditions of corporeal marking with which they were familiar and the contemporary marking practices that were part of their everyday experience. As sixteenth- and seventeenth-century writers crafted the mark into a viable material sign of a witch's collusion with Satan, they drew on their vast knowledge and experience of models of corporeal marking, both past and present. The maturity of the devil's mark at the threshold between the sixteenth and seventeenth centuries coincided with wider developments in marking practices across modernizing Europe—both corporeal and otherwise—that deeply informed its genesis and gave it viability as an authoritative sign. Of the numerous marking traditions that influenced the creation and acceptance of the devil's mark in this period, three emerge with particular frequency in discussions of the devil's mark: Christian signs of belonging or election, notably the baptismal mark; material signs worn on clothing to signal status or stigma; and the branding of people and products for purposes of recognition and control.[29] All marks of identity and authority, they served as models for the making of the mark placed upon the devil's own.

Sacred signs

The devil's mark developed within a culture that espoused deep-seated belief in the body as inscribed or imprinted with signs through which a person's identity, character, and destiny could be known, as examined in the introduction to this book. The revival of the sciences of physiognomy, metoposcopy, chiromancy, and moleoscopy in this period established a relationship between exterior signs and interior essence that informed the thinking surrounding the devil's mark as a visible sign of the corruption of the witch's soul.[30] Moreover, a vast folkloric tradition saw in birthmarks—to which devil's marks were so often compared—innate signs of identity that allowed for the recognition and identification of exceptional individuals.[31] For example, belief that French monarchs bore on their bodies a royal sign attesting their God-given power to heal—first the vermillion cross, later the fleur-de-lis—was widespread.[32] So powerful was the sign on skin as proof of identity that itinerant healers regularly displayed supposedly innate birthmarks to validate their claim of belonging to illustrious families endowed with special healing powers. The *Saludadores* or *Ensalmadores* of Spain, self-proclaimed descendants of Saint Catherine, wore the martyr's wheel, while the *Pauliani* or *Salvatori* of Italy, ostensibly descendants of Saint Paul, wore an image of the snake whose venomous bite Saint Paul had overcome.[33]

This vision of the mark on skin as a powerful identifying sign did not limit itself to the occult sciences and to folk culture. Roman Catholic doctrine itself offered up similar marks of belonging. Catholic theologians defended the idea that all Christians bore upon their bodies the sign of Christ, inscribed or imprinted upon them at the moment of baptism, a belief reaffirmed by the Council of Trent in 1547.[34] As Jesuit Théophile Raynaud

(1583–1663), author of an encyclopedic 1647 treatise on corporeal marking, asserts, "in baptism, the faithful are signed with an indelible character, by which they are transcribed into the family of God, and surrendered into His eternal service."[35] The permanent impression of the baptismal character, a Christian rewriting of the corporeal sign made through circumcision in Hebrew tradition, thus made an individual a member of the Christian family and enrolled her into God's service; it communicated its bearer's belonging and signaled the authority to whom she owed allegiance. While period theologians affirm that this mark was a spiritual, interior, and thus invisible sign because it was imprinted on the soul, rather than the body, they use highly corporeal language to describe it, and mention its effectiveness for warding off demons, for whom they believe the mark was clearly visible.[36] Moreover, the baptismal mark on the soul of the newly minted Christian corresponded to the more material, exterior sign of the cross made on the body by the officiating priest during the rite of baptism: the ceremony concluded with the priest physically drawing the cross upon the forehead of the person receiving the sacrament with the holy chrism—a sanctified perfumed oil made for this express purpose—thus lending external visibility to what was otherwise a hidden imprint. Dominican prior and inquisitor Sebastien Michaëlis (1543?–1618) emphasizes this dual nature of the signature on Christians made during baptism: God "marks them internally with his Holy Spirit by the baptismal character, and externally on the forehead with the holy chrism and the sign of the cross."[37] The Christian was thus doubly marked with the sign of Christ, which identified him and made him Christ's own.[38]

If God marked his faithful with a sign, it was, then, only logical that the devil—"God's ape"—did so as well, in imitation.[39] As all things demonic, the devil's mark was, first and foremost, a perversion of God's own actions. Raynaud explains:

> [A]ll whom [the devil] claims as slaves and members of his household, he marks equally, perversely imitating God, who impresses a character onto the soul of all those who have been enrolled into his family by the sacrament of baptism. To this is analogous the corporeal character on Satan's slaves.[40]

De Lancre traces the common lineage of these corporeal signs—from circumcision, to the character of baptism, to the devil's mark—but singles out the devil's mark as a recent development. While God had always marked his servants with a permanent sign, he notes, Satan had only recently begun to mark his own:

> God's servants under the Old Law were marked [through circumcision], and still are today with the sign and character of baptism that cannot be erased. The ape of God also wanted to mark his servants. . . . *And recently the devil took up this custom [Nouvellement le Demon a prins*

cette coustume], that he imprints ordinarily certain notes and insensitive marks, in the form of characters, on the bodies of magicians and witches, as our experience has shown us many times.[41]

Like baptismal marks on Christians, devil's marks served purposes of recognition and identification; they allowed the devil to know his faithful—"those he has enrolled in his militia."[42] A later skeptic, François Gayot de Pitaval (1673–1743), even suggests ironically that the sabbat begins with a roll call, where the devil checks all attendees for his sign: "The Devil begins the exercises by examining all those who attend the Sabbat, to see if they have the marks through which he enrolled them in his service."[43] But for Fontaine and his contemporaries, the devil marks his followers not only for purposes of identification but also to display his arrogance and authority:

> These marks are not engraved by the Demon on the bodies of witches only to recognize them, . . . but to imitate the creator of all things, to show his arrogance, and the authority that he has won over the miserable humans who allow themselves to be caught by his tricks and ruses to be held in his service and subjugation.[44]

Though both marks of identity, the characters imprinted by God and those imprinted by the devil are nonetheless distinct in their signification. Demonologists insist that while the divine sign promises eternal life, the demonic announces only death and damnation: "Almighty God marks those who belong to his flock with saintly and divine marks that give eternal life. The evil spirit marks those whom he has captured with those of death."[45] These dueling divine and demonic characters sparked significant debate among demonologists as to whether the devil's mark, when placed upon a Christian, could effectively overwrite the mark of baptism: "[I]t has seemed to some," writes Raynaud, "that the aim of imprinting this magic character is the abolition of the fortifications of baptism, that is, of the baptismal character, through this contrary symbol, which they otherwise call *eradicationem chrismatis* [the eradication of the chrism]."[46] Judge Nicolas Rémy of Lorraine (1530–1616) sees the process as one of reimpression, wherein

> the devil brands and seals those whom he has newly claimed as his own . . . , marking them especially . . . on that part of the body which was anointed by the priest on the day of their baptism; just as thieves change the brand on stolen cattle to their own mark.[47]

Accused witches, their narratives fed by their prosecutors' leading questions, effectively testified that during the sabbat "the demon scraped their forehead to erase . . . the character of baptism or of confirmation," just as one would scrape parchment to write new text upon it.[48] This erasure and rewriting symbolically encapsulated the transformation of identity that took place through the sabbat initiation, where witches renounced their Christian baptism, former names, and godparents; underwent a baptism by the devil; and took new names.[49]

In creating the devil's mark on witches, demonologists thus staged a battle between God and the devil over the authority to mark the human body, a struggle that they saw as ultimately culminating in the corporeal marking by God or Satan announced in the Apocalypse. Michaëlis underlines the material nature of this final act of marking and the importance of the mark as a sign of identity:

> Saint John often predicts in the Apocalypse that at the end of the world there will be a certain cast of people who will wear the mark or character of the beast, which we should understand corporeally and literally, like the texts intend it to mean, because it is said that by such a mark they will have entry with the perverted men who wear the aforesaid mark on their hands or foreheads.[50]

Just as the infamous "mark of the beast" placed upon the bodies of Satan's faithful would be recognized at the end of the world and ensure the damnation of those who bore it, so too contemporary witches could be recognized by the physical sign impressed upon them.[51]

In addition to the mark of baptism and the mark of the Apocalypse, another, more contemporary religious tradition of corporeal marking invoked by early modern demonologists as they theorized the devil's mark must not escape mention here. During the Catholic Counter-Reformation of the sixteenth and seventeenth centuries, stigmatic phenomena, made famous by the celebrated thirteenth-century example of Saint Francis of Assisi, found new prominence.[52] Even as exterior signs of devotion met with increased skepticism under Protestant criticism of Catholic materialism, cases of stigmatization multiplied, especially among women. It is thus not surprising that stigmata surface as a model in De Lancre's treatment of the devil's mark, as they were very much alive in contemporary theological discourse.[53] Like the cross of baptism upon all believers, stigmata were God-given signs of identity, distinguishing particularly worthy Christians by corporeal signs that imitated the bodily wounds of Christ. De Lancre underlines as follows the parallels and distinctions between God-given stigmata and the devil's mark:

> By this mark it seems that Satan wants to imitate our Lord, who sometimes gave and imprinted stigmata to saintly people who were his most favored servants, to whom he wanted to impart the holy marks of his martyrdom. . . . [N]evertheless his imitation is imperfect: because God gives to his own the same wounds that were made by the five nails

in his precious members, and wants them to be visible, to attract by such a worthy example holy souls to so great a glory, and to so a sweet a reward: on the contrary Satan gives them in secret, and even when having imprinted them, buries and hides them.[54]

The usefulness of stigmata as a model for the devil's mark was, however, undoubtedly limited, since stigmata were reserved for a spiritual elite, while the devil's mark was believed to be made on all witches. Still, stigmata occupied an important place in the early modern imaginary of body marking, and links between the devil's mark and stigmata would know an important destiny in the demonic possession cases of the seventeenth century, as I examine in Chapter 2.

Vestimentary signs

While theological understandings of marking deeply informed early modern demonologists' descriptions of the devil's mark, they were by no means their sole point of reference. As they attempted to define the various functions of the devil's mark, demonologists inevitably invoked numerous marking traditions, both permanent and nonpermanent, past and present. Among these were the particular clothing and signs worn upon it that commonly identified individuals and allowed for their visual recognition, a vestimentary tradition of the Middle Ages that persisted well into the early modern era.[55] In the sixteenth and seventeenth centuries, people were known first and foremost by the exterior signs they wore. Fontaine compares the devil's mark to colored helmets worn by soldiers to recognize their allegiance on the battlefield and to the special hats and uniforms identifying servants of a particular household, marked with the family's coat of arms.[56] Distinguishing signs, commonly embroidered onto clothing or attached as metal, cloth, paper, or parchment badges, knew wide use and recognition. Traveling pilgrims marked their identity by wearing badges affixed to their cloaks and hats, as shown in this 1664 engraving by Sébastien Le Clerc (1637–1714) of a pilgrim destined for Santiago de Compostela, who wears the shrine's well-known scallop shell symbol on his shoulders, hat, and collar, clearly identifying him as a pilgrim (see Figure 1.2).[57] Distinctive signs worn on the body also communicated a person's membership in a particular religious group, professional guild, fraternal organization, or honorable order. As Antoine Furetière (1619–1688) attests in his 1690 *Dictionnaire universel*, "All the chivalric orders each have marks that distinguish them. The cross of Malta, of the Holy Spirit, the Cordon Bleu, the Garter."[58] Holy Land pilgrims who became Knights of the Holy Sepulcher or Knights of Saint Catherine of Mount Sinai during their travels won the right to wear the Jerusalem Cross and a wheel-shaped emblem—the symbol of Saint Catherine's martyrdom—respectively, which they received upon induction and had embroidered on their cloaks, making

Figure 1.2 A Saint James of Compostela pilgrim, Sébastien Le Clerc (1664). Bibliothèque Nationale de France.

them recognizable to all who encountered them.[59] Pierre Palliot's 1661 *Vraye et parfaite science des armoiries* includes detailed descriptions and engravings of numerous orders' insignia and often specifies the precise location where they should be placed on the body.[60] Vestimentary signs sometimes became cutaneous signs as well, through tattooing—in the case of Holy Land pilgrims—or branding—in the case of members of the Order of Saint John who founded hospitals for their care. De Lancre explicitly compares the devil's mark to the latter group, who, he writes, wore "a cross lightly marked on the skin with a hot iron," in addition to citing the marking rites of several other religious sects described by Renaissance pilgrims.[61] These insignia—signs of identification and belonging placed on the body during initiation rituals and worn to indicate membership— find their echo in the sabbat narrative of the marking of witches, who receive the mark upon initiation into the Satanic order. Indeed, De Lancre reports that, much like the signs worn by members of confrater- nities, the mark of a toad's foot could be found in the left eye of all the witches of Biarritz.[62]

Like the devil's mark, vestimentary signs also stigmatized. New reiterations of medieval laws requiring that members of specific groups wear apparent signs of their inferior status were common into the eighteenth century.[63] In many places, Renaissance Jews, like their medieval ancestors, were required to wear a distinguishing mark signaling their identity as non-Christians. This sign most often took the form of a yellow wheel, or *rouelle*, made with cord, paper, or cloth and affixed to the breast of the cloak, as portrayed in this 1612 print from the Basel *Stammbuch* (see Figure 1.3).[64] Prostitutes were also required to wear certain colored clothing, arm bands, or *aiguillettes*— decorative tips for ribbons or braided cords similar to those that serve to ornament uniforms today—that signified their profession, as were members of other marginalized groups.[65] The Cagots, a discriminated minority of disputed origin who inhabited western France and the Pyrenees, were forced to wear a red cloth in the shape of a goose foot sewn on their garments to signal their identity, while lepers, with whom they were associated, wore bells.[66] Given the widespread use of signs worn on the body to confer not only identity but also stigma, it is not surprising that early modern theoreticians of the devil's mark thought it natural that accused witches, who were often people who lived at the margins of society to begin with, wore a mark of shame upon their bodies.[67] However, while these other populations, once distinguished with vestimentary markings, could remain part of society, the witch could only be eradicated.[68]

Brand marks

The ultimate badge of shame, burned permanently into the flesh, the brand was often evoked by period demonologists to characterize the devil's mark, as already evident in examples quoted above. Though they

Figure 1.3 Jewish men of the Upper Rhine, the *rouelle* plainly visible on the cloak of
the figure at right, from the Basel *Stammbuch* (1612), reprinted in the
Jewish Encyclopedia (New York: Funk and Wagnalls Company,
1901–1906), vol. 4, 295. Bowdoin College Library.

maintained divergent theories as to how exactly the devil marked his
faithful—citing his use of his claw, hoof, horn, teeth, or little finger as
possibilities—those who wrote about the devil's mark commonly
described it as an imprint left by a hot iron.[69] Raynaud, for example,
after considering various marking methods, concludes that given the
brand's great efficacy and assurance of permanence, "an actual cauteriz-
ing iron or white-hot iron seems more suitable and convenient for
Satan's purpose."[70] Though the engraving from Guazzo's 1608 *Compendium maleficarum* represents the devil marking the forehead of an initiate
with his claw (see Figure 1.1), his textual description of marking suggests
the devil's use of a branding iron instead.[71] Fontaine imagines an even more

complicated two-step process that combines the use of a hot iron and treatment with a penetrating salve to numb the marked spot once it is made. For him, the devil adopts branding for two reasons:

> One, to terrify witches, and to better impress in their imagination this action and marking, which is of great importance for the belief he wants to inspire in witches. The other, so that the ointment responsible for numbing the area penetrates more easily and more deeply. It is not necessary to prove that this is possible, because nothing hinders Satan, who has knowledge of the virtues of all medicines, from having the strongest among them to deaden the area. As for the scar, he is such a good surgeon that he is able to apply the fire close to the body without producing a scab.[72]

The devil thus uses the branding iron to make a strong impression on witches, both literally and figuratively. Branding offers Satan, qualified by Fontaine as a knowledgeable doctor and skillful surgeon, the means to create deep and enduring marks upon the bodies of his chosen adepts. Testimonials reported by Fontaine's contemporaries confirm the cauterization thesis, condemned witches confessing that "as the devil makes his mark, you feel a little heat that penetrates more or less deeply into the flesh."[73]

Early modern demonologists traced the practice of branding back to the ancients, whom they believed had used branding both to stigmatize and to identify their slaves or prisoners, methods Rémy recalls with dismay:

> It is said that in olden times the cruelty and barbarity of masters towards their slaves was in many ways grievous, but its most intolerable manifestation was that they scarred them with marks as a precaution against their possible escape, so that they could be easily recognized and recaptured.[74]

De Lancre too calls on the example of the Romans, while Michaëlis and Boguet cite more contemporary examples of slaves in Turkey and Spain who "wear the mark of their masters on the forehead, cauterized with a hot iron."[75] Since "slaves are normally marked," it went without saying that the devil, a merciless slave master, marked the bodies of his followers not only for recognition but also as a material reminder of their debased state of servitude, as Boguet underlines: "Satan marks them like this to make them understand that they are his slaves forever."[76]

Though French demonologists and judges consistently situated branding in the distant past or in foreign lands, branding was also very much a part of their own contemporary landscape. Ironically, they shudder in horror at an ancient practice that was in fact commonplace in their own time both in

Europe and on the plantations of the French and British Atlantic colonies. The very same period that saw the rise of the devil's mark also knew the revival of branding for the punishment of noncapital crimes, which gained in frequency during the seventeenth century and expanded its geographical reach through the development of the royal galleys and the Atlantic slave trade. In France, state authorities reinstituted criminal branding beginning in the mid-sixteenth century as a mechanism for identifying repeat offenders when they came before the courts a second or third time, a practice common to many European states. The brand, which in France first took the shape of the fleur-de-lis on the shoulder, permanently marked an individual as an ex-convict, a sign that made him forever identifiable as having transgressed the laws of society.[77] Those condemned to service in the royal galleys, who became slaves of the crown, were marked with the letters GAL.[78] In the French Antilles, the brands on enslaved Africans indicated their provenance and owner, while fugitive slaves were also marked with the fleur-de-lis.[79]

Though period demonologists refrain from making the comparison with contemporary criminal or slave branding, they surely had the practice in mind when they envisioned the devil's marking of witches. The judges among them would have commonly handed down sentences of branding for noncapital crimes and the spectacle of branding itself was commonplace in public squares throughout France, as it was in English courtrooms and elsewhere in Europe. Moreover, the search for the devil's mark by the courts had its corollary in the search for the brand mark that was systematically conducted upon apprehending a thief to determine if he was a repeat offender and thus punish him accordingly. Physician Johann Weyer (1515–1588), famous for his fervent opposition to the witch trials of the period, displays his own awareness of branding as an increasingly common and effective judicial method, proposing branding witches as an alternative to their execution.[80] Weyer suggests that rather than consigning wayward women to the flames, judges should seek to reeducate them and make them renounce any pact, a process culminating in the removal of any identifiable devil's mark and its replacement with a Christian sign by impression or branding:

> Then, let any vestige of the Devil's mark be removed—if it should appear—and let the Sign of the Cross or that of the letter *Tau* be firmly imprinted in its place, or let a mark in the shape of the cross be burned upon her if this seems good.[81]

In suggesting a replacement mark, Weyer seems to acknowledge a need for the impression of a material sign to complete the woman's conversion, performing a reversal of the rebranding early modern theologians commonly attributed to the devil, as discussed above. The cross-shaped brand served as a new visible mark of baptism through which Catholic authorities could signal the former witch's recuperation into the fold.

As a sign of identification and ownership, the devil's mark also found models in the widespread practice of marking household possessions, livestock, artisanal products, and other goods to identify their owners or producers. Brands, punches, and stamps impressed personal belongings and commercial goods with distinctive marks so that they could be recognized if stolen and identified as they traveled the roads.[82] Like the devil's mark, these marks indicated an object's ownership or the authority that exercised control over it; they allowed an individual to recognize his property on sight and to claim rights concerning it. Demonologists reference such marks of ownership to argue that since God would never allow anyone else to mark his possessions, a person can never be innocent if he bears the devil's mark. Michaëlis asks, "who is the patriarch who would allow his lamb or ox to wear the mark of another?"[83] Fontaine similarly invokes the coat of arms to prove his point:

[J]ust as a man of power and credibility will never allow the coat of arms of his enemies to be engraved on what belongs to him, in the same way God who is all powerful will never allow the marks of the devil, his sworn and obstinate enemy, to be put upon a person who does not belong to him but to God [as indicated] by the Christian character.[84]

Pacts, seals, signatures, and skin

The devil's mark, closely linked to the paper or parchment pact, whose signature it followed in the sabbat ritual, also rose out of a cultural moment where official documentation, with its requisite seals and signatures, became increasingly prominent in the courtroom as well as in everyday life.[85] In this era characterized by the explosion of paper, writing, and print commonly referred to as the "rise of print culture," when demonologists wrote of the devil's mark, their textual metaphors demonstrated their acute consciousness of the new importance accorded to contracts, seals, and signatures in the legal realm. The proliferation of written and printed texts that characterized the early modern period not only spurred the publication and wide circulation of countless books, pamphlets, and broadsheets—among them, numerous texts on witchcraft and demonic possession—but also satisfied the needs of a modernizing state and judicial system that saw paper documents as important vehicles of authority and key pieces of material evidence in court proceedings.[86] The pact of servitude concluded between witch and devil, newly valorized by demonologists as a central element in the sabbat narrative and paired with the cutaneous mark, constituted an eternally binding agreement that was very much in keeping with the legal contracts of the time, complete with written promises, terms, and signatures.[87] Signed by the witch, and sometimes by the devil, the pact condemned her to a life of enslavement in exchange for special powers, knowledge, or assistance. Indeed, De Lancre characterizes the devil as able to draw up contracts so tight "that there is almost no way at all to escape them and to get out of them."[88] The written pact produced as evidence against priest Urbain Grandier (1590–1634), tried and executed for bringing on the demonic possession of a whole convent of Ursuline nuns in Loudun (1632–1637), provides an example of one such contract (see Figure 1.4).[89] In it, Grandier renounces God and the Catholic Church and declares his allegiance to the devil, promising to obey and worship him, to perform as much evil as possible, and to bring others into the fold, signing his name and his life away to the devil should he not fulfill his pledge.

In the French courts of the sixteenth and seventeenth centuries, contracts and other certified documents carried strong probative value in judicial proceedings and were considered "literal proof" of the accused party's guilt or innocence.[90] The problem faced by witch trial judges, however, was that in most cases, the written pact, which would have proven a witch's guilt, failed to materialize during the trial. The devil's mark thus became the sole material evidence for what was otherwise an undocumented event, a powerful corporeal double of the signature on the absent pact. As folklorist François Delpech points out, the mark may even have represented "the transposition for the illiterate of the signature on the pact written in blood, reserved for more academic magicians, the body and the skin of the witch taking the place of parchment."[91] Moreover, in the case of a verbal agreement, which demonologists thought common among the illiterate, the mark gave the act materiality and longevity, as Rémy explains: "it is not enough for Demons to hold Men bound and fettered by a Verbal Oath: but they furthermore mark them . . . as an Enduring Witness of the Servitude to which they have subjected them."[92] Judges thus established what literary scholar Marie-Luce Demonet calls a "relationship of necessity (every witch's mark leads without fail to a pact with the devil)," in which they linked the visible mark—or if invisible, nonetheless localizable—to the invisible ceremony of the pact.[93] As French jurist and Calvinist theologian Lambert Daneau (ca. 1535–ca. 1590), one of the first to theorize the devil's mark in 1564, asserts, the physical mark on the witch's skin testified to the pact's existence and thus to the witch's guilt:

> There exists no Witch . . . who has not made a pact with the devil, and who has not given himself to him. And as testimony to this, they have and wear a mark, which the devil made on them in some part of their body.[94]

In a curious slippage from paper pact to cutaneous sign, De Lancre even suggests that the devil's mark no longer simply confirmed the pact's conclusion but took on a contractual function itself: "these marks are made as a kind of pledge that one will be a good and faithful friend to the Devil one's whole life."[95]

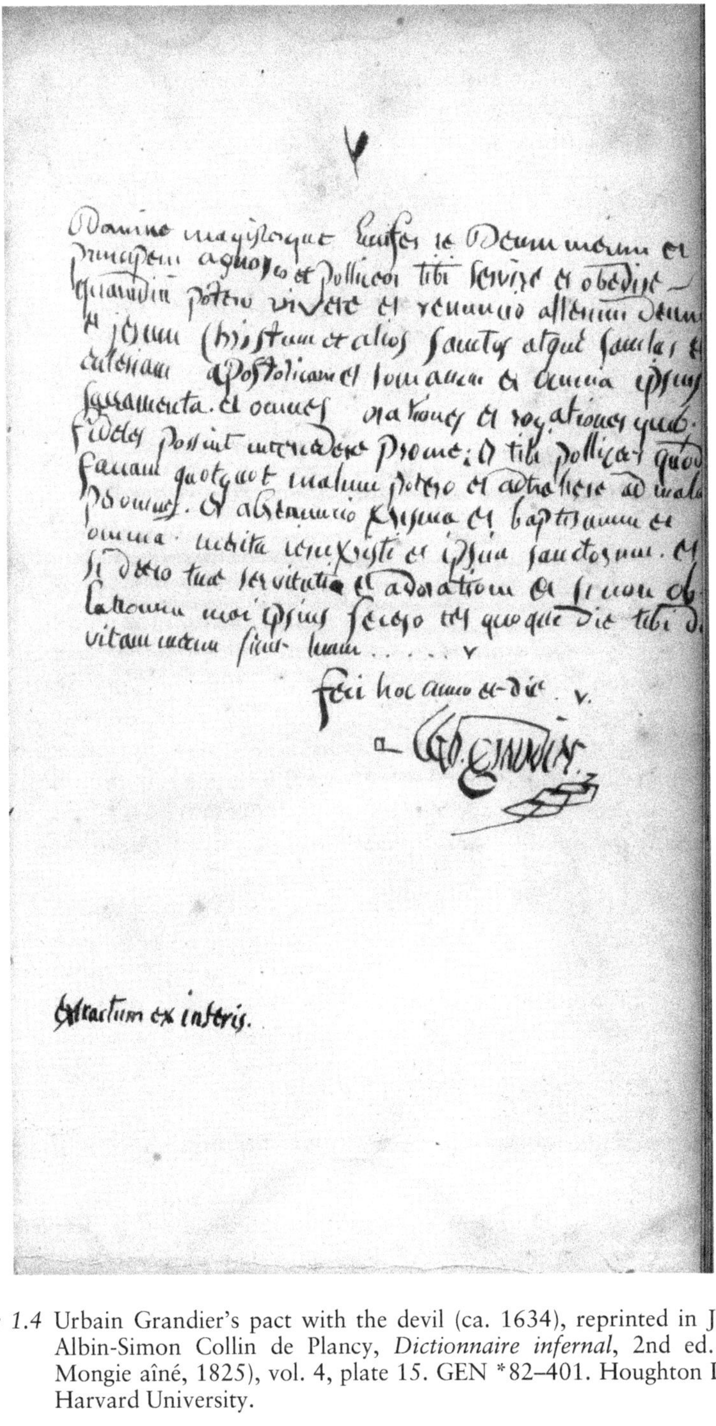

V

Domine magisterque Lucifer te Deum meum et
principem agnosco et polliceor tibi servire et obedire —
quamdiu potero vivere et renuncio alterum deum
et Jesum Christum et alios sanctos atque sanctas et
ecclesiam apostolicam et romanam et omnia ipsius
sacramenta. et omnes orationes et rogationes quib.
fideles possint intercedere pro me; et tibi pollicear quod
faciam quotquot malum potero et attrahere ad mala
omnes. et abrenuncio chrisma et baptismum et
omnia merita Jesu Christi et ipsius sanctorum. et
si desero tuae servituti et adorationi et si non ob-
lationem mei ipsius fecero ter quaque die tibi do
vitam meam sicut tuam. v

feci hoc anno et die . v.

Urb. Grandier

Extractum ex infris.

Figure 1.4 Urbain Grandier's pact with the devil (ca. 1634), reprinted in Jacques-Albin-Simon Collin de Plancy, *Dictionnaire infernal*, 2nd ed. (Paris: Mongie aîné, 1825), vol. 4, plate 15. GEN *82–401. Houghton Library, Harvard University.

In addition to standing in for or reinforcing the oral or written pact, the devil's mark, impressed upon the witch's skin, also closely resembled the seals and signatures of the period that gave legitimacy to paper and ink documents, public and private. Legislation governing seals and signatures, as well as that controlling the paper upon which they were embossed or inscribed, increased significantly beginning in the sixteenth century, only intensifying as the French crown sought to centralize judicial protocols. As Furetière's definition of *sceau* attests, each public authority had its own distinctive seal, "whose imprint serves to make an act authentic and legally binding," the color of the wax used to seal a document also communicating the particular power behind the mark.[96] Early moderns marked all things of judicial value, from edicts and contracts to pieces of evidence—even human corpses were sealed to mark them as belonging to the jurisdiction of the courts.[97] As jurist Claude Le Brun de la Rochette (1560–1630) relates in his 1607 *Procès civil et criminel*, written and printed documents, both public and private, had to be properly sealed and signed to be admissible in court and the signs upon them recognized as authentic by the interested parties and competent judicial authorities.[98] He cites numerous sixteenth-century laws that enforce these protocols, governing documents of all kinds, including edicts, contracts, wills, letters, and accounting books. A letter, for example, is only valid as a piece of evidence if it is "recognized, or verified, written, underwritten, or sealed with the seal of the party against whom it is produced."[99] The devil's mark—often called the "devil's seal" [*sigillum diaboli*]—was assuredly seen by writers living in a time when all things official were sealed as a similar type of authenticating sign. Raynaud suggests as much, defining both the mark of baptism and the devil's mark by comparing them to official state seals:

> [T]he character of baptism is like a seal, with which is sealed the pact concerning a new life that is entered into with God and that is strengthened by the apposition of a royal seal, as is customary in the making of official documents. . . . Likewise the apposition of this [devil's] mark, just like the impression of a public seal, attests that a firm and inviolable pact has been entered into with Satan, which is truly a pact with death.[100]

In both cases, the mark effectively certifies the pact, be it with God or with the devil. Trial accounts reinforce this parallel between official seals and devil's marks as well. De Lancre, for example, describes the mark received on the buttocks by two men accused as werewolves as "a round mark in the shape of a little seal," impressed by a broach the devil happened to have on hand.[101]

Alongside its more ancient cousin, the signature rose in importance in this period and served as another point of reference for demonologists, who often compared the devil's mark to the signature on a contract. Construed in the sixteenth century more as a seal or an emblem than as a product of writing, the signature likewise carried an authenticating value.[102] At the beginning of the seventeenth century, Jean Nicot's 1606 *Thresor de la langue francoyse* defines *signer* as "*To make a sign or mark for the recognition and assurance of something.*"[103] A *seing*, or signature, was, then, most often figurative: a symbol, an object associated with one's trade, even a self-portrait, as visual examples attest.[104] A second pact from the Loudun possession, the demonic response to Grandier's original pact, represents the signatures of a whole legion of devils as a series of heterogeneous assemblages of written and figurative signs that, though written backward and containing oddities due to their purported demonic origin, were true to the signatures of the time (see Figure 1.5).[105] Even at the close of the seventeenth century, when the signature had greater affinity with an act of writing and actually signing one's name on legal documents had become common, *signe* still retained a more figurative meaning, as a synonym of "seal"—"the mark that each individual has chosen to mark the legal documents to which he has consented"—or, as the signature of the illiterate—"a mark that those who do not know how to write make, with the imprint of a seal."[106] The devil's mark on the body of the witch thus closely resembled both the signatures and seals that appeared on contracts of the period in its diverse figurative forms and was invested with a similar authenticating power.

The transposition of the mark from paper to skin that took place during the witch trials of the late sixteenth and seventeenth centuries surprises less when we consider how early modern demonologists wrote about both paper pacts and the devil's marks that so often replaced them. They drew frequently on textual metaphors for describing corporeal marking, often going so far as to conflate body and text. On the most basic level, the vocabulary of engraving and impression they used to describe the devil's marking of witches suggests important links between marking the body and the world of print: the devil's mark is *gravé* [engraved] or, more often, *imprimé* [printed, imprinted, impressed] upon the witch's body. Demonologists make use of scriptorial metaphors for the devil's mark as well, as the body of the witch replaces the paper or parchment pact as a surface for the inscription of the demon's signature. In discussing the Aix case, Michaëlis vividly evokes the resemblance between human skin and parchment—animal skin—when he writes that at the place of the accused Magdaleine de Demandouls's mark, her skin makes "a sound like that of parchment when you pierce it."[107] De Lancre enlarges this observation, transposing it more generally to the moment of marking itself: "And when the Devil puts needles in like this, and when he wants to make them enter, you would say that someone is piercing parchment."[108]

If the witch's skin became the devil's parchment, the written pact, as early modern demonologists conceived of it, was itself intensely corporeal. The paper or parchment pact bore traces of the bodily presence of both the witch and the devil, material vestiges of the witch's history of intimate

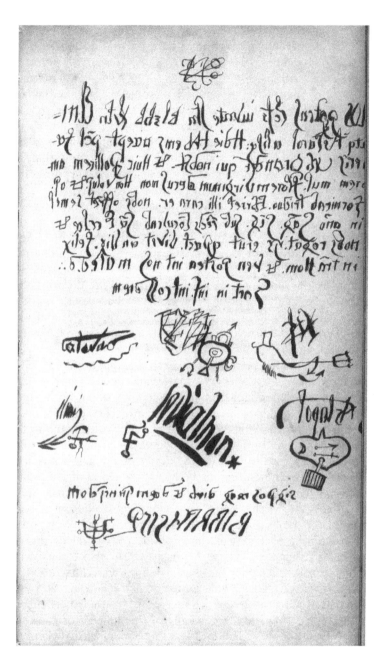

Figure 1.5 Demonic response to Urbain Grandier's pact, written backward with demons' signatures (ca. 1634), reprinted in Jacques-Albin-Simon Collin de Plancy, *Dictionnaire infernal*, 2nd ed. (Paris: Mongie aîné, 1825), vol. 4, plate 16. GEN *82–401. Houghton Library, Harvard University.

physical contact with him during the sabbat ritual.[109] As noted earlier, the pact was signed—or even written in its entirety—in the witch's blood.[110] Demonologists even suggest that some devil's marks were in fact the scars left on the place where he drew the witch's blood for the pact's signature, thus intimately linking the pact and the mark. De Lancre recounts that when Magdaleine makes her pact, her mentor Gaufridy, "in Beelsebub's presence, pricked her with a little punch in the shape of a needle in between the third and fourth fingers, to draw blood."[111] This physical proximity between paper pact and corporeal mark is also reflected in some early accounts of pact-making, where the signed document was worn against the body like an amulet, in direct contact with the flesh, or even lodged underneath the skin.[112] In an early example from Vevey, Switzerland, Jaquet Durier testified in 1448 that he wore a pact, written in his blood, sewn into his arm "between the skin and the flesh."[113] Another young man's pact magically inserted itself into his arm upon its conclusion at the spot where the devil had wounded him to obtain blood for its signing.[114]

Intimately linked to the witch's body, the pact also commonly contained traces of the devil's physical presence in the signs he left upon it, evidence of his often-debated ability to take corporeal form. As Robert Munchembled argues, "[f]or the judges, the mark was at least as important as a way of affirming the physical presence of the devil as it was in proving the guilt of the prisoners."[115] Durier testifies that his pact was soaked with the devil's sweat, and, given the bawdy revelries of the sabbat, one might imagine other bodily fluids imbibing pacts as well.[116] Traces of demonic "signatures" on paper pacts reproduced by Dutch Calvinist theologian Gijsbert Voet (1589–1676) suggest the reality of the devil's physical presence (see Figures 1.6 and 1.7).[117] One reproduction displays figurative signs that appear to be burned into the paper as a result of the devil laying a hand upon it and then tracing a cross. Holes burned through the paper of the second pact, apparently made by the demon's maleficent touch, penetrated much as the devil's mark emblazoned the witch's skin. The engraver of this pact chose to display it with the corner folded back to reveal its judicial seal, apparently to reinforce his viewer's belief in the document's legitimacy as a piece of evidence. A material vestige that signaled a now absent presence, the *marque* was "the trace, the impression that a body leaves behind when it has passed over another, either because of its weight, or its viscosity, or its malignity" and as such, it became a "proof, testimony" of a past event.[118] Here, the devil leaves a paper trail.

The body as evidence

As the comparisons used by early modern demonologists to describe the devil's mark attest, its creation and rise to prominence during the second half of the sixteenth century was, in part, the product of long-standing customs and beliefs. The baptismal sign, vestimentary badge, and brand

G Signum I° Manus, cum
grosse, a spina Huella appa-

figno Crucis ap-
rette, relictum.

FIGURES LAISSÉES PAR UN ESPRIT SUR UN PACTE.

Extrait du livre de Gilbert de Vos. 1625.

Figure 1.6 Signs of a hand and a cross made by a spirit upon a pact, Gijsbert Voet (1625), reprinted in Paul Regnard, *Sorcellerie, magnétisme, morphinisme, délire des grandeurs. Les Maladies épidémiques de l'esprit* (Paris: E. Plon, Nourrit et Cie, 1887), 11. Bibliothèque Nationale de France.

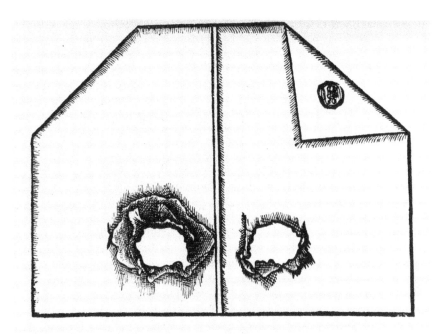

TRACES LAISSÉES PAR UN ESPRIT SUR UN PACTE.

Extrait du livre de Gilbert de Vos. 1625.

Figure 1.7 Traces left by a spirit on a pact, Gijsbert Voet (1625), reprinted in Paul
Regnard, *Sorcellerie, magnétisme, morphinisme, délire des grandeurs. Les
Maladies épidémiques de l'esprit* (Paris: E. Plon, Nourrit et Cie, 1887), 10.
Bibliothèque Nationale de France.

mark all placed *stigma* upon the body as signs of identification, indicating
membership, ownership, social status, or past transgression. The devil's
mark and its corresponding paper pact drew inspiration as well from more
contemporary developments: the advent of a legal culture that placed great
value on contracts, seals, and signatures and the proliferation of a variety of
modern marking practices that had the goal of identifying, validating, and
controlling people, paper, and products across Europe. The devil's mark,
which identified Satan's own and communicated his authority over them,
drew its materiality and meanings from all of these traditions. Indeed, given
the ubiquity and widespread use of the material mark in the early modern
period to identify, authenticate, and indicate ownership or belonging, it
would have been inconceivable that the devil did not mark his followers.

While these influences deeply informed the theoretical development of
the devil's mark and facilitated its acceptance as a determinant sign in the
witch trials of the sixteenth and seventeenth centuries, the invention and
proliferation of the devil's mark also responded to the demands of a newly

professionalized judicial system that, influenced by the growth of scientific empiricism, placed increasing value on material evidence to establish truth.[119] Early moderns viewed the devil's mark as providing tangible, materially verifiable proof of the reality of the accused's commerce with Satan, much like we place faith in DNA testing to prove guilt or innocence today. As Delpech puts it, the mark provided concrete proof of a witch's intimate contact with Satan—"*an immanence . . . of the demon in the body of the witch.*"[120] It furnished, in the words of Demonet, "an element accessible to the senses that testifie[d] to the alliance of the devil with a person's soul and body."[121] Paradoxically, then, the creation and rise of the devil's mark, which seems so irrational to our modern sensibilities, responded at least in part to a highly rational desire on the part of judges, influenced by scientific empiricism, for materially verifiable signs by which they could determine guilt.[122] As Brian Levack demonstrates, continental Romano-canonical law held sixteenth-century judges to high standards of proof that confronted those faced with the prosecution of a witch with serious hurdles.[123] Few people could ever actually testify that they saw a witch commit a crime and the crimes attributed to witches left little or no incriminating physical evidence behind.[124] Though the widespread perse-cution of witches brought about the relaxation of these rigid standards of proof—witchcraft was considered a *crime d'exception* and therefore subject to its own rules—judges may nonetheless have seen in the mark an answer to the problem of proof posed by the occult nature of the alleged crimes.[125] Faced with stories of unseen events, intangible offences, and witnesses who were themselves implicated in the crime, judges found in the mark the material evidence they needed to corroborate crimes and an answer to critics of the witch trials who saw these narratives as questionable sources upon which to base a conviction. Moreover, if the mark was real, so too was the sabbat, as De Lancre unequivocally affirms: "the mark with which the devil stigmatizes witches and children at the sabbat is a very strong proof of the reality of transport [to the sabbat]."[126] The mark's material existence thus reinforced the legitimacy of the judges' otherwise exceptional enterprise, providing a tangible trace of questionable and hidden crimes.

Placing value in the material sign thus conformed to judicial best practices of the day, which encouraged judges to privilege evidence that could be empirically verified by the senses. Bodin presents this evidentiary standard in his 1580 *Démonomanie des sorciers*:

> It is necessary to limit oneself to the truth of the established facts, which the judge sees or recognizes, or touches, or perceives, or knows through one of his five senses; such evidence is never excluded by edicts, sentences, or customs.[127]

Bodin's empiricism was shared by his fellow demonologists who based their treatment of the devil's mark, and of witchcraft in general, on their own experience as judges, creating what Hélène Hotton has aptly named a new "empirical demonology."[128] While Boguet admits in his preface that he has been helped in writing his treatise by reading the works of others, he insists on having drawn his conclusions "principally from experience"—from all he has "seen, heard, and probed most carefully" during his two years of presiding over witch trials.[129] De Lancre too insists on the empirical nature of the findings he communicates in his treatise, offering his reader "the ocular view of all the secrets that we have seen with our own eyes."[130] Demonologists' emphasis on sensory experience in the pursuit of understanding echoed that expressed by Renaissance anatomists and physicians, who saw in the observation of the open body a source of truth that surpassed that of ancient authorities.[131]

When discussing the devil's mark, these men underline their lived experience of it, using sensory language and highlighting their empirical methods: "we . . . discovered visibly;" "experience shows manifestly that;" "as we have seen with our own eyes, and proven with a needle or pin."[132] Rémy, who insists that he bases his conclusions on witches' lived experience of marking, invites anyone skeptical of the marks' validity to see, touch, and test them for himself:

> [T]he fact itself is beyond all doubt. For not only is it admitted by various persons who, in different places and at different times, have to their own loss experienced it, but they have even proved it by showing the traces of the marks visible to the eye. . . . The matter is, moreover, proved by the scars themselves, which are shown by a slight hardening of the skin, if anyone is doubtful and wishes to test the truth of it.[133]

Demonologists not only used empirical language but, as Rémy's description of the marks suggests, looked to medical discourse specifically to reinforce their claims. The fact that the only treatise of the period devoted solely to the devil's mark was penned not by an ecclesiastic or a judge but by a physician—Jacques Fontaine—testifies to this medicalization of the mark.[134] In his treatise, Fontaine deploys his scientific knowledge, comparing the physiological characteristics of devil's marks to those of other cutaneous abnormalities or insensitivities caused by disease. He concludes that any difficulty his predecessors and contemporaries have in distinguishing between natural and supernatural marks must be attributed to their own medical incompetence: "[B]ecause these authors do not place much confidence in the recognition of marks, they say it is difficult to distinguish them from a natural mark, in which they display clearly that they are not good doctors."[135]

To refute critics who claimed probable confusion between the devil's mark and natural cutaneous marks such as birthmarks, demonologists drew on the authority of scientific discourse, attributing to the devil's mark a set of particular anatomical and physiological characteristics to establish a distinct pathology. They concurred that all places that the devil touched were, without fail, dead; they were therefore insensitive, emitted no blood or serum when probed, and did not react following pricking, as Fontaine describes:

> As for the essence and the nature of witches' marks, they are found to be without any sensation, and without any humor at all, without any elevation of the skin, but at its surface. Testing proves the validity of what I say: because in piercing them more or less deeply with a needle, no sensation or humor is to be found coming out of the punctured spot, nor does any inflammation follow. From whence we can conclude that the part so disposed is dead. . . . It follows that they are dry, also that they are quite hard, and as difficult to pierce as boiled and dried leather.[136]

While Fontaine's reliance on scientific language to describe the mark does not surprise given his profession, other demonologists without Fontaine's training made regular use of the medical lexicon to justify their position. Rémy, for instance, concludes:

> Finally, speaking in surgical terms, an abrasion or excoriation of the skin only consists, unless there is any further complication, in the skin alone, and lies no deeper: whereas in the case of even the slightest wound of the sort we are discussing, every part beneath it for as far as the longest pin can penetrate is entirely drained of all feeling.[137]

Rémy's choice to "speak in surgical terms" betrays the magistrate's desire to ground solidly the truth of the devil's mark in corporeal reality. To do so, he calls on the authority of scientific discourse to give weight—and even depth—to his defense of the mark.

As Rémy's and Fontaine's descriptions suggest, the determinant characteristics of the devil's mark, as they came to be defined by early modern demonologists, could not be verified by sight or touch alone but required the penetration of the skin for their confirmation. With the invention of the insensitive mark that did not bleed, demonologists located truth not only upon the body's surface but beneath it as well. By creating a pathology that relied on scientific methods for its confirmation, court officials situated the devil's mark within the increasingly authoritative domain of medicine, effectively professionalizing the search for the mark.[138] Court-appointed medical professionals became natural and necessary allies in establishing the mark's validity as an empirically verifiable sign. Ironically, in probing the body of an accused witch in search of the devil's mark, medical professionals themselves marked the body in a kind of "counter-ritual, as if the investigator, taking his turn at attacking the skin of the accused, also wanted to leave his imprint and therein signify that the body had found a new master."[139]

Medical reports of examinations seek to reinforce the objectivity of the pricking process, locating the mark anatomically, describing its physical characteristics, and noting the depth to which the needle was inserted. An excerpt from the detailed report of Gaufridy's medical exam, performed on March 10, 1611, serves as an example:

> We, the undersigned doctors and surgeons, . . . visited sir L. Gaufridy, on whose body we noticed three small marks little different in color from the rest of the skin. One in the lower middle part of his left thigh, into which we having pushed a needle about two finger widths, he felt no pain, nor did any blood or other fluid come out of the spot. The second mark is in the region of the lower vertebrae, on the right side, one thumb length away from the spine and four fingers above the muscles of the buttocks, into which we drove the needle three finger widths, left it, as we had done with the first one, implanted in that place for a certain time, without the aforementioned Gaufridy feeling any pain or any blood or humor at all coming out of it.[140]

The doctors and surgeons performed a second examination the following day, during which they "did not recognize in the pricked parts either swelling, or redness," the wounded skin's lack of response leading them to conclude that the accused priest's marks were not the result of a preexisting skin condition but were clearly supernatural.[141] Accepted as scientifically conclusive, their empirical tests apparently convinced even Gaufridy himself and, when coupled with other testimony against him, sealed his fate.

In calling upon medical personnel to search for the devil's mark upon the skin, early modern magistrates extended what was already a standard role for surgeons in the courts: the shaving and physical inspection of criminals of all stripes prior to judicial torture for the purpose of finding "characters"—small, magically endowed paper amulets—hidden on their bodies to protect them from pain, thus impeding confession.[142] The Sieur de Bouvet, Provost-Marshal of the Armies of Louis XIV in Italy, describes the practice for all accused criminals as follows:

> [The judge] will have all his clothes taken off to his undergarment, and having therein stripped him naked, something will be put on him to cover his nakedness. Then, he will be examined in all the parts of his body, and particularly in the nostrils, the ears, the genitals, or even in any wounds or cuts, if any little slips of paper, or of membrane called virgin parchment can be found, in which there is sometimes enveloped a very little bit of wax, and some words inscribed.[143]

This commonly performed search clearly informed the later development of pricking for the devil's mark. In the case of witchcraft, shaving accused witches and clipping their nails for this purpose had already been recommended in the late fifteenth-century *Malleus Maleficarum*. Since the stripping of the accused and the probing of all orifices by a surgeon was already standard court procedure, it was, as William Monter points out, "a relatively short step to have professional surgeons shave and search suspected witches in order to discover the place where the Devil had marked them at the time of their pact."[144]

As court experts and examiners, doctors and surgeons thus became active participants in defining and defending the devil's mark as an empirically verifiable sign. A doctor himself, Fontaine finds the courts' recourse to medical professionals highly appropriate, given that cutaneous marks "were accidents of the human body, whose contemplation most rightly belonged to doctors than to many others of diverse professions."[145] In the dedication of his work to the Queen Mother and Regent, Marie de Médicis, Fontaine celebrates the growing investigative role of medical personnel in cases involving witchcraft and its corollary, demonic possession: "the judgment of a large number of such questions belongs to those who are medical professionals, as is evident by the reports that doctors in medicine make daily in similar circumstances."[146] Indeed, the involvement of physicians and surgeons as medical experts in cases of witchcraft was part of a much larger movement of judicial empiricism, as courts increasingly employed medical professionals to aid them in their determinations. For example, much like today, cases of homicide required that a surgeon examine the cadaver and report on the

> number of wounds he found in it . . . , their depth, length, and in what parts of the body they are imprinted, which ones are mortal and which ones are not, and with what kind of weapon the wounds were made.[147]

The surgeons and doctors who participated as medical experts in witchcraft cases, and those who supported their work, were, in effect, among the founders of modern forensic science.

The vanishing mark

The celebration of the mark as a tangible, empirically verifiable, sign and its widespread use as material evidence in the witch trials of the sixteenth and seventeenth centuries masked numerous uncertainties that persisted even for the demonologists who invented it. Faith in the mark as a determinant sign was not universal. Important voices both Catholic and Protestant spoke out against the extraordinary probative value many of their contemporaries attributed to it and questions and contradictions abounded, even within the accounts of defenders of the mark themselves.[148] Are all witches necessarily marked? Are children and youth who are brought to the sabbat marked? Can the devil mark a person without her consent? Can the devil erase his marks, hide them temporarily, or renew their sensitivity, once made? If a witch converts, are his marks erased? Demonologists wrestled with these theoretical problems with varying responses, and some went to great rhetorical lengths in their attempt to uphold the validity of the devil's mark as a sign of proof. Fontaine's treatise on the devil's mark, an exercise in tautological argument, is a case in point: if a witch does not appear to be marked, he argues, it is either because she is already so faithful to the devil that he did not feel the need to mark her, or he has hidden his mark so well that it cannot be found, or he has erased it so that the witch cannot be convicted, or the surgeons employed to look for it are simply incompetent.[149] Similar rhetorical gymnastics characterize other demonologists' treatment of the mark. Even Boguet, who openly testifies that, despite his experience, he has never actually seen a devil's mark, remains resolute in his judgment that it exists:

> As for me, I was never able to see even one of these marks, despite the fact that I was very conscientious about it, and that the witches I was trying even confessed that Satan marked them, to the point where George Grandillon showed me the place where the devil had touched him, that is to say on the left shoulder, without me being able to perceive anything.[150]

For Boguet, the mark lies just beyond his ability to apprehend it. Yet he wants so much to support the mark's reality that he attributes his inability to see it to his court's temporary lack of a proper medical expert to empirically verify its existence: "even so I lay the blame on the fact that we had no expert surgeon at that time."[151]

One of the major problems that plagued early modern doctors and judges throughout the witch trials was that of the vanishing mark. As Boguet asserts, not only are devil's marks "very difficult to find because they are not very apparent," but "the Devil most often erases them once the witches are in judicial hands."[152] Marks visible one day often disappear the next, creating a problem for the witch's prosecutors. Bodin recounts two such instances:

> Aubert of Poitiers, a Lawyer in parlement, told me that he had attended the pretrial investigation of a high-ranking Witch of Thieri Castle, who was found to be marked on the right shoulder, and the next day the devil had erased the mark. Mr. Claude Deffay, the King's prosecutor in Ribemont, told me of a similar case, that he had seen the mark of the Witch Jehanne Heruillier, whose whole trial transcript he sent me, and the next day the mark was found to be erased.[153]

Numerous cases of vanishing marks surface in trial accounts, and those who write about the mark devote significant attention to the question as to whether or not the devil can erase his marks from a witch's skin to avoid her conviction or simply to confound her judges.[154] Much as the mark's potential to disappear allowed jurists greater flexibility—it explained why the mark could not be found on some witches and enabled judges to argue that the mark was once present, but through demonic ruse had since disappeared—marks here today, gone tomorrow posed difficulties for the positioning of the devil's mark as an infallible material sign upon which condemnation or acquittal could depend. Between the potential for the mark's erasure by the devil and the many examples of invisible marks, discernable only through their insensitivity to the needle, the devil's mark proved to be, in fact, a remarkably capricious and elusive sign.

These disappearing acts seem to foreshadow the mark's destiny, and ultimately that of witch prosecutions as a whole, as the seventeenth century wore on. The demise of the devil's mark, while an abundance of other marking practices continued to proliferate into the modern era, was, of course, part of the larger decline of witch belief and increase in skepticism characteristic of what would become the Enlightenment, especially among the elite who ran the courts. A growing distaste for torture contributed as well to the gradual elimination of the degrading and painful process of pricking itself, without which the mark could not exist. Even De Lancre, a committed witch hunter and a major proponent of the devil's mark, found fault with the torturous process after extensive experience in the Labourd region. Already in the second edition of his *Tableau de l'inconstance des mauvais anges et démons*, published in 1613, he inserts a scathing assessment of pricking as a flawed and barbaric method for discerning truth, masquerading under the guise of cold empiricism:

> But now after many consultations by our doctors and surgeons, those who are charged to examine them have become accustomed to pricking them with an awl or a needle in several places in their bodies, and if by chance they find the whole body to be insensitive, . . . they have no regard for anything other than seeing if the needle is bloody, or if in the place that they make the prick there is some appearance or demonstration of blood. This is done both with a kind of cruelty and uncertainty throughout. Because if the Witch has a dozen or more little signs or marks on her body, they prick her everywhere almost as deeply as in the mark itself, so much so that sometimes she is all bloody. If she is insensitive everywhere, they are looking for the insensitivity of the mark in vain, given that her whole body is one sole mark. . . . So, since all things have their limits, I would readily believe that pushing the needle in further is not the best test. Because pricking in places where the true mark is not, and always pushing the needle in so far and to such an extent, it is a kind of torture.[155]

As early as 1610, the Paris Parlement, which had jurisdiction over nearly half of France and had never been enthusiastic in its use of the mark, had stopped considering the devil's mark as evidence. But if the mark quickly lost ground in France's center, it continued its career as an important evidentiary sign in many provincial courts in France, elsewhere in Europe, and in the North American colonies, as numerous cases testify.[156] In the 1640s, the Paris Parlement condemned several lower regional courts for continuing to prick witches.[157] French-speaking Switzerland continued to search for the mark through the 1660s and 1670s.[158] By the end of the seventeenth century judges across Europe had become increasingly reluctant to admit the devil's mark—the main proof of the existence of a pact between witch and devil—as viable evidence, making witchcraft quite difficult to prove.[159] In France, a 1682 royal decree, the product of long-standing debate, marked an official end to the vast majority of witch trials across the country and eliminated the "true witch" on a juridical level, shifting attention to the prosecution of diviners, poisoners, and imposters for their malevolent actions against others.[160]

One of Furetière's 1690 dictionary definitions of *marquer* testifies to the climate of skepticism in France as the seventeenth century drew to a close: "Some also claim that the Devil *marks* Witches, that they have a part of their body that is insensitive."[161] Furetière's use of the verb *prétendre*—to claim, but with the implication that the person doing so is wrong—is a far cry from the certainty that so many judges had expressed a century earlier. Just as it appeared and disappeared on the skin of countless witches, the devil's mark, prominent at the turn of the seventeenth century, faded from visibility at the turn of the eighteenth. Yet, while the imaginary of the sabbat and all of its trappings, which filled demonological treatises and fueled witchcraft persecutions, may seem the stuff of extraordinary and ill-intentioned fantasy that we wish to relegate to some dark past, the devil's mark itself was very much a product of modern times. Built not only on well-established traditions of corporeal marking associated with identity, recognition, and belonging but also on the models offered by widespread contemporary marking practices in the commercial and judicial realms, the devil's mark took its place alongside the seals, signatures, brands, and badges that characterized the modernizing state. Like these signs, devil's marks upon the body identified the witch, enabled his recognition, and verified the authenticity of his pact with the devil through the use of a material sign. Moreover, they provided physical, empirically verifiable evidence of the existence of the pact; gave material reality to the sabbat ceremony itself; and declared a witch's guilt according to a new standard of proof. This recourse to the corporeal for the material expression of an otherwise hard to establish truth finds echoes in contemporary discourses on demonic possession, pilgrimage tattooing, and judicial branding, examined in subsequent chapters of this book, discourses that made the body a powerful medium for the expression of truth and identity. Indeed, the theorization of the devil's mark and the methods used for its detection directly informed the spectacular convent possessions of the 1640s, examined in the next chapter, where a novel set of cutaneous signs emerged once again to declare truths about the bodies that bore them.

Notes

1 Claude Caron, *L'Antechrist demasque* (Tournon: Guillaume Linocier, 1589), 57ff. Throughout this chapter, I will refrain from constantly qualifying actions that are attributed to demons or the devil by source texts and instead present events as period writers reported them.

2 This scenario of possessed demons as accusers repeats itself in many infamous cases of the period, including a case at Laon (1566–1578) and the convent cases at Aix-en-Provence (1609–1611), Loudun (1632–1637), Auxonne (1658–1663), and Louviers (1642–1647). See Chapter 2.

3 On the development of the sabbat narrative, see Nicole Jacques-Chaquin and Maxime Préaud, eds., *Le sabbat des sorciers en Europe, XVe-XVIIIe siècles* (Grenoble: Jérôme Millon, 1993), Stuart Clark, *Thinking with Demons: The Idea of Witchcraft in Early Modern Europe* (Oxford and New York: Oxford University Press 1997), 139–42, and Brian P. Levack, *The Witch-Hunt in Early Modern Europe* (London and New York: Longman, 1988), 26.

4 Caron, *L'Antechrist demasque*, 65–66.

5 Ibid., 66–67. Henry Boguet retells Caron's difficult search in his own *Discours execrable des sorciers* [1602], 2nd ed. (Paris: Denis Binet, 1603), 107. For comparison, see the method described by Pierre de Lancre, *Tableau de l'inconstance des mauvais anges et démons* (Paris: Jean Berjon, 1612), 186.

6 The devil's mark is touched on throughout the expansive body of scholarship on the European witch trials. For in-depth treatment of the mark itself, see François Delpech's seminal analysis, "La 'marque' des sorcières: logique(s) de la stigmatisation diabolique," in *Le Sabbat des sorciers*, ed. Jacques-Chaquin and Préaud, 347–68. Marie-Luce Demonet builds on Delpech's study, expertly examining Pierre de Lancre and Jacques Fontaine's treatment of the devil's mark in relationship to the larger context of Renaissance semiology in "Les marques insensibles, ou les nuages de la certitude," *Littératures Classiques* 25 (Fall 1995): 97–134. Martine Ostorero offers an important perspective on the mark's origins and role in early Swiss trials in "Les Marques du diable sur le corps des sorcières (XIVe-XVIIe siècles)," in *La pelle umana. The Human Skin, Micrologus* 13 (2005): 359–88. Most recently, see Hélène Hotton's doctoral dissertation, *Les marques du diable et les signes de l'Autre: rhétorique du dire démonologique à la fin de la Renaissance*, Doctoral thesis, Université de Montréal, 2011. On the judicial history of the devil's mark see: Heikki Pihlajamäki, "Swimming the Witch, Pricking for the Devil's Mark: Ordeals in the Early Modern Witchcraft Trials," *Journal of Legal History* 21.2 (April 2000): 35–58 and Orna Alyagon Darr, "The Devil's Mark: A Socio-Cultural Analysis of Physical Evidence," *Continuity and Change* 24.2 (August 2009): 361–87. On the judicial status of sabbat, see Alfred Soman, "Le sabbat des sorciers: preuve juridique," in *Le Sabbat des sorciers*, ed. Jacques-Chaquin and Préaud, 85–99. Useful encyclopedia entries are Rossell Hope Robins, "Devil's Mark" and "Witch's Mark" in *The Encyclopedia of Witchcraft and Demonology* (New York: Crown Publishers, 1959), 135–37 and 551–53 and William Monter, "Devil's Mark" and Vincinzo Lavenia, "Witch's Mark," in *The Encyclopedia of Witchcraft: The Western Tradition*, ed. Richard M. Golden, 4 vols. (Santa Barbara, CA: ABC-Clio, 2006), vol. 1, 275–77 and vol. 4, 1220–21. See also: Montague Summers, *The History of Witchcraft and Demonology* (New York: Alfred A. Knopf, 1926), 76–77; Lynn Thorndike, *A History of Magic and Experimental Science*, 8 vols. (New York: Macmillan, 1923-1958), vol. 7, 353–59; Henry Charles Lea, *Materials Toward a History of Witchcraft*, ed. Arthur C. Howland (New York and London: Thomas Yoseloff, 1957), vol. 2, 888–92; Étienne Delcambre, *Le concept de la sorcellerie dans le duché de Lorraine au XVIe et au XVIIe siècle*

(Nancy: Société d'archéologie lorraine, 1948), vol. 1, 86–96; William Monter, *Witchcraft in France and Switzerland: The Borderlands during the Reformation* (Ithaca and London: Cornell University Press, 1976), 157–66; Jean-Thierry Maertens, *Ritologiques I. Le Dessein sur la peau. Essai d'anthropologie des inscriptions tégumentaires* (Paris: Aubier Montaine, 1978), 109–14; Robert Mandrou, *Magistrats et sorciers en France au XVIIe siècle. Une analyse de psychologie historique* (Paris: Éditions du Seuil, 1980), 99–104; and Robert Munchembled, *A History of the Devil from the Middle Ages to the Present* [Paris: Seuil, 2000], trans. Jean Birrell (Cambridge, UK: Polity Press, 2003), 64–66. In the late nineteenth century, Jean-Martin Charcot and his colleagues took an avid interest in the devil's mark in relationship to the cutaneous symptoms of hysteria. Gilles de la Tourette, *Traité clinique et thérapeutique de l'hystérie d'après l'enseignement de la Salpêtrière* (Paris: E. Plon, Nourrit et Cie, 1891), begins his chapter on cutaneous anesthesia with a treatment of the devil's mark. See Steven Connor, *The Book of Skin* (London: Reaktion Books, 2004), 120–35.

7 I use masculine and feminine pronouns alternately throughout this chapter to refer to accused witches. Though far more women than men were executed as witches across Europe, men were also present among them and, as William Monter shows, France was remarkable in that half of the witches executed there were men; Bengt Ankarloo, Stuart Clark, and William Monter, *Witchcraft and Magic in Europe: The Period of the Witch Trials* (Philadelphia, PA: University of Pennsylvania Press, 2002), 42.

8 Monter, *Witchcraft in France and Switzerland*, 163. The belief in the possibility of multiple marks was undoubtedly fueled by metoposcopic ideas about multiple planetary marks, some visible, some hidden. See, for example Girolamo Cardano, *La Metaposcopie*, trans. C.M. de Lavrendiere (Paris: Thomas Jolly, 1658), 184–221 and Richard Saunders, *Treatise of the Moles of the Body of Man and Woman*, in *Physiognomonie and Chiromancie, Metoposcopie* (London: Nathaniel Brook, 1653, 2nd ed. 1671), 2nd ed., 307–69. In the 1653 edition of his work, Saunders provides a map of moles on the face that links them with lines to corresponding signs elsewhere on the body to the point of illegibility; 262.

9 On the demonologists of the period in the context of witch trails, see: Nicole Jacques-Chaquin's introduction to her and Philippe Huvet's edition of Henry Boguet, *Discours exécrable des sorciers* [Paris: Denis Binet, 1602] (Paris: Le Sycomore, 1980); Sophie Houdard, *Les Sciences du diable. Quatre discours sur la sorcellerie (XVe-XVIIe siècle)* (Paris: Les Éditions du Cerf, 1992); Clark, *Thinking with Demons*; Jonathan L. Pearl, *The Crime of Crimes: Demonology and Politics in France, 1560–1620* (Waterloo, Ontario: Wilfrid Laurier University Press, 1999); and Jan Machielsen, *Martin Delrio: Demonology and Scholarship in the Counter-Reformation* (Oxford: Oxford University Press, 2015). Though less known today, the *Compendium Maleficarum* was widely regarded in its day as an authoritative textbook on witchcraft; Summers, "Introduction," in Francesco Maria Guazzo, *Compendium Maleficarum* [1608], ed. Montague Summers, trans. E.A. Ashwin (Secaucus, NJ: University Books, 1974), vol. 1, xv. On marking's place in the sabbat ritual, see Guazzo, vol. 2, 15–16 and Martin Antoine Delrio, [*Disquisitionum magicarum* (Louvain: Gerard Rivius, 1599–1600)] *Les Controverses et recherches magiques*, ed. and trans. André Du Chesne (Paris: Regnauld Chaudière, 1611), 121–22.

10 "Judicial torture," conducted during trial proceedings as an investigative method, differed in its goals from torture accompanying the punishment of a sentenced criminal; Levack, *The Witch-Hunt*, 70. For physician Jacques

Fontaine, medical examiner in the Aix-en-Provence trial of Louys Gaufridy, the mark proved so conclusive that other evidence was certain to be forthcoming; Fontaine, *Discours des marques des sorciers* (Paris: Denis Langlois, 1611), 11. See also Aix inquisitor Sébastien Michaëlis's defense of the mark as a sure sign of guilt; Michaëlis, *Histoire admirable de la possession et conversion d'une penitente* [1613], 3rd ed. (Paris: Charles Chastellain, 1614), part 2, 79. On the infallibility of the mark, see also Peter Ostermann, *Commentarius juridicus ad L. Stigmata C. de Fabricensibus* (Cologne: Petrus Metternich, 1629), 51, in *Materials Toward a History of Witchcraft*, Lea, vol. 2, 888–92.

11   Monter, "Devil's Mark," 276.
12   Boguet, *Discours execrable*, 108.
13   De Lancre, *Tableau de l'inconstance*, 181–82; see also 189.
14   Guazzo, *Compendium Maleficarum*, vol. 2, 15, Delrio, *Controverses magiques*, 224 and 760, and Ludovico Maria Sinistrari, *De Dæmonialitate* [1699, first circulated in manuscript form in 1680], qtd. and trans. in *The History of Witchcraft*, Summers, 71–72, available in a modern edition, *De la Démonialité et des animaux incubes et succubes,* ed. Isabelle Hersant and Xavier Carrère, trans. Isidore Lisieux (Toulouse: Éditions Ombres, 1998). For an eighteenth-century skeptic's take, see François Gayot de Pitaval, *Causes célèbres et intéressantes, avec les jugemens qui les ont décidées*, 20 vols. (Paris: Theodore Legras et al., 1734–1748), vol. 6, 197–98. See also Maertens, *Ritologiques I*, 113, and Delpech, "La 'marque' des sorcières," 359–60 on the lack of orthodoxy in the marks' presentation. Critics of the devil's mark cite the inconsistencies in its shape and its potential confusion with natural marks. See, for example, Delrio, *Controverses magiques*, 760, and Fontaine, who refutes this critique at length in his *Discours des marques*, 13–17. One distinction must be made from the outset between the types of devil's marks described in continental European treatises and the teat-like protuberances at which familiars were thought to suckle, described only in the British Isles and in New England. This type of mark never appeared in France. See Summers, *The History of Witchcraft*, 75–77, Darr, "The Devil's Mark," 361–87, and the entries for "Devil's Mark" and "Witch's Mark" in Robins, *The Encyclopedia of Witchcraft* and Golden, *The Encyclopedia of Witchcraft*. On familiars, see Charlotte Rose Miller, "The Witch's Familiar in Sixteenth-Century England," *Melbourne Historical Journal* 38 (2010): 113–30, Darr, "The Devil's Mark," 364–66, and "Familiars" in Golden, *Encyclopedia of Witchcraft*.
15   De Lancre, *Tableau de l'inconstance*, 186.
16   Boguet, *Discours execrable*, 106. Boguet thus contradicts himself, affirming here the universality of the mark. On locations and forms of the mark, see: Lambert Daneau, *Les Sorciers* (Geneva: Jacques Bourgeois, 1574), 68–69; Jean Bodin, *De la démonomanie des sorciers* (Paris: Jacques du Puys, 1580), fols. 79v–80r; Guazzo, *Compendium Maleficarum*, vol. 2, 15; Nicolas Rémy, *Demonolatriæ libri tres* [Lyon: Vincentii, 1595], trans. E.A. Ashwin, *Demonolatry*, ed. Montague Summers (Secaucus, NJ: University Books, 1974), vol. 1, 9; Fontaine, *Discours des marques*, 13; and Théophile Raynaud, *De stigmatismo, sacro et profano, divino, humano, daemoniaco* [1647], 2nd ed. (Lyon: Antoine Cellier, 1654), 372–75. Some gender differentiation occurs, as women are more often marked on the breasts and genitals while men on the shoulder and anus. On this, see Delrio, *Controverses magiques*, 760, Guazzo, *Compendium Maleficarum*, vol. 2, 15, and Sinastrari, in Summers, *The History of Witchcraft*, 71–72. Magdaleine de Demandouls, accused as a witch in Aix-en-Provence in 1611, testifies that all witches ordinarily bear devil marks on their brains, hearts, and kidneys, with those of high-ranking witches buried deep within the body to hide them; Michaëlis, *Histoire admirable*, part 2, 30.

17 Fontaine, *Discours des marques*, 7.

18 De Lancre, *Tableau de l'inconstance*, 183.

19 Ibid. Of course, this theorization of the devil's mark as hidden also provided a way out for prosecutors who could not locate the mark.

20 On the birthmark in popular belief, see François Delpech, "Les Marques de naissance: Physiognomonie, signature magique et charisme souverain," in *Le Corps dans la société espagnole des XVIe et XVIIe siècles*, Augustin Redondo, ed. (Paris: Publications de la Sorbonne, 1990), 27–49 and Karl Jaberg, "The Birthmark in Folk Belief, Language, Literature, and Fashion," *Romance Philology* 10.4 (1957): 307–42.

21 Members of the local elite also often engaged in efforts to educate the population regarding the mark and witches' activities more generally during witch hunts; Levack, *The Witch-Hunt*, 26.

22 Fontaine, *Discours des marques*, 5.

23 Bodin, *De la démonomanie*, bk. 2, ch. 4, fol. 80r.

24 De Lancre, *Tableau de l'inconstance*, 186. De Lancre is quick, however, to reassure his readers that despite the women's best efforts, "all this did not hinder us from visibly discovering the mark;" ibid.

25 Monter, *Witchcraft in France and Switzerland*, 157 and Levack, *The Witch-Hunt*, 49. Heinrich Kramer and Jakob Sprenger, *The Maleficarum of Heinrich Kramer and James Sprenger*, ed. and trans. Montague Summers (London: Pushkin Press, 1971) and in French translation (under Kramer's commonly Latinized last name), Henry Institoris and Jacques Sprenger, *Le Marteau des Sorcières*, trans. Amand Danet (Grenoble: Jérôme Millon, 1990).

26 Ostorero, "Les Marques du diable," 383. By 1550, authorities in these regions systematically searched accused witches for the mark. Kurt Baschwitz dates the earliest mentions of the mark to 1428; *Procès de sorcellerie: histoire d'une psychose collective* (Paris: Arthaud, 1973), 225. Ostorero and Monter both date the mark's profusion in Vaud and Geneva regions to 1534; Ostorero, "Les Marques du diable," 368 and 383 and Monter, *Witchcraft in France and Switzerland*, 157–66. See also Delpech, "La 'marque' des sorcières," 350–51, nn. 8 and 9 and Demonet, "Les marques insensibles," 102.

27 For an overview of the varied positions and practices regarding the devil's mark across Europe, England, and New England, see Monter, "Devil's Mark" and Lavenia, "Witches Mark." Demonet examines the contradictions within De Lancre's and Fontaine's own presentations of the mark in "Les marques insensibles," as does Hotton for a larger corpus in *Les marques du diable*, esp. 281–363. The Paris Parlement, whose authority extended to about half of France, was far more reticent in their use of the mark than were many regional courts; Soman, "Le sabbat des sorciers," 95–96, Robert Munchembled, *La Sorcière au village (XVe-XVIIIe siècle)* (Paris: Gallimard-Julliard, 1979), 261–69, and Levack, *The Witch-Hunt*, 85–89.

28 Clark, *Thinking with Demons*. A case in point is Jean Bodin, whose *Six livres de la République* (Paris: Jacques du Puys, 1576) is famous for providing the foundations for modern government. He was also the author of the 1580 *Demonomanie des sorciers*, the most often reprinted of his works, with ten editions before 1604.

29 In discussing these marking practices, I draw and continue to build on the important studies by Delpech, "La 'marque' des sorcières," and Demonet, "Les Marques insensibles." I am also grateful to Hélène Hotton who generously shared with me her doctoral dissertation, *Les marques du diable et les signes de l'Autre*, during the final stages of the writing of this chapter.

30 See the Introduction, Delpech, "La 'marque' des sorcières," 356–57, and Demonet, "Les marques insensibles," 103–4.

31   On the idea of the innate sign and folk traditions surrounding the birthmark, see Delpech, "Les Marques de naissance" and Jaberg, "The Birthmark."

32   Marc Bloch traces this belief from the medieval period in *Les Rois thaumaturges. Étude sur le caractère surnaturel attribué à la puissance royale particulièrement en France et en Angleterre* (Paris: Armand Colin, [1924] 1961), 246–56 and 300–3. There are numerous literary examples of the birthmark as proof of identity, among them Honoré d'Urfé (1567–1625), "Histoire de Rosanire, Celiodante, et Rosileon," in *L'Astrée* [1607–1627] (Geneva: Slatkine Reprints, 1966), vol. 4, bk. 10, 569–645 and Pierre Augustin Caron de Beaumarchais (1732–1799), *La Folle Journée ou le Mariage de Figaro* [1785] (Paris: Garnier, 1985), Act III, Scenes 15 and 16. See also Gaston Paris, "Le cycle de la gageure," ed. J. Bédier, *Romania* 32 (1903): 481–551.

33   These healers were widely rebuked as con men by period authors. See Raynaud, *De stigmatismo*, sect. 2, ch. 4, 311–26; Leonard Vair, *Trois livres des charmes*, trans. Julian Baudon (Paris: Nicolas Chesneau, 1583), bk. 2, ch. 11, 275–76; Delrio, *Controverses magiques*, bk. 1, qu. 4, 49–52; De Lancre, *Tableau de l'inconstance*, 190–91 and *L'incrédulité et mescréance du sortilège plainement convaincue* (Paris: Nicolas Buon, 1622), 156; and Jean-Baptiste Thiers, *Traité des superstitions* (Paris, Antoine Dezallier, 1679), 431–33. On the *Pauliani*, see Katharine Park, "Country Medicine in the City Marketplace: Snakehandlers As Itinerant Healers," *Renaissance Studies* 15.2 (2001): 104–20 and David Gentilcore, "Charlatans and Medical Secrets," in *Healers and Healing in Early Modern Italy* (Manchester and New York: Manchester University Press, 1998), 96–124.

34   "Characters" were also believed to be divinely imprinted by the rites of confirmation and ordination, as reaffirmed by the Council of Trent; "Decree on the Sacraments," Canon 9, March 3, 1547, *The Council of Trent. The Canons and Decrees of the Sacred and Oecumenical Council of Trent*, ed. and trans. J. Waterworth (London: C. Dolman, 1848), 55; see also Session 23, Canon 4 of July 15, 1563. The recent 1992 catechism still places emphasis on the character as conferring identity and membership to its bearer; *Catechism of the Catholic Church* (Vatican City: Libreria Editrice Vaticana, 1993), part 2, sect. 1, ch. 1, art. 2.2, 1121, accessed June 27, 2012, www.vatican.va/archive/ ENG0015/_INDEX.HTM.

35   Rayaud, *De Stigmatismo*, 352. All translations from the original Latin text are by Erika Nickerson and Samantha Waxman, and verified by Barbara Weiden Boyd.

36   Le Loyer, *Discours de spectres*, 2nd ed. (Paris: Nicolas Buon, 1608), bk. 8, ch. 7, 901–2.

37   Michaëlis, *Histoire admirable*, part 2, 80. See also part 2, 172.

38   Galations 6:17. Devotional literature often used the divine character as metaphor. For the 1691 *Dictionnaire chrétien*, being a good Christian meant carrying "the idea of God imprinted like an indelible seal on our heart," following the biblical injunction, "Set me as a seal upon thine heart, as a seal upon thine arm" (Song of Solomon 8:6); "Cachet," in Nicolas Fontaine, *Le Dictionnaire chretien* (Paris: Elie Josset, 1691), 90. See also *Trois Sermons de S. Augustin*, trans. M. René Benoist (Paris, Jean Poupy, 1579), fol. 3.

39   Boguet, *Discours execrable*, 106. See also De Lancre, *Tableau de l'inconstance*, 183 and Guazzo, *Compendium Maleficarum*, vol. 2, 15–16. On this idea, see Clark, *Thinking with Demons*, 80–93.

40   Raynaud, *De Stigmatismo*, 364; see also 352–53.

41   De Lancre, *L'incrédulité et mescréance*, 410. My emphasis. See also De Lancre, *Tableau de l'inconstance*, 182. In contrast, Guazzo asserts that the devil has

marked heretics from the earliest times; *Compendium malieficarum*, vol. 2, 15–16. Michaëlis too cites biblical sources for the mark to bolster its authority, *Discours des esprits*, 172–73.

42 Fontaine, *Discours des marques*, 7.
43 Gayot de Pitaval, *Causes célèbres*, vol. 6, 197.
44 Fontaine, *Discours des marques*, 6; see also 18.
45 Ibid., 6.
46 Raynaud, *De Stigmatismo*, 390. Raynaud cites Rémy on this question, though he will ultimately disagree with this assertion; see 390–94. While demonologists affirm the devil's ability to mark Christians, most ultimately deny him the capacity to erase the baptismal mark. See, for example, De Lancre, *Tableau de l'inconstance*, 183–84 and 192. This denial ultimately transfers full responsibility to the witch, for if the devil cannot impose his mark without the witch's express cooperation in renouncing her Christian baptism, no one who bears it can be innocent. On the larger question, see: Raynaud, *De Stigmatismo*, 392 and 404; Rémy, *Demonolatry*, 9; and Delrio, who changes his take on the issue between 1608 and 1611, *Investigations into Magic*, ed. and trans. Peter G. Maxwell-Stuart (Manchester, UK: Manchester University Press, 2000), 75 and *Les Controverses magiques*, 122. See also 759, where Delrio critiques those who believe the devil can scrape off the mark of baptism.
47 Rémy, *Demonolatry*, 9.
48 Louis Lalement, *Mémoire sur la manière de juger les sorciers* [1671], rpt. in Robert Mandrou, *Possession et sorcellerie au XVIIe siècle. Textes inédits* (Paris: Fayard, 1979), 226. On the demonic chrism, see also De Lancre, *Tableau de l'inconstance*, 800 and 802.
49 See, for example, Delrio, *Controverses magiques*, 121–22 and Guazzo, *Compendium maleficarum*, vol. 2, 15–16.
50 Michaëlis, *Discours des esprits*, 172–73.
51 See, for example, Boguet, *Discours execrable*, 106, Fontaine, *Discours des marques*, 6, and Raynaud, *De stigmatismo*, 364. The early writings of Tertullian (ca. 155–ca. 240) and Irenaeus (died in 202) also include mention of the mark upon Satan's faithful. On the mark of the beast, see Revelation 13:16–17, 14:11, 16:2, 19:20, 20:4. On the seal of God, see Revelation 7:2–8, 9:4. See also Clark, *Thinking with Demons*, 381–82.
52 See Jacques Le Brun, "Les discours de la stigmatisation au XVIIe siècle," in *Stigmates*, ed. Courcelles, *Les Cahiers de l'Herne* 75 (Paris: Éditions de l'Herne, 2001), 103–18 and Nicole Pellegrin, "L'écriture des stigmates. (XVIe-XVIIIe siècles)," in *La Blessure corporelle. Violences et souffrances, symboles et représentations*, ed. Pierre Cordier and Sébastien Jahan, *Les Cahiers du Gerhico* 4 (2003): 41–62, republished as "Fleurs saintes. L'écriture des stigmates (XVIe-XVIIIe siècles)," in *Femmes en fleurs, femmes en corps. Sang, Santé, Sexualités du Moyen Âge aux Lumières*, eds. Cathy McClive and Nicole Pellegrin (Saint-Étienne: Publications de l'Université de Saint-Étienne, 2010), 101–22. For further discussion, see Chapter 2.
53 Raynaud's monumental 1647 treatise devotes several chapters to divine stigmata; *De stigmatismo*, ch. 8–14.
54 De Lancre, *Tableau de l'inconstance*, 182–83.
55 See also Delpech, "Les 'marques' des sorcières," 352–53 and 355–56, Demonet, "Les marques insensibles," 104–5 and Hotton, *Les marques du diable*, 236–39.
56 Fontaine, *Discours des marques*, 6, 8 and 10. See also Boguet, *Discours execrable*, 106.

57 On pilgrim badges, see also Chapter 4 and Figure 4.13, another visual representation of pilgrim badges in Lucas van Leyden's *Resting Pilgrims* (ca. 1508).

58 "Marque," Antoine Furetière, *Dictionnaire universel,* 3 vols. (La Haye and Rotterdam: Arnout & Reinier Leers, 1690). The first three orders listed by Furetière are prestigious French chivalric orders, each with their own highly distinctive insignia. The *Most Noble Order of the Garter* is the highest British chivalric order. For a seventeenth-century treatment of these, see Louvan Geliot, *La Vraye et parfaite science des armoiries,* ed. Pierre Palliot (Paris: Chez Helie Josset, 1661), esp. 483–507. The 1660 edition is also available in facsimile (Paris: Édouard Rouveyre, 1895).

59 See Chapter 4 for further treatment of Holy Land orders. See Palliot, *La Vraye et parfaite science des armoiries,* 486–87 and 505 on the Knights of the Saint Sepulcher and Saint Catherine.

60 See Palliot, *La Vraye et parfaite science des armoiries,* 483–507, for several examples.

61 De Lancre, *Tableau de l'inconstance,* 183. De Lancre mentions the initiation practices of three other groups: the Jacobites, who baptized by fire, branding the cross onto the initiate's forehead; the ancient gnostic Carpocrates, who branded their faithful with an initiation sign below the ear and were, for early modern demonologists, the forbearers of modern witches; and another sect he does not identify, who branded on the forehead, citing Tertullian; Ibid., 182–83. On treatment of the marking practices of these sects by Holy Land pilgrims and on pilgrim tattooing, see Chapter 4.

62 De Lancre, *Tableau de l'inconstance,* 184 and 187–88. On the importance of the toad as a familiar in Basque country, see Delpech, "Les 'marques' des sorcières," 359.

63 See Ulysee Robert, *Les signes d'infamie au Moyen Âge: Juifs, Sarrasins, hérétiques, lépreux, Cagots et filles publiques* (Paris: Honoré Champion, 1891). On the importance of clothing itself as a marker of identity, see Isabelle Paresys, "Corps, apparences vestimentaires et identités en France à la Renaissance," *Apparence(s)* 4 (2012), accessed July 26, 2013, http://apparences.revues.org/1229.

64 The practice of marking Jews with a yellow wheel endured, a precursor to the infamous star required in the twentieth century by the Nazi regime. Article 20 of a July 15, 1776 edict of the Bishop of Cavaillon specifies "[t]hat Jews are obligated to wear a yellow mark that distinguishes them from others and to wear it at all times and in all places;" qtd. in Jean Giroud, *De la rouelle à l'étoile. La présence des Juifs à Cavaillon* (Cavaillon: Imprimerie Rimbaud, 2010), 15; see also 52 and 156. Catholic authorities compared the mark imposed on Jews to the Old Testament story of God's mark on Cain (Genesis 4:15). On the marking of Jews, see: Robert, *Les signes d'infamie,* ch. 1, 6–113; Diane Hughes, "Distinguishing Signs: Ear-Rings, Jews and Franciscan Rhetoric in the Italian Renaissance City," *Past and Present* 112 (August 1986): 3–59; and Robert Michael, *A History of Catholic Antisemitism: The Dark Side of the Church* (Palgrave Macmillan, 2008), 80–82 and 107. I thank Jennifer Perlmutter for her assistance on this question. On signs worn by Muslims and other "heretics" in the medieval period, see Robert, *Les signes d'infamie,* ch. 2, 113–46.

65 Bonnie S. Anderson and Judith P. Zinsser, *A History of Their Own: Women in Europe from Prehistory to the Present* (Oxford: Oxford University Press, 1999), vol. 1, 434, Vern and Bonnie Bullough, *An Illustrated Social History of Prostitution* (New York: Crown Publishers, 1978), 144, and Robert, *Les signes d'infamie au Moyen Âge,* ch. 4, 175–89. In fifteenth-century Dijon, prostitutes were required to wear a white cloth band around their arm, while in Lyon and

Amiens, they wore on their arm an aiguillette on red cord of specific measurements; Ibid., 182–83. The French expression "courir l'aiguillette" has its origins in this practice. In early eighteenth-century England, actual blemishes and moles on the skin themselves were seen as signs of a loose woman and associated with prostitution, leading women to attempt to get rid of any such skin marking; Philip K. Wilson, *Surgery, Skin and Syphilis: Daniel Turner's London (1667–1741)* (Amsterdam and Atlanta: Rodopi, 1999), 61.

66 Paola Antolini, *Au-delà de la rivière. Les cagots: histoire d'une exclusion* (Paris: Éditions Nathan, 1989), Michel Fabre, *Le mystère des cagots, race maudite des Pyrénées* (Pau: M.C.T., 1987), Françoise Bériac, *Des lépreux aux cagots. Recherche sur les sociétés marginales en Aquitaine médiévale* (Bordeaux: Fédération historique du Sud-Ouest, 1990) and *Histoire des lépreux au Moyen-Age. Une société d'exclus* (Paris: Imago, 1980), and Robert, *Les signes d'infamie*, ch. 3, 146–74.

67 Delpech, "La 'marque' des sorcières," 355. Emphasis in original.

68 Hotton, *Les marques du diable*, 236–39.

69 Rémy cites the devil's claw or talons; *Demonolatry*, 8–9. For Daneau, *Les Sorciers*, 69, the devil uses his teeth. On the little finger, see Fontaine, *Discours des marques*, 17, De Lancre, *Tableau de l'inconstance*, 191, and Gayot de Pitaval, *Causes célèbres*, vol. 6, 217. De Lancre cites a witness who saw children being branded at the sabbat with a hot iron; *Tableau de l'inconstance*, 182. In a 1661 Lille case chronicled by Antoinette Bourignon, the accused also reported that the devil had branded them; qtd. in Summers, *The History of Witchcraft*, 79, n. 56.

70 Raynaud, *De Stigmatismo*, 406. For Raynaud, the devil is only spirit so cannot mark with a part of his body, 404–7.

71 Guazzo, *Compendium maleficarum*, vol. 2, 15.

72 Fontaine, *Discours des marques*, 17–18.

73 De Lancre, *Tableau de l'inconstance*, 191; see also 183 and 189 and Gayot de Pitaval, *Causes célèbres*, vol. 6, 217.

74 Rémy, *Demonolatry*, 8–9. In fact, the ancients had used tattoos. See C.P. Jones, "Stigma and Tattoo," in *Written on the Body: The Tattoo in European and American History*, ed. Jane Caplan (Princeton, NJ: Princeton University Press, 2000), 1–16; 1–5.

75 De Lancre, *Tableau de l'inconstance*, 183, Michaëlis, *Histoire admirable*, part 2, 80, and Boguet, *Discours execrable*, 106.

76 Boguet, *Discours execrable*, 106. See also Delrio, *Controverses magiques*, 223.

77 For more in-depth treatment of branding, see Chapter 5.

78 On the *galères*, see Nicole Castan and André Zysberg, "Galères et galériens en France à la fin du XVIIe siècle," *Criminal Justice History* 1 (1980): 49–115, Marc Vigié, *Les Galériens du Roi, 1661–1715* (Paris: Fayard, 1985), André Zysberg, *Les Galériens. Vies et destins de 60 000 forçats sur les galères de France, 1680–1748* (Paris: Le Seuil, 1987), and Nicole Castan and André Zysberg, *Histoire des galères, bagnes et prisons en France de l'Ancien Régime* (Paris: Privat, 2002).

79 Branding and other mutilating punishments are listed in article 38 of the *Code Noir* (Paris: Veuve Saugrain, 1685), 8. On the branding of enslaved Africans see Katrina H.B. Keefer, "Marked by Fire: Brands, Slavery, and Identity," *Slavery & Abolition* (2019), DOI: 10.1080/0144039X.2019.1606521; Gabriel Debien, *Les Esclaves aux Antilles françaises* (Basse-Terre: Société d'Histoire de la Guadeloupe, 1974), 70; Orlando Patterson, *Slavery and Social Death: A Comparative Study* (Cambridge, MA and London: Harvard University

Press, 1982), 58–59; Hugh Thomas, *The Slave Trade: The Story of the Atlantic Slave Trade: 1440–1870* (New York: Simon and Schuster, 1997), 396–97; Michael Harrigan, *Frontiers of Servitude: Slavery in Narratives of the Early French Atlantic* (Manchester, UK: Manchester University Press, 2018), 259–61; and Craig Koslovsky's ongoing work on the uses and meanings of country marks and slave branding.

80   On the debate between Johann Weyer and Jean Bodin, see Rebecca M. Wilkin, *Women, Imagination and the Search for Truth in Early Modern France* (Aldershot, UK and Burlington, VT, 2008), chs. 1 and 2.

81   Johann Weyer, *De Præstigiis dæmonum et incantationibus ac venificiis* (Basel: Joannes Oporinus, 1563), ed. George Mora and Benjamin Kohl and trans. John Shea as *Witches, Devils, and Doctors in the Renaissance* (Binghamton, NY: Medieval and Renaissance Texts and Studies, 1991), 552.

82   See Furetière's many examples in "marque," *Dictionnaire universel*. For more on commercial marks, see Chapter 5.

83   Michaëlis, *Histoire admirable*, part 2, 80. For Raynaud, the devil signs his chosen vessels; *De Stigmatismo*, 349.

84   Fontaine, *Discours des marques*, 8.

85   For treatment of the pact, see: Delrio, *Controverses magiques*, 118–30; Guazzo, *Compendium Maleficium*, 13–19; and De Lancre, *Tableau de l'inconstance*, 169–80. For English and German sources, see "Pact with the Devil," in Robbins, *The Encyclopedia of Witchcraft*, 369–79. On the rise in importance of the signature, see Beatrice Fraenkel, *La Signature. Genèse d'un signe* (Paris: Gallimard, 1992).

86   Legislation concerning the preparation and dissemination of judicial documents is cited in Chapter 5. On the development of official documentation for personal identification, see Valentin Groebner, *Who Are You? Identification, Deception, and Surveillance in Early Modern Europe*, trans. Mark Kyburz and John Peck (New York: Zone Books, 2007).

87   Bodin, *De la démonomanie*, fol. 79v.

88   De Lancre, *Tableau de l'inconstance*, 170.

89   On Loudun, see Chapter 2. Two supposed pacts were presented as evidence during Grandier's trial. The first contained Grandier's vows (see Figure 1.4); the second was a demonic response (see Figure 1.5). For another example, see De Lancre's transcription of Louys Gaufridy's pact; *Tableau de l'inconstance*, 178.

90   Claude Le Brun de la Rochette, *Le procès civil et criminel* (Rouen: Pierre Calles, [1607] 1611), bk. 1, 140.

91   Delpech, "La 'marque' des sorcières," 350. See also Bodin, *De la démonomanie*, bk. 2, ch. 4, fol. 79r.

92   Rémy, *Demonolatry*, 8. See also Pierre Marescot, *Traité des marques des Possedez* (Rouen: Claude Osmont, 1644), 13 and Bodin, *De la démonomanie*, bk. 2, ch. 4, fol. 79r.

93   Demonet, "Les marques insensibles," 113. On the probative value of the pact, see Delpech, "La 'marque' des sorcières," 354–55. Darr underlines the greater emphasis in the English context on wrongdoing as evidence, "The Devil's Mark," 364.

94   Daneau, *Les Sorciers*, 68. Daneau's text first appeared in Latin in 1564 as *Dialogus de veneficiis*, and then in French (1574) and English (1575) editions. On the important role Protestant demonologists played in the theoretical development of the mark, see Monter, *Witchcraft in France and Switzerland*, 156–66.

95   De Lancre, *Tableau de l'inconstance*, 191. See also Boguet, *Discours execrable*, 108.

96 "Sceau," Furetière, *Dictionnaire universel.*

97 Ibid.

98 Le Brun de la Rochette, *Le procès civil et criminel*, bk. 1, 140–41 and bk. 3, 184. Le Brun assures his reader that "in this kind of recognition all Judges are competent;" bk. 1, 142. He also examines all the ways in which a contract can be nullified, notably if the proper seals or signatures are missing; bk. 1, 148–52.

99 Ibid., bk. 1, 142.

100 Raynaud, *De Stigmatismo*, 397–98.

101 De Lancre, *Tableau de l'inconstance*, 259.

102 Fraenkel, *La Signature.* On the link between the devil's mark and the signature, see also Demonet, "Les marques insensibles," 106.

103 "Signer," Jean Nicot, *Thresor de la langue francoyse, tant ancienne que moderne* (Paris: David Douceur, 1606). Emphasis in original.

104 Fraenkel reproduces several sixteenth- and seventeenth-century signatures. See *La Signature*, figs. 86–90, and her appendix of notaries' signs, 279–88.

105 See the figures reproduced in Fraenkel, *La Signature*, for comparison. In often abbreviated Latin, the text is transcribed and translated by Collin de Plancy, *Dictionnaire infernal* and Robbins, *The Encyclopedia of Witchcraft and Demonology*, 377–79.

106 "Signe," Furetière, *Dictionnaire universel.*

107 Michaëlis, *Histoire admirable*, part 2, 102; see also part 2, 70. Gayot de Pitaval also cites this example; *Causes célèbres*, vol. 6, 217.

108 De Lancre, *Tableau de l'inconstance*, 191.

109 On the corporeality of the sabbat ritual and the question of the devil's corporeal presence, see, among others, Munchembled, *A History of the Devil*, 60–68.

110 See, for example: Boguet, *Discours execrable*, 108; Bodin, bk. 2, ch. 4, fol. 79r; and Raynaud, *De Stigmatismo*, 366. Just who signs the pact, the witch, the devil, or both, differs among accounts.

111 De Lancre, *Tableau de l'inconstance*, 178. See also Delpech, "La 'marque' des sorcières," 350, who cites further examples.

112 On textual amulets, see Don C. Skemer, *Binding Words: Textual Amulets in the Middle Ages* (University Park, PA: Pennsylvania State University Press, 2006) and my "Prêt à porter: Textual Amulets, Popular Belief and Defining Superstition in Sixteenth and Seventeenth-Century France," special issue on *Wearing Images*, edited by Diane Brodart, Espacio, Tiempo y Forma 6 (2018): 84–114.

113 Martine Ostorero, *"Fôlatrer avec les démons." Sabbat et chasse aux sorciers à Vevey (1448)* (Lausanne: Université de Lausanne, 1996), 218–19. See other early pact stories in Ostorero, "Les Marques du diable," 377 and Claude Seignolle, *Les Évangiles du diable* (Paris: Robert Laffont, 1998). See also Delpech, "La 'marque' des sorcières," 350 and Hotton, *Les marques du diable*, 275.

114 Seignolle, *Les Évangiles du diable*, 185.

115 Munchembled, *A History of the Devil*, 66.

116 Ostorero, *"Fôlatrer avec les démons,"* 218–19.

117 Paul Regnard, *Sorcellerie, magnétisme, morphinisme, délire des grandeurs. Les Maladies épidémiques de l'esprit* (Paris: E. Plon, Nourrit et Cie, 1887), 10–11. Though Regnard labels these engravings as taken from an unidentified 1625 text by Gijsbert Voet (1589–1676), whom he calls Gilbert de Vos (also known by his Latin name, Gisbertus Voetius) this text remains unlocatable. Voet did publish a text on demonology, *Selectarum disputationum . . . de natura & operationibus daemonum* (Utrecht: Aegidius Roman, 1638), but no engravings appear in this edition.

118 "Marque," Furetière, *Dictionnaire universel* and "Marque," *Dictionnaire de l'Académie françoise* (Paris: Jean-Baptiste Coignard, 1694).

119   On empiricism's influence on the return of ordeals for proving guilt or innocence, especially in Scandinavia, see Pihlajamäki, "'Swimming the Witch,'" 39.
See Darr, "The Devil's mark," on evidentiary standards in England.

120   Delpech, "La 'marque' des sorcières," 349. Emphasis in original.

121   Demonet, "Les marques insensibles," 102. The rise in demonic possession as
evidence of witchcraft, with its visible, physical manifestations in the bodies of
its victims, may also have responded to this need for material proof of
malevolent activity. See Chapter 2.

122   This is the central argument of Hotton's dissertation, *Les marques du diable*;
see esp. 192–227 and 353–55. See also Delpech, "La 'marque' des sorcières," 354–55 and Pihlajamäki, "'Swimming the Witch'." On the development of body marks as evidence, see Groebner, *Who Are You?*, 102 and
115, where he examines the role of the scar in the 1560 trial of Martin
Guerre.

123   Standards of proof were much lower in England and Scotland; Levack, *The
Witch-Hunt*, 69.

124   Ibid., 69–70 and Soman, "Le sabbat des sorciers," 85–86.

125   See also Delpech, "La 'marque' des sorcières," 354–55.

126   De Lancre, *Tableau de l'inconstance*, marginal note, 103.

127   Bodin, *De la démonomanie*, bk. 4, ch. 2, fol. 173. Bodin does not, however,
put much value in the devil's mark as a judicial sign, as discussed below.

128   Hotton, *Les marques du diable*, 191.

129   Boguet, *Discours execrable*, "Preface," n. pag. He cites French demonologists
Bodin and Rémy, cited above, and German Catholic theologian and bishop
Peter Binsfeld (ca. 1545–1598). A prominent witch hunter, Binsfeld published
the *Tractatus de confessionibus maleficorum & Sagarum* (Trier: Heinrich
Bock, 1589) and the *Tractat von Bekanntnuß der Zauberer und Hexen*
(Munich: Adam Berg, 1591).

130   De Lancre, *Tableau de l'inconstance*, "Avertissemens," n. pag.

131   On the new model of inquiry offered by period anatomists, see Johanthan
Sawday, *The Body Emblazoned: Dissection and the Human Body in Renaissance Culture* (London: Routledge, 1995).

132   Michaëlis, *Discours des esprits*, 171–72.

133   Rémy, *Demonolatry*, 9.

134   Fontaine, *Discours des marques*, 5. On Fontaine's goals and the important
differences between his approach and those of his nonmedical predecessors, see
Hotton, *Les marques du diable*, esp. 351–63.

135   Fontaine, *Discours des marques*, 13–17; 13.

136   Ibid., 15. See also: De Lancre, *Tableau de l'inconstance*, 181; Rémy, *Demonolatry*, 9; Raynaud, *De Stigmatismo*, 377–80; and Michaëlis, *Discours des
esprits*, 171–73.

137   Rémy, *Demonolatry*, 10.

138   Delpech, "La 'marque' des sorcières," 354–55 and Mandrou, *Magistrats et
Sorciers*, 101–2. On pricking in Europe, see Pihlajamäki, "'Swimming the
Witch,'" 43–44. It is important to acknowledge here that, though rarely the
case in France, not all those who searched for the mark were accredited
medical professionals but were sometimes professional "prickers," paid on
a case-by-case basis and thus encouraged to find the marks they sought. On
professional prickers, prominent in England and Scotland, see: Malcolm
Gaskill, *Witchfinders: A Seventeenth-Century English Tragedy* (Cambridge,
MA: Harvard University Press, 2005); Peter G. Maxwell-Stuart, *Witch Hunters:
Professional Prickers, Unwitchers & Witch Finders of the Renaissance* (Gloucestershire, UK: Tempus Publishing, Ltd., 2003), ch. 5, 98–122; Pihlajamäki,

"Swimming the Witch;" and Robbins, "Pricking," *The Encyclopedia of Witchcraft and Demonology*, 395–401. Monter cites examples of abuse in *Witchcraft in France and Switzerland*, 160–61 and "The Devil's Mark," 276. See Summers on Scottish charlatans, *The History of Witchcraft*, 74–75. Though medical professionals are most often cited as doing the pricking in the French treatises, there are examples to the contrary. Boguet mentions that a well-qualified surgeon was not always present to perform examinations; *Discours execrable*, 8. De Lancre relates that his surgeon, an "estrangier," had become arrogantly proud of his abilities after much success. De Lancre also used a seventeen-year-old girl, Morguy, to prick some witnesses to avoid the potentially arousing experience that the physical examination of young women may represent for a male surgeon. He even allows visiting dignitaries to experience firsthand the mark's validity by taking up the needle themselves; De Lancre, *Tableau de l'inconstance*, 185–86. One French charlatan pricker, Jean Minard, was charged in 1601 with collusion in the death of over two hundred persons; Alfred Soman, "Decriminalizing Witchcraft: Does the French Experience Furnish a European Model?," article XV in *Sorcellerie et justice criminelle: Le Parlement de Paris, 16e-18e siècles* (Hampshire, UK and Brookfield, VT: Variorum, 1992), 14–15 [reprinted articles individually paginated]. The Parlement of Toulouse warned lower courts against using self-appointed professionals in 1644–1645; Pihlajamäki, "'Swimming the Witch,'" 44. German Jesuit Friedrich Spee also condemned abuses; Friedrich Spee, *Cautio Criminalis, or a Book on Witch Trials* [1631], trans. Marcus Hellyer (Charlottesville: University of Virginia Press, 2003), 167–70.

139 Delpech, "La 'marque' des sorcières," 349. See also Demonet, "Les marques insensibles," 124.

140 Summer's transcription, *The History of Witchcraft*, 79, n. 59.

141 Ibid. Doctors were called on as experts to make the same distinction between natural and supernatural causes through the medical examination of individuals thought to be demonically possessed. On doctor Michel Marsecot and the Marthe Brossier case, see ch. 3 of Sarah Ferber, *Demonic Possession and Exorcism in Early Modern* France (London: Routledge, 2004), esp. 48–54, and Hotton, *Les marques du diable*, esp. 345–50. Some treatises composed by medical experts in these cases include: for Marthe Brossier in Paris, Michel Marsecot, *Discours véritable sur le fait de Marthe Brossier* (Paris: Mamert Patisson, 1599); for Loudun, Marc Duncan, *Discours sur la possession des religieuses ursulines de Lodun* (N.p.: N.p., 1634); for Louviers, Pierre Yvelin, *Examen de la possession des religieuses de Louviers* (Paris: N.p., 1643) and *Apologie pour l'autheur de L'Examen de la possession des religieuses de Louviers* (Rouen and Paris: N.p., 1643). On demonic possession, see Chapter 2.

142 Several demonologists make links between textual amulets and devil's marks in their texts: De Lancre, *Tableau de l'inconstance*, 184; Delrio, *Controverses magiques*, 223; and Boguet, *Discours execrable*, 105–6.

143 Bouvet, *Les Manieres admirables pour découvrir toutes sortes de crimes et sortileges* (Paris: Jean de la Caille, 1659), 196.

144 Monter, "Devil's Mark," 275.

145 Fontaine, *Discours des marques*, 5.

146 Ibid., 1–2.

147 Le Brun de la Rochette, *Le procès civil et criminel*, bk. 2, 61. On medical examination in duels, see Bouvet, *Les Manieres admirables*, 110–11.

148 Delrio, Weyer, and Spee were outspoken critics of the mark. Delrio lists the devil's mark under "Other less urgent and certain indications in the crime of

witchcraft," as the twenty-fifth of twenty-six possible signs of witchcraft, and then only to denounce its validity; Delrio, *Controverses magiques*, 748–76 and 759–60. Weyer believes there is not enough proof that these marks come from the devil and even if there were such proof, if the accused has done no harm to others, God will forgive her; Weyer, *De praestigiis daemonum*, 551–52. Spee cautions judges of the abuses inherent in the system of pricking; Friederich Spee, *Cautio Criminalis*, 167–70. Other opponents of the mark include Augustin Nicolas (1622–1695), who critiques the opinions of Boguet in *Si la torture est un moyen seur a verifier les crimes secrets* (Amsterdam: Abraham Wolfgang, 1682), 161–62 and 222–23 and Lalement, *Mémoire sur la manière de juger les sorciers*, 223. Though Jean Bodin qualifies the mark among "very strong presumptions of guilt" he does not consider it a "notable proof," because he believes that witches are only marked if Satan doubts their fidelity; Bodin, *De la démonomanie*, fol. 79v. and Hotton, *Les marques du diable*, 256–57. For a summary of these disagreements across Europe, see Monter, "Devil's Mark," 275–76 and Lavenia, "Witch's Mark," 1221. On the debate in England, see Darr, "The Devil's Mark," 370–80. Others see the mark as corroborating evidence rather than absolute proof or question, like Bodin, whether all witches are marked: Delrio, *Controverses magiques*, 759; Guazzo, *Compendium Maleficarum*, 15; and Boguet, *Discours execrable*, 108. Daneau, despite how some later authors read him, firmly affirms the marking of all witches: "But the truth is that, without exception, he marks them all;" *Les Sorciers*, 69.

149 Fontaine, *Discours des marques*, 11–13. See also Boguet, *Discours execrable*, 107–8. On the mark's possible erasure by Satan, see also Delrio, *Controverses magiques*, 759–60.

150 Boguet, *Discours execrable*, 107.

151 Ibid., 107–8.

152 Ibid., 107.

153 Bodin, *De la démonomanie*, fol. 80r.

154 See, for example: Delrio, *Controverses magiques,* 759–60; Boguet, *Discours execrable*, 107 and 108; and Fontaine, *Discours des marques*, 18–20.

155 De Lancre, *Tableau de l'inconstance* (Paris: Nicolas Buon, 1613), 190.

156 Demonet, "Les marques insensibles," 118 and Soman, "Decriminalizing Witchcraft." Demonet points out that Fontaine and De Lancre, major proponents of the evidentiary value of the mark, were writing at a time when marking was already no longer universally accepted in France. The last known case of pricking for the devil's mark in England was in 1712, though Reginald Scot mocked it as early as 1584 in his *The Discoverie of Witchcraft* (London: W. Brome, 1584); Darr, "The Devil's Mark," 363–64.

157 Soman, "Le sabbat des sorciers," 87 and 95–96 and Soman, "Aux origines de l'appel de droit dans l'ordonnance criminelle de 1670," article VI in *Sorcellerie et justice criminelle*, 29 and n. 33. See also Demonet, "Les marques insensibles," 118. On the decriminalization of witchcraft and the differences between the Paris Parlement and lower courts in France, see Mandrou, *Magistrats et sorciers*, 313–63 and Soman, "La décriminalisation de la sorcellerie en France," article XII in *Sorcellerie et justice criminelle*. On the relative decline of witch trials throughout Europe, see Soman, "Decriminalizing Witchcraft" and Levack, *The Witch-Hunt*, 212–37.

158 Monter, "Devil's Mark," 276 and *Witchcraft in France and Switzerland*, 157–66.

159 Levack, *The Witch-Hunt*, 216.

160 Mandrou, *Magistrats et sorciers*, 425–86.

161 "Marquer," Furetière, *Dictionnaire universel*. Emphasis in original.

2 Demonic marks, divine stigmata
The female body inscribed

Few episodes in the history of witchcraft and demonic possession are as notorious as the events surrounding the Loudun possession, which captured public attention in France and across Europe in the seventeenth century and have inspired the interest of scholars, doctors, writers, and filmmakers ever since.[1] From 1632 to 1637, the Ursuline monastery of Loudun became a theater for the spectacular exorcism of several demonically possessed nuns, first among them the convent's Mother Superior, Jeanne des Anges (1602–1665). The women displayed all the signs of possession: they exhibited unnatural strength, suffered terrible convulsions and contortions, behaved immodestly, revealed hidden truths, and proffered blasphemous and scandalous speech. Fueled by the venom of Protestant-Catholic clashes and political tensions between local and centralized control, the tragic events of the Loudun possession ultimately led to the burning for witchcraft of a controversial local priest, Urbain Grandier (1590–1634), on August 18, 1634. He was accused by the nuns' demons during exorcisms of having made a pact with the devil to bring on the women's possession. Grandier's execution did not spell the end to the nuns' torment, however, and exorcisms continued for three more years after his death.

Though the most highly publicized possession case of seventeenth-century France, Loudun was only one among several instances of mass possession that erupted in female monasteries across Europe during the early modern period, not to mention countless cases of individual possession, as important work on the question by both Sarah Ferber and Mosche Sluhovsky has demonstrated.[2] While, as Sluhovsky has shown, the vast majority of group convent possessions occurred in private, behind closed doors in female monasteries, a small minority became highly public events. In their exceptional theatricality, Loudun's exorcisms drew on the earlier elaborately staged exorcisms of a young woman, Nicole Obry, in Laon (1565–1566) and of Ursulines Louise Capeau and Magdaleine de Demandouls in Aix-en-Provence (1609–1611).[3] Physical possession by demons, with rare exceptions, afflicted women exclusively throughout the early modern period, and recent scholarship has brought to light just how fraught with gender issues possession and exorcism were in the Catholic Counter-Reformation context.[4] The exorcisms that took place at the Ursuline convents of Loudun and Auxonne (1658–1663), and at the Hospitaller convent in Louviers (1642–1647), had as a central goal the material display of Catholic truth on the bodies of women. Masters in the art of spectacle, priests performed public exorcisms in churches, seeking to render the nuns' signs of possession visible to assembled spectators, to identify and map the locations of the demons inhabiting each woman, and to bring about their ultimate expulsion in a staged performance of ecclesiastical authority over the demonic.[5] Female bodies, violently controlled from within by masculine gendered demons, and from without by male exorcists, became the material media through which exorcists affirmed the truth of their systems of knowledge and belief. During exorcisms, demons were forced by God to reveal truths through the mouths of the possessed, and exorcists vividly demonstrated the superiority of the Catholic faith over Protestantism by controlling demons within the women's bodies and driving them out, notably through the use of the consecrated Eucharist, relics, and the invocation of saints.

Contrary to most mass possessions, these cases owed their fame to their unusual transformation into witch trials, which provoked controversy and raised their stakes in the public eye during a period that marked the beginnings of the waning of the witch craze in France. In Loudun, Auxonne, and Louviers, demons, speaking through the possessed nuns, accused a third party of bringing on the women's possession through a pact with the devil. In Loudun, Grandier was executed for witchcraft, just as priest Louys Gaufridy had been in Aix, largely as a result of testimony given during exorcism. Though quieter than the Loudun affair, the Louviers possession saw the exhumation and destruction of former spiritual director and priest Mathurin Picard's body from its convent burial spot; the burning of the nuns' current spiritual director, priest Thomas Boullé; and the life imprisonment of Hospitaller Magdaleine Bavant on charges of witchcraft in 1647.[6] In Auxonne, demons repeatedly accused the prioress Barbe Buvée of witchcraft through the mouths of her spiritual daughters, though she eventually gained acquittal thanks to the intervention of the Parlements of Dijon and Paris.[7] However, while the association of these convent possessions with witch trials is important to understanding their unique dynamics, a distinction must be made between the possessed women, who were largely cast by exorcists as the innocent victims of demons, and their "guilty" witch counterparts, who had purportedly made a deliberate pact with the devil that caused their possession.[8] It was the demoniac's innocence that made her an ideal vehicle for the propagation of the particular truth exorcists sought to communicate.

This recuperation of the bodies of women took place not only during exorcism before throngs of spectators but also in print, in scores of published texts that further affirmed and stabilized their reading.[9] In Loudun, each successful exorcism saw the swift publication and distribution of its minutes. Medical doctors, too, provided their scientific expertise on the women's condition, performing evaluations and writing opinions according to their own diagnostic systems. Other visitors came—laypeople, Protestants, digni-taries, and aristocrats—all curious to see and judge for themselves the strange events they had heard about. They too subsequently wrote and published their impressions. The female body was thus read and reread, written and rewritten, onlookers and examiners offering interpretations of the visible and tangible signs manifested in the nuns' unruly bodies according to their own codes and epistemologies. They produced and circulated in great numbers pamphlets, medical and theological treatises, *histoires admirables*, memoirs, *relations*, letters, news reports, and popular songs, a vast propagandistic enterprise that sought to render the possessed body legible to the public and to secure meaning for the troubling events.

Alongside and in dynamic interplay with the countless paper and ink testimonies these possession cases inspired, another set of texts emerged that will be the focus of this chapter—signs written directly upon the women's bodies. Figurative and textual engravings, cast as the work of demons, appeared etched in the flesh of the possessed, materializing the more metaphorical inscription of the female body that went on throughout these events. During the exorcisms that took place from 1632 to 1647 at the Ursuline convent in Loudun, the Hospitaller convent in Louviers, and, with variations, the Ursuline convent in Auxonne, the skin of several possessed women functioned quite literally as a site for the physical impression of signs by demons, who indicated their final expulsion from the women's bodies by carving wounds, symbols, names, and words into their skin.[10] Though so-called *signes de sortie*, or "exit signs," negotiated and agreed upon in advance by demon and exorcist, were an important component of early modern exorcism ritual, never before had they assumed such corporeal form. These signs of submission, required as crucial confirmation of the spirit's final defeat at the hands of the exorcist, and thus of the Church's victory over the forces of evil, had traditionally been transient—the appear-ance of wind, fire, or an insect exiting the possessed individual's mouth, the shattering of a glass pane, an object falling or flying across the room.[11] In the exorcisms that took place at Loudun and elsewhere, however, such conventional, fleeting signs were eclipsed by others of a far more permanent quality—they were engraved upon the women's flesh.

The case of Ursuline prioress and prominent demoniac Jeanne de Belcier (1605–1665), known in religion as Sœur Jeanne des Anges, who toured France with her inscribed hand in the aftermath of the possession at the Loudun convent, is well known.[12] According to published summaries of the events written by her exorcists, and later, by the prioress herself, originally host to seven demons, Jeanne des Anges received three wounds in the form of lines below her heart from the first trio of demons to exit her body on May 20, 1634—Asmodée, Aman, and Grésil. In so marking her, the demons fulfilled a written contract between their hierarchical leader, Asmo-dée, and Jeanne des Anges's exorcists, a document purportedly drafted and signed by Asmodée himself through the intermediary of the prioress, whose distinct handwriting graces the page (see Figure 2.1). The demon's paper and ink pledge represented a reversal of typical pacts believed to be concluded between humans and the devil made famous by the witch trials of the period.[13] Here, the demon assumed the role of signatory and promised submission to Church authorities, an agreement he then sealed in Jeanne des Anges's blood upon marking her skin. On November 5, 1635, another demon, Léviathan, left his mark on the prioress's forehead, a large bloody cross that remained visible for two weeks, engraving in the flesh the sign of her baptism and imitating the cross that would have been traced there repeatedly by her exorcist's finger as a standard gesture in the rite of exorcism.[14] These first signatures on Jeanne des Anges's skin also recall the lines and crosses commonly used by the period's illiterate on official documents in lieu of their name, further underlining the link between the signature on the original paper contract and the signing of the skin. Figurative marks gave way to letters as Jeanne des Anges's exorcisms haltingly progressed through changes in exorcists, long periods of debilitating illness, and resistance from demons. From November 29, 1635, through her last demon's exit on October 17, 1637, each of Jeanne des Anges's

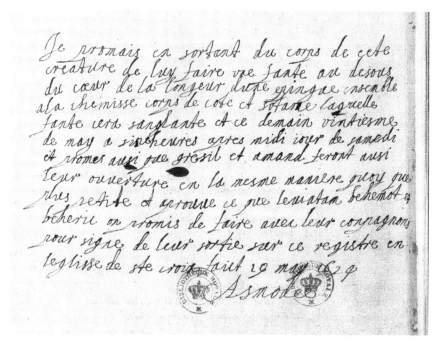

Figure 2.1 Pledge written and signed by the demon Asmodée in Sœur Jeanne des Anges's hand, complete with the authoritative seal of the Bibliothèque Royale where it was kept (May 19, 1634), Ms. Fr. 7618, fol. 20v. Bibliothèque Nationale de France.

remaining demons literally signed her body as they left it. However, in place of their own signatures, exorcists forced them to replace their own names with holy names, because

> it was not reasonable that he who had been banished from paradise for eternity write his name on the hand of a girl who was consecrated to God. . . . That it should not be that his name, which had been crossed out of the book of life, be carried back by her to the place from whence he had fallen because of his rebellion.[15]

The demon thus became God's reluctant scribe, forced to sign the woman's consecrated skin indelibly with the name of each sainted figure who interceded to expulse him. By the time the last of the devils left the prioress, her hand displayed a total of four names: those of the members of the holy family—Jesus, Mary, and Joseph—and that of Catholic Counter-Reformation bishop, mystic, and devotional writer François de Sales (1567–1622), who would be beatified in 1661 and canonized in 1665 by Pope Alexander VII.[16] All of the names were "written in Roman characters, raised, and the color of fresh blood, and vermilion," and placed in hierarchical order, each of them proportionally smaller than the one above it.[17]

While documentation of Jeanne des Anges's corporeal inscription, provided by the prioress herself, her exorcists, and other contemporary observers is certainly the richest and most copious, hers was not an isolated case. In Loudun alone, at least four other possessed women received or were promised figurative wounds from their departing demons. The *Demonomanie de Loudun*, published by Loudun exorcists two years into the exorcisms there, lists *signes de sortie* either already executed or agreed to by demons, often, as with Asmodée, in the form of a written and signed paper contract. In addition to several more traditional signs of departure, the list includes many figurative corporeal marks, from the drawing of a heart on one nun's left temple to that of a ring on the forehead of another, both symbols of divine love and commitment.[18] Sœur Claire's demon Verrine even agreed to "make a fleur-de-lis on her left hand, to remain there throughout the girl's lifetime," effectively marking her with the seal of royal authority.[19] The Louviers case also boasted a dramatic example of symbols and words engraved on the chest of a demoniac upon her deliverance, the narrative of which I will examine further in this chapter.

Similar textual production took place during the later exorcisms at Auxonne. There, however, the names of saints appeared not on the demoniacs' skin but imprinted in blood on pieces of cloth worn against the body or expelled from its orifices. When demoniac Humberte Borthon, known in religion as Sœur de Saint-François, was freed of her demons in 1661 on the feast of the Presentation of the Virgin, as a sign of her deliverance [she] expelled from her mouth a piece of folded taffeta, upon which appeared written in red letters the name of Mary, and four other capitals that marked the name of Saint Hubert, and that of the Blessed François de Sales.[20]

Following Sœur de la Purifications's successful exorcism that same day, that nun's white headband suddenly displayed, "in large characters, as if made of blood, JESUS, MARIE, JOSEPH." Later, when she was delivered from another demon on the feast day of Saint Gregory, "as a sign of this grace [she] rendered by the mouth a piece of cloth encircled by copper, on which was written the name of Gregorius," miraculously producing an amulet-like memento of that saint's intervention.[21] In Auxonne, the women's bodies thus produced texts that affirmed their deliverance, their demons clearly borrowing from the signs produced years earlier on the skin of Jeanne des Anges, as well as creating new ones. Indeed, the eighteenth-century historian of the Loudun case, P.-J.-Baptiste de la Ménardaye, reads this textual production of names at Auxonne as divine confirmation of the truth of the corporeal marks made in Loudun:

> Certainly this was a very remarkable event, through which it seems that God wanted to justify the miracle of the engravings of Loudun against ridiculous and slanderous speech, which the Protestants had sown in the world to destroy belief in them.[22]

Texts produced by the body thus intervened to justify earlier corporeal signs, claiming greater authority than any who would contradict them.

Impressionable women

Engraved upon or issuing forth from the bodies of women, this new, literal incarnation of the demon's *signe de sortie* that first appeared in Loudun and reemerged in Louviers and Auxonne must be understood within larger established traditions of female impressionability. Demons' marks drew their rhetorical power and viability as a genre and tool for promoting belief from the fact that their media were women. The very plausibility of this new sign's appearance was guaranteed by a philosophical-medical characterization of the female body and mind as both impressionable and impressionist. Theories expounded by medical, theological, and philosophical writers of the Renaissance cast the female sex as "soft," "malleable," and "impressionable" in body and mind, making of women ready surfaces for the inscription and retention of text and image. French-trained Dutch physician Johann Weyer (1515–1588) offered in 1563 an often invoked false etymology of the Latin word for "woman," which he drew from Augustine: "[T]he word 'woman' [*mulier*] seems to be derived, rather appropriately, from 'softness' [*mollities*], with one letter changed and one removed, as though the word should have been *mollier*."[23] Softness, accompanied by a compatible humoral definition as cold and moist, was a fundamental feminine characteristic for early modern writers, who were quick to make the leap, as did their ancient models, from discussion of soft bodies to that of soft minds. In contrast to men, whose bodies were hot, hard, and dry, women's cold and wet humors made them penetrable and pliant, and therein more vulnerable to both supernatural and natural influences. Women and their equally supple imaginations were like wax, ready to receive the impression of any seal.[24] Demonologist, linguist, and poet Pierre Le Loyer (1550–1634) employs this often-used metaphor to explain why women are so easily frightened—in French, *impressionnées*—in his 1586 *Discours et histoires des spectres*:

> Just as soft wax so easily receives many different characters and figures under the seal or the finger of he who makes something out of wax, so too do people who are naturally fearful and apprehensive easily receive all impressions.[25]

Anti-feminist exploitations of the idea of female softness permeated the seventeenth-century debates of the *Querelle des femmes*—literally, the "quarrel about women"—to explain everything from women's vulnerability to demonic influence to their inability to lead lives outside the home. At the same time, defenders of women made use of the concept of female impressionability, even to argue women's particular fitness for learning. Borrowing a vision of memory as a wax tablet from Plato's *Theaetus*, and from their contemporary, René Descartes (1596–1650), they argued that women's cold and moist minds were far better suited than those of men to receiving and retaining the knowledge impressed upon them. The anonymous author of the 1643 *Femme généreuse* provides a vivid illustration of this line of reasoning:

> [T]hat which is moist is better suited to receive the impression, imprint and engraving of the images and the portrait of things that are the object of science, without whose idea and representation we cannot know them. And it is much easier to engrave unto something moist that is always soft, than onto something dry that is usually hard. And [woman] being colder (or less hot) than man, the cold retains the brain's humor, holding this liquid intact and keeping it from flowing, thus preserving the engraving of images of this sort.[26]

Women's memories and imaginations, physically construed, were, then—like the rest of their soft bodies—especially capable of receiving and maintaining impressions.[27] Anti-feminist writers, while they cast female impressionability in the negative, arguing that it made women particularly vulnerable to imprinting by evil influences, also maintained the indelibility of marks received by the female brain. Le sieur de Ferville, for example, compares a woman's mind to "a Painter's canvas, that receives indiscriminately the impression of all colors, and none is more sure than black that once laid down can never be erased."[28] Blank canvases, pages, or wax tablets, women were well suited for the inscription and preservation of impressions of all genres.

As examined briefly in the Introduction, the centerpiece for the discussion about female impressionability was the pregnant woman's imagination, thought to be particularly susceptible to impression by external images and then capable of reproducing those images onto the even softer flesh of her fetus within.[29] A woman's supposed ability to receive and impress upon the fetus she carried a representation of an object of fear, desire, or intense contemplation in the form of a birthmark or deformity served as the paradigmatic argument for the impressionability of bodies more generally throughout the period. So powerful was this idea for early modern thinkers that demonologists, theologians, philosophers, and physicians cited it again and again to defend or refute the validity of a wide range of corporeal inscriptions, including the devil's marks made on witches and divine stigmata on the bodies of saints.[30] Indeed, critics of the Loudun case were quick to offer the argument that the demoniacs' corporeal marks might be the natural product of their overactive imaginations rather than a supernatural force, leading Loudun exorcist Jean-Joseph Surin (1600–1665) to respond that this was impossible, "because there is nothing similar in nature," citing as proof the extraordinary textual form of the saints' names on Jeanne des Anges's hand.[31]

To borrow Monique Wittig's term, early modern women carried the "mark of gender," in their very susceptibility to marking.[32] It is not surprising, then, that female bodies offered ideal media for the impression and circulation of demonic, divine, and ultimately ecclesiastical texts of truth in seventeenth-century cases of demonic possession. With women's susceptibility to impression already a commonplace for their early modern audience, exorcists saw in their charges ready surfaces for the inscription of authoritative texts and model memorials to the truth of Catholicism's victory over the demonic and the heretical.

A new hybrid sign

With its visual appeal and greater staying power, the novel physical sign of departure that emerged in the contested possession cases of the seventeenth century responded to exorcists' desire to provide visible material proof of the supernatural. Corporeal inscription offered rhetorically potent, flesh and blood testimony to the truth of a nun's possession and deliverance and thus to the Catholic Church's power over demons. In demanding a new, corporeal *signe de sortie* of the demons who occupied their charges, Loudun exorcists sought a sign free of ambiguity that boasted greater endurance so that it could be seen by more witnesses over a longer period of time. In the words of Surin, these new physical marks distinguished themselves from typical signs of departure in that they "were not ambiguous but real;" for him, their corporeal nature guaranteed their authenticity. Surin's description of the decision to force the demon Léviathan to engrave the sign of the cross on Jeanne des Anges's forehead highlights his and his fellow exorcists' motives in inventing the new sign:

> The advice of his Eminence the Bishop of Poitiers, who had exorcised the Mother Superior and had had her exorcised with me, was to propose as a sign of their departure results that would subsist and would not be over in an moment; to this end he commanded that Léviathan, who was the first demon among them and the head of the band, would upon leaving make a cross on the forehead that would cut into the skin, like the marks that are made on the bark of trees or of pumpkins. This sign was executed according to the promise, the cross was engraved on the skin as though with a sharp metal object, and remained there twelve or fifteen days during which everyone came to see it.[33]

As more demons left her body, Jeanne des Anges's marks increased in endurance and spectacular appeal. While the sign of the cross, visible for two weeks, eventually faded, beginning with her inscription of Joseph's name, the prioress's marks not only remained clearly imprinted on her body but renewed themselves periodically to regain their original appearance, thus providing even more effective and long-lasting testimony to the truth of her deliverance and of the Loudun possession as a whole.[34]

To create this new sign of departure, Loudun exorcists drew from widely known traditions of corporeal marking performed both by the devil and by God. Theorized by period theologians as mirror images, the devil's mark on witches represented Satan's inversion of God's mark of baptism or of the stigmata God granted his elect. Exorcists conflated devil's marks and divine marks to form a hybrid sign that referenced both the demonic source of its inscription and the divine power that made the women's final deliverance possible. The devil's mark thus found itself rewritten through the tradition of divine stigmata. As examined in Chapter 1, the *stigmata* or *sigillum diaboli* [devil's mark or devil's seal] on his faithful not only provided tangible proof of an individual's dealings with the devil—imprinted on the body to validate the written pact—but also marked the witch as the devil's possession. The physical trace of a demon's passage through the demoniac's body, the sign of departure fulfilled a similar purpose, testifying to the veracity of her former possession by that demon. Yet at the same time, rather than marking the now delivered woman as the devil's own, the marks that appeared on her skin as bleeding wounds signified the divine intervention that had freed her, closely resembling the stigmata of saints. While the accused witches of the possession cases of the period were found to bear devil's marks—proof of their guilty relationship with Satan—the possessed women of these cases, far from being condemned as the devil's conspirators and marked with his sign, became instead God's palimpsests.[35]

This borrowing from the mystical stigmatic tradition manifests itself clearly in the form taken by many demoniac's marks in Loudun. While the epigraphic and figurative engravings that appear on the demoniacs' skin depart in their presentation from what we normally think of as stigmata— the corporeal representation of Christ's five wounds—other acts of bodily marking promised or executed during exorcisms did follow traditional patterns of full or partial stigmatization, often coexisting on the same body with their more figurative and textual cousins.[36] Sœur Claire's demons promised not only to engrave her forehead permanently with the name of Jesus and to mark her left hand with the fleur-de-lis, but Ennemy de la Vierge would "pierce clear through her right hand, the width of a fingertip," while Concupiscence vowed to pierce her left foot, and Pollution, her right.[37] Isabelle Blanchart's five demons collectively pledged her complete stigmatization, with wounds that would pierce her feet, hands, and side, in perfect imitation of the crucified Christ.[38] Even Jeanne des Anges's initial markings might be seen as following a stigmatic pattern. The "three openings in her right side" recall Christ's lance wound, presented in the form of a trinity.[39] The existence of these clearly stigmatic wounds alongside the more figurative markings that these women wore calls the latter to be read as stigmata as well, cutaneous signs that resonated especially deeply with feminine ecstatic experience. Whether more representational imitations of Christ's wounds, mementos of the passion in the form of a cross, symbols of spousal union such as the heart and ring, or engravings of divine names in the flesh, the women's corporeal signs were legible within a largely feminine spiritual experience and mystical tradition.

Crucial to the ecclesiastical enterprise in Loudun, Louviers, and Auxonne was the clear recognition not only that the possessed women of these cases had been freed of their demons but also that they had been brought back into the Church's fold. Visible corporeal signs became central in ensuring that, in the reported words of one Louviers demon, "this place that had been marked as the residence of the devil, would find itself so admirable in the future."[40] By recasting the devil's mark through the tradition of divine stigmata, Loudun exorcists signaled the delivered women's passage from the realm of the sacrilegious to that of the sacred, from the domain of the demonic to that of the divine, a prerequisite for the realization of their propagandistic goals.

From skin to page

Among the cases of demonic inscription promised and executed during these seventeenth-century possessions, Jeanne des Anges's signed hand knew a particularly prolific textual destiny, becoming, as Scott Bryson puts it, "the banner, the billboard for the victory of the Counter Reformation over heresy and libertinage."[41] Throughout the Loudun prioress's exorcisms, crowds witnessed each event of her corporeal marking, fulfilling exorcists' propagandistic goals and affirming Jeanne des Anges's status as a memorial to the veracity of her possession and thus to the Church that delivered her. Final expulsions, like the public exorcisms that proceeded them, were carefully staged with respectable witnesses well placed so they could testify to their experience of the demoniac's deliverance. Loudun exorcists' account of the engraving of the name of Joseph by the demon Balam—the first to grace the prioress's hand—illustrates quite clearly their use of her inscription for the reinforcement of belief:

> The Demon resisted a great deal before wanting to render this act of obedience to the Church, but finally he made the promise, and executed it the twenty-ninth of that same month and year [November 1635], a day when Milor Montegu and some other Heretical English Noblemen were in Loudun, and with them holding the Nun's left hand, the Demon departed, and everyone saw the Letters of the name of JOSEPH appear and form themselves on that hand, one after the other in succession, to the great admiration of all the spectators who gave their testimony to the event.[42]

The centerpiece for the spectators' gaze, held by "heretical" Englishmen, Jeanne des Anges's hand was engraved, letter by letter, with the name of Joseph, whom she revered as her saintly protector. Onlookers observed the writing of the prioress's body firsthand, then furnished their own written accounts of their experience, or provided signed attestations to the truth of what they had witnessed at the end of the recorded minutes that were destined for publication. For instance, on the final page of Loudun exorcists' *Relation de la sortie du demon Balam*, Englishman Thomas Killigreu not only includes his signature among those of the other witnesses but adds additional testimony, writing a line in English above his signature, translated into French for the print version by Lord Montegu: "I saw the hand just as white as my collar, and then in an instant change color the whole length of the vein and become red, and just as quickly a distinct word appeared, and the word was Joseph."[43]

The rapid translation of the written body into written and printed testimony took place on a large scale in Loudun, as exorcists systematically published minutes of each instance of marking in inexpensive pamphlet form, furthering their political agenda and increasing their audience through the medium of print. Texts that began as ink-on-paper contracts, signed by demons, were thus transposed onto the nun's skin in their engraving and finally into print form for public consumption. Exorcists underlined the resemblance between the texts that appeared upon Jeanne des Anges's body and the written and printed texts that sought to reproduce them by employing a vocabulary inscription and impression. They described the names on the prioress's body as "written" or "engraved" on her flesh by her demons and referred to them as "inscriptions," "writing," "seals," and "signatures."[44] The vocabulary of writing ceded to that of print when exorcists emphasized the textual particularities of the nun's supernatural marks. As with the devil's mark on witches, a vocabulary of impression pervaded accounts of corporeal marking by demons, including the words "impression," "imprint," "print," "engraving," and "character." Moreover, exorcists emphasized the "Roman" form of the engraved characters—the choice type of the period that marked the departure from manuscript culture—therein signaling the modernity of the demons' textual enterprise. Testaments to the readability of the marks also underlined their status as legible texts.

If bodies could behave like texts, texts could also behave like bodies. Keen to bolster the validity of their own publications, exorcists emphasized the ability of their printed texts to reproduce the corporeal original to perfection and thus to stand in for the real thing. Through the use of printed engravings, they claimed to provide their readers with authentic replica of the marks themselves and to bring to life the experience of their impression, describing the imprinting and particulars of each cutaneous sign in graphic detail. They made use of scientific language—"the dermis and the epidermis were pierced," "without inflammation around the writing"—provided measurements—"two-inches high"—and indicated color—"vermillion."[45] Beginning with the cross on Jeanne des Anges's forehead, Loudun exorcists quickly reproduced each of the prioress's marks in print form, as life-size copies that leapt off the pages of their narratives (see Figure 2.2). The authors insisted on the accuracy of their reproductions, which they claim to be identical to the originals imprinted on the nun's flesh: "the first and second layer of skin, called dermis and epidermis, were wounded and opened to the same scale as they appear in this figure."[46] Their account of the formation of the name of Joseph, like those of the names that followed it, specified the equivalence in shape and size between the name's printed reproduction and its original appearance: "the aforesaid name is written in Roman letters of the form and size portrayed here" (see Figure 2.3).[47]

Following Jeanne des Anges's deliverance from her final demon, the translation of her marks from skin to page culminated in the publication of a broadsheet by Loudun exorcists during her post-possession visit to Paris (see Figure 2.4). As Jeanne des Anges explains, crowds of people flocked to see her marks,

> which forced the publication of a printed text in which the public was informed of all the most remarkable things that had happened in the entrance and departure of the demons from my body, and about the impression of the sacred names on my hand.[48]

The printed text was thus made to stand in for the corporeal text, providing a substitute for the overflow crowd or a souvenir for those lucky enough to see

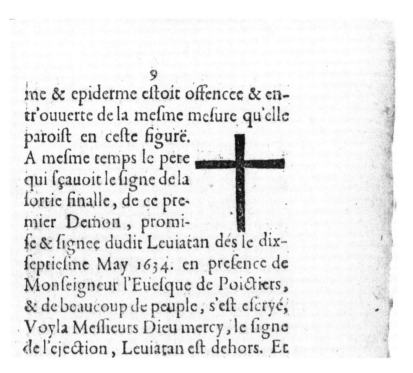

me & epiderme eſtoit offencee & en-
tr'ouuerte de la meſme meſure qu'elle
paroiſt en ceſte figurë.
A meſme temps le pere
qui ſçauoit le ſigne de la
ſortie finalle, de ce premier Demon, promi-
ſe & ſignee dudit Leuiatan dés le dix-
ſeptieſme May 1634. en preſence de
Monſeigneur l'Eueſque de Poiⅆiers,
& de beaucoup de peuple, s'eſt eſcryé,
Voyla Meſſieurs Dieu mercy, le ſigne
de l'ejeⅆion, Leuiatan eſt dehors. Et

Figure 2.2 Life-size reproduction of the cross made on Jeanne des Anges's forehead by the demon Leviatan upon leaving her body, Jean-Joseph Surin, *Lettre Escrite A Monseigneur L'Evesque de Poitiers* (Paris: Jean Martin, 1635), 9. Bibliothèque Nationale de France.

the prioress's sacred marks for themselves. The broadsheet, with an engraving of Jeanne des Anges displaying her signed hand at center, publicly memorialized the prioress's transformation from demoniac to mystic. She kneels before the altar in a serene, saint-like pose, while the three windows behind her call to mind the holy trinity. Holding a rosary in her right hand, with its reference to Mary and to specifically Catholic religious practice, she makes an offering of her inscribed left hand, extending it over the alter, upon which rests a book of prayers, reinforcing the sacred nature of her textual marks. Her eyes gaze at the effigy of the suffering Christ—the word made flesh *par excellence*—creating a relationship of identification with the crucified Christ, both in her wounded body and in her literal incarnation of divine word. Here, the demon's mark becomes the sacred sign that performs her transformation, calling on its readers to see her no longer as possessed by demons but instead by God. With the passage of demons through her skin, the Loudun prioress was not simply returned to her former state but underwent metamorphosis into a living relic, a sacred text of divine truth. At the same time,

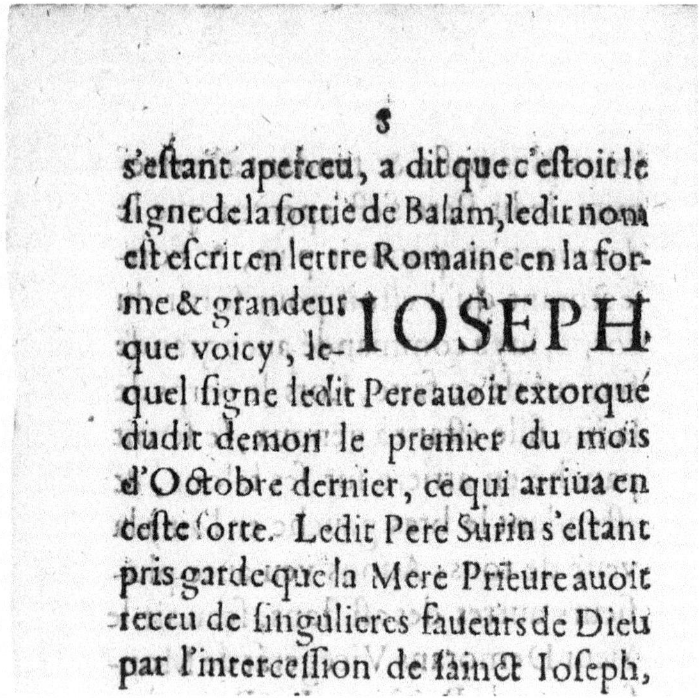

s

s'eſtant apeſceu, a diſque c'eſtoit le
ſigne de la ſortie de Balam, ledit nom
eſt eſcrit en lettre Romaine en la forme & grandeur **IOSEPH**
que voicy, le-
quel ſigne ledit Pere auoit extorqué
dudit demon le premier du mois
d'Octobre dernier, ce qui arriua en
ceſte ſorte. Ledit Pere Surin s'eſtant
pris garde que la Mere Prieure auoit
receu de ſingulieres faueurs de Dieu
par l'interceſſion de ſainct Ioſeph,

Figure 2.3 Life-size name of Joseph, written by the demon Balam on Jeanne des Anges's left hand upon leaving her body, *Relation de la Sortie du Demon Balam du corps de la Mere Prieure* (Paris: Jean Martin, 1635), 8. Bibliothèque Nationale de France.

as the layout of the broadsheet suggests, the lengthy and detailed ecclesiastical account of her marks' appearance that frames the engraving of Jeanne des Anges's body in print symbolically contains it within the Church's walls and within an approved, official reading.

Perhaps the most eloquent example of the conversion of possessed body into sacred text is that of Sœur Marie du Saint Sacrement of the Hospitaller convent in Louviers. According to Esprit du Bosroger (†1655), the Capuchin provincial who participated in exorcisms there and became the case's historian, Marie du Saint Sacrement was delivered of her demon Putiphar through the intercession of the Virgin Mary on Good Friday, March 25, 1644, a date heavy with significance in the liturgical calendar, especially for stigmatic experience. Upon leaving her body, the demon was forced to speak the words "Vive Jesus sur la Croix" [Long Live Jesus on the Cross]—calling up the decidedly Catholic iconography of the crucifix and a frequent header for spiritual correspondence in the period ("Vive Jesus †")—and to imprint those words on the woman's skin. Marie du Saint Sacrement's body, lifted two or

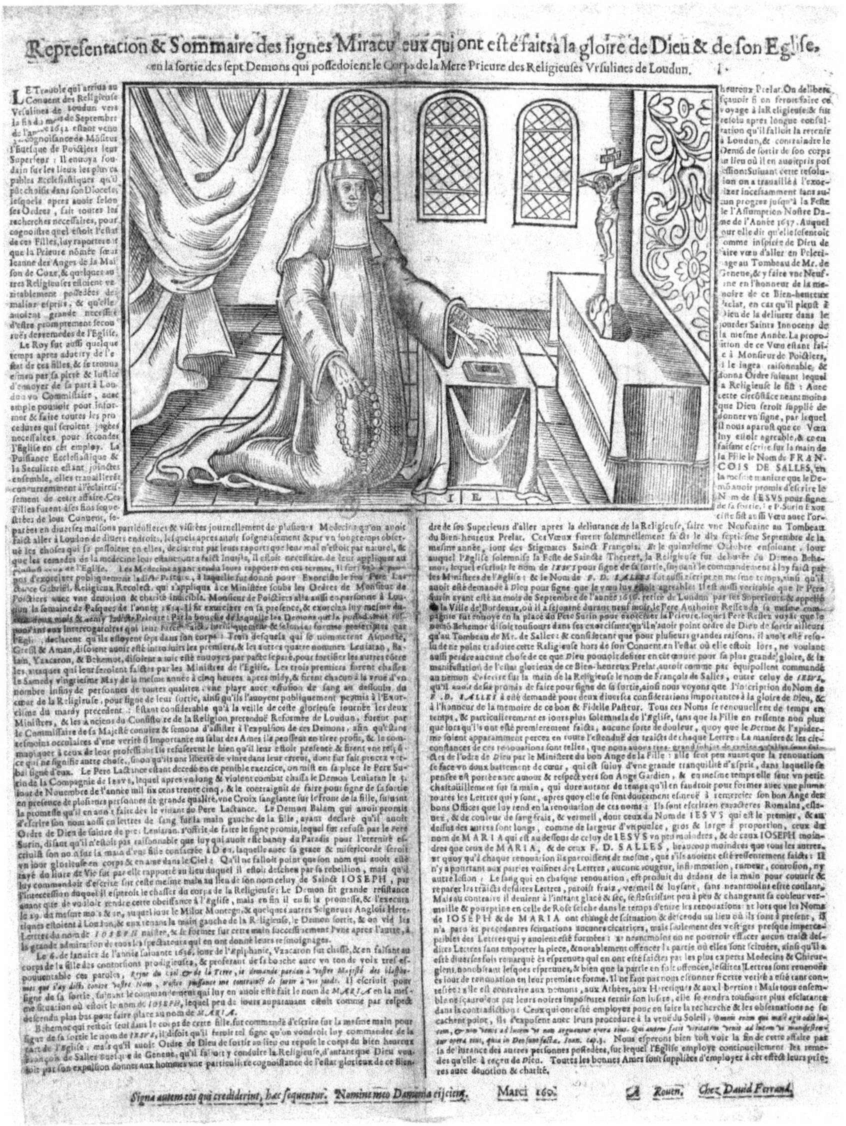

Representation & Sommaire des signes Miraculeux qui ont esté faits à la gloire de Dieu & de son Eglise, en la sortie des sept Demons qui possedoient le Corps de la Mere Prieure des Religieuses Vrsulines de Loudun.

Signa autem eos qui crediderint, hæc sequentur. Nomine meo Dæmonia eijcient. Marci 16. A Rouen, Chez David Ferrand.

Figure 2.4 Broadsheet published following the departure of Jeanne des Anges's last demon, *Representation et Sommaire des Signes Miraculeux* (Rouen: David Ferrand, n.d.). Bibliothèque Nationale de France.

three feet into the air by the demon and then fallen to the ground faint, was promptly searched for the demon's sign of departure, engraved in the place he had previously occupied—her chest:

> They quickly unveiled the breast of the girl, who had fainted and lay there as though dead, and according to the knowledge they had of the place of the charm, they found there freshly imprinted, still wet, and smoking in bright red letters in the white flesh, without inflammation around the writing, these admirable characters (*Vive Jesus sur la Croix*), represented here in this figure and description. . . . An astounding and truly miraculous thing it was, because nothing more was needed but to see the blood flowing and streaming, and there was a heart above, and the Cross below. Now during all of this, while everyone looked at this marvel, the girl remained a quarter of an hour without speaking, nor moving, her face quite beautiful and agreeable, and afterwards she remained so feeble and weak, that five or six people were needed to carry her, since she could not put any weight at all on her feet.[49]

This voyeuristic unveiling of the nun's body attained the desired effect, for the woman's wounds, visible and alive, spoke for themselves; seeing was believing: "nothing more was needed but to see" in order to be convinced. In contrast to her possessed state, where she had exercised strength, sexuality, will, and voice, the delivered nun was struck mute and motionless upon deliverance, reduced to the role of passive medium for the conveyance of the word. The bleeding text, "Vive Jesus," accompanied by the symbols of heart and cross, both declared an evangelical message and confirmed the formerly possessed nun's reinscription within the sacred, marking her as belonging to God. The apologetic treatise specifies that the cross she bore was "exactly the same length and width of the true cross of Monsieur the Bishop of Evreux that he was constantly applying to the place of the charm during exorcism," suggesting that her soft body had been imprinted with the shape of the cross so often held against it.[50] Like Jeanne des Anges's marks, Marie du Saint Sacrement's flesh and blood "impressions" were reprinted to scale in ink on paper (see Figure 2.5). Moreover, Esprit du Bosroger qualified her elaborate corporeal marking as being "of completely freshly impression, still wet," calling to mind wet ink on paper.[51]

Identity on the line

As work by medieval and early modern historians of possession and mysticism has demonstrated, the distinction between "bad" possession by demons and "good" possession by the divine, and thus between identification of a person as a demoniac or as a mystic, was far from clear.[52] Moche Sluhovky has shown how the interior spiritualities that dominated this period, especially popular among women, found themselves consistently scrutinized because it was difficult to define the origins of ecstatic experience; the outward signs of

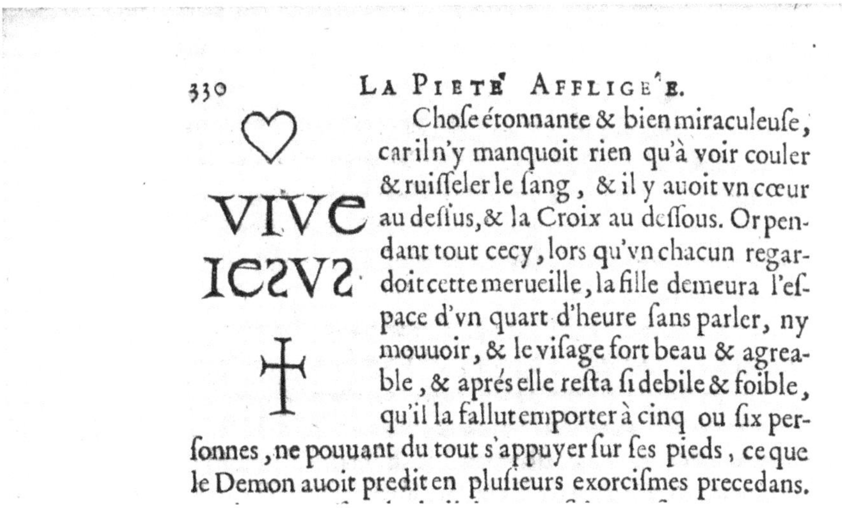

330   LA PIETÉ AFFLIGÉE.

♡

VIVE

IC2V2

✝

Chofe étonnante & bien miraculeufe, car il n'y manquoit rien qu'à voir couler & ruiffeler le fang , & il y auoit vn cœur au deffus, & la Croix au deffous. Or pendant tout cecy, lors qu'vn chacun regardoit cette merueille, la fille demeura l'efpace d'vn quart d'heure fans parler, ny mouuoir, & le vifage fort beau & agreable, & aprés elle refta fi debile & foible, qu'il la fallut emporter à cinq ou fix perfonnes, ne pouuant du tout s'appuyer fur fes pieds, ce que le Demon auoit predit en plufieurs exorcifmes precedans.

Figure 2.5 Life-size reproduction of the text and symbols as engraved on Marie du Saint Sacrement's chest, Esprit du Bosroger, *La Pieté Affligée* (Rouen: Jean Le Boulenger, 1652), 330. Bibliothèque Nationale de France.

demonic and divine possession were similar, often indistinguishable.[53] Indeed, female mystics were almost all accused of demonic possession at some point in their lives or at the very least had to fear such an accusation. While the women of the seventeenth-century cases examined here were clearly understood as having suffered from possession of the demonic kind, upon deliverance they were consistently reaffirmed as having lived through a deeply trying ordeal that ultimately brought them closer to God. Indeed, the resemblances between their experience of demonic possession and that of ecstatic experience as described by sixteenth-century mystic Teresa of Ávila and her late-medieval predecessors, whom women religious of seventeenth-century France celebrated as esteemed models, are striking.[54] Marie du Saint Sacrement's post-deliverance state of mutism and physical weakness mimics that of mystics following ecstatic experience. The demoniac's liberation from her demons was, after all, an intense encounter with the divine, as God intervened directly to drive the malevolent forces from her body. Just as the cutaneous marks themselves left by demons resembled the stigmata of saints, so too the moment of deliverance resonated with the experience of mystical union sought after by many spiritual figures of the period, women prominently among them.

If Church authorities highlighted the extraordinary outward signs of the inner conversion that signaled each demoniac's liberation, the women religious who suffered demonic possession undoubtedly saw too in their corporeal marking a crucial indicator of their transformed identity. These women, who had undergone the long, debilitating, and humiliating experience of demonic possession, had reputations to maintain both within and beyond the convent walls that they sought to reestablish in its aftermath. Their physical wounds played an important role in rewriting their demon-filled bodies in accordance with the feminine stigmatic tradition and devotional practices with which they were familiar. Their marks helped recast what had been "bad" possession as "good" possession. Indeed, the demoniacs of Loudun and Louviers may even have seen in them a guarantee of their innocence. Given the close association of these mass convent possessions with witch trials, and despite the more frequent casting of demoniacs as victims of another's wrongdoing, the danger that a diagnosis of possession might be transformed into an accusation of witchcraft always loomed. In the earlier 1611 Aix possession case, demoniac Magdaleine de Demandouls had come frighteningly close to being punished as a witch and, after years of penance, was again accused of witchcraft and imprisoned for life in 1653.[55] In Louviers, Magdaleine Bavant, transformed from demoniac into witch thanks to the accusations of her Hospitaller sisters, met the same fate and died in prison.[56] Cutaneous signs, well known to convict in cases of witchcraft, here authenticated virtue. Significantly, in Aix, it was by transforming the devil's marks that would condemn her into stigmata that Demandouls sought to establish her innocence of the crime of witchcraft during her possession. She directed the surgeons searching her body for the devil's mark to invisible marks on her feet and on her left side by her heart, highly unusual places for devil's marks to hide, following instead a stigmatic pattern. Her marks would then be removed by God on Easter, with Demandouls suffering terrible pain in these places, which bled when pricked. Her sensitivity and bleeding proved that they were no longer devil's marks, making her innocence manifest, a transformation of her marks that her medical examiner Jacques Fontaine calls "a divine miracle."[57] Inscription with holy signs thus assured demoniacs' safe passage from identification with the devil to identification with the divine and enduring recognition as God's own, a guarantee without which they risked serious material hardship, even persecution. Eager to dismiss accusations of fraud, to shed their identities as demoniacs, and to make manifest their election by God, formerly possessed women, in cooperation with their exorcists, saw in their corporeal marking a way to rewrite themselves within a more positive, feminine mystical tradition and to ensure their safety from future condemnation.

The case of Jeanne des Anges provides, thanks to the survival of her memoir, rare and extensive testimony to what corporal inscription may have meant to a woman's experience of possession and exorcism both as it occurred and in the years that followed it. As might be expected, given the extravagance of Jeanne des Anges's tale and Loudun's tragic consequences, the prioress and her signed body drew fire from critics of her own time and, until only recently, have also consistently met with severe judgment by historians and literary critics.[58] The Loudun prioress has inspired accusations of self-aggrandizement, manipulation, fame-seeking, and misguided abuse of self and others. Jeanne des Anges's identity as a nun and professed mystic has only fueled her detractors' demonization of her self-promotion, branding her a "manipulator" or "hypocrite" and judging her against standards of religious humility and piety. Interpreters of her corporeal inscription have variously portrayed it as the product of maniacal egotism, a symptom of apparent madness, or a sign of the prioress's ultimate subjugation to masculine authority.[59] Her inscription has become the emblem of a scandal that put an innocent priest to death, as Stephen Greenblatt underlines in his foreword to Michael B. Smith's English translation of Michel de Certeau's *Possession de Loudun*, describing Jeanne des Anges's signed hand as "devastating evidence of miserable fraud."[60] The fact that the only print edition of Jeanne des Anges's memoir of her possession experience is still that of 1886—penned by doctors Gabriel Legué and Gilles de la Tourette, followers of the famed neurologist and nineteenth-century father of hysteria, Jean-Martin Charcot (1825–1893)—has also gone a long way to perpetuating her enclosure within a diagnosis as "possessed hysteric."[61] In addition, popular novels like Aldous Huxley's *The Devils of Loudun* (1952) and Ken Russell's 1971 film, *The Devils*, based on Huxley's work, paint a picture of a mentally disturbed, sex-starved nun out for vengeance. Only recently has there been a significant lifting of the condemnatory tone so prevalent in discussions of Jeanne des Anges and an effort to provide a fuller contextualized image of the Loudun prioress and her importance in the spiritual community of her time.[62] As Elizabeth Goldsmith notes:

> Readings of Jeanne that dismiss her as either deluded or criminally insincere remain fixed within the limited range of interpretive options originally established by seventeenth-century diatribes against her, and continued in the nineteenth-century medical discourse on hysteria. These readings isolate her, moreover, from the mystical circles in which she functioned and was taken very seriously as an advisor, spiritual director, and conduit to the divine.[63]

In large part, Jeanne des Anges's unfortunate fate in the hands of many modern readers owes its origins to her consideration in isolation, as the emblematic figure of an infamous *cause célèbre*. But, as we have seen, her corporeal marking, though extraordinary in its extensive nature and in the ample attention it inspired, was not unique among demoniacs, nor was it unknown among women religious of her time. Once resituated within the movement of devotional corporeal inscription that informed it, and understood as part of a larger process of self-definition, the prioress's marking can no longer be read solely as an experience of subjugation, though she does experience it within a particular set of constraints of which she is highly conscious. Nor can her participation in determining and promoting her corporeal marks be simply condemned as fraudulent or inappropriate, though she undoubtedly pushed the limits of her authority. Jeanne des Anges's corporeal and textual enterprise must be understood as means through which she refashioned her identity within well-known feminine spiritual traditions, restored her reputation, and secured financial stability for her convent in the aftermath of the Loudun possession.

"Set me as a seal upon thy heart"

As Carolyn Walker Bynum points out, despite the fame of Francis of Assisi's stigmata, from the late medieval period forward, stigmatization was almost exclusively experienced by women.[64] Women religious identified not only with the humanity of Christ but especially with his suffering, bleeding body, and stigmata were one part of what Bynum calls a very "literal" pursuit of the imitation of Christ:

> Stigmatic women clearly saw themselves as imitating Christ's bleeding flesh both as it hung on the cross and as it was consecrated in the wafer. . . . Thus, it was women's bodies almost exclusively that bled as Christ bled. . . . Holy women imitated Christ in their bodies; and Christ's similar bleeding and feeding body was understood as analogous to theirs.[65]

Identification with Christ's body was thus all the more salient among women, who sought various means to relive and commemorate in their bodies Christ's physical suffering. During the Catholic Counter-Reformation, stigmatic phenomena flourished—along with practices of corporeal mortification and asceticism—as a specifically feminine miracle among women religious in Spain, Italy, and France.[66] Daily meditation, as advanced by François de Sales and many women mystics of the period, encouraged vivid contemplation of Christ's passion and wounds; blood miracles and visions of the body of the bleeding Christ played an important role in women's religious experience. Devout Catholic women actively sought to share their savior's corporeal pain, as had the saints and martyrs whose lives they read about in hagiographical texts and celebrated in their devotions.[67] As Jean-Pierre Albert's study of the preponderance of blood in female mystical experience makes clear, "Far more than those of their masculine counterparts, the lives of holy women are placed under the sign of blood."[68]

While several seventeenth-century women religious reported having received stigmata—both visible and invisible—even more women deliberately chose to inscribe their skin with devotional symbols or the name of Jesus.[69] More important than its role as a penitential practice that inflicted punishment on the flesh, self-inscribed stigmata served these women as a way of materializing and making permanent in their own bodies their union with the suffering Christ.[70] Those inspired to make such marks themselves used knives or hot irons to cut or burn names and symbols into their flesh. Historian Jacques Le Brun has described such sacrifices as "an attempt to found certitude on the body itself and on the cut that gashes it, to go beyond . . . the equivocal nature of symbols and imaginative powers, making of the wounded body the symbol and the image."[71] With a gesture that maimed their unworthy flesh yet simultaneously valorized it as a powerful signifying surface, these self-inscribing women made of their bodies the sign of their object of devotion, permanent memorials to Christ's passion. In so marking their own bodies, they sought to bridge the distance physically separating them from Christ's absent body, "to render Jesus Christ present in [them] in a visible, readable way, therefore immune to doubt, to deception."[72]

The celebrated Jeanne-Françoise Frémyot de Rabutin, baronne de Chantal (1572–1641), served as a prominent model for the formerly possessed Ursulines and Hospitallers of Loudun, Louviers, and Auxonne as they navigated their own reinscription into the sacred. Co-founder of the Order of the Visitation with François de Sales, whose name, we recall, figured on Jeanne des Anges's hand and on one of the texts produced from the mouths of the nuns at Auxonne, Jeanne de Chantal was well known to women religious of her time for her exemplary devotion, which included a prominent act of self-marking. As a widow of twenty-nine, Jeanne de Chantal used a red hot iron to inscribe her chest with the name of Jesus in order to manifest her preference for her chosen religious vocation over a proposed remarriage to a family friend. Flemish engraver Theodoor van Merlen's (1609–1672) illustration of the event portrays her powerful gesture as an act of sublime submission, consistent with mystical narratives of ecstatic rapture (see Figure 2.6). Christ stands before her, his hand guiding the iron that forms his name, as she, eyes closed, seems to sleep, her inert body supported by a smiling and contrastingly alert angel. Though the engraving eloquently expresses the much sought-after experience of losing oneself to Christ, the mise-en-scène effaces any agency on the part of the nun in her inscription.[73] But Jeanne de Chantal's act was, according to her seventeenth-century biographer, Bishop Henry de Maupas du Tour, a highly deliberate one, performed in full consciousness and motivated by self-preservation, religious conviction, and ambition to accomplish her goal of founding a new order in Annecy with François de Sales.

In contrast to Van Merlen's engraving, Maupas du Tour's 1644 biography, published just three years after Jeanne de Chantal's death, underlines the nun's active role in the engraving of her chest. He portrays her by then well-known act as a method for overcoming the temptations of the world and affirming her commitment to God by "imprint[ing] his eternal word more deeply into her heart."[74] He marvels at how Jeanne de Chantal

> had the courage and fortitude to take a hot iron, red from the fire, which she used like a burin, engraving herself with the holy and sacred

Mets moy comme un cachet sur ton cœur et sur ton bras, car
L'amour est fort comme la mort. *Cantique chap. 8. vers 6.*

Figure 2.6 Jeanne de Chantal inscribing her chest with the name of Christ, engraving
by Theodoor van Merlen in Henry de Maupas du Tour, *La Vie de la
Venerable Mere Jeanne Francoise Fremiot* (Paris, Simeon Piget, 1672),
facing p. 1. Bibliothèque Nationale de France.

Name of Jesus on her chest, so deeply that she would have endangered her life, if love had not been stronger than death, and if these holy characters, like a sacred balm spreading, had not healed her in wounding her with this loving and painful lesion, with whose blood she wrote new vows and new promises, making therein an eternal sacrifice to her adored beloved, since her heart and body would remain forever innocent victims, and would be eternally marked with this divine seal, which made her enemies fear her the rest of her days, and made her invincible to all the powers of Hell.[75]

Like the many women who followed her, Jeanne de Chantal thus took literally the lover's invitation of the Song of Solomon 8:6: "Set me as a seal upon thy heart, as a seal upon thine arm: for love is stronger than death." Through corporeal inscription, she signed an ultimate vow of fidelity, visibly and indelibly marking herself as God's and therein guaranteeing her immunity to any forces that would oppose her. Maupas du Tour emphasizes the permanence of her mark; it is a seal that will last "forever," "eternally," "the rest of her days," an endurance of message only the corporeal medium can ensure. Far from being a passive recipient, Jeanne de Chantal knew what she was doing; the bishop even suggests "that she was knowledgeable in anatomy, and that she had studied just how deeply she could exercise these saintly cruelties, without killing herself."[76] Moreover, the fact that both her family and her spiritual mentor, François de Sales, expressed shock and disapproval at her self-inscription confirms its transgressive and solitary nature.[77]

Jeanne de Chantal's dramatic self-inscription inspired many women to sign their bodies with the name of Christ. Le Brun cites numerous cases of self-inscribed women among the Visitandine nuns whose biographies he has surveyed, and similar phenomena surface in the pages of the chronicles and lives written by other orders well into the eighteenth century.[78] Often kept secret and discovered only after a nun's death, these signs of sanctity were highlighted in the biographies featured in intra-order *circulaires*, newsletters that became evidence in cases for canonization. For example, the Visitandine sisters of Margueritte Angelique Cadeau (†1717) described the deep devotion that inspired her to

> engrave on her heart with an iron, the sacred and holy Name of Jesus in capital Letters half the length of a finger (as we saw after her death) and . . . this divine seal forever barred the entrance to anything that could be detrimental to the perfection of the love that God demanded of her.[79]

Another Visitandine, Anne Angelique Loppin (†1707), made extensive use of corporeal mortification, inflicting upon herself "cruel punishments to the point of making her body the palpable image of the Ecce Homo." She too "used the iron and the fire to imprint his sacred Name upon her heart."[80]

Two of the more well-known of Jeanne de Chantal's seventeenth-century imitators were mystics Jeanne Marie Bouvier de la Motte Guyon (1648–1717) and Marguerite-Marie Alacoque (1647–1690).[81] In recounting her spiritual journey in her memoir, Guyon chose to include her attempt at marking as a young girl, who, "not yet twelve," was already an avid reader of François de Sales's works and determined in her pursuit of a deep interior spirituality. Inspired by Jeanne de Chantal's self-inscription, which she had read about in the Visitandine foundress's biography, yet unable to brand her flesh in the same way, Guyon substituted a piece of paper on which she wrote the name of Jesus, fastening it to her chest with pins and ribbons:

> Everything I saw written in the biography of Madame de Chantal enchanted me, and I was such a child that I thought I had to do all that I saw there. . . . One day I read that she had put the name of Jesus upon her heart to follow the advice of the Spouse: *Set me as a seal upon thy heart*, and that she had used a red hot iron engraved with the saintly Name, I was terribly upset not to be able to do the same. I decided to write the sacred and adorable Name in large characters on a piece of paper. With ribbons and a large needle I attached it to my skin in four places and it stayed attached in this way for a long time.[82]

Guyon thus carried out a youthful imitation of her spiritual heroine by wearing the name of Jesus in paper and ink form, a text that nonetheless penetrated her skin through the pins that held it in place.[83] Her contemporary, Visitandine Marguerite-Marie Alacoque, waited until her early thirties to perform her inscription but went further, twice cutting the name of Jesus into her chest with a knife, first in December 1678 and again in the fall of 1679.[84] The account Alacoque provides in her memoir suggests a blurring of skin and paper, as she wrote new vows first in her own blood on paper and then carved the name of Jesus on her chest.[85]

Inscribing the body, fashioning the self

Jeanne des Anges and her Ursuline sisters may well have been Jeanne de Chantal's first imitators. Though the corporeal signs that appeared on Jeanne des Anges's skin and were promised to other Loudun nuns, as well as those that reemerged in the possession cases that followed in Louviers and Auxonne, were clearly cast as the work of demons, not nuns, at the very least, the women who received the stigmata surely saw their inscription as in line with Jeanne de Chantal's example. Her prominence among women religious and the similarity between her marks and those that appeared on the skin of the Loudun and Louviers nuns certainly suggests that the latter may in fact have actively participated in their own inscription. Indeed, in the case of Jeanne des Anges, a later Ursuline account of the prioress's marking does not hesitate to attribute to her full agency in their inscription, citing the act as evidence of her extraordinary devotion to the suffering Christ. The *Life* that figures in the 1686 volume of the *Journal des Illustres Religieuses de l'Ordre de Sainte Ursule* proclaims that the prioress's intense love of God "gave her the inspiration and the strength to engrave the Holy names of Jesus and of Mary numerous times on the flesh of her arms with a knife."[86] The Ursuline biographer thus places Jeanne des Anges in Jeanne de Chantal's lineage, seeing her gesture of self-inscribing stigmata as a testament to her deep commitment to her divine spouse. Moreover, the author's naming of the tool she used to engrave the names—a *ganif*, defined by Jean Nicot as "a sort of little knife for cutting writing quills," spelled *canif* today—makes a symbolic connection between this powerful act of corporeal inscription that defines her and the other major pillar of Jeanne des Anges's self-fashioning enterprise: the writing of her autobiography.[87] Whether or not she actually took up the knife herself to inscribe her body, or whether—as she describes it—the writing and rewriting of her body took place through the divine intervention of a guardian angel, Jeanne des Anges took a leading role in decisions regarding how her body would be marked and in the promotion of her stigmata following her possession. She clearly understood writing—both on paper and on skin—as a potent medium for making a new identity for herself among the women mystics of her time in the aftermath of her possession.

The same year that Jeanne de Chantal's biography saw publication, Jeanne des Anges completed her own unique memoir of her possession experience that circulated in manuscript form.[88] Having obtained permission to continue the account begun by her exorcist, Jesuit Jean-Joseph Surin, when he became ill, Jeanne des Anges rewrote the story of her possession as a tale of inner struggle, physical suffering, penitence, and conversion, modeled on the *Life* of Saint Teresa of Ávila.[89] She thus took control of the written record of her possession, ultimately exceeding the text's initial goals by emphasizing her own failings, her spiritual growth, her deliverance, and the events following her possession. Her language is that of interiority and self-examination, consistent with the unique approach of meditative prayer and personal development her exorcist-turned-spiritual-director had taken to freeing her of her demons, replacing more violent methods that focused exclusively on the exorcist tormenting the demons that inhabited his charge.[90] In her memoir, Jeanne des Anges recounts her personal battle against the demonic forces within as well as against her own "bad inclinations" that rendered her possession possible, making of her suffering a test of faith as well as an opportunity for intense inner work.[91] From the beginning, she sees victory over her own weaknesses as essential to her eventual freedom from her demons: "The thought often came to me that I should fight my enemies in my own nature and take out on myself all the disorders that I felt, without looking for foreign causes."[92] Her conviction is confirmed by a divine message that told her that "it is time that you work towards your perfection at your own expense, and that you apply yourself in strongly combatting your enemies in yourself and in your passions."[93] In accepting this challenge, Jeanne des Anges thus takes responsibility for her own cure, placing herself, rather than her exorcists, on the front lines in the battle against her demons, making her memoir the tale of her own hard-won victory over the demonic. She highlights her acts of resistance and penance and recounts the divine favors and miracles she experienced intimately both during and in the years following her ordeal, crafting a narrative of personal struggle and communication with the divine in line with the experiences of other women mystics of her time. She describes in detail the divine voices she hears and the visits of a guardian angel who counseled and supported her constantly in her battle, as well as the miraculous cures of self and of others brought about through traces of a sacred unction left on her nightdress by Saint Joseph when he had miraculously cured her of a near-fatal illness.[94]

While the choices Jeanne des Anges makes in writing the story of her possession attest to her desire to position herself among women mystics, past and present, in her interior quest for perfection and union with God, her memoir also reveals the importance she attributed to her exterior corporeal marking as part of her enterprise of self-fashioning and her confidence in the power of her inscriptions to guarantee her identity as a woman touched by God. Throughout her possession and beyond, Jeanne des Anges refused the role of passive relic and became a protagonist in the signing of her body and the defense and preservation of her signatures. She participated in decisions regarding her marking both during and following her exorcisms, defended her marks before critics, and used them to bolster her own reputation as well as that of her convent, ensuring its future prosperity.

Jeanne des Anges provides ample evidence in her memoir of her personal investment in decisions as to how her body was to be indelibly marked by her demons, an involvement corroborated by ecclesiastical accounts of her inscription. She recounts how, with the aid of Surin as a supportive exorcist, regular visits from a guardian angel, and divine visions, she took a leading role in transforming the original exit signs promised by her demons so as to increase their permanence and associate herself with the holy rather than the demonic. She writes that following her first two inscriptions with the lines and the cross, she prayed to Saint Joseph to change the next promised sign, one that would have forever tied her to her former demon—the writing of the demon's name, Balaam, upon her hand: "I spoke to him once again to ask him to force Balaam to change the sign of his departure, which was to write his name on my hand, which I would wear my whole lifetime."[95] As a result of ardent prayer, mortification, and masses said to convince Saint Joseph to intervene, the name of Jeanne des Anges's patron saint and deliverer was instead successfully memorialized in her flesh.[96] Having obtained this favor, the prioress continued her devotions, praying that he "obtain [for her] the grace to be able to have the names of Jesus and Mary, by changing the signs that the demons had proposed," a transformation that she also secured.[97] Even the official ecclesiastical narrative of the demon Behemot's departure assigns her complete responsibility for the transformation of her inscriptions:

> Now is important to note regarding the name of JESUS, which Behemot received the order to write on the hand of the Mother Superior, that besides the sign he had promised the Church to make when leaving the body, . . . the Mother Superior had desired to wear on her hands the name of JESUS along with those of MARY and JOSEPH, to have before her eyes during her whole lifetime these three principal objects of her devotion, and had asked this of Our Savior through the intercession of S. JOSEPH, so that without any other commandment made by the Church, upon the simple wish of this good woman, the Demon was enjoined to reconcile this second sign to the first, already promised, in accordance with this pious desire.[98]

Given the prioress's agency behind her inscription, it hardly seems accidental, then, that her deliverance from Behemot took place on the feast day of Saint Teresa of Ávila, the already canonized saint with whom Jeanne des Anges closely identified and shared a particular affection for Saint Joseph.[99]

Jeanne des Anges thus effectively bypassed ecclesiastical authority in her choice of her stigmata, making a compact with God and the demon through prayers said directly to Joseph to bring about the transformation of previously designated exit signs. During her possession, she intervened in a power struggle normally waged exclusively between demon and exorcist, taking an active role in the negotiation over how her body would be signed.[100] As for the inscription of François de Sales's yet to be sainted name, according to Jeanne des Anges, it appeared in private, "without the Father [Surin] noticing. A few nuns who were close by saw [it] formed," again suggesting the prioress's initiative behind that choice and highlighting the engraving as a miracle shared among women.[101] Moreover, Jeanne des Anges's selection of her inscriptions—the names of the members of the holy family and that of the foremost spiritual father of her time—is highly significant. Rather than sealing her subjugation to the hierarchies of the family and the church, as Mitchell Greenberg has argued, it celebrates a particularly feminine emphasis on the holy family and makes a memorial to one of the most influential spiritual writers of the period, whose works women in particular read widely and whose methods of devotional meditation they adopted and developed.[102] Jeanne des Anges's choice to add the name of François de Sales to her hand also underlines her identification with his spiritual partner, Jeanne de Chantal, whose approbation the Loudun prioress sought and received following her possession through pilgrimage to the nun's convent of the Visitation in Annecy. There, Jeanne de Chantal opened her monastery and the grave of her mentor and collaborator François de Sales to Jeanne des Anges. The Loudun prioress writes that the two women shared "very long conversations together about everything that had happened during the possession, and especially, I told her a very exact story of what had happened in the appearance of Saint Joseph when he miraculously cured me with the holy unction."[103] Jeanne de Chantal's nuns, dignitaries of Annecy, and the people of the city and surrounding countryside all came to see the names on Jeanne des Anges's hand and the cloth stained with Saint Joseph's sacred unction, and to touch objects to them, as was commonly done with relics: "There was a great eagerness to have rosaries, crosses, medallions, cotton and paper touched against them."[104] The cloth dirtied from so much use that the Visitandine nuns even laundered it for their Ursuline visitor.[105]

The visit to Annecy was just one stop in a post-possession pilgrimage that Jeanne des Anges initiated and organized to give thanks for her deliverance, and to which she devoted a substantial portion of her narrative.[106] Shortly after her final liberation from her demons, despite initial resistance from her male superiors, Jeanne des Anges obtained permission for and carried out an extensive post-possession trip that took her from Loudun to Tours, Paris, Lyon, Grenoble, Chambéry, and finally to Annecy. Her travels, which lasted five months, had all the allure of a star going on tour, with stops in several smaller cities and convents of diverse orders along the way. Jeanne des Anges recounts each of these visits in detail, as well as the numerous miracles that took place in various locations thanks to the cloth containing Saint Joseph's healing unction that she carried with her. She writes how she was greeted everywhere by groups of local dignitaries as well as mobs of people, who, eager to see her signed hand, even broke down the doors of her lodgings. During her initial trip to Paris, the curious crowds were such that she had to remain at a window, her hand displayed on a pillow, from four in the morning until ten at night:

> They put me in a room on the lower level where there was a window at eye level that opened onto one of the house's courtyards. I was sitting, my arm on a pillow, and my hand was stretched out, outside the window, to be seen by the people. Persons of the highest rank could not enter the room because the common people were occupying the avenues. I was not even given the time to hear mass or take my meals. It was extremely hot and the crowd of people raised the temperature so much that I felt faint with dizziness and even fell unconscious onto the floor.[107]

Jeanne des Anges writes that "more than twenty thousand people visited me each day during my stay in Paris," an excess that

> required the publication of a printed text in which the public was instructed about all the most considerable things that had happened in the entrance and the exit of the demons from my body and about the impression of the sacred names on my hand [see Figure 2.4].[108]

She recounts that her marks were even plagiarized—"It happened that an unfortunate soul wanted to imprint on his hand and forge the names that I wear on mine"—but is quick to assure her readers that God revealed the inauthenticity of those inscriptions, for "such an inflammation developed on his hand that he thought he would lose his arm, and even his life, God showing that no one could make that impression by natural means."[109]

If Jeanne des Anges's ecclesiastical entourage realized the potential of her sacred inscription, and made the most of it, the prioress too gained notoriety through their display, both for herself and for her convent. She was received not only by Cardinal Richelieu and other Church authorities, aristocrats, and dignitaries who examined her hand and offered material and financial aid to her and her Ursuline establishment, but also by King Louis XIII and Anne of Austria, who, pregnant, asked her to return to be at her side for the birth of the future Sun King. Jeanne des Anges's detailed record of each visit reveals her awareness of her marks' importance, her careful negotiation of their use and examination, and the position she acquired as the bearer of these signatures. Like a seal that bestowed veracity and authenticity to a paper document, her sacred signatures validated her importance as one who had been touched by the divine. Significantly, she reports that during her audience with Richelieu, "[s]ome courtiers suggested to the cardinal to have my hand wrapped in a glove, and to seal it with his seal" as a sign of his endorsement. But, as Jeanne des Anges underlines, the cardinal saw no need to add such a sign of authority, stating that "'[o]ne would have to be crazy or impious to doubt the truth of what we have seen; it would be tempting God to do what you suggest.'"[110] Already imprinted with a seal that exceeded in power the official mark of the prime minister, Jeanne des Anges needed no further stamp of approval.[111]

Throughout her travels, the prioress promoted and defended the validity of her corporeal text, and thus of her own transformed identity, inviting the examination of her hand while carefully controlling what could be done with it in order to protect herself from physical harm and to prevent damage to the sacred names.[112] In order to silence detractors, she even allowed numerous doctors and clerics to perform tests on her marks— rubbing with scalding cloths, the strongest alcohols, and oils—and recorded in detail the results of these experiments in her memoir: "after all these efforts, the characters, instead of a coming off or undergoing alteration, took on a new luster and appeared more beautiful than before."[113] Jeanne des Anges recounts that upon seeing this, an examining surgeon "gave at that very moment a double testimony, one with his eyes that broke into tears of joy and devotion, and the other with his mouth that said loudly and clearly 'That God's finger was present here.'"[114] According to Jeanne des Anges, the doctors' and surgeons' published reports about her stigmata achieved their desired end and "imposed silence on the heretics and the libertines, and encouraged the good souls to believe, respect and honor this great miracle."[115] Yet the prioress also placed limits on what she would endure. When Cardinal Richelieu's skeptical brother, Alphone-Louis du Plessis de Richelieu, archbishop of Lyon, went too far, attempting to remove her marks with scissors and razor, she protested, invoking the authority of her protector, the prime minister himself, who, she said, had not ordered her to suffer such torments.[116]

Jeanne des Anges's deep involvement in the writing of her body continued for years after her possession ended, her marks frequently renewing themselves on holy days, regaining their original vermilion color throughout the prioress's lifetime, and thus regularly validating her legitimacy as a mystic. A Loudun exorcist describes this process:

> [W]henever these sacred names begin to fade, and seem to want to disappear, they never fail to refresh and renew themselves in an instant, without our being able to discern the cause. And what gives even more consolation, is that this renewal happens on Saturdays, which are days consecrated to the Saint Virgin, so that . . . on Friday evenings, we see on the hand of the Mother Superior these characters dry and discolored, and in part removed, and then on Saturday mornings when she leaves her Prayers, or Communion, we find them completely fresh as they were the first days, moist and vermilion, and glowing like coral.[117]

Such periodic bleeding of stigmatic wounds, claimed only for women throughout history, was present in Louviers as well.[118] Esprit du Bosroger writes that the mark inscribed on Marie du Saint-Sacrement's chest grew:

> redder and redder during first year of its impression, increasing in the flesh according to the nourishment of the body and retaining its redness in its extension. . . . [A]nd [it] appears brighter on Fridays from three in the afternoon on, the hour it was first engraved, and at present you can still see it, well expressed, even though more than five years have gone by.[119]

The timing of the renewals, frequent on Friday evenings and on Saturdays, days devoted to the Virgin Mary, was shared by most female stigmatics, for whom Mary was a preeminent model of feminine devotion. Easter week, which commemorates Christ's bleeding body, was also a common period of renewal for many, including Jeanne des Anges. For female stigmatics, as Jean-Pierre Albert has suggested, on a symbolic level "a liturgical rhythm [came] to substitute for the natural cycle of menstruation."[120] Of course, for former dermoniacs, the regular regeneration of the symbols and names they bore, which took place at significant times in the Catholic calendar, made their inscriptions all the more rhetorically powerful as texts of propaganda, for the constant reappearance of these signs affirmed each time anew the women's liberation and the authority of the Catholic Church that had enabled it. Nonetheless, more often than not, in contrast to the highly public events of their original inscription, the renewal of these women's marks took place most often in private or among women, in spaces removed from the male gaze, as Jeanne des Anges's testimony attests. She describes the intimacy and spiritual nature of the renewal experience, performed, in her case, by her guardian angel:

> This happens ordinarily on the eve of important feast days or during the night, when I am praying or on the feast day when I am taking communion . . . [b]ecause, then, my mind is turned toward God, and my soul receives interior consolation. . . . [O]n the outside, the operation is quite gentle. During it I feel a very delicate tingling in the hand; sometimes, my guardian Angel, invisible, even pulls off the glove I wear on that hand; not that I see the glove being removed, but that I realize that it is removed.[121]

Sometimes, she writes, her angel "makes a movement as though someone were writing on my hand. . . . During this time, my soul is in great interior contemplation."[122] On another occasion, one of her Ursuline sisters shared in her experience:

> [W]hen [Sœur Agnes] saw that the glove had been removed, she put her cheek against my hand and felt the little tingling that I have described, and, having looked at my hand, she saw the characters that were renewed, which were very beautiful and very vermillion.[123]

While the initial marking in these cases was nothing short of spectacular, renewal was thus a more private affair, an intense spiritual experience shared among women or more often solitary, relatively removed from ecclesiastical control, determined and reported solely by the women who bore the stigmata.

Jeanne des Anges announced the periodic renewal of her stigmata throughout her lifetime and "elected a new engraver," a guardian angel, to do the work.[124] Moreover, she sought to continue her corporeal inscription beyond the sacred names on her hand, this time directly at the hands of the divine. In her *imitatio Christi*, and also in imitation of earlier saints such as Chiara de Montefalco († 1308), much admired by the women mystics of her time, she prayed for her heart to be imprinted with the instruments of the passion.[125] In letters to her confessor, Jean-Baptiste Saint-Jure (1588–1657), Jeanne des Anges relates that from April through December 1645, beginning in the week of Christ's passion, her heart was engraved with each of the *arma Christi*, save for the lance, which she was told she would receive only upon death, for it would transpierce her heart. These figurative marks, like those that came before them, renewed themselves periodically, with "effusions of blood" to reinforce her determination.[126] Jeanne des Anges describes her desire to live Christ's sufferings using a mystical vocabulary:

My very dear Father, Our Lord ties me more and more to his sufferings, and, despite any pain my body feels in it, my heart ardently desires to suffer. I ask God the Father that he complete his work in me, and that he make inside me a portrait of Jesus Christ crucified. Night and day, I feel this desire; I long ceaselessly for this happiness; no matter what I am doing, I find myself in these thoughts.[127]

Jeanne des Anges provides a detailed account of each of the violent engravings of her heart that follow as painful but fulfilling ecstatic experiences, emphasizing their role in her pursuit of spiritual union with Christ. Her guardian angel appears to her at the moment of the engraving of the first instrument, that of the cross:

Shortly thereafter, I felt a great internal upheaval, with pain so violent that it is impossible for me to express. It lasted five hours. The pain spread throughout my body, but was sharpest in my heart. The effect on me was so great that that same day I vomited up nearly three pints of blood, and, in truth, I thought I was going to die. The pain in my heart still has not left me; I have remained in such a debilitated state that I fall from weakness and faint at nearly any hour of the day. As for my soul, it remains tranquil in the presence of God, and it seems to me that it finds ever-greater attachment to and union with Jesus Christ.[128]

Jeanne des Anges's mystical devotion was widely recognized among women of her order as exemplary, a model to be imitated, as her Ursuline biographer attests:

[H]er Angelic way incited others in their Devotion, and her example alone invited them to adore and prostrate themselves before the Divine Majesty; she prayed holding a Crucifix in her hand, which she sometimes pressed against her chest, as though she wished to imprint her heart with the characters of crucifying love.[129]

An engraving of Jeanne des Anges made upon her death in 1665 reflects the image of serene devotion and sanctity preserved in these Ursuline chronicles and her place as an important spiritual figure of her time (see Figure 2.7). Her gaze turned toward the viewer, she smiles, her right hand holding a crucifix against her chest and her inscribed left hand resting upon it, prominently displayed. Jeanne des Anges's guardian angel gazes upon her, smiling, his left hand identically positioned over his heart while his right gestures toward heaven, from which descend rays of light, suggesting her divine election.

Though, because of her prominent role in the scandalous Loudun affair and her subsequent cult following, Jeanne des Anges remained far too

Portrait de la sœur Marie Ieanne des anges, vrsuliñe; decedeé le 29.me Ianuier 1665.

V.S.f

Figure 2.7 Portrait of Jeanne des Anges following her death, attributed to Mathias van Somer, 1665. Private collection. Image courtesy of Dr. Yu Watanabe.

controversial to ever be canonized, the recognition she gained through her stigmata and her own rewriting of herself as mystic allowed her to remain prioress of a prosperous convent throughout her lifetime, to become a frequently consulted authority on spiritual matters, and to maintain numerous relations with those in power.[130] Publicly regarded as an insider expert on the discernment of spirits—able to communicate with the deceased and benefitting from a direct channel to divine truth through communion with her guardian angel—her opinions were sought after and highly respected, and the maxims of her angel were published.[131] So many visitors frequented the Loudun convent to see her marks and to seek her advice that Surin warned her against running "a sort of shop . . . a sort of office for finding out what one must do concerning marriages, trials, and other things of this nature."[132] While never completely free from the criticism of detractors and skeptics, far from marginal, Jeanne des Anges held a place of importance for the larger public and among the religious authorities of her time, both female and male.[133]

As for her stigmata, toward the end of her life, it was Jeanne des Anges herself who asked God that they be removed. With no further explanation, another seventeenth-century Ursuline biographer writes simply:

> She wore these names as they have been described here for twenty-six or twenty-seven years, until two and a half years before her death, when she prayed to God to erase them entirely; and he who had inspired this prayer, fulfilled it.[134]

Whether fueled by a burst of humility in her old age, fatigue with the numerous visitors who distracted her from her devotions, or simply, as one Protestant critic suggested, disappointment at the sight of her marks' increasing illegibility as the skin of her hand aged, Jeanne des Anges erased the signatures of her holiness on the eve of her death.[135] By denying her exterior signs this ultimate permanence, she rendered her hand's otherwise likely preservation as a relic far less desirable, and indeed, it never did end up displayed under glass. She thus refused eventual mutilation at the hands of others after her death, maintained control over her external self and its signifying power beyond the grave, and shifted emphasis to her inner self, whose cultivation and development she had so carefully chronicled in her autobiographical project.

Leaving one's mark

The claim I have made in this chapter that wounding the body represented, at least for some women religious of the seventeenth century, a tool for the expression of devotion and identity, remains troubling for our modern sensibilities, especially when we consider a religion in which the female body was loaded with connotations of impurity. But far from representing the experience of a few "hysterical" nuns, corporeal marking was an experience shared and valued by many women religious in this period. Indeed, among the women who received or engraved such marks were several of the most respected spiritual authorities of their day. Despite the obvious pain early modern women suffered or inflicted upon themselves in the marking of their bodies, it is then difficult to see this penetrating gesture as driven by madness or masochism, hatred of the corporeal self, or submission to Church authority. These nuns' marks were instead visible and legible markers of identity and belonging, vehicles of meaning that published a message about the women who wore them. Moreover, corporeal inscription was clearly a transgressive rather than a conformist act, for it consistently met with disapproval on the part of the nuns' male confessors, as did other "excessive" exterior signs of devotion that were often celebrated by female writers. It did nothing to efface the women's corporeality—the objective of bodily mortification—but, on the contrary, highlighted it. By inscribing themselves with readable texts, these nuns attempted not so much to hurt their bodies as to sanctify them, to make of them signifying surfaces that could communicate their direct union with Christ both to themselves and to others, a goal confirmed in their choice of visible, intelligible signs. In so doing, these women ultimately protested the model of the docile feminine body touted by their ecclesiastical superiors. They made materially manifest a form of control over their bodies that they were normally denied, even as they affirmed their desire to lose themselves in union with the divine lover whose sign they chose to bear.

In the case of the nuns of Loudun and Louviers, their corporeal inscription allowed them to shed their identities as demoniacs and to reintegrate the domain of the holy. Jeanne des Anges's corporeal marking clearly brought her fame and credibility within the religious circles of her time and played a central role in her self-defining autobiographical project. While the destinies of many other former demoniacs remain relatively unknown, what emerges most prominently in considering these women is that even on the stage of exorcism, corporeal inscription represented a tactic through which they were able to renegotiate their spiritual status and transform their identity, becoming makers of meaning within a world of established constraints.[136] In all their complexity and contradiction, these "impressionable women" leave on history their own indelible mark.

Notes

1 Aldous Huxley's 1952 *The Devils of Loudun*, a play by John Whiting (*The Devils*, 1965), an opera by Krzysztof Penderecki (1969), and a film by Ken Russell (*The Devils*, 1971) are among the many works inspired by the events at Loudun. Scholarship on early modern demonic possession and on Loudun in particular is vast, and I cite here only work that deals directly with the French context. Wide-ranging studies include: Robert Mandrou, *Magistrats et sorciers en France au XVIIe siècle. Une analyse de psychologie historique* (Paris: Éditions du Seuil, 1980); D.P. Walker, *Unclean Spirits: Possession and Exorcism in France and England in the Late Sixteenth and Early Seventeenth Centuries* (London: Scholar Press, 1981); Alfred Soman, *Sorcellerie et justice criminelle (XVIe-XVIIIe siècles)* (Hampshire, UK: Variorum, 1992); Jonathan L. Pearl, *The Crime of Crimes: Demonology and Politics in France, 1560–1620* (Waterloo, Canada: Wilfrid Laurier University Press, 1999); Sarah Ferber, *Demonic Possession and Exorcism in Early Modern France* (London and New York: Routledge, 2004); Moche Sluhovsky, "The Devil in the Convent," *American Historical Review* 107.5 (2002): 1379–1411 and *"Believe Not Every Spirit": Possession, Mysticism, and Discernment of Spirits in Early Modern Catholicism* (Chicago: University of Chicago Press, 2007). Studies focused exclusively on Loudun include: Michel de Certeau, *La Possession de Loudun*, 2nd ed. (1970; Paris: Gallimard/Julliard, 1990); Roland Villeneuve, *La mystérieuse affaire Grandier. Le Diable à Loudun* (Paris: Payot, 1980); Michel Carmona, *Les Diables à Loudun. Sorcellerie et politique sous Richelieu* (Paris: Fayard, 1988); and Scott Bryson, "La Chair devenue parole: Aliénation et raison d'État dans la possession de Loudun," in *Le Labyrinthe de Versailles. Parcours critiques de Molière à La Fontaine. À la mémoire d'Alvin Eustis* (Amsterdam and Atlanta: Rodopi, 1998), 133–55.

2 See Ferber's eloquent analysis of several cases involving women in *Demonic Possession*. On the spectacular nature of the cases examined here as highly atypical of group convent possession, see Sluhovsky, "The Devil in the Convent," and *"Believe Not Every Spirit*," 233–64. Sluhovsky cites about forty-five cases of mass possession during the period; "The Devil in the Convent," 1380 and 1383–86 and *"Believe Not Every Spirit,"* 238–39. He provides an excellent analysis of the overarching characteristics and potential causes of mass convent possessions. Among other reasons behind these outbreaks, he points out that most cases of mass possession took place in convents of recently founded or reformed orders, forced into enclosure following the Council of Trent; *"Believe Not Every Spirit,"* 244–45. This was notably the case of the Ursulines and the Hospitallers discussed here.

3 On exorcism as Catholic propaganda: Mandrou, *Magistrats et sorciers*; Walker, *Unclean Spirits*; Henri Weber, "L'Exorcisme à la fin du XVIe siècle, instrument de la Contre Réforme et spectacle baroque," *Nouvelle revue du seizième siècle* 1 (1983): 79–101; Irena Backus, *Le Miracle de Laon. Le Déraisonnable, le raisonnable, l'apocalyptique et le politique dans les récits du miracle de Laon (1566–1578)* (Paris: Librairie Philosophique Jean Vrin, 1994); Pearl, *The Crime of Crimes*; and Ferber, *Demonic Possession*. The Laon event was not a mass possession but played a crucial role in setting the stage for public exorcism in the century that followed. On the Aix-en-Provence case in particular: Jules Michelet's lyrical 1862 *La Sorcière* (Paris: Garnier-Flammarion, 1966), 179–93; Jean Lorédan's early study, *Un grand procès de sorcellerie au XVIIe siècle. L'abbé Gaufridy et Madeleine de Demandolx (1600–1670) d'après les documents inédits* (Paris: Perrin et Cie, 1912); Mandrou, *Magistrats et sorciers*, esp. chs. 4 and 5; Weber, "L'Exorcisme," 95–101;

Walker, *Unclean Spirits*, 75–77; Pearl, *Crime of Crimes*, 41–57; Anita M. Walker and Edmund H. Dickerman, "A Notorious Woman: Possession, Witchcraft and Sexuality in Seventeenth-Century Provence," *Historical Reflections/Réflexions Historiques* 27.1 (2001): 1–26; Ferber, *Demonic Possession*, 70–88; and my "Ventriloquism and the Voice of Authority: Nuns, Demons, and Exorcists in Early Seventeenth-Century France," in *Early Modern Convent Voices: The World and the Cloister*, ed. Thomas M. Carr, Jr., *EMF: Studies in Early Modern France* 11 (2005): 75–112.

4 Work on gender and possession includes: Anita M. Walker and Edmund H. Dickerman, "'A Woman Under the Influence': A Case of Alleged Possession in Sixteenth-Century France," *Sixteenth Century Journal* 22.3 (1991): 535–54 and "The Haunted Girl: Possession, Witchcraft and Healing in Sixteenth-Century Louviers," *Proceedings of the Annual Meeting of the Western Society for French History* 23 (1996): 207–18; Ferber, "The Demonic Possession of Marthe Brossier, France 1598–1600," in *No Gods Except Me: Orthodoxy and Religious Practice in Europe, 1200–1600*, ed. Charles Zika (Melbourne: University of Melbourne Press, 1991), 59–83 and *Demonic Possession*; Lyndal Roper, *Oedipus and the Devil: Witchcraft, Sexuality and Religion in Early Modern Europe* (London: Routledge, 1994); Moche Sluhovsky, "A Divine Apparition or Demonic Possession? Female Agency and Church Authority in Sixteenth-Century France," *Sixteenth Century Journal* 27.4 (1996): 1039–55 and "The Devil in the Convent;" Denis Crouzet, "A Woman and the Devil: Possession and Exorcism in Sixteenth-Century France," in *Changing Identities in Early Modern France*, ed. Michael Wolfe (Durham, NC: Duke University Press, 1997), 191–215; and Ronnie Po-chia Hsia, *The World of Catholic Renewal, 1540–1770* (Cambridge: Cambridge University Press, 1998), 138–51. For Spain: Alison Weber, *Teresa of Avila and the Rhetoric of Femininity* (Princeton: Princeton University Press, 1990), "Between Ecstasy and Exorcism: Religious Negotiation in Sixteenth-Century Spain," *Journal of Medieval and Renaissance Studies* 23.2 (Spring 1993): 221–34, "Demonizing Ecstasy: Alonso de la Fuente and the Alumbrados of Extremadura," in *The Mystical Gesture: Essays on Medieval and Early Modern Spiritual Culture in Honor of Mary C. Gilles*, ed. Robert Boenig (Brookfield, VT: Ashgate, 2000), 147–65, and "Spiritual Administration: Gender and Discernment in the Carmelite Reform," *Sixteenth Century Journal* 31.1 (2000): 123–46. On medieval women, see Nancy Caciola, *Discerning Spirits: Divine and Demonic Possession in the Middle Ages* (Ithaca, NY: Cornell University Press, 2003). Children, who shared women's supposed vulnerabilities, were also prone to possession. The rare men to experience demonic influence were considered "obsessed" (with brief spells of possession or a kind of demonic madness) rather than "possessed." Sluhovsky uncovered only two cases of diabolic attack on monks, one from the thirteenth century and the other from the seventeenth century; "The Devil in the Convent," 1405–7. Male exorcists, notably Jean-Joseph Surin, the Loudun prioress's exorcist and spiritual director, sometimes experienced a sort of "demonic contagion," caught like an illness from contact with their charges. See Surin's letter 52 in *Correspondance*, ed. Michel de Certeau (Paris: Desclée De Brouwer, 1966), 263; Surin, *Triomphe de l'amour divin sur les puissances de l'enfer et Science expérimentale des choses de l'autre vie (1653–1660)* (Grenoble: Jérôme Millon, 1990); Sophie Houdard, "De l'exorcisme à la communication spirituelle: le sujet et ses démons," *Littératures Classiques* 25 (1995): 187–99; Nicholas Paige, *Being Interior: Autobiography and the Contradictions of Modernity in Seventeenth-Century France* (Philadelphia, PA: University of Pennsylvania Press, 2001), 179–225; Laura Verciani, *Le Moi et ses diables*.

Autobiographie spirituelle et récit de possession au XVIIe siècle (Paris: Honoré Champion, 2001), 109–53; Sluhovsky, *"Believe Not Every Spirit,"* 156–64 and 234–35; Bernadette Höfer, "Possession, Exorcism, and Madness: The Context of Jean-Joseph Surin's Illness," in her *Psychosomatic Disorders in Seventeenth-Century French Literature* (Farnam, UK and Burlington, VT: Ashgate, 2009), 59–94, and my "Médiations, figures et expériences de l'autre vie: Jean-Joseph Surin à la rencontre du démoniaque," in *L'autre au dix-septième siècle*, ed. Ralph Heyndels and Barbara Woshinsky (Tübingen: Gunter Narr, 1999), 375–84.

5 For an example of how exorcists mapped the possessed body, see *La Demono-manie de Lo[u]dun*, 2nd ed. (La Flèche: George Griveau, 1634), which names each demon and his "residence" within the bodies of eleven possessed nuns.

6 On Louviers, see: Mandrou, *Magistrats et sorciers*; Daniel Vidal, *Critique de la Raison Mystique. Benoît de Canfield: Possession et dépossession au XVIIe siècle* (Grenoble: Jérôme Millon, 1990); Ferber, *Demonic Possession*, 89–112; and Sluhovsky, *"Believe Not Every Spirit;"* ch. 5, 137–65, esp. 150–56. At issue in Louviers were worries over interior spiritual practices tinged with Illuminism, which ecclesiastical authorities perceived as circumventing Church hierarchy in favor of direct contact with the divine. Ferber's chapter on Louviers focuses on these issues; *Demonic Possession*, 89-112. On Illuminism, similar movements, and their close ties to spirit possession, see Sluhovsky, *"Believe Not Every Spirit."*

7 On Auxonne, see: Samuel Garnier, *Barbe buvée, en religion sœur Sainte-Colombe et la prétendue possession des ursulines d'Auxonne (1658–1663). Étude historique et médicale d'après les manuscrits de la Bibiothèque nationale et des Archives de l'ancienne province de Bourgogne* (Paris: Aux Bureaux du Progrès Médical, Félix Alcan, 1895); Mandrou, *Magistrats et sorciers*, 404–22; and Benoit Garnot, *Le Diable au couvent. Les Possédées d'Auxonne (1658–1663)* (Paris: Imago, 1995).

8 On witches and their pact with the devil, see Chapter 1.

9 For an extensive bibliography of the primary source texts, see Mandrou, *Magistrats et sorciers*, 13–70 and Ferber, *Possession and Exorcism*, 198–206.

10 Throughout this chapter, I will refrain from constantly qualifying actions that are attributed to demons by source texts and instead present events as period writers reported them.

11 Lists of typical signs of departure are included in the widely used *Manuale Exorcismorum*, compiled by Maximilian van Eynatten and published in 1618, 1626, and 1648 and in several editions of the *Thesarus Exorcismorum* (Cologne: Laar Zezner, [1608] 1626); presented in a bilingual edition, *Manuale exorcismorum/Manuel d'exorcismes* [Antwerp: Plantiniana B. Moreti] (Paris: Édition Communication Prestige, 1995). In Loudun, for example, one of Sœur Louise's demons promised to "leave from her mouth, in the form of a flame of fire the length of two forearms and two fingers in diameter that will last the time of a Miserere, and will break one diamond-shaped pane of the Church's stained-glass window;" *La Demonomanie de Lo[u]dun*, 58. Several other demons promised to levitate objects or the demoniac herself for brief periods or carry objects to other locations; 58, 59, and 60. Surin discusses the practice of demanding a sign of departure; *Science expérimentale*, 135.

12 In addition to scholarship on Loudun cited above, see also Ferdinand Caval-lera, "L'autobiographie de Jeanne des Anges d'après des documents inédits," rpt. in Jeanne des Anges, *Autobiographie (1644)* (Grenoble: Jérôme Millon, 1990), 291–300; Mino Bergamo, *Jeanne des Anges. Autobiographia. Il punto di vista dell'indemoniata* (Venice: Marsilio Editori, 1986); Sarah E. Miller,

"Bringing up Demons," *Diacritics* 18.1 (Spring 1988): 2–17; Mitchell Greenberg, "Passion Play: Jeanne des Anges, Devils, Hysteria and the Incorporation of the Classical Subject," in *Subjectivity and Subjugation in Seventeenth-Century Drama and Prose: The Family Romance of French Classicism* (Cambridge: Cambridge University Press, 1992), 65–86; Giovanna Malquoiri Fondi, "De l'irrationnel diabolique au surnaturel angélique: *l'Autobiographie* de Jeanne des Anges," *Littératures Classiques* 25 (1995): 201–11; Elizabeth C. Goldsmith, "Public Sanctity and Private Writing: The Autobiography of Jeanne des Anges," in *Publishing Women's Life Stories in France, 1647–1720: From Voice to Print* (Aldershot, UK and Burlington, VT: Ashgate, 2001), 42–70; and Verciani, *Le Moi et ses Diables*, 73–107.

13 On witches' pacts with the devil, see Chapter 1.

14 *Representation et Sommaire* (Rouen: David Ferrand, n.d. [1637]), col. 1; "Extrait du Procez verbal" in Jean-Joseph Surin, *Lettre Escrite A Monseigneur L'Evesque de Poitiers* (Paris: Jean Martin, 1635), 8–9; and Jeanne des Anges, *Autobiographie d'une hystérique possédée, d'après le manuscrit inédit de la Bibliothèque de Tours, annoté*, ed. Gabriel Legué and Gilles de la Tourette (Paris: Aux Bureaux du Progès médical, 1866), rpt. as *Autobiographie (1644)* (Grenoble: Jérôme Millon, 1990), 157. All subsequent references are to the Millon edition.

15 *Representation et Sommaire*, col. 1. On the book of life, see Revelation 20:12 and 15.

16 Bishop of Geneva, François de Sales was well known as the author of popular devotional works, including the *Introduction à la vie dévote* (1608–1619) and the *Traité de l'amour de Dieu* (1619). Both texts appear in François de Sales, *Œuvres de saint François de Sales*, ed. André Ravier and Roger Devos (Paris: Gallimard, La Pléiade, 1969).

17 *Representation et Sommaire*, col. 2.

18 *La Demonomanie de Lo[u]dun*, 59–60.

19 Ibid., 61. The exorcist also demands that Sœur Agnes's possessing demon make a fleur-de-lis on her left hand; ibid., 59. As examined in Chapter 5, the fleur-de-lis was also used in the period to brand certain convicted criminals, in a gesture that reclaimed their bodies for the state. On the branding of convicts, see also Marguerite Rateau, "La Récidive et sa preuve dans l'ancien droit français," *Revue internationale de criminologie et de police technique* 25.3 (July–September 1961): 168–77 and Marc Vigié, "La Flétrissure des forçats au XVIIIe siècle. Un exemple de justice emblématique," *Revue de science criminelle et de droit pénal comparé* 3 (July–September 1986): 809–17. This sign differs from the others presented here and suggests the important royal backing of the highly politicized Loudun case.

20 *Jugement . . . sur la prétendüe possession des filles d'Auxonne*, written in Paris, January 12, 1662 (Chalon-sur-Saône: Philippe Tan, 1662), qtd. in Garnier, *Barbe buvée*, 65; this printed text is also BN Mss fds fs, 20973, fol. 252. The choice of "capitals" to describe the letters that appeared explicitly connects them to the printed word. The *Grand Robert* provides a 1690 definition of the word "capital" as a "[p]rinted letter" or a "[m]anuscript letter . . . whose form recalls the printed letter;" *Le Grand Robert* (Paris: Le Robert, 1985).

21 *Jugement*, qtd. in Garnier, *Barbe buvée*, 65–66.

22 P.-J.-Baptiste de la Ménardaye, *Examen et discussion critique de l'histoire des diables de Loudun* (Paris: Debure l'aîné, 1747), 242–43.

23 Johann Weyer, *Witches, Devils, and Doctors in the Renaissance. (De praestigiis daemonum)*, ed. George Mora of the 6th edition of 1583, trans. John Shea (Binghamton, NY: Medieval and Renaissance Texts and Studies, 1991), 182.

Weyer's *De praestigiis daemonum*, first published in 1563 in Latin and translated into French by Jacques Grévin, *Cinq livres de l'imposture et tromperie des diables* (Paris: J. Du Puys, 1567), knew considerable success. Writing to defend women accused as witches, Weyer's goal in underlining feminine softness was to cast the female sex as easy prey to a combination of demonic and melancholic influences that made them believe they had actually engaged in demonic acts that they had only fantasized. This argument was a mainstay in the defense of witches from Weyer on. See also Augustine, Sermon 243 "On Time."

24 See Marie-Hélène Huet, *Monstrous Imagination* (Cambridge, MA: Harvard University Press, 1993) and Rebecca M. Wilkin, "Feminizing the Imagination in France, 1563–1678," (PhD diss., The University of Michigan, 2000) on this characterization of the feminine imagination. On its importance in the witchcraft debate, see Rebecca M. Wilkin, *Women, Imagination and the Search for Truth in Early Modern France* (Aldershot, UK and Burlingon, VT: Ashgate, 2008), chs. 1 and 2.

25 Pierre Le Loyer, *Quatre livres des spectres* (Angers: Georges Nepveu, 1586), 101.

26 L.S.D.L.L., *La femme généreuse* (Paris: François Piot, 1643), 91–92.

27 See Ian Maclean, *Woman Triumphant: Feminism in French Literature, 1610–1652* (Oxford: Oxford University Press, 1977), 47–49, for other seventeenth-century authors who make this argument.

28 Le sieur D.F.D.L. de Ferville, *La méchanceté des femmes* (Paris: Pierre Rocolet, 1618), 61–62.

29 See the book's Introduction, 12–15.

30 See defenses of the devil's mark by demonologist Pierre de Lancre, *Tableau de l'inconstance des mauvais anges et démons* (Paris: Jean Berjon, 1612), 181, and doctor Jacques Fontaine, *Discours des marques des sorciers* (Paris: Denis Langlois, 1611), 13–14. Pietro Pomponazzi used the female body's capacity for impression to refute divine cause for stigmata in his *De naturalium effectuum causis*, composed in 1520, first published 1556; ed. and trans. Henri Busson, *Les Causes des merveilles de la nature ou Les Enchantements* (Paris: Les Éditions Rieder, 1930), 149. François de Sales used the idea to support the opposite position, as an illustration to explain the first stage in the formation of Francis of Assisi's stigmata; *Traité de l'Amour de Dieu* in *Œuvres*, 657–59. On the devil's mark on witches, see Chapter 1. On the argument of the power of the imagination in the seventeenth-century debate over stigmata, see Jacques Le Brun, "Les discours de la stigmatisation au XVIIe siècle," in *Stigmates*, ed. Dominique de Courcelles, *Les Cahiers de l'Herne 75* (Paris: Éditions de l'Herne, 2001), 103–18; esp. 106–8.

31 Surin, *Science expérimentale*, 136.

32 Monique Wittig, "The Mark of Gender" (1985), in *The Straight Mind and Other Essays* (Boston: Beacon Press, 1992), 76–89.

33 Surin, *Science expérimentale*, 136.

34 Ibid., 137–38. Jeanne des Anges describes each inscription and renewal in her memoir, as discussed further.

35 On Urbain Grandier's marks as proof of his guilt, see *Recit veritable de ce qui s'est passé à Loudun. Contre Maistre Urbain Grandier, Prestre Curé de l'Eglise de S. Pierre de Loudun* (Paris: Pierre Targa, 1634), 4. As discussed in Chapter 1, during the earlier Aix-en-Provence case, physician Jacques Fontaine wrote an entire treatise on the subject of devil's marks where he transcribes the minutes of his examination of Gaufridy's marks; *Discours des marques des sorciers*.

36 On the forms and meanings of stigmata, see E. Amann, "Stigmatisation," in *Dictionnaire de théologie catholique*, ed. A. Vacant, E. Mangenot, and

E. Amann (Paris: Librairie Letouzey et Ané, 1941), vol. 14, cols. 2616–24; Pierre Adnès, "Stigmates," in *Dictionnaire de spiritualité ascétique et mystique*, ed. Marcel Viller, F. Cavallera, and J. de Guibert, 17 vols. (Paris: G. Beauchesne, 1932–95), vol. 14, 1211–43; and Dominique de Courcelles, ed., *Stigmates, Les Cahiers de l'Herne 75* (Paris: Éditions de l'Herne, 2001). See also the following, who are useful despite extravagances: Herbert Thurston, *The Physical Phenomena of Mysticism* (London: J. H. Crehan, 1952); Montague Summers, *The Physical Phenomena of Mysticism, with Especial Reference to the Stigmata, Divine and Diabolic* (London and New York: Rider, 1950); and Antoine Imbert-Gourbeyre, *Les Stigmatisées* (Paris: Palmé, 1873) and *La Stigmatisation* (Clermont-Ferrand: L. Bellet, 1894). For the first history of stigmata, see Théophile Raynaud, *De stigmatismo, sacro et profano, divino, humano, daemoniaco* [1647], 2nd ed. (Lyon: Antoine Cellier, 1654). Adnès affirms the existence but rarity of figurative and epigraphic stigmata among those reported: "'Figurative' stigmata are exceptional, produced, as the term indicates, in figurative form: crosses, hearts, flowers, crowns of thorns, hosts. . . . Sometimes the crosses bleed. . . . Even more rare are 'epigraphic' stigmata, which consist of inscriptions on diverse parts of the body;" col. 1226. He also provides examples for later periods taken from Imbert-Gourbeyre, *La Stigmatisation*, vol. 2, 21 and 74 and Thurston, *Physical Phenomena*, 160–73. Both Imbert-Gourbeyre's controversial texts provide descriptions of women's textual and figurative stigmata through the twentieth century, reproduced in drawings.

37   *La Demonomanie de Lo[u]dun*, 60–61.
38   Ibid., 63.
39   Ibid., 57.
40   Esprit du Bosroger, *La Pieté Affligée* (Rouen: Jean Le Boulenger, 1652), 329.
41   Scott Bryson, "La chair devenue parole: Aliénation et raison d'État dans la possession de Loudun," in *Labyrinthe de Versailles. Parcours critiques de Molière à La Fontaine*, ed. Alvin Eustis and Martine Debaisieux, 133–55; 154.
42   *Representation et Sommaire*, col. 1.
43   *Relation de la Sortie du Demon Balam* (Paris: Jean Martin, 1635), 13.
44   See, for example, *Relation de la sortie du demon Balam, Representation et Sommaire*, and *La Gloire de S. Joseph* (Paris: Sébastien Huré, 1636). See also, for Louviers, Esprit du Bosroger, *La Pieté Affligée*, 329.
45   Ibid.
46   "Extrait du Procez verbal" in Surin, *Lettre Escrite*, 8–9. Printers' errors, however, complicate this desire for reproducing corporeal marks accurately, as seen in Figure 2.5.
47   *Relation de la Sortie du Demon Balam* (Paris: Jean Martin, 1635), 7–8 and 10.
48   Jeanne des Anges, *Autobiographie*, 202.
49   Esprit du Bosroger, *La Pieté Affligée*, 329–30.
50   Ibid., 331.
51   Ibid., 329–30. The reversal of the letters "S" in "JESUS" is likely a printer's error, ironic considering the author's desire to replicate the corporeal text exactly.
52   See Weber, "Between Ecstasy and Exorcism," "Demonizing Ecstasy," and "Spiritual Administration;" Ferber, *Demonic Possession*; and Sluhovsky, "A Divine Apparition," "The Devil in the Convent," and "*Believe Not Every Spirit*." For the medieval period, see Caciola, *Discerning Spirits*.
53   See Sluhovsky, "*Believe Not Every Spirit*" on the copious literary production on the discernment of spirits in the late sixteenth and early seventeenth centuries.

54 On Teresa of Ávila, see Jodi Bilinkoff, *The Avila of Saint Teresa: Religious Reform in a Sixteenth-Century City* (Cornell University Press, 1989) and Weber, *Teresa of Avila*. On the saint's influence in France, see Alphonse Vermeylen, *Sainte Thérèse en France au XVIIe siècle, 1600–1660* (Louvain: Publications Universitaires de Louvain, 1958).

55 On Demandouls's destiny, see Walker and Dickerman, "A Notorious Woman" and Ferber, *Demonic Possession*, 83. Already in 1599, demoniac Marthe Brossier was searched for the devil's mark during her examination by doctor Michel Marescot. Hélène Hotton presents the curious slippage in Marsecot's treatment of Brossier and convincingly argues that the properties of the witch's mark (insensitivity and not bleeding) are transferred here onto the body of the possessed; *Les marques du diable et les signes de l'Autre: rhétorique du dire démonologique à la fin de la Renaissance*, Doctoral thesis, University of Montréal, 2011, 345–50.

56 On Bavant, see Verciani, *Le Moi et ses diables*, 155–90, Ferber, *Demonic Possession*, 89–112, and Sluhovsky, *"Believe Not Every Spirit,"* 150–56. See also additional sources cited above for Louviers, including Bavant's autobiography.

57 Fontaine, *Discours des marques*, 18–19 and Sébastien Michaëlis, *Histoire admirable de la possession et conversion d'une penitente* [1613], 3rd ed. (Paris: Charles Chastellain, 1614), part 2, 102.

58 Goldsmith points out how very different the scholarly treatment of Jean-Joseph Surin, Jeanne des Anges's exorcist, has been. Surin experienced demonic "obsession"—meaning he was severely debilitated by demons without being inhabited by them; "Public Sanctity," 63–64.

59 Even Mitchell Greenberg's insightful reading, which does not question Jeanne des Anges's motives, casts the signing of her body as masochism, signaling the nun's renewed subjection to the celestial, religious, and political hierarchies of the family and the Church, and sees in her submission to language the effacement of her body as a recalcitrant force; "Passion Play," 80–82.

60 Stephen Greenblatt, "Foreword," Michel de Certeau, *The Possession at Loudun*, trans. Michael B. Smith (Chicago: The University of Chicago Press, [1996] 2000), x.

61 See Goldsmith, "Public Sanctity," esp. 62–64. The 1886 edition of Jeanne des Anges's memoir, edited by Gabriel Legué and Gilles de la Tourette and produced by the *Bureau du Progrès médical* [Office of Medical Progress], is dedicated to Charcot, who wrote the preface. The nineteenth-century *Bureau* created a series called the "Bibliothèque Diabolique" [Diabolical Library], publishing numerous early works dealing with witchcraft and possession. The Introduction and extensive footnotes of their edition of Jeanne des Anges's memoir perform a retroactive diagnosis of the nun's suffering and symptoms to affirm the validity of the newly invented malady of hysteria. The 1990 Jérôme Millon edition reprints the nineteenth-century text in full. See Frank Bowman, "From History to Hysteria: Nineteenth-Century Discourse on Loudun," in *French Romanticism: Intertextual and Interdisciplinary Readings* (Baltimore, MD: Johns Hopkins University Press, 1990), 106–21, Jean-Martin Charcot and Paul Richer, *Les démoniaques dans l'art* [Paris: Adrien Delahaye and Émile Lecrosnier, 1887] (Paris: Macula, 1984), and Georges Didi-Huberman, *Invention de l'hystérie. Charcot et l'Iconographie photographique de la Salpêtrière* (Paris: Macula, 1982).

62 See Goldsmith, "Public Sanctity," Verciani, *Le Moi et ses diables*, 73–107, Ferber, *Demonic Possession*, 124–47, and Antoinette Gimaret, *"L'Autobiographie* de Jeanne des Anges (1644): histoire d'une âme ou réécriture d'une affaire

de possession?" in *Les Femmes témoins de l'histoire*, ed. Armel Dubois-Nayt and Claire Gheeraert-Graffeuille, *Études Épistémè* 19 (2011): 22–49.

63 Goldsmith, "Public Sanctity," 64.

64 As Bynam asserts, "he and the modern figure Padre Pio are the only males in history who have claimed all five visible wounds. . . . Francis . . . may indeed have been the first case (although even this is uncertain); but stigmata rapidly became a female miracle;" Caroline Walker Bynum, *Fragmentation and Redemption: Essays on Gender and the Human Body in Medieval Religion* (New York: Zone Books, 1992), 186–87; See also her *Holy Feast and Holy Fast: The Religious Significance of Food to Medieval Women* (Berkeley, CA: University of California Press, 1987). Numerous scholars have affirmed the preponderance of the phenomenon reported among women across periods: Imbert-Gourbeyre, *La Stigmatisation*; Amann, "Stigmatisation," col. 2619; Thurston, *Physical Phenomena*; Thierry Maertens, *Ritologiques I. Le Dessin sur la peau. Essai d'anthropologie des inscriptions tégumentaires* (Paris: Aubier Montaigne, 1978), 99; André Vauchez, *Sainthood in the Later Middle Ages*, trans. Jean Birrell (Cambridge: Cambridge University Press, 1997), esp. 439–43; Jean-Pierre Albert, *Le sang et le Ciel. Les saintes mystiques dans le monde chrétien* (Paris: Aubier, 1997), 202–13; and Courcelles, *Stigmates*, 13–14 and several essays in that volume. On stigmata among women in the seventeenth century, see esp. the important work of Jacques Le Brun and Nicole Pellegrin, including: Le Brun, "Les discours de la stigmatisation;" "L'institution et le corps, lieux de mémoire, d'après les biographies spirituelles féminines du XVIIe siècle," *Corps écrit* 11 (1984): 111–21; and "À corps perdu. Les biographies spirituelles féminines du XVIIe siècle," in *Corps des dieux. Le temps de la réflexion*, ed. Charles Malamoud and Jean-Pierre Vernant (Paris: Gallimard, 1986), 389–408. Nicole Pellegrin's insightful essay, "L'écriture des stigmates. (XVIe-XVIIIe siècles)," in *La Blessure corporelle. Violences et souffrances, symboles et représentations*, ed. Pierre Cordier and Sébastien Jahan, *Les Cahiers du Gerhico* 4 (2003): 41–62, builds on Le Brun and Albert's studies, rpt. as "Fleurs saintes. L'écriture des stigmates (XVIe-XVIIIe siècles)," *in Femmes en fleurs, femmes en corps. Sang, Santé, Sexualités du Moyen Âge aux Lumières*, ed. Cathy McClive and Nicole Pellegrin (Saint-Étienne: Publications de l'Université de Saint-Étienne, 2010), 101–22.

65 Bynum, *Fragmentation and Redemption*, 102.

66 Suspicion of such "exterior" signs of devotion increased as the seventeenth century progressed, and evidence of the repression of the body in spiritual practice of the period only further underlines its prevalence. See Isabelle Poutrin, "Les Stigmatisées et les clercs: Interprétation et répression d'un signe–Espagne, XVIIe siècle," in *Les Signes de Dieu aux XVIe et XVIIe siècles*, ed. Geneviève Demerson and Bernard Dompnier (Clermont-Ferrand: Faculté des Lettres et Sciences humaines de l'Université Blaise-Pascal, 1993), 189–99; Micheline Cuénin, "Fausse et vraie mystique: Signes de reconnaissance, d'après la *Correspondance* de Jeanne de Chantal," in *Les Signes de Dieu*, 177–87; Sophie Houdard, "Des fausses saintes aux spirituelles à la mode; les signes suspects de la mystique," *Dix-septième siècle* 50.3 (1998): 417–32; and Le Brun, "Les discours de la stigmatisation," 103–18.

67 On the importance of physical suffering in the period, see Antoinette Gimaret, *Extraordinaire et ordinaire des Croix. Les représentations du corps souffrant, 1580–1650* (Paris: Honoré Champion, 2011).

68 Albert, *Le sang et le Ciel*, 200.

69 On women religious who inscribed their bodies, see Le Brun, "L'institution et le corps," "À corps perdu," and "Les discours de la stigmatisation" and Pellegrin, "L'écriture des stigmates." Raynaud included a chapter on "pious

voluntary stigmata" in his *De stigmatismo*, 165–76, which cites numerous examples. For medieval examples, see Bynum, *Fragmentation and Redemption*, 131–32. Adnès, "Stigmates," lists persons who self-imposed stigmata, cols. 1229–30. The only known self-inscriber prior to the Catholic Counter-Reformation was a man, Henry Suso (ca. 1295–1366), who engraved "IHS" on his chest. Significantly, artists deliberately feminized him in their depictions; Jeffrey F. Hamburger, *Nuns as Artists: The Visual Culture of a Medieval Convent* (Berkeley, CA: University of California Press, 1997), 65. Suso's marks were reproduced as bleeding letters in a manuscript illumination, as were Jeanne des Anges and Marie du Saint Sacrement's three centuries later in print; ibid., 178–80. Suso's female spiritual companion, Elsbeth Stagel, contented herself with wearing a cloth substitute against her skin, upon which she had embroidered "IHS" in red letters; 178.

70 On the desire for and practice of various forms of corporeal mortification see several articles by Le Brun: "L'institution et le corps;" "*Cancer serpit. Recherches sur la représentation du cancer dans les biographies spirituelles féminines du XVIIe siècle,*" *Sciences Sociales et Santé* 2.2 (June 1984): 9–31; "À corps perdu;" "Mutations de la notion de martyre au XVIIe siècle d'après les biographies spirituelles féminines," in *Sainteté et martyr dans les religions du livre*, ed. Jacques Marx (Brussels: Université de Bruxelles, 1989), 77–96; and "Les discours de la stigmatisation." See also: Gwénael Murphy, "La dévotion corporelle dans les couvents de femmes (XVIIe-XIXe siècles)," in *La Blessure corporelle*, 63–76; Pellegrin, "L'écriture des stigmates;" and Albert, *Le sang et le Ciel*.

71 Le Brun, "À corps perdu," 399–400.

72 Ibid., 399.

73 See also Le Brun's reading of the engraving in "À corps perdu," 401. Jean-Pierre Albert, "Hagio-graphiques. L'écriture qui sanctifie," *Terrain* 24 (March 1995): 75–82 also reproduces and briefly comments the image, 75.

74 Henry de Maupas du Tour, *La Vie de la Venerable Mere Jeanne Francoise Fremiot* [1644] (Paris, Simeon Piget, 1672), 170.

75 Ibid., 170–71. Jeanne de Chantal's cutaneous marks thus functionned much like relics and amulets that were commonly worn at the time and believed to have apotropaic properties. In presenting Jeanne de Chantal as possessing "le courage & la generosité" to perform such an act, Maupas du Tour borrows terms that were gendered masculine at the time.

76 Ibid., 172–73.

77 Hsia, *The World of Catholic Renewal*, 143.

78 Le Brun, "À corps perdu," 399–400 and Pellegrin, "L'écriture des stigmates."

79 "Abregé de la Vie & des Vertus, de feuë Nôtre-trés honnorée Sœur MARGUERITTE ANGELIQUE CADEAU" in *Circulaires des Religieuses de la Visitation de Ste-Marie*, vol. 24 (Blois, 1717), 6.

80 "Abregé de la vie et des vertus de nôtre tres honorée Sœur & ancienne Mere Anne Angelique Loppin décedée en ce Monastére de la Visitation Ste. Marie de Beaune le 17. May 1707," in *Circulaires des Religieuses de la Visitation de Ste-Marie*, vol. 21 (1707), 5.

81 See also Pellegrin, "L'écriture des stigmates," esp. 51–52 and Le Brun, "À corps perdu."

82 Jeanne Marie Bouvier de la Motte Guyon, *Vie par elle-même*, ed. B. Sahler (Paris: Dervy-Livre, 1983), 39–40. In Guyon's rendition of Jeanne de Chantal's marking, the metal burin Chantal used becomes a full-fledged branding iron, ready-made in the shape of the name of Jesus, similar to the letter brands used

on convicted criminals and slaves in the period as a means of identifying them, as discussed in Chapter 5.

83 On the practice of attaching textual amulets to the body, see Don C. Skemer, *Binding Words: Textual Amulets in the Middle Ages* (University Park, PA: Pennsylvania State University Press, 2006) and my *"Prêt à porter*: Textual Amulets, Popular Belief and Defining Superstition in Sixteenth and Seventeenth-Century France," special issue on *Wearing Images*, edited by Diane Brodart, *Espacio, Tiempo y Forma* 6 (2018): 84–114.

84 Marguerite-Marie Alacoque, *Vie et Œuvres de Sainte Marguerite-Marie Alacoque*, ed. François-Léon Gauthey, 3 vols. (Paris: Ancienne Librairie Poussielgue, 1920), vol. 1, 174 and vol. 2, 95–96. The nun's inscription later disappeared, divinely erased ostensibly because she had disobeyed her mother superior by not showing her the engraved name; vol. 1, 189–91 and vol. 2, 110–12. Alocoque's writing of the contract in blood on paper followed by the marking of the flesh itself vividly recalls pacts with the devil written in blood, followed by the impression of the devil's mark on the skin, examined in Chapter 1.

85 Ibid., vol. 1, 174.

86 Jeanne de Cambounet de la Mothe, *Journal des Illustres Religieuses de l'Ordre de Sainte Ursule*, 4 vols. (Bourg en Bresse: Joseph Ravous, 1684–1690), vol. 3 (1686), 135–36.

87 "Ganif," Jean Nicot, *Le Thresor de la langue francoyse* (Paris: David Douceur, 1606).

88 Jeanne des Anges, *Autobiographie*. Her memoir was not presented in published form until the nineteenth-century "Bibliothèque diaboloque" edition, cited above. On her autobiographical enterprise, see Bryson, "La chair devenue parole," Goldsmith, "Public Sanctity," and Ferber, *Demonic Possession*, 135–47. On spiritual autobiography and the increasing valorization of interiority in this period, see Paige, *Being Interior*. On women's spiritual autobiography in particular, see Le Brun, "Les biographies spirituelles françaises du XVIIème siècle: Écriture féminine? Écriture mystique?" in *Esperienza religiosa e scritture femminili tra medioevo ed età moderna*, ed. Marilena Modica Vasta (Palermo: Bonanno, 1992), 135–51, and Hélène Trépanier, "Entre amour-propre et anéantissement: le 'je' des autobiographies mystiques féminines," in *La femme au XVIIe siècle*, ed. Richard G. Hodgson (Tübingen: Gunter Narr, 2002), 301–13. At least three other memoirs of possession were written during the period by demoniacs; they are those of Jeanne Fery (Mons), Elizabeth de Ranfaing (Nancy), and Magdelaine Bavant (Louviers). Twenty-five-year-old Fery, of the couvent des Sœurs noires of Mons, wrote her account at the request of her superiors. It was printed in the Archbishop of Cambray's account of her possession, *Discours admirable et veritable, des choses advenues en la ville de Mons en Hainaut, à l'endroit d'une religieuse possessee, et depuis delivree* (Douay: Jean Bogart, 1586), 90–129 and reedited as part of the "Bibliothèque Diabolique" by Désiré Magloire Bourneville, *La Possession de Jeanne Fery, religieuse professe du couvent des sœurs noires de la ville de Mons (1584)* (Paris: Adrien Delahaye and Émile Lecrosnier, 1886). On Fery, see: Ferber, *Demonic Possession*, 36–37, 116, and 119–20; Verciani, *Le Moi et ses Diables*, 22–43; and Marianne Closson, "Avaler le pacte, être possédée," in *Écritures du corps. Nouvelles perspectives*, ed. Pierre Zoberman, Anne Tomiche, and William J. Spurlin (Paris: Classiques Garnier, 2013), 174–88. Ranfaing, a widow, hindered from becoming a nun because of her familial obligations, was subject to demonic obsessions from 1618–1625 in Nancy. She was protected and exorcised by Jesuits and went on to found a religious sect at the convent of the Refuge, whose practices later came under extreme scrutiny, though Ranfaing maintained a pious reputation. Nicholas

Paige affirms that her memoir, written shortly after delivery from her demonic struggle, is now lost; "Je, L'Autre et la possession; ou pourquoi l'autobiographie démoniaque n'a jamais constitué un genre," in *L'autre au dix-septième siècle*, ed. Ralph Heyndels and Barbara Woshinsky (Tübingen: Gunter Narr, 1999), 385–92; n. 2, 385. On Ranfaing, see Christian Pfister, *L'énergumène de Nancy, Élizabeth de Ranfaing et le couvent du Refuge* (Nancy: Berger-Levrault, 1901); and Étienne Delcambre and Jean Lhermitte, *Un cas énigmatique de possession diabolique en Lorraine au XVIIe siècle: Élizabeth de Ranfaing, l'énergumène de Nancy* (Nancy: Société d'Archéologie Lorraine, 1956). Bavant, Louviers demoniac accused of witchcraft, died in prison. Her memoir, first published by her confessor, Charles Desmarets, *Histoire de Magdelaine Bavant* (Paris: J. Le Gentil, 1652), was reedited twice: Magdelaine Bavant, *Récit de l'histoire de sœur Magdelaine Bavent* (Rouen: Deshays, 1878); and *Histoire de Magdelaine Bavent*, ed. Roger Dubos, in *Les Possédées de Louviers. Histoire de Magdelaine Bavent d'après les documents de l'époque* (Mondeville: Charles Corlet, 1990), 14–99. Marianne Closson and Nicole Jacques-Lefèvre are preparing a new critical edition. On Bavent's writings, see Paige, "Je, L'Autre et la possession," Ferber, *Demonic Possession*, 105–6, Verciani, *Le Moi et ses Diables*, 155–90, and Closson, "Avaler le pacte." On the memoir of possession as a genre, see Paige, "Je, L'Autre et la possession" and Verciani, *Le Moi et ses Diables*.

89 On Teresa of Ávila's influence in France, see Vermeylen, *Sainte Thérèse en France*.

90 Surin's own account of the Loudun possession was the *Triomphe de l'amour divin* in which he describes his unique approach to freeing Jeanne des Anges of her demons. On Surin's methods, see, among others, Houdard, "De l'exorcisme à la communication spirituelle" and my "Médiations, figures et expériences de l'autre vie."

91 Jeanne des Anges, *Autobiographie*, 125 and 119.

92 Ibid., 119.

93 Ibid., 120.

94 Saint Joseph had also intervened to cure Teresa of Ávila, whom Jeanne des Anges held as an esteemed model, of paralysis. Jeanne des Anges's choice of saintly protector is thus another way in which she seeks to identify herself with her predecessor.

95 Jeanne des Anges, *Autobiographie*, 159.

96 Ibid., 163.

97 Ibid., 169.

98 *La Gloire de S. Joseph*, 33.

99 Teresa of Ávila was canonized in 1622.

100 Jeanne des Anges, *Autobiographie*, 190.

101 Ibid., 191.

102 Greenberg, "Passion Play," 80–82. This feminine emphasis on the holy family dates from the later Middle Ages; Bynum, *Fragmentation and Redemption*, 56. On François de Sales, see above.

103 Jeanne des Anges, *Autobiographie*, 230.

104 Ibid.

105 Ibid., 231.

106 Ibid., 193–234.

107 Ibid., 203.

108 Ibid., 201.

109 Ibid., 221.

110 Ibid., 207.

111 Ibid., 220.

112 See also Goldsmith, "Public Sanctity," 54–59.

113 Jeanne des Anges, *Autobiographie*, 220.

114 Ibid.

115 Ibid., 221.

116 Ibid., 224.

117 *La Gloire de S. Joseph*, 34.

118 On the regular bleeding of stigmata, see: Imbert-Gourbeyre, *La Stigmatisation*; Amann, "Stigmatisation," vol. 14, cols. 2617–19; and Thurston, *Physical Phenomena*, esp. 69, 95–99, and 123. Women religious saw themselves as coming closer than men to *imitatio Christi* in their everyday gendered lives, and the experience of menstruation no doubt informed their stigmatic manifestations. For the medieval period, see Carolyn Walker Bynum, *Jesus as Mother: Studies in the Spirituality of the High Middle Ages* (Berkeley, CA: University of California Press, 1982), 257; for a cross-period study, see Albert, *Le sang et le Ciel*, 202–13.

119 Esprit du Bosroger, *La Pieté Affligée*, 330.

120 Albert, *Le sang et le Ciel*, 211. Albert posits that the periodic bleeding of stigmata allowed women a sacred substitute for menstrual bleeding, a sign of impurity. On the tradition of stigmatic renewal, see 209–13.

121 Jeanne des Anges, *Autobiographie*, 192–93.

122 Ibid., 246.

123 Ibid., 193.

124 François Gayot de Pitaval, *Causes célèbres et intéressantes, avec les jugemens qui les ont décidées*, 20 vols. (Paris: Theodore Legras et al., 1734–1748), vol. 2 (1734), 533.

125 Alacoque, discussed above, also cites Chiara de Montefalco as an esteemed model; *Vie et Œuvres*, vol. 1, 174. The instruments of the passion Jeanne des Anges lists as imprinted on her heart are the cross with the *Titulus Crucis*, the nails, crown of thorns, pillar, ropes, whips, ladder, pincers, hammer, coins, dice, sponge, and lance; *Autobiographie*, 266. On Chiara de Montefalco, whose heart was removed by her fellow nuns following her death and found to be imprinted with each of the instruments, see Imbert-Gourbeyre, *La Stigmatisation*, vol. 2, 48–56; Summers, *The Physical Phenomena of Mysticism*, 129–141; Vauchez, *Sainthood*; and Katharine Park, "The Criminal and the Saintly Body: Autopsy and Dissection in Renaissance Italy," *Renaissance Quarterly* 47.1 (Spring 1994): 1–33.

126 Jeanne des Anges, *Autobiographie*, 267.

127 Ibid., 253. Religious writers commonly used the language of portraiture to describe spiritual growth. For example, Alacoque's mother superior tells her to "'put [herself] before Our Savior like a canvass waiting before a painter.' The divine Master had long ago begun tracing upon that waiting canvass the sketch of his 'suffering image;'" *Vie et Œuvres*, vol. 1, 24–25.

128 Jeanne des Anges, *Autobiographie*, 249.

129 *Journal des Illustres Religieuses*, 135.

130 On Jeanne des Anges as an often-consulted spiritual authority see Ferber, *Demonic Possession*, esp. 135–36 and 140–44.

131 An anonymous Jesuit published the maxims of the angel in *La Gloire de S. Ursule* (Valentiennes: Jean Boucher, 1656), 329–38.

132 Surin, *Correspondance*, letter 211, 713. See also Ferber, *Demonic Possession*, 140–44 and Michel de Certeau, "Jeanne des Anges," in Jeanne des Anges, *Autobiographie*, 301–44.

133 Surin recounts that she faced accusations as late as 1662; Ferber, *Demonic Possession*, 135, who cites his *Histoire abrégée de la possession des Ursulines*

de Loudun, et des peines du Père Surin (Paris: Bureau de l'Association Catholique du Sacré-Cœur, 1828), 97.

134 Marie de Pommereu, *Les chroniques de l'Ordre des Ursulines*, 2 vols. (Paris: J. Henault, 1673), vol. 2, 461–62.

135 Nicolas Aubin, *Histoire des diables de Loudun* (Amsterdam: Abraham Wolfgang, 1694), 469.

136 I use the term "tactic" as defined by Michel de Certeau, *The Practice of Everyday Life*, trans. Steven F. Rendall (Berkeley, CA: University of California Press, 1984), xix and 29.

3 The Amerindian tattoo

Signs of identity in New France

The tattoo has long been thought an exotic eighteenth-century import to Europe, brought back on the skin of sailors from the islands of South Seas.[1] Indeed, the words "tattoo," *tatouer*, and *tatouage* that we use today first came into English and French in the late eighteenth century through two sea captains' accounts of their Polynesian voyages: French admiral Louis-Antoine de Bougainville's (1729–1811) published narrative of his travels from 1766 to 1769 and the official account of English Captain James Cook's (1728–1779) three voyages from 1769 to 1779.[2] Bougainville includes the word *nreou-tataou* in his glossary of Tahitian vocabulary, meaning "color for pricking; it is this that serves to make the permanent characters that they imprint on different parts of their bodies," while Cook invents *tattow*, the ancestor of the modern English word, based on the Polynesian word *tatau* meaning "to hit."[3] The French translator of the account of Cook's second voyage writes in 1778 that he must invent a new French word to represent what he casts as an apparently yet unknown, and therefore unnamed, foreign practice: "We thought it necessary to create this word to express the little holes that are made on the skin with wooden points."[4] Yet while the word "tattoo" was new to the European lexicon in the eighteenth century, the practice of painting, pricking, or incising the skin to mark the body had existed in Europe from earliest times and had figured prominently in the written accounts and artistic production of many a New World traveler since the early sixteenth century. Better known to early modern French readers by the nouns *marques* or *picqueures* [marks or pricks] and the verbs *marquer, piquer*, or *graver* [to mark, prick, or engrave] tattooing for the French had long been associated not with the far-off peoples of the South Pacific but with the far more familiar "Sauvages d'Amérique"—the native inhabitants of New France.[5] Indeed, Bougainville himself compares the tattooing he witnesses in the South Pacific to the practices of the indigenous peoples of Canada.[6] By the time the verb *tatouer* appeared in the 1798 edition of the *Dictionnaire de l'Académie française*, French travelers, missionaries, merchants, artists, and soldiers had been living among, trading with, and representing in word and image the native peoples of North America for over two hundred years. Samuel de Champlain (1574–1635) had traveled inland in 1603 and 1608—following the path Jacques Cartier (1491–1557) had charted nearly sixty years earlier—to found Québec, which would become the center for the French colonial enterprise. The Recollets had served as the first Catholic missionaries in New France, accompanying Champlain to Québec in 1615, closely followed by the more militant and better funded Jesuits in 1625, who would take the leading role in the French civilizing mission in North America for years to come. When eighteenth-century French academicians defined the verb *tatouer*, then, they did not emphasize its Polynesian origins but situated it in a specifically French colonial context, as a "travel term, which designates the American Savages' practice of painting, pricking, rubbing their bodies with different patterns and diverse colors."[7]

For the French, whose image of New World inhabitants was shaped by plentiful, widely circulated narrative and artistic accounts as well as by elaborate public spectacles featuring them, Amerindians' alterity was inscribed upon their very skin. As missionaries lived among the native peoples of New France in their attempt to convert them to Catholicism and to assimilate them into French society, they wrote extensively about their customs, communicating events and observations to the reading public back home through their *Relations*, accounts published regularly from 1610 through the late eighteenth century.[8] While these narratives were written to cultivate continued popular and royal support for the development and conversion of New France, their ethnographic richness reflected a distinctly French approach to the colonial project.[9] In contrast to the English who also colonized Canada, the French went much further into North America, learned the native languages, and saw knowledge of Amerindian cultures as essential to the success of their colonial enterprise.[10] Recollet missionaries such as Gabriel Sagard-Théodat († 1636) and erudite travelers like Marc Lescarbot (ca. 1570–1641) adopted an ethnographic and comparative approach to understanding the practices of the Amerindians they frequented, a methodology that Jesuits such as Paul Le Jeune (1591–1664) and Joseph-François Lafitau (1681–1746) would later follow.[11] To be sure, these French colonists saw alterity in the bodies of the Amerindians they encountered, clearly associating painting, tattooing, and other body ornamentation practices with the savage other whom they were charged to civilize. Yet they also admired and sought to make meaning of the corporeal signs the Amerindians wore, to document their ornamentation processes, and to understand the forces that motivated their creation. In so doing, they found not only difference but also similarity between Amerindian and European marking practices. Indeed, this resemblance was a necessary prerequisite to the success of the French assimilationist model in which the "savage other" and the French were to become, in the words of French Minister of Finances Jean-Baptiste Colbert (1619–1683), "a single people and a single blood."[12] It was also a source of troubling questions about the communication and potential transformation of identity for both Amerindians and Frenchmen in an ethnically diverse New France.

The mark of the other

By the dawn of the seventeenth century, writers and artists had established corporeal marking—whether through hair style, jewelry, feathers, body greasing, painting, or tattooing—as a distinctive sign of Amerindian otherness. Physical characteristics were the first to strike early French colonists upon meeting the native peoples of the New World, and methods of bodily ornamentation provoked strong reactions and keen interest from their French witnesses.[13] Linking "savage" identity directly to unfamiliar adornment practices, many described their shock upon first seeing painted and tattooed Amerindians, whose colors and lines transformed them into "monsters" and "demons," like masks worn during Mardi-Gras.[14] Nearly a century following Cartier's first encounter with the marked bodies of Amerindians, Sagard's description, provided in the narrative of his year spent among the Hurons and Petuns from 1623 to 1624, remained typical:

> They paint their bodies and faces with a variety of colors—black, green, red, purple—and in several different ways. Others have their bodies and faces engraved in compartments, with the shapes of serpents, lizards, squirrels and other animals, and particularly those from the nation of Petun, who almost all have their bodies decorated this way, which makes them terrifying and hideous to those who are not accustomed to it.[15]

Amerindians' physical markings provoked fear and distaste in those who were not used to seeing them—in other words, in the uninitiated Frenchman, Sagard's reader. Even Sagard, well-accustomed to their appearance, reports having trouble gazing upon them, adding in his later 1636 *Histoire du Canada* that the corporeal marks many Amerindians wear still frighten him, despite his years among them.[16] He finds their practice of tattooing particularly shocking, though he admires their ability to withstand the painful process:

> But what I found stranger, and eminently crazier, were those who, in order to be thought courageous and terrifying to their enemies, took a bone of a bird or a fish that they sharpened like razors, with which they engraved and drew shapes upon their bodies, but several times over. . . . In which they showed admirable courage and patience greater than that of most men, not because they did not feel the pain well, because they are not insensitive, but because they remained motionless and mute during such fierce sensation, then they wiped off the blood

that ran from their incisions, which they quickly rubbed afterwards with a black-colored powder that penetrated the scars so that the shapes they engraved remained on their body forever, without ever being able to be erased.[17]

Sagard wonders over Amerindian stoicism during a process that inflicts such terrible pain that it must be done in several sittings, causing fever and loss of appetite:

> [T]hey decorate them in several sittings, because these prickings cause them great pain, and [they] often fall sick from them, to the point of having fever, and losing appetite, and despite all this they do not stop, but have them continue until the whole has been completed, and according to their desires, without manifesting any impatience or irritation during the most extreme pain.[18]

Though Sagard, like many of his contemporaries, admires the Amerindians' tolerance for pain, he worries about the health risks of tattooing and, especially, its permanence, an anxiety reflected in his 1632 *Dictionnaire de la langue huronne*.[19] Consisting of phrases apparently used with enough frequency by missionaries to merit translation, dictionary entries dealing with corporeal ornamentation reinforce his distaste for the Amerindian practice. The basic phrase, "He is painted. *Ottocahouy*," is followed by translations of two sentences that cast painting in the negative: "You do not oil or paint yourself. *Stan techerenonquasse*" and the moralizing "It is beautiful to not be painted or oiled. *Ongyandé stan téerenonquasse*."[20] Sagard worries in particular over the permanence of marks that, as colonial officer Jean-François Benjamin Dumont de Montigny (1696–1760) later put it, "you carry . . . to the grave."[21] Five entries in a row under the heading for bodily decoration provide translations of French sentences having to do with the erasability, or lack thereof, of body markings, suggesting that Sagard must have often asked the question, "Does it come off?":

> It is erasable, it will come off. *Atasoüache, Quathronheyse.*
> Don't erase it. *Ennon choüam.*
> You erase it, erase it. *Sauhathronha.*
> I erase it, he erases it, it comes off. *Auhatrhonha.*
> It does not come off. *Stan tesquatrhonhey*.[22]

For Sagard and his contemporaries, Amerindians' corporeal markings represented permanent signs of a persistent and resistant otherness that posed a threat to their assimilation into French society.

Body marking was so essential a signifier for the Amerindian among seventeenth-century writers that several felt the need to address the practice even in its absence among the peoples they personally encountered in

New France. While Lescarbot, for example, in his "Description des mœurs des souriquoises comparées à celles d'autres peuples" (1609), clearly states that the Micmacs he has lived among and whom he calls "our savages" do not engage in tattooing, he immediately turns to discussion of other Native American peoples who do, drawing extensively on his own reading of other earlier writers' accounts:

> Concerning the body, our Savages do not apply paint, but the Brazilians do this very much, and those of Florida, who for the most part have painted torsos, arms and thighs, in quite beautiful compartments, the paint of which can never be removed because it is pricked into the flesh. . . . Those of Virginia, who are further north, have marks on the back.[23]

No description of Amerindians was complete without some mention of practices of bodily adornment, and writers readily borrowed from their predecessors in order to round out the picture. Close textual similarities between accounts of body painting and tattooing among a wide variety of peoples and even across the American continent suggest that many based their descriptions as much or even entirely on their readings of earlier accounts of the practice as they did upon firsthand experience. Some even passed off their descriptions of corporeal marking as eye-witness testimony when they themselves never in fact encountered the practice. When reading about Amerindians, discussion of body marking was expected; for the French, Amerindian identity was emblazoned upon their skin.

Amerindians in art

Early paintings, drawings, and engravings made to represent the native inhabitants of North America joined the written narratives of the period in highlighting the Amerindian body in all its naked and marked alterity. The familiar prints of the Powhatan and the Timucua peoples produced simultaneously in French, English, and Latin in the last decade of the sixteenth century by engraver and editor Theodor de Bry (1528–1598) prominently displayed the bodies of Amerindians, greatly influencing the European vision of the New World and its inhabitants for centuries to come.[24] De Bry made his engravings from the paintings and drawings of Frenchman Jacques Le Moyne de Morgues (ca. 1533–1588), a native of Dieppe who had accompanied René de Laudonnière's attempt to found a Protestant colony in Florida from 1562 to 1565, and of Englishman John White (ca. 1540–ca. 1593), who took part in the Roanoke expeditions begun in 1584 for the English by Richard Grenville.[25] In De Bry's first two *America* volumes, and presumably in the drawings and watercolors by White and Le Moyne from which he made his engravings, tattoos appear on the bodies of high-ranking members of Amerindian society.[26] Le Moyne's commentary on a plate showing tattooing among Timucua leaders in Florida included in De Bry's 1591 volume draws the viewer's attention to the marking practices displayed, underlining their importance as a noteworthy sign of Amerindian identity:

> The reader should remember further that all these rulers and their wives decorate the skin of their bodies with a kind of tattooing in imitation of various painted designs (as he can see from the plates), and in consequence from time to time fall ill for seven or eight days. Nevertheless, they rub the places that have been pricked with a certain herb which adds an indelible stain. . . . They are also in the habit of painting round their mouths with a blue colour.[27]

In De Bry's text, these corporeal signs went hand in hand with rites that shocked European sensibilities—cannibalism and human sacrifice among them—prominently portrayed in his engravings.[28] It is the lavishly tattooed Timucua chief who initiates the French colonists—and the French reader— to Amerindian ceremonies. He sits or stands in the foreground with his European guests, explaining and gesturing reassuringly as his shocked French counterpart looks on, as in De Bry's rendering of a woman's sacrifice of her first-born child to the chief in accordance with Timucua tradition (see Figure 3.1).[29]

Visual sources from the seventeenth century build on the artistic tradition established by De Bry, reinforcing corporeal decoration as a primary marker of Amerindian identity for the European eye. Like the authors of New World travel narratives, artists borrowed elements from earlier engravings as well as from each other, perpetuating an image of the Amerindian of New France that was most often generic and paint- or tattoo-bearing. In fact, many of the artists who drew or engraved images of Amerindians never actually set foot in New France. Their representations are therefore all the more indicative of how the uninitiated French imagined the Amerindian body. The engravings published by Jesuit François Du Creux, who himself never traveled to Canada, are a case in point. Commissioned by the Jesuit order to record the notable events of their mission there for dissemination to a cultivated readership whose support they sought in their efforts overseas, Du Creux's 1664 *Historiae Canadiensis seu Novae Franciae* was an eight-hundred-page history of the Jesuit mission drawn largely from published relations. Such an elegant volume would not have been complete without a decorative frontispiece and several engravings. Of the four warriors portrayed two are painted or tattooed.[30] These engravings do not show Amerindians of a specific nation but rather "a type, that of the 'savage man'" who is characterized by, among other markers, his painted and pricked body.[31] The first of these leans against a boulder, his body covered with geometric designs, with the figures of the sun and the moon prominently displayed upon his breast (see Figure 3.2).[32] The other figure, though

Primogeniti folennibus ceremonijs Regi   XXXIIII.
facrificantur.

Figure 3.1 "Solemn ceremony sacrificing a first-born child to the king," Theodor de
Bry after Jacques Le Moyne de Morgues, *Brevis Narratio* (Frankfurt:
Johann Wechel, 1591). Beinecke Library, Yale University.

more Europeanized—clad in a long cape and elaborate loin covering—also
sports extensive tattooed or painted designs on his legs (see Figure 3.3).[33]
    Another artist, Jesuit missionary Louis Nicolas (1634–1682?), who tra-
veled throughout Canada from 1664 to 1675, adorned each of his drawings
of Amerindians with extensive tattoo work.[34] One figure, for example,
appears to have his entire body embroidered with geometric patterns
forming dots, lines, and shapes, as well as a large tortoise on his thigh
and a serpent on his chest (see Figure 3.4). Here, as in De Bry, tattoos are
associated with foreign rites and religious beliefs: the figure holds a snake
used in ceremonial dancing, whose scales and decoration resemble the
Amerindian's tattoos. In contrast to Du Creux, Nicolas, whose drawings
were assembled in the 1701 *Codex Canadiensis*, ostensibly attempted to
differentiate among Amerindian populations, specifying the tribal identity
of his subjects and suggesting that they were made from life: "in my
presence" (see Figures 3.4, 3.5, 3.6, and 3.7).[35] However, even this on-

Figure 3.2 Amerindian displaying sun and moon tattoos on his chest, François du
Creux, *Historia Canadensis* (Paris: Sébastien Cramoisy, 1664). Beinecke
Library, Yale University.

Figure 3.3 Amerindian with cape and bow and arrows, François du Creux, *Historia Canadensis* (Paris: Sébastien Cramoisy, 1664). Beinecke Library, Yale University.

Figure 3.4 Drawing of a "representative sent from the village of Gannachiouavé," attributed to Louis Nicolas, in *Codex Canadensis* (ca. 1670), 11. Ink on paper, overall 13¼ x 8½ in. (33.7 x 21.6 cm), accession No. 4726.7, Gilcrease Museum, Tulsa, OK.

Figure 3.5 Drawing of a "Savage of the Onneiothehaga Nation," attributed to Louis Nicolas, in *Codex Canadensis* (ca. 1670), 10. Ink on paper, overall 13¼ x 8½ in. (33.7 x 21.6 cm), accession No. 4726.7, Gilcrease Museum, Tulsa, OK.

Figure 3.6 Drawing of the "King of the great Nation of the Nadouessiouek," attributed to Louis Nicolas, in *Codex Canadensis* (ca. 1670), 8. Ink on paper, overall 13¼ x 8½ in. (33.7 x 21.6 cm), accession No. 4726.7, Gilcrease Museum, Tulsa, OK.

Figure 3.7 Drawing of an "Iroquois Savage of the Gandaouaguehaga Nation in Virginia," attributed to Louis Nicolas, in *Codex Canadensis* (ca. 1670), 7. Ink on paper, overall 13¼ x 8½ in. (33.7 x 21.6 cm), accession No. 4726.7, Gilcrease Museum, Tulsa, OK.

Figure 3.8 Amerindian with bow and arrows and shield, François du Creux, *Historia Canadensis* (Paris: Sébastien Cramoisy, 1664). Beinecke Library, Yale University.

the-ground witness borrowed from already published sources. The artist clearly modeled some of his drawings on the engravings that appear in Du Creux's earlier volume, tracing the poses of these figures, borrowing some elements, and then making changes or additions as he saw fit, as comparison of Figures 3.2 and 3.6 suggests.[36] Nicolas removed the capes and transformed or added further native accouterments such as long tobacco pipes, headdresses, and tomahawks, supposedly representing the specific nation to which each figure belonged. Significantly, he also increased the number of corporeal markings that covered the Amerindians' bodies, suggesting a "correction" of their initial portrayal (compare Figures 3.3 and 3.7). Moreover, figures that had originally appeared unmarked in Du Creux's volume received numerous figurative and geometric designs (compare, for example, Figures 3.5 and 3.8). Nicolas apparently saw the addition of more extensive body work as necessary for the creation of an accurate, "true-to-life" representation of Amerindian bodies, one that his public expected when viewing representations of the native inhabitants of New France.[37]

Amerindians on display

Paper and ink texts and images were not the only sources feeding the French imaginary of the Amerindian body. Amerindians left the printed page and circulated among the French, as captured or "invited" members of native populations were brought back to Europe and put on public display in the royal court and beyond. As early as 1508, French shipowner, adventurer, and governor of the important port city of Dieppe, Jehan Ango (1480–1551), a close companion to King François I (1494–1547), captured and returned to France from Newfoundland with seven "savage men" who wore tattoos on their faces.[38] In 1534, during his first voyage to Canada, Cartier kidnapped Domagaia and Taignoagyny, the sons of Saint Lawrence Iroquois chief Donnacona, to have them learn French and serve as interpreters and guides for his next voyage. The following year, he brought Donnacona himself, his sons, and several others back to France permanently for the King to entertain and display, as was in vogue among European rulers with colonial ambitions.[39] Just as early modern artists overdrew Amerindian bodies with their addition of tattooed signs in their drawings and engravings, so too court displays and elaborate spectacles featuring captured Amerindians overemphasized their corporeal otherness. Amerindians served like curiosity cabinets for the demonstration of social status, taking their place alongside exotic objects that period monarchs and aristocrats avidly collected and put on display.[40] A wide audience was party to events such as the lavish 1550 royal *entrée* of King Henry II and Catherine de Médicis to Rouen, which featured an extraordinary Brazilian *fête*, where Tupinamba warriors, brought to France for the occasion, mixed it up with nearly fifty French sailors who stripped down and painted their bodies to adopt the role of "savages."[41] Louis XIV kept Iroquois and their canoes as curiosities in his Grand Canal at Versailles to exhibit his cultural and economic capital.[42] At the close of the century, the marked Amerindian body remained a fetish, as surgeon Dière de Dièreville (fl. 1699–1711), who spent the year 1699–1700 in Acadia, attests. He relates how the tattooed skin of a dead Amerindian was fashioned by surgeons into an object fit for display on the wall of a curiosity cabinet: "I saw a savage who was marked in this way die at the Hôtel Dieu of Paris. The Surgeons flayed him and had the skin dressed, without any change taking place in it."[43]

Public spectacles showcasing Amerindian bodies also served as powerful means of celebrating French Catholic progress in the Americas and rallying support for the French civilizing mission. On April 12, 1613, Paris was treated to another Brazilian spectacle as Capuchin missionary Claude d'Abbeville, Admiral François de Rasilly, and six feather-clad Tupinamba men arrived triumphantly in the capital after a long voyage back from the young French colony on the island of Maragnan. Throngs of excited onlookers and dignitaries greeted them.[44] The Frenchmen were returning after a short month on the island to report on their mission's progress and to ask for further royal support for their fledgling French settlement in territory largely controlled by Portugal; they had brought the Tupinamba along to help sway popular and royal opinion in their favor.[45] Their elaborately staged visit—which included a parade through the streets, a speech before the royal family, a music and dance presentation by the Tupinamba men, their recitation of Catholic prayers in their native language, baptism, and marriage to French women—was all part of a well-orchestrated publicity campaign. The "savage others" passed through a kind of magical civilizing process to become French Catholics in a spectacular demonstration of the effectiveness of the French assimilationist model.[46] In Abbeville's estimation, the Tupinamba's entry was a complete success with the Parisian crowds and dignitaries. He contentedly marvels over the popular frenzy inspired by their arrival in Paris, carefully prepared by the troupe's earlier visits to Le Havre and Rouen on their way to the capital:

> But who would ever have thought that the people of Paris, so accustomed to seeing rare and new things, would have been as moved as they were by the arrival of these Indians? How many times have we seen barbarous and foreign nations come to the city without anyone making a fuss? And here it was that upon the arrival of these poor Indians *Commota est universa civitas*, all of Paris is in an uproar, each person feeling in his heart an indefinable rejoicing that it could no longer be held back in its constraints and limits, it had to burst out so that he could have the satisfaction of seeing with his own eyes that after which his poor heart trembled. All the streets were full of huge crowds of people running to see what could scarcely be believed.[47]

According to Abbeville, so transported were the Parisians by their desire to gaze on the Amerindians that they flooded the Capuchin convent, and "[e]ven those who saw them could almost not be satiated by looking at them and admiring them."[48]

One of the Tupinamba men, a sixty- or seventy-year-old warrior named Carypyra, wore an elaborate full-body tattoo design, making him a star specimen in Abbeville's performance of the civilizing power of conversion. Indeed, if the Capuchins could inspire one so visibly identified as "other" to convert, then their success with the Tupinamba population as a whole was all but guaranteed. Abbeville tells Carypyra's story in his *Histoire de la Mission des Pères Capucins en l'Isle de Maragnan et terres circonvoysines*, which he published in 1614 to celebrate the dramatic events and to secure continued funding for the mission.[49] Though the warrior was the first of three Brazilians to succumb to pneumonia while in France, Abbeville chronicled his successful transformation from "savage" to French Catholic in a lengthy obituary. Indeed, Carypyra's extreme difference, immediately visible in the marks he wore upon his skin, did not impede his incorporation into the French social body but instead reinforced the extraordinary civilizing power of conversion. Abbeville chooses to highlight the warrior's corporeal alterity, providing a vivid description of his tattoos, their place in Tupinamba culture, and the process of their creation.[50] He then puts Carypyra's body on display once more in an engraving that he asserts is "made from life" (see Figure 3.9).[51] While the male figure's features and pose are Europeanized, the native weapons he wears, piercings on his chin and ears, loin covering decorated with feathers, and, most prominently, the geometric tattoo pattern that runs, as Abbeville points out, from the top of his cheekbones to just above his knees, mark foreignness on his otherwise naked body.[52] Unlike clothing and accessories that could be swapped for French styles, as was the case for several men in his party whom Abbeville portrays in "before" and "after" engravings, redressed as Frenchmen, Carypyra's cutaneous markings "remain on the body without ever being able to be removed."[53] Conscious of his protégé's marks as a potentially troubling remainder in the transformation of his identity from savage to French Catholic, Abbeville finds a radical solution, which he casts explicitly in terms of corporeal marking. He symbolically replaces Carypyra's tattoos that represent the twenty-four "names" the warrior has obtained for courageous actions in battle with a newly acquired baptismal name, François, chosen in honor of François de Rasilly who had led the mission, but also meaning "French."[54] Through baptism, Abbeville thus explicitly renames Carypyra as French and replaces his corporeal marks—their meaning intimately tied to Tupinamba society and culture—with a new mark: a Christian sign of belonging, the mark of baptism both literally and figuratively inscribed on his body during the baptismal rite.[55] Abbeville casts this ceremony of remarking in which Carypyra voluntarily submits himself for reinscription by the welcoming French Capuchins as an event supremely satisfying to both parties:

FRANÇOIS CARYPYRA.

Figure 3.9 Tupinamba warrior François Carypyra, Claude d'Abbeville, *Histoire de la Mission des Pères Capucins en l'Isle de Maragnan* (Paris: François Huby, 1614), fol. 347v. Bibliothèque Nationale de France.

It was marvelous to see the mutual pleasure that reigned between us, on our side in receiving him to give him a more beautiful mark than the one he had and to make him a soldier of a new militia; and on his side in giving himself over to us to be made a Christian.[56]

Carypyra's identity is thus transformed through an overwriting of his original marks of identity with those of the Catholic faith and the French state, the process of conversion enabling his inscription into the celebratory narrative of the French colonial project. Abbeville's Parisian triumph was only the first in a series of public baptisms of Amerindians that continued throughout the seventeenth century as France turned its colonial aspirations further north to Canada, providing vivid displays of French Catholic progress in the New World that brought the colonial project of conversion and assimilation—and the Amerindian tattoo—closer to home.

Making meaning of marking

As the relations, images, and public spectacles already examined attest, for the French, the Amerindian tattoo clearly represented, as Gorden Sayre has argued, "an enduring mark of primitivism."[57] A highly visible and permanent mark of the "savage," tattooed skin had to be rewritten by French Catholicism in order to be incorporated into the social body, as dramatized in the story of Carypyra's conversion. However, ambivalence characterized French accounts of Amerindian tattooing, which provoked fascination and admiration as much as it did fear and repulsion. Though French colonists clearly saw the colors, figures, and patterns that ornamented Amerindian bodies as signs of their otherness, most did not stop at the surface but sought to decipher the meaning behind the marks. Indeed, giving Amerindian markings meaning was the first step in rendering their bearers less "savage," thus initiating the civilizing process the French hoped to bring to fruition in New France.[58] For French missionaries, the marks born by their Amerindian charges functioned within a signifying system that they had to decode if they were ever to win over souls for Catholic France. For traders and military men, understanding and deploying tattoos proved as essential to their success and survival as did learning the languages of the Amerindian nations they frequented. As the French made sense of the signs born by their Amerindian hosts, they inevitably questioned the assumed difference between the inhabitants of the New and Old Worlds and consciously linked marking traditions on both sides of the Atlantic.

On the most basic level, when writing about Amerindian body marking practices, French chroniclers made them legible to their readers through comparison with the arts of engraving, embroidery, and leatherwork as practiced in Europe, all of which made use of sharp tools to create images and designs. D'Abbeville vividly describes the initial step of Carypyra's tattooing in his homeland as akin to that of decorating armor:

> Concerning the most valiant and greatest warriors, [the Tupinamba] have this custom . . . to take a bone from the leg of certain birds, which they sharpen like razors, with which they engrave themselves & decorate the body in diverse ways like we do here a beautiful breastplate with the burin . . . rubbing all the incisions right away with some black color, either powder or sap or anything else, it mixes with the blood that runs from them everywhere & seeps into the scars, so that the figures that they have engraved stay on the body without ever being able to be removed.[59]

According to Abbeville, Carypyra's body was decorated "with characters and figures so new that you would have taken the surface of his flesh for damask armor" and "the same marquetry could be seen around his neck."[60] Sagard too compares tattooing to decorative metalwork, writing that the Amerindians engrave signs on their skin "like we here make a coat of arms with the burin."[61] This comparison continues into the eighteenth century when Lafitau treats what he calls "caustic paintings on live flesh." He relates the technique he witnessed during his time spent among the Iroquois from 1712 to 1718, borrowing vocabulary from leather making, marveling at how Amerindians turn the cutting and pricking techniques they use on animal hides on their own skin:

> It is not only the art of making these kinds of Caustic paintings on the skins of Deer and other animals that the Savages inherited from their fathers; they also learned from them that of making magnificent embroideries on live flesh, and to compose a piece of clothing that truly costs them dearly, but that has the practical value of lasting as long as they do. The work is in itself the same as that which is done on hides. You first draw on the flesh the design of the shapes you wish to engrave, then you go over all these lines by pricking the flesh until the blood flows out, with needles or little bones. Finally, you introduce into the prick marks red lead, ground up wood ash, or some other color that you wish to apply.[62]

Making links between tattooing and artisanal processes known to their readers laid the groundwork for a larger examination of the cultural meanings of corporeal marking that foregrounded comparison between Amerindian and European practices, providing French readers with an interpretive structure that followed a grammar with which they were familiar. The art of engraving itself, to which tattooing practices were often compared, engaged in reproducing and interpreting the meaning of tattoos observed on Amerindian bodies.[63] A well-known plate engraved by De Bry for his 1590 edition of Thomas Harriot's (1560–1621) *A Briefe and True Report of the New Found Land of Virginia*, which relayed Harriot's observations during an 1585 English expedition there, interprets the Algonquian tattoo as having a role in personal identification similar to that played by the coats of arms and vestimentary insignia that proliferated on the European continent.[64] De Bry's "The Marckes of sundrye of the Cheif mene of Virginia" provides a composite rendering of seven distinctive marks by which Europeans could ostensibly identify various native inhabitants, one of which adorns the back of the Algonquian at center (see Figure 3.10). Harriot's text explains that "[t]he inhabitants of all the cuntrie for the most parte have marks rased on their backs, wherby yt may be knowen what Princes subjects they bee, or of what place they have their originall," asserting the function of tattoos as marks of identification.[65] De Bry furnishes his reader with a legend for the marks displayed in the engraving, attributing each one to a particular nation or chief, creating a key that the traveler could fancifully hold up for comparison when confronted with his Amerindian hosts.[66] De Bry's plate thus establishes Amerindian tattoos as a meaningful sign system and stakes the claim that they could be successfully translated for their European viewers, providing what Mairin Odle has called "a visual vocabulary list for tattoos" that, in a significant reversal of the European-

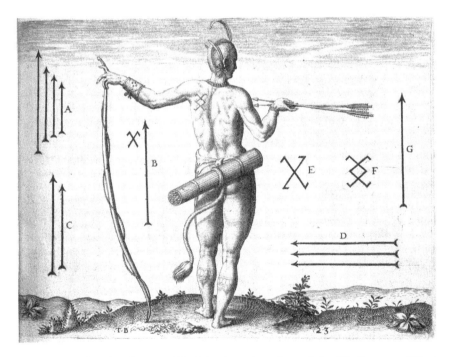

Figure 3.10 Theodor de Bry, "The Marckes of sundrye of the Cheif mene of Virginia," in Thomas Harriot, *A Briefe and True Report of the New Found Land of Virginia* (Frankfurt: Theodor De Bry, 1590). William L. Clements Library, The University of Michigan.

Amerindian literacy hierarchy, teaches Europeans how to read the bodies of the Amerindians they encounter.[67] This interpretation of the tattoo as a legible sign of identity traverses seventeenth-century accounts as well. When Lescarbot, referencing Harriot's work in his own 1609 account, discusses body marking among the Algonquians, he refers to tattoos as being "like [the marks] our merchants imprint on their merchandise" so that it can be identified, or those slaves were made to wear in ancient times so they could be recognized as belonging to a particular owner.[68]

Lafitau's early eighteenth-century work crystalizes this European desire to make meaning of the marks on skin they encountered in the Americas, highlighting anew the role of corporeal marks in identifying the Amerindian, presenting them as "characteristic marks [*nottes*], that distinguish him personally."[69] Going beyond the relatively simple graphic designs razed on the backs of Algonquian men as depicted by De Bry, Lafitau explains tattoos as participating in a highly sophisticated signifying system that uses symbols "that serve them as Hieroglyphics, writings, and memoirs," a substitute for "the missing Alphabet."[70] Not only do tattoos identify individual warriors, but, as distinctive signs, they can also be transferred to other surfaces to record and publish that warrior's accomplishments and to mark his territory. In the engraving that accompanies Lafitau's analysis, an Amerindian at center carves signs in a tree, "writing in his own way what he wants to make known," the symbols reproduced in a separate engraving below it, "each of which can be considered a Letter" (see Figure 3.11).[71] In place of a typical portrait representing facial features, the Amerindian

> traces marks that he has had pricked on [his face], as well as those that are engraved on his chest, and that being unique to him, make him recognizable, not only to those who have seen him, but also to all those who only know him by reputation, knowing his hieroglyphic symbol, just as we in the past distinguished a person in Europe by his motto, and as we today identify a family by its coat of arms.[72]

Lafitau thus inscribes Amerindian tattooing into both past and contemporary European identification practices through his comparison of tattooing with family insignia that could be recognized, as he writes, even by those who had never seen an individual but knew him only by reputation. Like De Bry, he attempts to categorize—and thus master—each symbol, labeling it, and linking it to a corresponding key that explains its meaning. Dumont de Montigny similarly compares Amerindian tattoos to European coats of arms, providing a description of how Amerindians leave calling cards that identify them with a reproduction of the corporeal mark worn by their leader on the site of successful attacks:

> These are little wooden clubs, upon which they engrave with the point of their knife, either the sign that designates their village, . . . or that

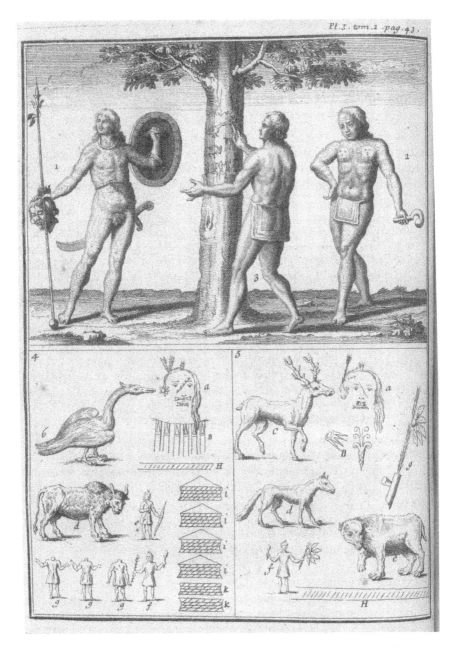

Pl. 3. tom. 2. pag. 43.

Figure 3.11 Amerindian inscribing a tree trunk with "hieroglyphics," flanked by a Pict on the left and another Amerindian on the right, Jean-François Lafitau, *Mœurs de sauvages américains* (Paris: Saugrain l'aîné and Charles Estienne Hochereau, 1724), vol. 2, plate 3, facing p. 43. Beinecke Library, Yale University.

which the leader of their group wears on his stomach. These marks are like their coat of arms.[73]

Translated from skin to wood, animal skins, and the bark of trees, tattoos were, for these writers, signs of identity not so foreign from those that had currency in Europe.

In casting Amerindian tattoos as distinguishing marks of identity, many writers also draw parallels with European signs of honor, citing the use of tattoos for recognizing the accomplishments of "the most valiant and great warriors."[74] Abbeville likens Carypyra's extensive markings to the honors and memorials that both the ancients and the Frenchmen of his day inscribed onto various surfaces to celebrate military exploits:

> What is most remarkable, is that his names were accompanied by their praises and written like Epigrams, not on paper, nor on bronze, nor on the bark of a tree, but on his own flesh; his face, his stomach and the entirety of both his thighs were the marble and the porphyry upon which he had had his life engraved . . . , more honorable for this soldier, given his status as a brave soldier, than all the world's precious stones.[75]

French soldiers in particular likely saw in tattoos a merit system of awards given for acts of bravery that they found both recognizable and attractive.[76] Henri de Tonti (1649–1704), who accompanied Robert Cavelier de la Salle (1643–1687) on his trip down the Mississippi in 1682, specifies that "you must have distinguished yourself by the death of some enemy in order to earn it. While here we crown our Heroes, there they imprint on the stomach an infinity of black, red, and blue stripes."[77] Naval officer Jean-Bernard Bossu, who traveled three times to Louisiana, up the Mississippi Valley and through Alabama and Illinois country between 1751 and 1762, treats extensively the role of tattooing as an honor for valiant warriors and a register of their exploits. Citing the example of an Osage man who had killed a giant snake plaguing the tribe and wore its image imprinted on his body, he explains that tattooing conferred

> a type of knighthood on only those who have done extraordinary deeds, and one endures it with pleasure in order to be considered a valiant man. The more brave deeds a warrior does, the more such marks of distinction he bears on his body.[78]

Like Tonti, Bossu is quick to compare this signifying system to medals and other signs of distinction worn by military officers in France, arguing that "[w]e often find in the customs of the Savages the equivalent of those of Europeans, no matter how much difference there might seem to be between them."[79] To prove his point, he provocatively joins two true stories of men who falsely appropriated signs of honor, one Amerindian, one French:

> I knew an Indian who, although he had never done anything out-standing in defense of his tribe, decided to have himself tattooed with one of these marks of distinction in order to impress those who judge others by outward appearances. This show-off wanted to pass himself off as a valiant man so that he could marry one of the prettiest girls of the tribe. . . . Just as the match was about to be concluded with the girl's relatives, the warriors, who were indignant upon seeing a coward display a symbol of military merit, called an assembly of war chiefs to deal with this bit of audacity. The council decided, in order to prevent such abuses which would remove the distinction between courageous men and cowards, that this false hero who unjustly decorated himself with the tomahawk, without ever having struck a blow in battle, would have the design torn off him, skin and all, and that the same would be done to all others like him.[80]

Bossu compares this story to one he dates from 1749 of an officer in the Île-de-France regiment who fell in love with a woman, but her mother would only approve the marriage if he were first decorated with the Royal and Military Order of Saint-Louis, established in 1693 by Louis XIV to honor exceptional officers. Like the Amerindian youth, he falsely assumed the military badge of honor in order to win the woman's hand. When found out, the medal were taken away and the officer were demoted and imprisoned for twenty years.[81] Bossu underlines the resemblance between the two cases, deliberately repeating the verb "arracher"—used in the Amerindian story to describe the ripping of skin and, in the French, the tearing off of the medal from cloth—thus emphasizing both the violence of social correction and the value of the corporeal mark as a status symbol common to both Amerindian and European cultures.

In decoding Amerindian body marking practices, then, early modern writers, for all their initial emphasis on difference, highlighted similarities between European and Amerindian arts, customs, and signifying systems. Indeed, in their readings of the decorated bodies of the natives they encountered in New France, most writers sought not to distance them from peoples and practices of European descent, but, in fact, to establish relationships between them, relationships that were key to justifying the French colonial project. As further examination of the treatment of body marking by French chroniclers of the Americas will reveal, the very tattoos that would initially seem to distance the Amerindians from their French counterparts in fact found their most common points of reference in European tattooing practices both ancient and modern.

New World tattoo meets Old World tattoo

As its title suggests, Lescarbot's 1609 *Description des mœurs souriquoises comparées à celles d'autres peuples* provides a model example of the comparative approach taken by many seventeenth- and early eighteenth-century French ethnographers. In his chapter on Amerindian "Painting, Marking, Incising and Body Ornamentation," Lescarbot in fact spends little time on the description and analysis of New World practices but instead devotes the overwhelming majority of his chapter to the discussion of European traditions of corporeal inscription and their heritage. Far from distancing Amerindian customs from European ones, Lescarbot places them in immediate parallel, comparing marked Amerindian bodies to the bodies of ancient European peoples who tattooed their skin, notably the Picts—who had once inhabited present-day England—and the Pictons (*Pictones* in Latin)—who formerly occupied France's Poitou region:

> Now these peoples were called Picts because of the paintings they applied to their naked bodies, which . . . they did not want to cover with any clothing, so as not to hide and obscure the beautiful damask paintings they had applied to them, in which were represented the forms of animals of all kinds, and imprinted with sharp tools so deeply that it were impossible to take them off. Which they did . . . beginning in childhood, so that as a child grew, the figures grew also, just as happens with marks that you engrave on young pumpkins.[82]

Lescarbot establishes, then, an early French heritage for tattooing, calling the Pictons "our Poitouvian Celts" and asserting that they were "very ancient Gauls beginning in the time of Julius Caesar."[83] By offering his own version on "nos ancêtres les Gaulois," bolstered by references to ancient and medieval authorities, Lescarbot suggests that his reader look at the Amerindian corporeal rites he describes not as a curiosity of foreign lands but instead through the lens of France's own early history of body marking: "This taste for painting oneself having been so generalized here [in France], there is no reason to ridicule it if the peoples of the West Indies did and still do the same."[84] Though Lescarbot asserts that the French ancestors he cites, the Poitouvian Pictons, are not of the same "race" as the Picts, he posits that they got their name for the same reason: "I venture to believe that this name was given to them for the same reason that the Picts were given theirs," namely because they displayed pictures on their skin.[85] He draws a continuous line between these "very ancient Gauls" and the seventeenth-century Amerindians he encounters in New France:

> And because customs once introduced among a people are not lost but over many centuries (just as we still see persist today the madness of

Mardi Gras), in the same way the vestiges of the paintings [on the skin] we have talked about have remained in some North American nations.[86]

For Lescarbot, then, Frenchmen were no less descendants of nations who painted and tattooed their bodies than were Amerindians: "we recognize that the world here [in France] was in ancient times just as unformed and savage as that of the West Indies."[87] Though his implication that Europe is now "formed" and "civilized" while Amerindian culture is not does not flatter, he nonetheless asks his reader to see the present-day practices of the indigenous peoples of New France as endurances of a past they share with the French.

The relationship Lescarbot draws between the Amerindians of New France and ancient European peoples articulates in writing earlier visual representations that had first juxtaposed images of ancient Picts with those of modern-day Amerindians. Lescarbot references engravings published in De Bry's 1590 edition of Harriot's *A Briefe and True Report of the New Found Land of Virginia*, which deliberately placed figures of decorated Picts directly following engravings of Amerindians and their markings: "[T]here are still old portraits that he who made the history of the English travels in Virginia engraved, where Picts of both sexes are shown with their beautiful incisions, and with their swords hanging from their naked flesh" (see Figures 3.12 and 3.13).[88] De Bry thus presented engravings of ancient Picts sporting ink work, battle accouterments, and, in the case of the male Pict, a slain enemy's head as a trophy, in direct relationship with representations of marked Amerindians "for to showe how that the Inhabitants of the great Bretannie have bin in times past as sauvage as those of Virginia."[89] By the early eighteenth century when Lafitau published his *Mœurs des Sauvages Américains, Comparés aux Mœurs des Premiers Temps* (1720), the parallel between European Pict and Native American was well established. Lafitau reproduced De Bry's earlier engraving of the male Pict opposite that of an Amerindian borrowed from Du Creux's 1664 *Historiae Canadiensis*.[90] The ancient Pict and the modern Amerindian pose on either side of the engraved tree, displaying their tattooed bodies (see Figure 3.11). The plate's legend reinforces the intentionality of the juxtaposition of the figures at left and right: "Painted savage, parallel to the Pict."[91]

Cited by authors and artists from the late sixteenth century through the eighteenth century, the tattooed ancient Pict thus became an emblematic figure of French ethnographers' "premiers temps" approach, which looked to the ancient past to establish relationships between the French and the native inhabitants of New France. By asserting their common ancestry and a shared heritage of body marking, these writers and artists lent hope for the ultimate success of the French assimilationist model; if the Picts and Pictons had evolved into present-day Europeans, then so too could the

Figure 3.12 Male Pict, Theodor de Bry in Thomas Harriot, *A Briefe and True Report of the New Found Land of Virginia* (Frankfurt: Theodor de Bry, 1590). William L. Clements Library, University of Michigan.

Figure 3.13 Female Pict, Theodor de Bry in Thomas Harriot, *A Briefe and True Report of the New Found Land of Virginia* (Frankfurt: Theodor de Bry, 1590). William L. Clements Library, University of Michigan.

Amerindians. Moreover, by claiming that the Amerindians had, in effect, always been French, they strategically bolstered France's claims to this part of the world over those of its colonial competitors.[92] The tattoo, then, for all its apparent significance as a mark of difference, became an unexpected ally in establishing a shared lineage that ultimately justified the colonization of New France.

The figure of the Pict played an essential role in linking the Old World and the New, as early modern travelers looked to the distant past for evidence of a body marking culture on the European continent. But these writers also referenced a contemporary and widely accepted European tattooing tradition: the Holy Land pilgrim tattoo.[93] When Recollet missionary Sagard describes tattooing methods among the Hurons and the Petuns, he is quick to provide his French reader with what was apparently an easy point of reference for understanding the practice: the cross of Jerusalem that, along with several other designs, commonly adorned the bodies of pilgrims returning from the Holy Land. Sagard thus presents the Amerindian tattoo to his reader in European terms, referencing a well-known and accepted Christian practice prevalent in his own time: "[I]t is pricked and made in the same way as are made and engraved on the flesh's surface the Crosses that those returning from Jerusalem have on their arms, and it lasts forever."[94] Rather than encountering the tattoo on the body of the Amerindian other, Sagard's readers were already familiar with similar body markings on European skin.

Ultimately, the very marks that would seem to powerfully represent the Amerindian's otherness and resist his incorporation into the French social body are rewritten by these early ethnographers so as to show resemblance, rather than difference, a unity essential to the success of France's assimilationist model. Perhaps, as Jesuit historian Joseph Jouvency (1643–1719) provocatively affirms, Amerindians had "the same complexion as the French" underneath their paint and grease, for even their practices of corporeal ornamentation could be linked to European traditions both past and contemporary.[95] They were then not as unlike the French as they might first have seemed, a key concept of the Catholic universalism that provided the ideological framework for the French assimilationist enterprise.[96] Yet, while such assertions of resemblance were essential for Amerindian integration into the French social body, assimilation was meant to work one way only—Amerindians becoming more like the French. Of course, as an examination of the adoption of body marking practices by the French living in Canada and Louisiana attests, this neat unidirectional model was not always quite so clear cut. Indeed, the state-encouraged intermingling of French and Amerindian populations in New France raised serious concerns for missionaries and colonial authorities as to the dangers of "contamination" of the French colonists by the native Amerindian populations with which they lived, a phenomenon that found material confirmation upon the Frenchmen's skin.[97]

Incorporating the other: *coureurs de bois*

French travelers to the Americas were no less enthusiastic than their Holy Land pilgrim counterparts in their experimentation with the customs of corporeal inscription that they encountered in New France.[98] Even short-term visitors to the colony often submitted themselves to the Amerindian needle, returning to France with their tattoo as a souvenir, as surgeon Dièreville, who chose not to get tattooed himself, observes: "[s]ome Frenchmen have undergone the ordeal, who could testify to the experience. For my part, I was not interested in wearing such marks."[99] Despite taboos—or perhaps in part because of them—the entrepreneurial Frenchmen who represented the lifeblood of the colony's fur trade, long-term residents living alongside and trading with the Amerindians, became adepts of tattooing.[100] As Henri de Tonti recounts,

> Our French settled in Louisiana, who are travelers by profession, easily contract savage ways. They run through the woods in stockings and shoes, without pants and with a simple loin covering. They are especially fond of having themselves pricked, and there are many who, except for the face, have them on almost their whole bodies.[101]

Referred to as *coureurs de bois*—literally, "wood runners"—these Frenchmen, like many of the Amerindian tribes they frequented, lived a nomadic life, a quality that Europeans associated with the savage and uncivilized.[102] Recollet missionary Sagard bemoans that living among the Amerindians caused the physical transformation of these Christian Frenchmen into savages: "the French themselves, better educated and brought up in the school of the faith, become savages just by living with the savages, and nearly lose the shape of a Christian."[103] If these French born and raised Catholics lose their Christian appearance, even essence, through daily transient life with the Amerindians, how then, Sagard wonders, can missionaries expect to convert the Amerindians themselves? Colonial administrators expressed similar worries, complaining loudly about the "ensauvagement" of the French population of New France.[104] Jacques-René de Brisay, marquis de Denonville (1637–1710), who governed the colony from 1685 to 1689, relates the following impressions in 1685:

> We long thought that bringing the savages closer to our towns was a very considerable gain for making these peoples accustomed to living like us and to instructing themselves in our religion, but I have noticed, Your Grace, that the complete opposite has happened because instead of them growing accustomed to our laws, I assure you that they strongly communicate all they have that is the most evil, and do not take themselves but that which is bad and vicious in us.[105]

In an attempt to control what they saw as the contamination of Frenchmen by Amerindian ways, French administrators went so far as to place limits on time spent in the woods by royal ordinance, prohibiting, for example, in 1673, colonists from spending more than twenty-four hours at a time in the woods without special permission.[106] Such measures, next to impossible to enforce, had little effect.

While, as we have seen, erudite ethnographers of the period justified the colonial enterprise by theorizing a common European-Amerindian ancestry through the practice of tattooing, on the ground, corporeal marking remained a sign of the desertion of "civilization" by the French inhabitants of Canada and Louisiana, a visible sign of the failure of the civilizing process.[107] While Sagard remains unspecific as to the practices of body ornamentation Frenchmen used as they morphed into "savages," other contemporary accounts provide evidence and even vivid descriptions of the adoption of tattooing by the French inhabitants of North America. When New France chronicler Claude-Charles Le Roy Bacqueville de la Potherie (1663–1736) discusses tattooing in the region of present-day Wisconsin, he includes the French inhabitants of Canada as adepts of the practice alongside the Amerindians: "The [Amerindian] men make themselves snakes that extend from the forehead to the nose. They prick most of their bodies, *as do the Canadians*, with a needle, until they bleed."[108] Henri Joutel (ca. 1643–1735), who served in the last expedition commanded by La Salle from 1684 to 1687, recounts his encounter in March 1687 with three deserters living among the Cenis, two of whom were tattooed. One he calls "the Provençal" had himself pricked, while another, whom he calls Reuter, is so transformed that when Joutel first encounters him, he takes him for an Amerindian:

> It seemed as though he had been a savage for ten years. He was naked and barefoot. All he had for clothing was an ugly covering that the savages of the region where they were make with turkey feathers and decorate with little strings, which they do quite well. But what I admired most, was that he had had himself pricked like them and marked on the face, so that he was in almost no way different from them, except that he was not as alert. As for religion, I think that was what bothered him the least; he liked this libertine life pretty well.[109]

While Joutel expresses a certain fascination at the Frenchman's metamorphosis, he also associates Amerindian corporeal adornment with an abandonment of Christianity—and thus civilization—for libertinism. For him, Reuter's external makeover signifies his internal transformation—the loss of his Christian faith. Joutel's reaction to meeting the last of the La Salle deserters, who has not undergone marking, is significant in this respect:

> The last one had not had himself marked in the savage manner, as the other had done, nor cut his hair like most of the savages. As a result this

last Frenchman seemed to me more reasonable than the other, seeming to have more religion.[110]

Despite complaints and constraints, the avidity of *coureurs de bois* for tattooing continued well into the eighteenth century. As New France army commander Louis-Joseph de Saint-Véran de Montcalm (1712–1759) asserts, by the mid-eighteenth century tattoos had become so common among the French population of New France that they represented one of the defining traits by which a *coureur de bois* could be recognized: "You recognize them easily . . . because all of them have themselves pricked with the image of some plant or animal."[111] Swedish naturalist Pehr Kalm (1716–1779) observes the same in 1749, though like Tonti, he claims that they avoid tattooing their faces, perhaps therein preserving to a certain degree their European identity:

> Several of the French, especially the common people, who travel frequently about the country in order to buy skins, have in fun followed the example of the natives. However, they never paint their faces as the natives do, but another part of the body, as their chest, back, thighs and especially their legs. . . . As a rule the natives who are masters of the art adorn the Frenchmen.[112]

As Kalm underlines, through tattooing the French voluntarily submitted themselves to inscription by the Amerindian artist, receiving the mark of the other upon their skin in a poignant reversal of the receipt of the "beautiful mark" of Christian baptism bestowed on Carypyra by Abbeville to replace the Tupinamba warrior's "savage" tattoos. Though Kalm casts the fur traders' decision to tattoo themselves as something done for fun, a more profound transformation took place as they put themselves under the Amerindian needle to permanently mark their skin. By adopting the body marking practices of the Amerindians they frequented, Frenchmen literally incorporated the other.[113] This penetration of the other is symbolized in the act of tattooing itself, which inserts a foreign body underneath the skin, operating a permanent change in the body of its recipient that determines how his body—indeed his very identity—is read.

Hybrid identities

The Frenchmen who chose to get inked in America—a group that by the late seventeenth century included not only more marginal figures such as fur traders and deserters but also French officers—saw in tattooing the opportunity to create new hybrid identities for themselves. While some may have wished to signal their departure from or rebellion against European institutions, others adopted tattoos to ease their integration into Amerindian society and their ability to move among the nations with which they negotiated. For historian Arnaud Balvay, "Tattooing thus made it possible for the French to be integrated into the indigenous social body," through which they could more easily do business or raise troops.[114] As Montcalm relates in 1758, in Amerindian culture, real men got tattoos—it was therefore incumbent upon European colonists to follow suit if they wished to command the respect of their hosts: "You would not be considered a man among the savages of the Upper Country unless you had yourself pricked."[115] The more culturally assimilated fur traders were, the more welcome and respected they were among Amerindians; the Frenchmen's own penetration by the needle facilitated their penetration of the market and thus led to greater economic gain, which was, after all, their ultimate goal in New France.[116]

Corporeal signs facilitated not only commercial relations but military conquest as well. French military officers seem to have used tattoos for colonial gain, at least from the mid-eighteenth century. Soldier Joseph-Charles Bonnefons testifies, for example, that during his military service from 1751 to 1761 he saw "among others an officer who spoke several native languages being very highly esteemed among them and who often served as their interpreter" who was "pricked in this manner . . . all over the body and in different colors."[117] Speaking the language, then, meant not only mastering Amerindian verbal linguistic cues but also wearing signs that had meaning in their culture upon one's body. Since tattoos most often served the Amerindians as signs of valor, representing heroic exploits, French soldiers were able to harness their signifying power to gain esteem among the native peoples, at least according to the Frenchmen's accounts.[118] Like pilgrim travelers who relied on their Jerusalem tattoos to offer them safe passage as they crossed potentially hostile territories, some French military officers also used tattoos as a kind of passport, an identifying mark that allowed them entry and gained them trust where they might otherwise have been greeted with hostility.[119] A story told by Bossu of his military exploits provides a fascinating, if undoubtedly embellished, account of the tattoo as offering identification and protection for a European traveling among the Amerindians.[120] In a letter to the Marquis de l'Estrade de la Cousse of Burgandy, he recounts at length his "adoption" by the Arkansas through the ceremonial engraving of a deer tattoo on his thigh, a sign that, he writes, will serve him well as he travels through the lands of other Amerindian peoples:

> Before ending my letter, I should like to tell you about an event which will seem strange to you, but which, in spite of its insignificance, could be very useful to me during my stay in America. The Arkansas have just adopted me. A deer was tattooed on my thigh as a sign that I have been made a warrior and a chief. I submitted to this painful operation with good grace. . . . They then told me that if I traveled among the tribes allied to them, all that I had to do to receive a warm welcome was to

smoke a peace pipe and show my tattoo. They also said that I was their brother and that if I were killed they would avenge my death. I am now a noble of the Arkansas nation. By adopting me, these people have shown me the greatest honor they can pay to a defender of their land. I consider it similar to the honor received by Marshal de Richelieu when his name was inscribed in the golden book among the names of the nobles of the Republic of Genoa.[121]

Bossu's inscription through tattooing seals his relationship with the Arkansas just as a signature in ink on the pages of a book had validated Richelieu's nobility; Bossu becomes one of them, his identity as their "brother" emblazoned upon his thigh. Though he rhetorically casts his tattooing as an "insignificant" event, he is obviously quite proud of his achievement, which has bought him the trust and esteem of the Arkansas: "You would never believe how attached to me these people have become since then."[122] By inscribing himself within the symbolic system of the other, he gains the privilege to circulate freely and securely among them. The tattoo apparently provides Bossu's body with legibility as friend rather than foe even as he moves through geographically and ethnically diverse terrain. Yet his tattoo, which he describes at length in his narrative, is also meant for a dual readership, identifying him to his European public as well, displaying his courage and ingenuity as a soldier.

In addition to adopting Amerindian iconography, French soldiers also used Native American tattooing methods to produce marks on their skin that, legible within the European sign system, affirmed or complicated their identities. Dumont de Montigny, who spent almost eighteen years in Louisiana from 1719 to 1738, had himself tattooed with the cross of the Royal and Military Order of Saint-Louis.[123] Though most military officers were awarded the cross after ten years of service, Dumont de Montigny, a rebel, never received the honor due to his altercations with his superior officers, including the colony's governor himself, which bought him some prison time.[124] His choice to emblazon the medal upon his skin—the very medal that both he and Bossu use in their narratives to compare the Amerindian tattoo to French signs of honor—was therefore quite presumptuous, replicating on his body the eight-pointed Maltese cross that distinguished officers wore on their coats in the form of an elaborate medallion with Saint Louis at center.[125] By adopting the Cross of Saint-Louis on his own terms through tattooing, and later removing it, Dumont de Montigny not only appropriates the medal otherwise denied him but ultimately makes a mockery of such status symbols and implicitly questions their validity and permanence.[126] His tattoo also situates him between two cultures and signifying systems. Though pricked by Amerindian hands, its design links him not to the nations that he lived among—as was the case for Bossu—but to the French monarchy, military hierarchy, and Catholic faith. Yet, in his choice to use a tattoo to flaunt his military accomplishments, he adopts an

Amerindian custom of displaying heroism upon the skin and makes the most of its value within a culture where the tattoo enjoyed greater symbolic capital.

While, as Balvay suggests, soldiers like Bossu may have "regarded tattooing only as a tool"—an expression of kinship with the Amerindians that was far more useful than heartfelt—and others used tattooing to assert their identities as courageous soldiers, many French inhabitants of Canada seem to have seen tattooing as an opportunity to express new identities upon their skin, forged in New France of Amerindian and European elements.[127] Tonti's colorful description of a certain well-known officer gone native—for him the epitome of the scandalous contamination of Frenchmen by Amerindian ways—suggests a will on the part of the elaborately tattooed soldier to inscribe signs upon on his skin that declare a newfound hybrid European-American identity:

> I saw many of them [tattooed Frenchmen], and especially a high ranking Officer, whose name you may know, who, in addition to an image of the Virgin with the baby Jesus, a large cross on his stomach with the miraculous words that appeared to Constantine, and an infinity of tattoos in the savage style, had a snake that encircled his body, whose tongue, pointed and ready to strike, came to end on an extremity that you will guess, if you can.[128]

For Tonti, while the officer's name may identify him, his body possibly no longer will, overtaken as it is by the influence of the ethnic other. But rather than representing an abandonment of his French Christian identity, this officer's body project suggests a will to fashion a new hybrid identity for himself, signaling through its use of signs borrowed from both traditions his esteem for and belief in elements of both cultures. As historian Gilles Harvard asserts,

> This hybrid composition translates in an exemplary manner, in the esthetic register, the mixing of cultures in the Upper Country. Here, the officer expresses, through Christian symbols, his attachment to European culture, even as he gives himself over to a pagan iconography he fully embraces.[129]

Though he covers his body with an "infinity of tattoos in the savage style," the officer uses the art to assert his Christian identity as well by displaying images of the cross, the Virgin Mary, and the infant Christ on his torso, symbols that may well have found their place on the skin of the most pious pilgrim. His entire body project refuses distinctions so often asserted by his contemporaries by placing French Christian and Amerindian elements side by side and even presenting composite symbols that have meaning in both traditions. Even his scandalous snake tattoo belongs to both Amerindian and European Christian iconography, positively symbolizing fertility in the former, negatively temptation in the latter. Indeed, the location of this hybrid sign on the reproductive organ itself might be read as a libertine challenge to mainstream ideas about the cultural reproduction of Frenchness that informed the colonial project, calling for the production of a new generation identified beyond the French-Amerindian binary.

The officer's prominent evocation of the Roman Emperor Constantine (272–337) is highly significant in this regard. Constantine, though known as the first Christian emperor, was himself a hybrid; his life, policies, and practices were characterized by both multi-theistic "pagan" religion and Christianity.[130] Legend has it that the sign and words that the officer inscribed on his stomach—"Hoc Signo ✝ Victor Eris" [By this sign you will conquer]—came to Constantine in a vision before battle, inspiring his conversion to Christianity.[131] The emperor adopted the powerful apotropaic sign as his army's talisman, creating a monogram of the name of Christ and the cross to mark all battle gear, and supposedly wore the symbol on his right arm.[132] Proud of his own military exploits in the name of Catholic France, the officer described by Tonti likely saw an appealing motto that referenced not only his own potential prowess on the battlefield but also his Christian identity and a crusader-like vision of his purpose in New France.

The French appropriation of Amerindian tattooing methods for the marking of signs drawn from European tradition must have been quite widespread, as narratives attest to a variety of tattoo designs that included both typical Amerindian motifs of animals and plants and figures inspired by Christian iconography, like the virgin and child emblazoned on the skin of Tonti's Louisiana officer.[133] Dièreville confirms that "they make all kinds of figures, crosses, names of Jesus, flowers; really anything that you want," underlining the flexibility of the medium and its allowance for custom-made designs.[134] Kalm's list of tattoo designs also includes Amerindian, Christian, and customized iconography: "The designs they paint are made up of stripes, or they represent the sun, our Crucified Saviour, or something else which their fancy may dictate."[135] Given the prevalence of Holy Land tattoos among European colonists in the period, it is likely that the French inhabitants of New France quite consciously imitated these well-known insignia to honor their European Christian roots, while also incorporating designs that more closely corresponded to their everyday life in North America. Indeed, historian Craig Koslofsky's ongoing research on tattoos worn by runaway servants in North America shows that the use of Jerusalem tattoos by non-pilgrims was widespread, even among the lower classes.[136] For them, the juxtaposition of cultural references they created upon their skin did not clash but accurately represented their identities and lived experience as French inhabitants of Canada and Louisiana, a recasting of their inherited blazons through the inscription of their flesh.

Ambivalence characterized written and artistic accounts of the Amerindian tattoo in early modern Europe. For the French in particular, who espoused an assimilationist model in which the foreign was to find integration into Frenchness, the tattoo became a powerful symbol of identity both affirmed and threatened, mapping upon the surface of the body the tensions and contradictions of the colonial encounter. From the first American voyages forward, painting and pricking of the skin became for the French a key characteristic identifying Amerindians as other and signaling their difference. Vivid narrative descriptions and artistic renderings fed an imaginary of the New World "savage" physically marked as inferior. At the same time, numerous early ethnographers and missionaries saw in Amerindian tattoos, rather than a mark of primitivism, a sophisticated sign system that they sought to decode in order to better understand, and hence convert and control, the native inhabitants of the new French colonies. In envisioning the Amerindian tattoo as a sign of distinction communicating identity, belonging, and social status, like the coats of arms and honorary insignia worn on the European body, these early ethnographers invested the tattoo with meaning. They therein made legible for their European audience a system of identification and distinction regularly appropriated by the soldiers and traders who lived among the Amerindians in New France for their personal safety as well as economic and military gain.

Ironically, under the pens, brushes, and burins of French writers and artists, the tattoo, for all its presumed importance as a sign of difference, became a mark that identified Amerindians' common heritage with the French. Comparison of Amerindian rites with those of the ancient Gauls performed a dual function: it both asserted the superiority of the now civilized French and justified France's claim to the territories of New France; if the Amerindians were already Gauls, then the French empire in North America was no less than natural. At the same time, this mythology of common ancestry and discourse of similarity between the peoples of the Old World and the New threatened the clear-cut distinctions and definitions of cultural identity that the French hoped to maintain even as they espoused an assimilationist approach to empire. As the success of their colonies grew, they faced the impossible bind characteristic of the colonial encounter, wherein the colonizer who would seek to conquer and convert is inevitably altered by the colonized. French colonists who engaged in tattooing not only signaled the porous and mutually transformative nature of the cultural exchange taking place on American soil—the sign of the other literally penetrating their skin—but expressed new composite identities formed of both Amerindian and European elements. As the primordial site of intimate exchange, the skin became the surface upon which the story of cultural interaction and influence was written in New France.

Notes

1 The idea that tattooing was imported to Europe from Polynesia in the eighteenth century has known remarkable endurance, despite overwhelming evidence to the contrary. Anna Felicity Friedman has catalogued and debunked the "Cook myth;" https://tattoohistorian.com/2014/04/05/the-cook-myth-common-tattoo-history-debunked and *Tattooed Transculturites: Western Expatriates Among Amerindian and Pacific Islander Societies, 1500–1900* (PhD diss., University of Chicago, 2012). Since the 1970s, authors of both popular and scholarly tattoo histories have testified to the practice of tattooing in Europe prior to the eighteenth century, including C. Bruno, *Tatoués, qui êtes vous . . . ?* (Brussels: Éditions de Feynerolles, 1970), Ronald W.B. Scutt and Christopher Gotch, *Skin Deep: The Mystery of Tattooing* (London: P. Davies, 1974), William Caruchet, *Tatouages et tatoués* (Paris: Tchou, 1976), Stephan Oettermann, *Zeichen auf der Haut. Die Geschichte der Tätowierung in Europa* (Frankfurt am Main: Syndikat, 1979), Philippe Dubé, *Tattoo-tatoué. Histoire, techniques, motifs du tatouage en Amérique française, de la colonisation à nos jours* (Montréal: Jean Basile, 1980), Jérôme Pierrat and Éric Guillon, *Les hommes illustrés. Le tatouage des origines à nos jours* (Clichy: Larivière, 2000), Kathlyn Gay and Christine Whittington, *Body Marks: Tattooing, Piercing, and Scarification* (Hong Kong: The Millbrook Press, 2002), David Le Breton, ch. 2, "Les marques corporelles dans les sociétés occidentales: histoire d'un malentendu," 23–62 in *Signes d'identité. Tatouages, piercings et autres marques corporelles* (Paris: Métailié, 2002), and Juliet Fleming, "The Renaissance Tattoo," in *Written on the Body: The Tattoo in European and American History*, ed. Jane Caplan (Princeton, NJ: Princeton University Press, 2000), 61–82, that first appeared in *Res: Anthropology and Aesthetics* 31 (1997): 34–52 and also appears in Fleming's *Graffiti and the Writing Arts of Early Modern England* (Philadelphia, PA: University of Pennsylvania Press, 2001), 79–112. All references here are to the Caplan edition.

2 Bougainville's account appeared as the *Voyage autour du monde, par la frégate du Roi La Boudeuse, et la flûte L'Étoile; en 1766, 1767, 1768 & 1769* (Paris: Saillant & Nyon, 1771). The official account of Cook's voyages was drawn from Cook's and his fellow captains' journals by John Hawkesworth, *An Account of the Voyages Undertaken by the Order of Present Majesty for Making Discoveries in the Southern Hemisphere*, 3 vols. (London: A. Strahan and T. Cadell, 1773). Cook's first voyage was published in French translation as *Relation d'un voyage fait autour du monde, Dans les années 1769, 1770 & 1771* (Paris: Nyon & Merigot, 1772–1776).

3 Bougainville, *Voyage*, 393. See 215–16 for his discussion of the Tahitian "custom of pricking the skin." The ancestor of the modern English "tattoo," *tattow* first appeared in Cook's 1769 manuscript, apparently derived from the Polynesian word *tatau* meaning "to hit;" "Tattoo, n.2," *Oxford English Dictionary*, 2nd ed., 1989; online version June 2012, accessed July 28, 2012, www.oed.com/view/Entry/198122.

4 Qtd. in Ernest Berchon, *Discours sur les origines et le but du tatouage* (Bordeaux: G. Gounouilhou, 1886), 5 and "Tatouer," Émile Littré, *Dictionnaire de la langue française*, 2nd ed. (Paris: Hachette, 1872–1877).

5 I reproduce here offensive terms such as "sauvages" because they were used in the period by Europeans to describe the native people they encountered across the Atlantic. For my own purposes, following First Nation historian Olive Patricia Dickason, I have chosen to use the term "Amerindian," widely accepted in French, when describing generally the native peoples of the Americas because of its geographical specificity, despite the term "Indian"

having its source in a case of mistaken identity. See Dickason's discussion of the pros and cons of various terms in Dickason and David T. McNab, *Canada's First Nations: A History of Founding Peoples from Earliest Times*, 4th ed. (Oxford: Oxford University Press, 2008), xii–xiii. Amerindians were also said to *figurer* their bodies and to wear *figures*. Marc Lescarbot calls tattoos *ferrements*, emphasizing the meeting of metal and skin, in his *Histoire de la Nouvelle-France* (Paris: Jean Millot, 1609). All references here are to Marie-Christine Pioffet's edition of book VI, chapter X of Lescarbot's work, "Description des mœurs souriquoises comparées à celles d'autres peuples," in *Voyages en Acadie (1604–1607) suivis de La Description des mœurs souriquoises comparées à celles d'autres peuples* (Québec: Presses de l'Université Laval, 2007), in which the term appears on 319. Gabriel Sagard-Théodat uses the verb *matachier* and the noun *matachia* to refer to both painting and tattooing, and, in his dictionary of the Huron language, lists both as represented by a single Huron word, *ononsan*, meaning "Picoter, & matachier son corps;" *Le Grand voyage du pays des Hurons suivi du dictionnaire de la langue huronne* [1632], ed. Jack Warwick (Montréal: Presses de l'Université de Montréal, 1998), 395. Leclercq, Tonti, and De Pauw, among others, all follow Sagard in their use of the term *matachier*: Chrestien Leclercq, *Nouvelle Relation de la Gaspesie* (Paris: Amable Auroy, 1691), ed. Réal Ouellet (Montréal: Presses de l'Université de Montréal, 1999), 253; Henri de Tonti, *Relation de la Louisiane* (Amsterdam: Jean Frederic Bernard, 1720), 1–34; and Cornelius de Pauw, *Recherches philosophiques sur les Américains* (Berlin: G. J. Decker, 1768–1769), vol. 1, 202.

6 Bougainville, *Voyage*, 215.

7 "Tatouer," *Dictionnaire de l'Académie françoise*, 5th ed. (Paris: J. J. Smits, 1798), vol. 2, 634. See also "Tatoué, ée," and "Tatouage." It is only in the 6th edition (Paris: Firmin Didot Frères, 1835) that "Nouvelle-Zélande, etc." is added to the definition of *tatouer*; vol. 2, 818.

8 Many of the Jesuit relations are collected and presented with translations by Reuben Gold Thwaites, ed., *The Jesuit Relations and Allied Documents: Travels and Explorations of the Jesuit Missionaries in New France, 1610–1791*, 73 vols. (Cleveland: Burrows Brothers, 1896–1901) and Lucien Campeau, ed., *Monumenta Novae Franciae*, 9 vols. (Rome: Monumenta Historica Societatis Jesu, 1967-2003). For extensive treatment of the Jesuit relations, see Sara E. Melzer, *Colonizer or Colonized: The Hidden Stories of Early Modern French Culture* (Philadelphia, PA: University of Pennsylvania Press, 2012) and Micah True, *Masters and Students: Jesuit Mission Ethnography in Seventeenth-Century New France* (Montréal and Kingston: McGill-Queen's University Press, 2015).

9 I use the term "ethnography" here conscious of its anachronism. Mary B. Campbell has coined the term "coloniology" to acknowledge the important role these writings played in furthering colonial aspirations; "The Illustrated Travel Book and the Birth of Ethnography: Part I of De Bry's *America*," in *The Work of Dissimilitude: Essays from the Sixth Citadel Conference on Medieval and Renaissance Literature*, ed. David G. Allen and Robert A. White (Newark, DE: University of Delaware Press, 1992), 177–95; 181.

10 Gorden M. Sayre, *Les Sauvages Américains: Representations of Native Americans in French and English Colonial Literature* (Chapel Hill and London: The University of North Carolina Press, 1997), 3 and 7. On the French assimilationist approach, see: Melzer, *Colonizer or Colonized*, "L'Histoire oubliée de la colonisation française: Universaliser la francité," *Dalhousie French Studies* 65 (Winter 2003): 33–44, "The Underside of France's Civilizing Mission:

Assimilationist Politics in 'New France'," *Biblio 17* 131 (2001): 151–64, "Une 'Seconde France'? Re-penser le paradigme 'classique' à partir de l'histoire oubliée de la colonisation française," in *La littérature, le XVIIe siècle et nous: dialogue transatlantique,* ed. Hélène Merlin-Kajman (Paris: Presses Sorbonne Nouvelle, 2008), 75–85, and "'Voluntary Subjection': France's Theory of Colonization/Culture in the Seventeenth Century," in *Structures of Feeling in Seventeenth-Century Cultural Expression,* 2nd ed., ed. Susan McClary, (Toronto, University of Toronto Press, 2013), 93–116; Cornelius J. Jaenen, *Friend and Foe: Aspects of French-Amerindian Cultural Contact in the Sixteenth and Seventeenth Centuries* (Ontario: McClelland and Steward Limited, 1976) and "Problems of Assimilation in New France, 1603–1645," *French Historical Studies* 4.3 (Spring 1966): 265–89; Gilles Harvard, *Empire et métissages: Indiens et Français dans le Pays d'en Haut, 1660–1715* (Sillery, QC: Les éditions du Septentrion, 2003); Brian Brazeau, *Writing a New France, 1604–1632: Empire and Early Modern French Identity* (Farnam, UK and Burlington, VT: Ashgate, 2009); and True, *Masters and Students.*

11 Sagard, *Le Grand voyage du pays des Hurons* [1632]; Lescarbot, *Histoire de la Nouvelle-France* [1609]; and Joseph-François Lafitau, *Mœurs des sauvages amériquains comparées aux mœurs des premiers temps,* 2 vols. (Paris: Saugrain l'aîné and Charles Estienne Hochereau, 1724).

12 Colbert to Talon, April 5, 1666, and April 5, 1667, *Rapport de l'Archiviste de la Province de Québec,* 45, 72. Qtd. in Melzer, *Colonizer or Colonized,* 12; Melzer's translation.

13 See, for example, Jacques Cartier, *Première relation* [1534], in *Relations,* ed. Michel Bideaux (Montréal: Presses de l'Université de Montréal, 1986), 101. On Cartier's encounters with Amerindians, see François-Marc Gagnon and Denise Petel, *Hommes effarables et bestes sauvaiges. Images du Nouveau-Monde d'après les voyages de Jacques Cartier* (Montreal: Boréal, 1986), esp. ch. 3, "Les hommes sauvaiges." For further examination of early European reactions to Amerindian body painting, see François-Marc Gagnon, "'Ils se peignent le visage . . .': Réaction européenne à un usage indien au XVIe et au début du XVIIe siècles," *Revue d'histoire de l'Amérique française* 30.3 (1976): 363–81.

14 See Paul Le Jeune, *Brieve relation du voyage de la Nouvelle France* (Paris: Sébastien Cramoisy, 1632), 16–17, in *Jesuit Relations,* ed. and trans. Thwaites, vol. 5, 22 and 23, and Lescarbot, *Description des mœurs,* 318–19.

15 Sagard, *Le Grand voyage,* 228–29. Writers often use the same terms indiscriminately to discuss both body painting and more permanent body marking together, though most differentiate tattooing for its permanence and the pain caused by the pricking process.

16 Gabriel Sagard-Théodat, *Histoire du Canada* (Paris: Claude Sonnius, 1636), 374. This is a revision and expansion of Sagard's earlier 1624 description in his *Grand voyage,* 228–29.

17 Sagard, *Histoire du Canada,* 373–74.

18 Sagard, *Grand voyage,* 229.

19 Numerous writers admire the apparent Amerindian tolerance for pain. See, for example, René Laudonnière, *L'Histoire Notable de la Floride* (Paris: Guillaume Auvray, 1586), 4.

20 Sagard, *Grand Voyage,* 395.

21 Dumont de Montigny, *Mémoires historiques,* vol. 1, 139–40. On permanence, pain, and the dangers of tattooing, see also: Laudonnière, *L'Histoire Notable,* 4; Francesco Gioseppe Bressani, *Breve relatione d'aucune missioni de PP. della Compagnia di Giesù nella Nuova Francia* (Macerata: Agosino Grisel, 1653),

rpt. in original Italian and trans. in *Jesuit Relations*, ed. Thwaites, vol. 38, 251 and 253; Lafitau, *Mœurs des sauvages amériquains*, vol. 2, 38–39; and Dière de Dièreville, *Relation du Voyage du Port Royal de l'Acadie* (Rouen: Jean-Baptiste Besongne, 1708), 175–76.

22 Sagard, *Grand voyage*, 395.

23 Lescarbot, *Description des mœurs*, 320. His source for Brazilian practices is Jean de Léry (1534–1611), *Histoire d'un voyage fait en la terre du Bresil* (La Rochelle: Antoine Chuppin, 1578). See Pioffet on Lescarbot's admiration for and reliance on Léry's work, *Voyages en Acadie*, 43–45. Thomas Harriot's *A Briefe and True Report of the New Found Land of Virginia* (London: R. Robinson, 1585) and Theodor De Bry's first two *America* volumes (1590 and 1591), cited and discussed below, were his sources for Florida and Virginia.

24 De Bry's *America* volumes parts I and II were published in Frankfurt in 1590 and 1591 respectively. The first reproduced Harriot's narrative, *A Briefe and True Report of the New Found Land of Virginia*, adding engravings made from the drawings by the expedition's artist John White, *Admiranda narratio, fida tamen, de commodis et incolorum ritibus Virginiae* (Frankfurt: Johann Wechel, 1590). The second contained relations by René de Laudonnière and his artist, Jacques Le Moyne de Morgues, of their expedition in Florida, featuring engravings of the Timucua made from Le Moyne's watercolors, *Brevis narratio eorum quae in Florida Americae provicia Gallis acciderunt* (Frankfurt: Johann Wechel, 1591). For a modern reproduction of De Bry's work, see *Le Théâtre du Nouveau Monde. Les Grands Voyages de Théodore de Bry*, ed. Marc Bouyer and Jean-Paul Duviols (Paris: Gallimard, 1992). On artists White and Le Moyne de Morgues, see Paul Hulton, *The Work of Jacques Le Moyne de Morgues, a Huguenot Artist in France, Florida, and England*, 2 vols. (London: British Museum Publications, 1977), *A Briefe and True Report of the New Found Land of Virginia. The Complete 1590 Edition* (New York: Dover Publications, 1972), and *America 1585: The Complete Drawings of John White* (Chapel Hill: University of North Carolina Press and London: British Museum Publications, 1984).

25 On Laudonnière's efforts to establish a Protestant colony in Florida, see D.B. Quinn, "The Attempted Colonization of Florida by the French, 1562–1565" in Hulton, *The Work of Jacques Le Moyne*, vol. 1, 17–44.

26 See plates 3–4, 6, 8, and 23 in De Bry's 1590 volume; rpt. in Thomas Harriot, *A Briefe and True Report of the New Found Land of Virginia. The Complete 1590 Edition with the 28 Engravings by Theodor de Bry After the Drawings of John White and Other Illustrations*, facsimile ed. Paul Hulton (New York: Dover Publications, 1972), 46–7, 49, 51, and 74. See plates 8, 11–12, 14, 16, 18, 32, and 34–35 in De Bry's 1591 volume, rpt. in Hulton, *The Work of Jacques Le Moyne*, vol. 2, plates 100, 103–4, 106, 108, 110, 124, and 126–27.

27 Le Moyne de Morgues, *Brevis narratio* (1591), trans. from the Latin by Hulton, *The Work of Jacques Le Moyne*, vol. 1, 151. Le Moyne's account appears in part II of De Bry's *America*, 6–30, rpt. and trans. in Hulton (Latin text, vol. 1, 89–113, trans., vol. 1, 119–38), as does his commentary on each plate (De Bry, *America* part II, plates 1–42; rpt. in Hulton, vol. 2, plates 93–134).

28 Examples include plates 11, 12, 16, 32, and 35 in De Bry, *America*, part II, rpt. in Hulton, *The Work of Jacques Le Moyne*, vol. 2, plates 103, 104, 108, 124, and 127.

29 Juliet Fleming has convincingly argued that Le Moyne playfully juxtaposes the figures of the Timucua chief and the Frenchmen in his watercolor

renderings to show their resemblance; "The Renaissance Tattoo," 71–72. See details of Le Moyne's suggestive renderings of corporeal decoration, plates 32 and 35 of De Bry's *America*, part II, rpt. in Fleming, 72, or rpt. in full in Hulton, *The Work of Jacques Le Moyne*, vol. 2, plates 124 and 127.

30 The identity of the artist is unknown and their placement in the work bears little relationship to passages in the text itself, suggesting that they were created independently.

31 François-Marc Gagnon, *Premiers peintres de la Nouvelle-France*, 2 vols. (Québec: Ministère des affaires culturelles, 1976), vol. 2, 63.

32 François Du Creux, *Historia Canadensis* (Paris: Sébastien Cramoisy, 1664); English edition: *The History of Canada or New France*, 2 vols., ed. James B. Conacher and trans. Percy J. Robinson (Toronto: The Champlain Society, 1951). On the engravings produced by Du Creux and other Jesuit sources, see Gagnon, *Premiers peintres*, vol. 2, 57–91.

33 See also Du Creux, *Historia Canadensis*, plate 4, facing page 70; rpt. in Gagnon, *Premiers peintres*, vol. 2, 34, plate 34. De Bry similarly Europeanizes the Amerindians portrayed in Le Moyne de Morgues and White's watercolor portraits. Joel Konrad reads such Europeanization of both bodies and customs as an effort to lessen the fear of the Amerindian other among potential colonists; Joel Konrad, "'Barbarous Gallants': Fashion, Morality, and the Marked Body in English Culture, 1590–1660," *Fashion Theory* 15.1 (2011): 29–48; 33–36.

34 Gagnon originally followed the text's first editor, Marc de Villiers, in attributing the drawings to Charles Bécart de Granville, who lived in Québec from 1675 to 1703, but corrected this attribution in his *The Codex Canadensis and the Writings of Louis Nicolas. The Natural History of the New World, Histoire naturelle des Indes occidentales* (McGill Queens University Press, 2011). The original manuscript is held by the Gilcrease Museum in Tulsa, OK.

35 *Codex Canadensis*, 7. For further visual examples, see Gagnon, *Premiers peintres*, vol. 2, 88–93 and his *The Codex Canadensis and the Writings of Louis Nicolas*. The *Codex Canadenis* is also available for view in full through the Library and Archives Canada at www.collectionscanada.gc.ca/codex/index-e.html, accessed June 15, 2017.

36 Gagnon makes this argument, providing a full set of comparisons: *Premiers peintres*, vol. 2, 63–65, plates on 78–85 and 88–89. See also his *The Codex Canadensis and the Writings of Louis Nicolas* and Dubé, *Tattoo-tatoué*, 27–30.

37 See also Du Creux, *Historiæ Canadensis*, plate 4, facing 70 and *Codex Canadiensis*, 6, rpt. in Gagnon, *Premiers peintres*, vol. 2, 84–85, plates 30 and 31.

38 Gagnon, "'Ils se peignent le visage . . .'," 366–67. Dickason suggests instead that it was one of Jehan Ango's captains, Thomas Aubert, who brought them to France; *The Myth of the Savage and the Beginnings of French Colonialism in the Americas* (Alberta: The University of Alberta Press, 1984), 209.

39 They had all died in France from sickness by the time Cartier undertook his third voyage, with the exception of one young girl, Donaconna's niece, whose fate is unknown; Daniel K. Richter, *Facing East from Indian Country: A Native History of Early America* (Cambridge, MA: Harvard University Press, [2001] 2003), 28–33.

40 Michael Wintroub, *A Savage Mirror: Power, Identity, and Knowledge in Early Modern France* (Stanford, CA: Stanford University Press, 2006).

41 See *L'entrée de Henri II à Rouen, 1550: A Facsimile with an Introduction by Margaret M. McGowan* (Amsterdam: Theatrum Orbis Terrum and New York: Johnson Reprint Corp., 1970), ed. Jean Ferdinand Denis, *Une fête brésilienne célébrée à Rouen en 1550* (Paris: J. Techener, 1850), Dickason, *Myth of the Savage*, 212–13, and Wintroub, *A Savage Mirror*.

42 A news report from Paris dated March 23, 1668, relates that the King had gone to Versailles to "se divertir" with several boats, including Iroquois in their canoes; Dickason, *Myth of the Savage*, 212. The French also experimented with the importation of Iroquois as slave labor in 1687, as reported in the November 1687 issue of the *Mercure Galant*; ibid., 222–23.

43 Dièreville, *Relation du Voyage*, 176.

44 For the colony's history from the French arrival in 1594, see Alfred Métraux and Jacques Lafaye, "Introduction" to the facsimile edition of Claude d'Abbeville, *Histoire de la Mission des Pères Capucins en l'Isle de Maragnan* ([Paris: François Huby, 1614] Austria: Akademische Druck- und Verlagsanstalt Graz, 1963).

45 Métraux and Lafaye, "Introduction," iv–vi.

46 Melzer, "France's Colonial History: From *Sauvages* into Civilized French Catholics," in *Colonizer or Colonized*, 91–121. See additional sources on the French assimilationist approach cited above. On Abbeville's work in Brazil, see also Laura Fishman, "Claude d'Abbeville and the Tupinamba: Problems and Goals of French Missionary Work in Early Seventeenth-Century Brazil," *Church History* 58.1 (March 1989): 20–35.

47 Abbeville, *Histoire de la Mission*, fols. 339v-340r.

48 Ibid., fol. 340r.

49 Abbeville's 1614 text was eagerly awaited as the sequel to his 1613 *L'arrivée des Pères Capucins en l'Inde Nouvelle appelée Maragnon*, published in Lyon and Paris, as well as in German and Italian translation the same year; Métraux and Lafaye, "Introduction," xliii. Following its publication, Marie de Médecis did allow more Capuchin missionaries to leave for the colony, but she provided Rasilly with less than a third of the financial support he had requested; ibid., vii.

50 Abbeville, *Histoire de la Mission*, fol. 272v.

51 Ibid., fol. 348v.

52 Ibid., fols. 348r and 348v.

53 Ibid., fol. 272v. For analysis of the redressing of Native Americans as French, see Melzer, *Colonizer or Colonized*, 91–121.

54 Ibid., fol. 347v. On the origin of his baptismal name, see fol. 352r.

55 On baptism as inscribing a mark, see the Introduction and Chapter 1.

56 Abbeville, *Histoire de la Mission*, fols. 348v and 349r. See Melzer, "Voluntary Subjection," on the French vision of conversion. Abbeville follows here the contemporary theorization of the baptismal mark as a sign of belonging. His substitution of one corporeal mark for another resembles the devil's replacement of God's mark of baptism with his mark (or vice versa) as a sign of possession. See the Introduction and Chapter 1.

57 Sayre, *Les Sauvages Américains*, 165.

58 Gagnon, "'Ils se peignent le visage . . .'," 367.

59 Abbeville, *Histoire de la Mission*, fol. 272v.

60 Ibid., fol. 348v. John Bulwer (1606–1656) similarly highlights in prose and engravings the resemblances between English styles of the day and the decorated bodies of Amerindians in his *Anthropometamorphosis* (London: William Hunt, 1653), 287, 537, 541, 535. For discussion, see the Conclusion. On the relationship between early modern English fashion and writing about the

foreign body, see Konrad, "'Barbarous Gallants.'" See also Fleming's reading of De Bry's engravings as highlighting resemblances between European clothing and Amerindian tattooing; "The Renaissance Tattoo," 71–72.

61 Sagard, *Histoire du Canada*, 373.

62 Lafitau, *Mœurs des sauvages amériquains*, vol. 2, 43. For further accounts of Amerindian tattooing processes, see: Lescarbot, *Description des mœurs*, 319; Abbeville, *Histoire de la Mission*, fol. 272v; Paul Le Jeune, *Relation de ce qui s'est passé en La Nouvelle-France* [1634], in *Monumenta Novae Franciae*, ed. Campeau, vol. 2, 531–740; 639—I thank Micah True for alerting me to this passage from Le Jeune's written *Relation* that was omitted from both the original published *Relation* and the Thwaites edition but is included in the Campeau edition; Henri Joutel, *Relation de Henri Joutel* [1687, first pub. 1713], in *Mémoires et Documents pour servir à l'histoire des origines françaises des pays d'outre-mer. Découvertes et Etablissements des Français dans l'Ouest et dans le Sud de l'Amérique Septentrionale (1614–1754)*, ed. Pierre Margry, 6 vols. (Paris: Maisonneuve et Cie, 1879–1888), vol. 3, 349; Dièreville, *Relation du Voyage*, 175–76; Pehr Kalm (1716–1779), *Peter Kalm's Travels in North America. The English Version of 1770*, ed. Adolph B. Benson, 2 vols. (New York: Dover Publications, 1964), vol. 2, 578; Claude-Charles Le Roy Bacqueville de La Potherie (1663–1736), *Histoire de l'Amerique septentrionale* (Paris: Jean-Luc Nion and François Didot, 1722 [written in 1702]), vol. 3, 43; Joseph-Charles Bonnefons, *Voyage au Canada fait depuis l'an 1751 jusqu'en l'an 1761*, ed. Claude Manceron (Paris: Aubier Montaigne, 1978), 168–69; Jean-François Benjamin Dumont de Montigny (1696–after 1753), *Mémoires historiques* (Paris: J. B. Bauche, 1753), vol. 1, 139–40; Dumont de Montigny, *Regards sur le monde atlantique, 1715–1747*, ed. Carla Zecher, Gordon M. Sayre, and Shannon Lee Dawdy (Sillery, Québec: Septentrion, 2008), 367–68, trans. as Jean-François-Benjamin Dumont de Montigny, *The Memoir of Lieutenant Dumont, 1715–1747: A Sojourner in the French Atlantic*, ed. Gordon M. Sayre and Carla Zecher, trans. Gordon M. Sayre (Chapel Hill, NC: University of North Carolina Press for the Omohundro Institute of Early American History and Culture, 2012), 348.

63 On engraving's role in early ethnography and De Bry's engraving examined below see Michael Gaudio, "Savage Marks: The Scriptive Techniques of Early Modern Ethnography" in his *Engraving the Savage: The New World and Techniques of Civilization* (Minneapolis: University of Minnesota Press, 2008), 1–43.

64 On signs meant for identification on clothing and commodities, see the Introduction and Chapters 4 and 5.

65 Harriot, *A Briefe and True Report*, ed. Hulton, plate 23, 74.

66 No watercolor of this engraving by White has survived, suggesting that this plate was of De Bry's own invention, perhaps with White's or Harriot's counsel.

67 Mairin Odle, conference presentation, "Pownced, Pricked, or Paynted: Tattooing and Indigenous Literacies," American Comparative Literature Association, Harvard University, March 20, 2016. Gaudio argues that De Bry's decoding of the tattoo constitutes its translation to a European alphabetic system and examines the implications of this move in "Savage Marks."

68 Lescarbot, *Description des mœurs*, 320. For similar comparisons regarding the criminal brand, see Chapter 5.

69 Lafitau, *Mœurs des sauvages amériquains*, vol. 2, 43.

70 Ibid. and 44. On this desire to render Amerindian markings alphabetic as evidenced in the earlier De Bry-Harriot text, see Gaudio, "Savage Marks" and Odle, "Powned, Pricked, or Paynted."

71 Lafitau, "Explication des planches et figures," *Mœurs des sauvages amériquains*, vol. 2, n. pag.

72 Lafitau, *Mœurs des sauvages amériquains*, vol. 2, 45.

73 Dumont de Montigny, *Mémoires historiques*, vol. 1, 185.

74 Abbeville, *Histoire de la mission*, fol. 272v.

75 Ibid., fols. 348r-348v.

76 Sayre, *Sauvages Américains*, 175. See also Arnaud Balvay, "Tattooing and Its Role in French-Native American Relations," *French Colonial History* 9 (2008): 1–14, esp. 2–3.

77 Tonti, *Relation de la Louisianne*, 13. For Dumont de Montigny, the Amerindian tattoo "is not only an ornament . . . , but more so a mark of honor and distinction that is only earned after several courageous acts;" Dumont de Montigny, *Mémoires historiques*, vol. 1, 139–40.

78 Bernard Bossu, *Nouveaux Voyages aux Indes Occidentales*, 2nd ed. (Paris: Le Jay, 1768), 187 and 188; Seymour Feiler ed. and trans., *Jean-Bernard Bossu's Travels in the Interior of North America, 1751–1762* (Norman, OK: University of Oklahoma Press, 1962), 95.

79 Bossu, *Nouveaux Voyages*, 191. My translation.

80 Ibid., 189–90; Feiler's translation, *Jean-Bernard Bossu's Travels*, 95–96. Bossu recounts that he saved the man from torture by using "French medicine" to remove the tattoo, sedating him with opium and applying cantharides, a topical skin irritant made from blister beetles, to the design; Bossu, *Nouveaux Voyages*, 190–91.

81 Ibid., 191–92.

82 Lescarbot, *Description des mœurs*, 317–18. On Celtic tattooing, see Charles W. MacQuarrie, "Insular Celtic Tattooing: History, Myth and Metaphor," in *Written on the Body*, ed. Caplan, 32–45. Pierrat and Guillon affirm that the Picts themselves first inhabited present-day French soil, occupying the north of Aquitaine before migrating over the channel in 400 BCE; *Les Hommes illustrés*, 18–19. On the Picts, their provocative portrayal by White and Le Moyne de Morgues, and their treatment in English sources, see Fleming, "The Renaissance Tattoo," 68–78. On the Pictones, see Venceslas Kruta, *Les Celtes. Histoire et dictionnaire. Des origines à la romanisation et au Christianisme* (Paris: Robert Laffont, 2000), 776.

83 Lescarbot, *Description des mœurs*, 318. Lescarbot cites Caesar, Herodianus, Tertullien, and Isidore of Seville; *Description des mœurs*, 317–19. The 787 AD Council of Calcuth, which condemned tattooing as pagan, also cited the Pict custom. For more on Caesar's account, see MacQuarrie, "Insular Celtic Tattooing."

84 Here I allude to a well-known catch phrase from France's national mythology about its historical resistance to Roman rule, "our ancestors the Gauls." Lescarbot, *Description des mœurs*, 319.

85 Ibid., 318. Englishman Bulwer's nearly identical description of the Picts and Pictons does not insist on their having been Gauls; *Anthropometamorphosis*, 464–66. Lescarbot, however, makes a point of underlining this French identity.

86 Lescarbot, *Description des mœurs*, 318.

87 Ibid., 321.

88 Ibid., 319. Hulton's facsimile edition includes reproductions of the five engravings; Harriot, *A Briefe and True Report*, 76–85.

89 De Bry in Harriot, *A Briefe and True Report*, ed. Hulton, 75. Hulton argues that the original Pict images were not by White as is usually asserted but by Le

Moyne de Morgues, since the third plate of the Picts portraying "A Young Daughter of the Picts," matches a ca. 1585–86 watercolor known to be his, currently held by the Yale Center for British Art; ibid., xii. The younger White, who likely exchanged work and ideas with Le Moyne in England, probably brought Le Moyne's drawings to De Bry.

90 See the originals that appear here as Figures 3.12 and 3.2, the latter of which has been reversed and slightly altered in the plate for Lafitau's text, for comparison. The original engravings figure in Harriot, *A Briefe and True Report*, as plate 1, Hulton edition, 77 and Du Creux, *Historia Canadensis*, facing 70, plate 1.

91 Lafitau, *Mœurs des sauvages amériquains*, vol. 2, plate 3, facing page 43 and "Explication des planches et figures," Planche III, n. pag. Like Lescarbot, Lafitau cites numerous references to the Picts; *Mœurs des sauvages amériquains*, vol. 2, 39–43. Many other early eighteenth-century accounts make this parallel with the Picts. See, for example, Pierre François Xavier Charlevoix, *Histoire et description générale de la Nouvelle France* [1722], 3 vols. (Paris: Nyon fils, 1744), vol. 3, 327, Dumont de Montigny, *Mémoires historiques*, vol. 1, 139, and Bougainville, *Voyage autour du monde*, 215–16.

92 On the "premier temps" approach as a justification of France's colonial rights, see Sayre, *Sauvages Américains*, 129–35.

93 See Chapter 4 on European pilgrim tattooing. See also Fleming, "The Renaissance Tattoo" and Mordechay Lewy, "Jerusalem unter der Haut. Zur Geschichte der Jerusalemer Pilgertätowierung," trans. Esther Kontarsky, *Zeitschrift für Religions und Geistesgeschichte* 55.1 (2003): 1–39, first published in Hebrew under the English title "Towards a History of Jerusalem Tattoo Marks among Western Pilgrims," *Cathedra* 95 (2000): 37–66.

94 Sagard, *Grand voyage*, 229. See also Sagard, *Histoire du Canada*, 374.

95 Joseph Jouvency, *De regione et moribus Canadensium seu barbarorum Novae Franciae*, part of his *Canadicae missionis relatio ab anno 1611 usque ad annum 1613, cum statu eiusdem missionis annis 1703 et 1710* (Rome: Georgii Plachi, 1710); rpt. and trans. in Thwaites, *Jesuit Relations*, vol. 1, trans. 279, original Latin 278.

96 See also Sayre, *Sauvages Américains*, 159–60 and Gagnon, "'Ils se peignent le visage . . .'," 370–73.

97 French missionaries regularly sent Amerindian children to France to be educated, some of whom never returned home and were adopted by French families. Intermarriage was also actively encouraged, though carefully monitored, in New France. See Melzer, *Colonizer or Colonized* and Dickason, *The Myth of the Savage*, 217–21.

98 For wider analysis of European expatriates' experiences of tattooing, see Friedman, *Tattooed Transculturites*.

99 Dièreville, *Relation du Voyage*, 175. He nonetheless subjects himself to the needle in verse by writing a poem about tattooing in the first person, 176.

100 On the *coureurs de bois* see Harvard, *Empire et métissages* and Philippe Jacquin, *Les Indiens Blancs. Français et Indiens en Amérique du Nord (XVIe-XVIIIe siècle)* (Paris: Payot, 1987). On the fur trader's corporeal transformation, see Gilles Harvard, "Virilité et 'ensauvagement': Le corps du coureur de bois (XVIIe et XVIIIe s.)," *Clio: Histoire, femmes, société* 27 (2008), entitled *Amériques métisses*, 57–74.

101 Tonti, *Relation de la Louisianne*, 13–14.

102 Antoine Furetière lists "errance" as a key characteristic of the "sauvage" in his *Dictionnaire universel*, 3 vols. (La Haye and Rotterdam: Arnout & Reinier Leers, 1690). Jesuit and Recollet missionaries often cite Amerindians' propensity for nomadism—though many nations were, in fact, at least partially

sedentary—as the prime difficulty they face in "civilizing" the native North American population. See, for example, Sagard, *Histoire du Canada*, 169–70 and Le Jeune, *Relation* [1634], ed. Campeau, vol. 2, 559–61.

103 Sagard, *Histoire du Canada*, 170.

104 On the problem of French "ensauvagement" as a consequence of France's assimilationist policies, see Melzer, *Colonizer or Colonized*, 115–18.

105 Qtd. in Harvard, *Empire et métissages*, 543.

106 Dubé, *Tatou-Tatoué*, 40, n. 21.

107 See also ibid., 41.

108 La Potherie, *Histoire de l'Amerique septentrionale*, 43. My emphasis.

109 Joutel in Margry, *Mémoires et Documents*, vol. 3, 349 and 353.

110 Ibid., 356.

111 Louis-Joseph de Saint-Véran de Montcalm, *Journal du Marquis de Montcalm*, vol. 7 of *Collection des manuscrits du maréchal de Lévis*, 12 vols., ed. Henri-Raymond Casgrain (Montréal: C.O. Beauchemin & fils, 1895), 466.

112 Kalm, *Peter Kalm's Travels*, vol. 2, 577–78.

113 On tattooing as the mark of a point of no return in the process of cultural integration, see Stephen Greenblatt's treatment of the story of Bernal Díaz del Castillo in *Renaissance Self-Fashioning: From More to Shakespeare* (Chicago and London: The University of Chicago Press, 1980), 184 and *Marvelous Possessions: The Wonder of the New World* (Oxford: Clarendon Press, 1992), 140–41. See also Sayre, *Les Sauvages Américains*, 166–67 and 171.

114 Balvay, "Tattooing and Its Role," 7.

115 Montcalm, *Journal*, 466.

116 See also Dubé, *Tattoo-tatoué*, 40.

117 Bonnefons, *Voyage au Canada*, 169.

118 See also Balvay, "Tattooing and Its Role," esp. 7–11 and Harvard, who argues that tattooing appeals to French soldiers "by magnifying the military *ethos,*" allowing them to gain prestige; *Empire et métissages*, 604. Emphasis in original.

119 See Chapter 4 for discussion of the Holy Land tattoo as a sign ensuring safe passage.

120 On Bossu's story, see also Balvay, "Tattooing and Its Role," 7–10 and Sayre, *Les Sauvages Américains*, 175–79.

121 Bossu's letter is dated November 6, 1751. Bossu, *Nouveaux Voyages*, 121–23; trans. Feiler, *Jean-Bernard Bossu's Travels*, 65–66. On the adoption of officers by Amerindian tribes see Balvay, "Tattooing and Its Role," 7.

122 Bossu, *Nouveaux Voyages*, 124; trans. Feiler, *Jean-Bernard Bossu's Travels*, 66.

123 Dumont de Montigny, *Regards sur le monde atlantique*, 367.

124 On Dumont de Montigny, see Sayre's introduction to both editions of his memoir and Gorden M. Sayre and Carla Zecher, "A French Soldier in Louisiana: The Memoir of Dumont de Montigny," *French Review* 80.6 (2007): 1265–77.

125 See Chapter 4 for a similar transcription of a chivalric medal onto pilgrim skin.

126 For Dumont's description of his tattoo's removal, see *Regards sur le monde atlantique*, 368–69 and *The Memoir of Lieutenant Dumont*, 348. Sayre believes that Bossu may have been satirizing Dumont de Montigny when he gave his own recipe for tattoo removal; *The Memoir of Lieutenant Dumont*, 348–49, n. 24 and personal communication with Sayre, June 28, 2011.

127 Balvay, "Tattooing and Its Role," 11.

128 Tonti, *Relation de la Louisianne*, 13–14. Balvay notes that Tonti may have been referring to Louisiana governor and New Orleans founder Jean-Baptiste

Lemoyne de Bienville (1680–1767), citing Jean-François Bertet de la Clue Sabran's travel journal: *A Voyage to Dauphin Island in 1720: The Journal of Bertet de la Clue*, ed. and trans. Francis Escoffier and Jay Higginbotham (Mobile, AL: Museum of the City of Mobile, 1974), 63–64; Balvay, "Tattooing and Its Role," 13–14, n. 38. Friedman makes the case that Tonti may be describing his own tattoos; *Tattooed Transculturites*, 115–22.

129 Harvard, *Empire et métissages*, 604.
130 Sayre points out the significance of the reference to Constantine, who "represents the transition from barbarism to Christianity." However, he sees the soldier as having undergone the opposite transition—from Christianity to barbarism—reading the juxtaposition of Christian and Amerindian symbols as rendering the whole "sacrilegious;" *Les Sauvages Américains*, 171.
131 Eusebius, *Vita Constantini* I. 27–28, qtd. and trans. in Charles Maston Odahl, *Constantine and the Christian Empire* (London and New York: Routledge, 2004), 105 and 98. See Odahl's discussion of Constantine's vision and its consequences, 105–6.
132 Pierre Massé, *De L'Imposture et Tromperie des diables* (Paris: Jean Poupy, 1579), fols. 45v-46r.
133 Charlevoix, *Histoire et description*, vol. 3, 328.
134 Dièreville, *Relation du Voyage*, 176.
135 Kalm, *Peter Kalm's Travels*, vol. 2, 577–78.
136 Craig Koslofsky, "A Deep Surface? Taking Stock of the History of Skin in Early American Studies" at the 23rd Annual Conference of the Omohundro Institute of Early American History and Culture, Ann Arbor, MI, June 15–18 2017 and "Tattooed Servants: The Jerusalem Arms in the Atlantic World" at the Renaissance Society of America Annual Conference, New Orleans, LA, March 22–24, 2018.

4   Jerusalem arms
The European pilgrim tattoo

At the very time Frenchmen were encountering the painted and tattooed bodies of Amerindians in the "New" Atlantic world, similar markings were already circulating back in the "Old" on the bodies of Europeans. As suggested by the references that seventeenth-century French colonizers and missionaries made to the "marks of Jerusalem" when they first described Amerindian tattoos to their readers back home, Holy Land pilgrims regularly got tattooed during their travels, and some even wrote about and replicated their tattoos in print.[1] While the number of pilgrims actually making the journey to Palestine in the sixteenth through eighteenth centuries was relatively small compared to its medieval heyday, pilgrimage undeniably remained an important form of travel in the early modern period, and the narratives Jerusalem pilgrims produced constituted a significant contribution to the travel literature of the period.[2] This copious literary production surrounding pilgrimage, as well as the intense debates regarding its religious value that characterized the Protestant Reformation and Catholic Counter-Reformation period, kept pilgrimage very much alive in the minds of the European reader.[3] Books by Western-going travelers lay side by side in booksellers' stands with those by Eastern-going pilgrims, forming, along with travel narratives of voyages to other distant lands, a vast corpus of popular, widely read literature.[4]

The voyage to the Holy Land—often referred to in the early modern period, along with the entire Middle East, as the "Levant," the place where the sun rises—required significant resources of time and money. Published testimonials to Levantine tattooing are necessarily, then, works authored by clergy, aristocrats, or successful bourgeois who were highly educated, had resources for travel, and could subsequently usher their narratives into print. Their written accounts of the pilgrim tattoo, coupled with surviving visual evidence, thus counter long-standing ideas about the history of the European tattoo as associated with sailors, soldiers, criminals, and members of the lower classes. It was in fact upon the bodies of members of the upper echelons of society—both Catholic and Protestant—that the tattoo circulated most prominently in early modern Europe.[5] Whether they knew someone who had gotten tattooed in the Holy Land or had only read about it, the Jerusalem tattoo was a familiar commodity for Europeans of this period, a legible and legitimate form of permanent body marking born by those Christians curious, brave, pious, or wealthy enough to have made the trip. While Holy Land pilgrims were by no means alone among their contemporaries in their experimentation with tattooing, their narrative and iconographic accounts provide unique glimpses into understanding the personal and public importance early moderns attributed to their tattoos within the spiritual and social hierarchies in which they moved.[6]

Sacred signs as souvenirs

From the late sixteenth century on, Holy Land pilgrims planned time into their travel itineraries to have themselves tattooed by Christian locals in Bethlehem or in Jerusalem at the site of the Church of the Holy Sepulcher.[7] A stop at the "tattoo parlor" was a standard halt on a pilgrim's travels, as Jean de Thévenot (1633–1665), the self-proclaimed world's most "perfect traveler," affirms in his popular 1665 *Relation d'un Voyage fait au Levant*.[8] "Getting marked" was something, he writes, that "all Pilgrims" did "ordinarily," much as they stopped at all the same monuments and shrines along the well-traced route they followed through the Holy Land.[9] It was an activity for leisure time, when other preoccupations lacked, as English chaplain Henry Maundrell (1665–1701), who traveled from Aleppo to Jerusalem for Easter in 1697, attests in his March 27 journal entry: "The next morning nothing extraordinary passed, which gave many of the pilgrims the leisure to have their arms marked with the usual ensigns of Jerusalem."[10] Thévenot provides a vivid account of the pilgrim experience of tattooing to which his party devotes a full day of their time in Bethlehem, highlighting it with its own distinct chapter heading, "On the manner in which to mark what one wants on one's arms":

> We took all of Tuesday April 29 to have our arms marked, as ordinarily all Pilgrims do, it is the Christians of Bethlehem following the Latin rite who do this. They have several wooden blocks, from which you choose the ones that please you the most, then they fill them with powdered charcoal, then they apply them to you, so that they leave the mark of what is engraved. After that with their left hand they hold your arm whose skin is stretched taut, and in their right hand they have a little cane where there are two needles, that they dip from time to time into ink mixed with ox bile, and prick you with it following the lines marked by the wood block. . . . This surely hurts, and ordinarily provokes a fever that lasts but a short time, and the arms stay swollen to about three times their normal size during two or three days. After they have pricked the whole length of all these lines, they wash the arm, and look to see if there is any error, and if so they start again, and sometimes they go back over it up to three times. When they are done, they wrap your arm very tightly, and a scab forms that falls off two or

three days later, and the marks remain blue, and never disappear, because the blood mixing with this pigment made of ink and ox bile still shows inside under the skin.[11]

The painful operation was not without its dangers, often causing fever and sometimes infection, as attested by Thévenot and several other pilgrim writers.[12]

The tattooing method Thévenot describes, though similar to those related by Europeans describing Amerindian practices, distinguishes itself by its inclusion of elements that bear the hallmark of print culture. Just as printers used carved woodblocks to reproduce images in early print texts, tattoo artists began their process by rubbing the raised figures of a block with charcoal and then printing the desired pattern onto the skin before pricking it with a needle and ink.[13] Not only materials but also language drawn from both print and writing characterizes descriptions of tattooing, as Maundrell's account in his highly popular and widely translated 1703 narrative illustrates:

> The artists who undertake the operation do it in this manner. They have *stamps in wood* of any figure you desire, which they first *print off* upon your arm with charcoal powder; then, taking two very fine needles tied close together, and dipping them often, *like a pen, in a certain ink . . .* they make small punctures with them all along the lines of the figure that they have *printed*, and then, washing the part in wine, conclude the work.[14]

Writers also likened tattooing to the arts of drawing and engraving, and compared the human skin to parchment or paper. Chaplain at the English embassy to the Great Mogul in India, Edward Terry (1590–1660) describes the famous English traveler Thomas Coryat's (ca. 1577–1617) Holy Land tattoos as looking "as if they had been drawn by some accurate Pencil upon Parchment."[15] Otto Friedrich von der Gröben (1657–1728), a native of Napratten who traveled to the Middle East at the age of seventeen, recounts a two-step tattooing process that echoes not only the gestures and vocabulary of print and writing but also those of early intaglio engraving in which holes were pricked along an image outline and ink rubbed into the indentations:[16]

> But first he washed the arm clean with wine, moistened the form a bit and sprinkled it with ground coals, after which *he pressed it* onto my arm, now that that had been done, he had tempered and prepared gun powder with vinegar in a glass jar, *almost like ink*, also two fine sewing needles stuck in a stick, which he dipped *like a quill* in the tempered powder, took my arm in one hand, and *stuck with the other [hand] prick by prick in the drawn figures*, so deep that blood followed every prick and a strongish pain was caused. Now that he had *completed a figure with several thousand pricks*, he washed my skin clean, and saw where it had not been pricked enough, which he then *improved with*

new pricks and pressed my arm afterward with his hands so that all the holes opened and the blood spritzed out as if out of a fire hose. Now that that was done, *he rubbed a copious amount of the tempered powder very forcefully into my arm, making it completely black as far down as the symbol went,* following which I had to wear a bandage on my arm for two days, after the two days had passed, he washed my arm clean with strong wine and began to tattoo the other design onto me, which he completed like the last one and then did the same with the third, fourth and fifth.[17]

While Gröben describes the tattooing process according to a lexicon drawn from writing and intaglio engraving, Lutheran theologian Johann Lund (1638–1686) writes that the marked arms of Hamburg native Ratge Stubbe were "very nice to look at and as well pricked as if [they] were a copperplate etching."[18] These associations between the methods of tattooing and engraving take on even greater significance when we consider that both Stubbe and Gröben, who traveled to the Holy Land in 1669 and 1675 respectively, actually had copper engravings made of their tattoos so that they could be reproduced in print, as did Scotsman William Lithgow (1582-ca. 1645), who made his pilgrimage to Palestine in 1612.[19] Cast by European pilgrims as similar to the familiar processes of writing, print, and engraving, the tattoo was an artisanal product and the skin, like paper, parchment, or copper, a ready surface for the impression or inscription of signs.

At the most basic level, the tattoo served as a souvenir, offered to travelers among numerous devotional objects and material vestiges of sacred sites that pilgrims hauled home and sent to friends and family even as far away as New France.[20] The Franciscans, who held the prestigious position of caretakers of the Holy Land from the fourteenth century on, accepted and encouraged tattooing as part of the pilgrim experience. Under their custody, Bethlehem developed as an important center of the commercial souvenir trade, providing income for the city's Christian inhabitants, who were well known for their skill as sculptors.[21] Tattooing was among the offerings by which Bethlehem Christians made their living, especially during the peak pilgrimage season of Easter. Toulousian Franciscan Henry Castela (ca. 1570–?) relates:

> This poor city is completely in ruins today, but when you see its foundations and old ruins you realize that it was of rather great expanse, though there is little more left of its old buildings than some small caverns and houses, where Mores and Sorien Christians live, who have no other livelihood other than trapping pilgrims by some method. It is true that some of them busy themselves with making crosses of Terebinth . . . or olive wood, along with crowns and rosaries that they then sell. Others serve as guides or interpreters, having learned for this purpose to speak the Italian language which they pass down from father to son. There are others who know very well how to sculpt little Holy

Sepulchers out of stone with the point of a knife alone, and beyond this they know how to imprint skillfully the Jerusalem seal on the arms of pilgrims.[22]

The same Christian artisans who carved wooden and stone figures thus diversified their offerings by turning their knives and needles on pilgrim skin as well, undoubtedly also carving the woodblocks that served to imprint tattoo patterns prior to pricking. As pilgrim Jean Doubdan, who traveled to the Holy Land in 1652, similarly attests, a pilgrim's tattoo artist may well have been the same local who served as his guide and translator, for Bethlehem Christians, he writes, made their living

> making Crosses, Rosaries, and other very pretty little pieces made of Olive and Terebinth wood that they sell to Pilgrims, also serving as Guides to lead them through all the Holy sites. It is also they who mark on Pilgrims' arms Crosses of Jerusalem, Mount Cavalries, Stars, Crowns, Names of Jesus, according to each person's devotion.[23]

In addition to supplying needle-wielding guides, Franciscan monks invited tattoo artists into their monasteries to perform their services or allowed them to set up shop on the grounds of shrines maintained by the Order.[24] Indeed, according to Stubbe's testimony, "the very monks" themselves sometimes tattooed pilgrims "for money."[25]

Pilgrim flash and custom designs

As Doubdan and Thévenot's descriptions suggest, pilgrims selected their marks according to their personal or religious preferences, choosing from a variety of models, the engraved woodblocks provided by tattoo artists serving as a kind of catalogue.[26] English traveler Georges Sandys (1577–1644) underlines the diversity of textual and iconographic signs that were available to pilgrims, writing that Holy Land tattoo artists "mark the Arms of Pilgrims, with the names of Jesus, Maria, Jerusalem, Bethlehem, the Jerusalem Cross, and sundry other characters."[27] While most pilgrims adopted standard patterns—symbols, images, and words that recalled the holy sites they visited and the stations of the *Via dolorosa* they walked in Jerusalem—some designed their own, as visual and textual evidence from the period attests. Unlike Amerindians and the French who imitated them, whose tattoos decorated many parts of their body, pilgrims usually wore tattoos on their inner forearms.[28]

Like so many of the title pages of the volumes recounting their voyages, Levantine travelers' skin most commonly bore the cross of Jerusalem, a large cross potent surrounded by four smaller Greek crosses (see Figure 4.1). Under the Franciscan custody, whose coat of arms included it, the cross of Jerusalem became the widely recognized sign that early modern Europeans associated with the Holy Land and those who traveled to it.[29] As the official caretakers of the Holy Land, the Order established itineraries, maintained pilgrimage sites,

Figure 4.1 Title page, Gabriel Giraudet, *Discours du Voyage d'Outre Mer au S. Sepulcre de Jerusalem* (Rouen: David Ferrand, 1637). Bibliothèque Nationale de France.

and provided guides, translators, and lodging for European pilgrims during their stay. They had, in short, a monopoly on Levantine pilgrimage.[30] The Jerusalem cross was, then, the obvious choice for a pilgrim when he got tattooed, commemorating his visit with the symbol that served as the emblem both for the holy city and the Franciscan custody. It appeared most often on the arms of pilgrims as the central component in a composite seal representing the cities of Jerusalem and Bethlehem.[31] Gröben, who returned from his 1675 voyage with an impressive collection of tattoos, bore this mark on his left inner arm, as depicted in the engraving he had made of it (see Figure 4.2). His tattoo features a Jerusalem cross flanked by the palm branches of Bethphage, the town on the outskirts of Jerusalem where Jesus first entered the city, welcomed by people laying palm branches on his path. Above these symbols are the three crowns of the Magi, and, at top center, the Bethlehem star, the whole framed above and below by the names of the two holy cities in Roman capitals. The same emblem also appears clearly on the right inner arm of the equally copiously tattooed Stubbe, along with the 1669 date of his pilgrimage, in a 1676 engraving made by Hans Martin Winterstein (see Figure 4.3).[32] A final visual example appears on the right arm of an unidentified pilgrim who traveled to the Holy Land in the 1660s, portrayed in an anonymous portrait that seems French or Flemish in style and composition (see Figures 4.4 and 4.5). The ship pictured in the background of the portrait, in addition to alluding to Holy Land pilgrimage, may suggest that he might have been a sea captain, merchant, or naval officer, identities that would have been consistent with his numerous tattoos, which could have been done over the course of several visits to Palestine.[33] The pilgrim bears the Bethlehem-Jerusalem composite seal on his right arm, partially obscured by the painter's perspective, with the incomplete year of his pilgrimage beneath it, "166 ." This playful omission of the year's final digit supports identifying the pilgrim as French, suggesting that he may have traveled to the Holy Land after 1665, when Louis XIV banned pilgrimage outside of France, and wanted to mask his transgression.[34]

Beyond the Bethlehem-Jerusalem tattoo, pilgrims chose from a variety of other patterns, most often scenes and sites from the passion, resurrection, and ascension of Christ. Stubbe's left arm tells, from wrist to bicep, the Easter story of Christ's death on the cross, triumphant resurrection, and ascension (see Figure 4.3).[35] Following typical iconography, the crucified Christ appears with the skull and crossbones below, symbolizing Adam's bones, the first sinner for whose absolution Christ's blood was shed. At the top of the crucifix are the letters "INRI," the abbreviation for "Jesus Nazarenus Rex Judæorum" [Jesus of Nazareth King of the Jews] that Pontius Pilate had nailed to the cross. Above this tattoo is a cartouche engraved with the letters "LVCFV," which stands for "Lapis Vbi Christus Fuit Vnctus" [The stone where Christ was anointed], representing the marble Stone of Unction, the place where Christ's body was laid following the crucifixion and prepared

Figure 4.2 Engraving of Otto Friedrich von der Gröben's tattoo of the arms of Jerusalem and Bethlehem, *Orientalische Reise-Beschreibung des branden-burgischen adelichen Pilgers Otto Friedrich von der Gröben* (Marlenwer-der: S. Reinigem, 1694). Burke Library, Hamilton College.

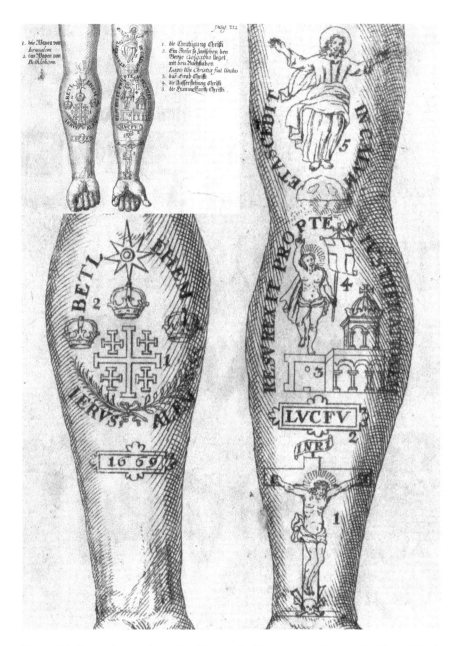

Figure 4.3 Engraving and detail of Ratge Stubbe's tattooed arms by Hans Martin Winterstein in Johannus Lundius, *Die Alten Jüdishchen Heiligtümer, Gottes-dienste und Gewohnheiten* (Hamburg: Liebernickel, 1701), facing p. 732. Universtitätsbibliothek Johann Christian Senckenberg, Frankfurt am Main.

Figure 4.4 Portrait of an unknown pilgrim who traveled to Palestine in the 1660s (ca. 1667). Private collection. Photograph by Andy Olenick, with the portrait owner's kind permission.

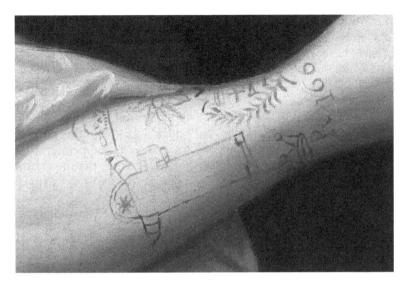

Figure 4.5 Detail of the tattoos on the pilgrim's right arm, his hand holding a certificate (ca. 1667). Private collection. Photograph by Andy Olenick, with the portrait owner's kind permission.

Figure 4.6 Engraving of Otto Friedrich von der Gröben's crucifixion tattoo, *Orientalische Reise-Beschreibung des brandenburgischen adelichen Pilgers Otto Friedrich von der Gröben* (Marlenwerder: S. Reinigem, 1694). Burke Library, Hamilton College.

for burial, located in the Church of the Holy Sepulcher.[36] Next, Christ appears, rising victorious over death above the recognizable building of the Church of the Holy Sepulcher, the image labeled "Resvrexit propter ivstificationem" [He rose again for our justification], from Romans 4:25. Finally, Christ ascends up into the heavens from the Mount of Olives, leaving his footprints behind, with the words "Et ascendit in caelum" [And he ascended into heaven].[37]

Three pilgrims supply visual examples of several other designs. While Gröben also sports the crucifixion scene on his right arm and the triumphant resurrection scene on his left (see Figures 4.6 and 4.7), his other tattoo choices are original among attested examples, though he writes that he chose them from "a whole sack full of forms cut from wood" that the tattoo artist carried with him from Bethlehem to Jerusalem, where Gröben had his ink work done.[38] On his right arm he wears both an image of Christ carrying his cross

Figure 4.7 Engraving of Otto Friedrich von der Gröben's tattoo showing a triumphant Christ ascending into heaven above the Church of the Holy Sepulcher, *Orientalische Reise-Beschreibung des brandenburgischen adelichen Pilgers Otto Friedrich von der Gröben* (Marlenwerder: S. Reinigem, 1694). Beinecke Library, Yale University.

with the words "Seqvere me" ["Follow me"] and a map of the *Via dolorosa*, complete with abbreviations labeling the various stations of the cross (see Figures 4.8 and 4.9).[39] Terry describes in detail the crucifix tattoo worn by Coryat on his right wrist as

> a single *Cross* made like that our Blessed Saviour suffered on; and on the sides of the *stem* or *tree* of that *Cross* these words written, *Via, Veritas, Vita*, some of the letters being put on the one side of that stem or tree, and some of them on the other; and at the foot of that *Cross* three *Nails*, to signifie those which fastned our *Saviour* unto it.[40]

The unknown pilgrim portrayed in the portrait presented above (Figure 4.4) wears several unique tattoos in addition to the Bethlehem-Jerusalem mark. One on his left inner arm commemorates his visit to Nazareth, a more removed and less frequented stop on the pilgrimage trail, having only been

Figure 4.8 Engraving of Otto Friedrich von der Gröben's "Sequere me" tattoo, *Orientalische Reise-Beschreibung des brandenburgischen adelichen Pilgers Otto Friedrich von der Gröben* (Marlenwerder: S. Reinigem, 1694). Beinecke Library, Yale University.

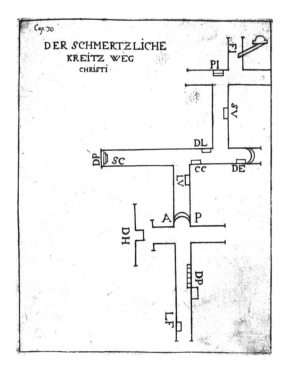

Figure 4.9 Engraving of Otto Friedrich von der Gröben's tattoo of a labeled map of the *Via Dolorosa, Orientalische Reise-Beschreibung des brandenburgischen adelichen Pilgers Otto Friedrich von der Gröben* (Marlenwerder: S. Reinigem, 1694). Beinecke Library, Yale University.

reopened by the Franciscans to Christians in 1620 after centuries of Arab control (see Figure 4.10).[41] The Virgin Mary's native city and Christ's childhood home would have been an exciting destination for seventeenth-century pilgrims since it was unknown by their sixteenth-century predecessors. The tattoo on his left inner wrist, labeled "NAZARET," symbolizes the site of the annunciation, a cave adjacent to the Church of the Annunciation, famous for its two marble pillars representing the spots where Mary and the Angel Gabriel supposedly stood when, in the words of Jesuit Michel Nau who traveled there in 1668, "the Angel concluded with her on behalf of God the greatest affair there ever was; and to put it better, the greatest affair of all times."[42] The object at center is likely the flaming Sacred Heart of Mary, though usually represented as pierced by swords.[43]

On the pilgrim's right arm, a prominently displayed rectangular shape with pointed appendages reproduces the floor plan of the Grotto of the Nativity in Bethlehem, the main chapel in a series of subterranean spaces that lie beneath the Church of the Nativity, celebrated as the birthplace of

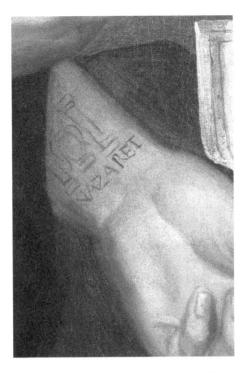

Figure 4.10 Detail of the pilgrim's Nazareth tattoo on his left wrist (ca. 1667). Private collection. Photograph by Andy Olenick, with the portrait owner's kind permission.

Christ (see Figure 4.5). Comparison with Franciscan Bernardino Amico da Gallipoli's detailed architectural drawings of the Grotto, first published in 1609, as well as with those that appear in the copiously illustrated 1615 *Pélerin Véritable*, allows the identification of many of its features (see Figures 4.11 and 4.12): stairs leading from both sides down into the space, the star marking the spot where Jesus was born; the side chapel of the Magi, where Christ was laid in the manger and presented with their gifts, complete with the stairs into it, altars, and the "Holy Crib."[44]

Two other symbols adorn the pilgrim's right arm (see Figure 4.5). The crown with initials below is a monogram, probably composed of three initials centered on the crown, the second and third of which are "I" and "R." While the crown figured in the Bethlehem seal and the Franciscan custody's coat of arms, it was also symbol commonly used in commercial marks, city arms, and personal monograms that proliferated in seventeenth-century Europe.[45] The tattoo may have paid homage to the ruler under whom the pilgrim served, like Lithgow's earlier 1612 tattoo honoring his sovereign, King of Scotland and England James I, consisting of a crown with the words "Vivat I R [Jacobus Rex]."[46] It may also

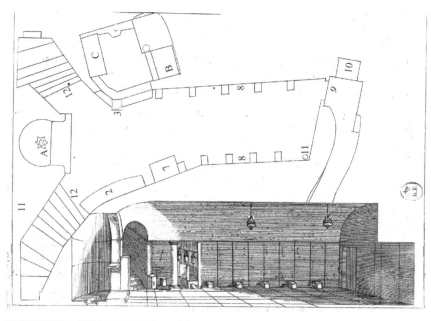

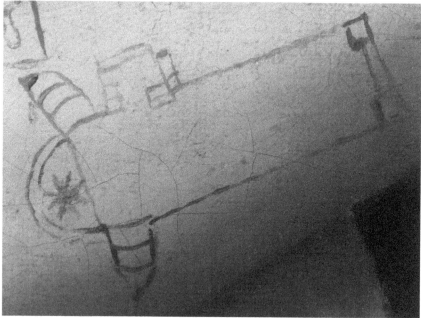

Figure 4.11 Detail of a tattoo on the unknown pilgrim's right arm (ca. 1667), compared to Bernardino Amico da Gallipoli's architectural drawings of the Grotto of the Nativity, *Trattato delle piante et imagini de' sacri edifizi di Terra Santa disegnate in Ierusalemme* (Florence: P. Cecconcelli, 1620), plate 11. Bibliothèque Nationale de France.

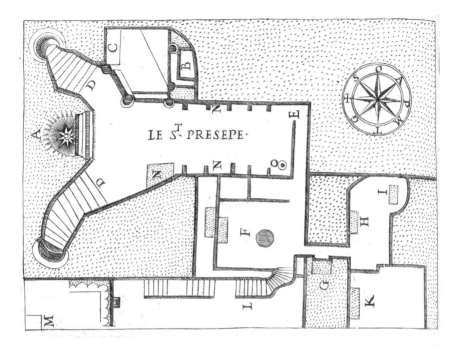

LE Sᵀ·PRESEPE·

A   *Le lieu de la Natiuité.*
B   *Le lieu du sainct Prefepe.*
C   *L'Autel des trois Roys.*
D   *Defcente au fainct Prefepe.*
E   *Entree au fainct Prefepe.*
F   *Chappelle des Innocens.*
G   *Sepulchre de fainct Eufebe.*
H   *Sepulchre de fainEte Paule,*

   & fa fille Euftochium.
I   *Sepulchre de S. Hierofme.*
K   *Chambre de S. Hierofme.*
L. *Efcallier du fainct Prefepe.*
M   *Eglife de fainEte Catherine.*
N   *Coffre de bois pour fe veftir*
   & deueftir,& les acoudoirs.
O   *Trou de l'Eftoille.*

Figure 4.12 Map of the Grotto of the Nativity in De Vergoncy, *Le Pelerin Veritable de la Terre Saincte* (Paris: Louys Febvrier, 1615), 364. Bibliothèque Nationale de France.

be the monogram of the portrait subject himself, his business, or his home city, engraved upon him as it would have been on his possessions or the products he made, transported, or sold. Monograms, including "IHS"—Christ's monogram, meaning "Jesus hominum salvator" [Jesus savior of men]—were often tattooed upon arms, as was the case for Lithgow as well. Finally, the skull and crossbones the pilgrim also wears may allude to Adam's bones, though their configuration is unusual. More likely, it commemorates the death of a loved one, its shape and symbol mimicking the upper portion of many seventeenth-century headstones, or serves as a *memento mori*, a reminder of the proximity of one's own death. The skull and crossbones was also a prominent symbol during the crusades of the Knights Templar, the medieval protectors of the Holy Land whose tradition lived on in the early modern period in other brotherhoods closely associated with the Holy Land and the Knights, an interpretation to which I return below.

Visual evidence and textual accounts of pilgrim tattoos from the seventeenth century thus reveal an iconographical canon of Christian symbols as well as departures from it. While some tattoo patterns were probably custom designed according to a pilgrim's desires, they remained linked, with rare exceptions, to Holy Land sites and specifically Catholic imagery. Those that did depart from the norm did not escape criticism. For instance, the tattoo honoring James I that Lithgow had marked on his skin earned him a reprimand from a Jerusalem official, since it displayed the coat of arms of an enemy of the Catholic Church.[47]

In contrast to most descriptions of Amerindian tattooing provided by European travelers to New France that usually describe the marking of another person's skin, Holy Land pilgrims who treat body marking recount by and large their own experience of being tattooed. Yet, despite the obvious importance pilgrims must have accorded to words and images that they chose to permanently emblazon on their skin and even reproduce in engravings and portraits, they rarely discuss their personal reasons for getting tattooed in their narratives. They do not fill pages or even paragraphs describing their motivations for getting inked, the rationale behind their choice of design, or their emotional reactions to the event.[48] Consistent with the pilgrimage narrative genre that set out to guide future pilgrims along their way, their accounts focus by and large on the practical and physical considerations of getting tattooed. The meanings with which pilgrims invested their marks must then be pieced together from scattered bits of evidence that appear in pilgrim accounts as well as analysis of certain pilgrims' decision to preserve their tattoos in engravings and portraits. Considered within the historical and religious contexts of which it was a part, the pilgrim tattoo reveals itself to be a multivalent sign linked to motivations ranging from practicality, to piety, to prestige.

Corporeal signs of identity

The pilgrim body was a body on the move and, as such, required identification, especially given the often treacherous lands through which it passed. Whatever other personal or spiritual significance tattoos may have had to the travelers who bore them, on a practical level they functioned as permanent marks of identification for pilgrims as they moved across time and space. The pilgrim tattoo thus represented the reverse positive image of the negatively stigmatized fleur-de-lis brand that commonly marked felons so that they could be recognized as past criminal offenders regardless of the passage of time or a change in location.[49] In choosing a corporeal sign to distinguish themselves as harmless pilgrims as they moved through potentially dangerous territory, pilgrim travelers may have found one model in the body markings used for identification among the peoples they encountered during their travels. Several pilgrim writers take note of the signs worn on the skin by their eastern Christian counterparts, both ancient and modern, as well as among other peoples of the Levant. Not long before the appearance of the first evidence of tattooing among European pilgrims in the late sixteenth century, French nobleman Greffin Affagart (ca. 1490–1557) describes the body marking practices that he observed among Christians, Turks, and Arabs during his 1533–1534 trip to Palestine in his *Relation de la Terre Sainte*. Eastern Christians used the baptismal brand, he writes, as a distinctive sign of Christian identity, enabling those branded to be recognized among non-Christians. The brand served "as a distinguishing sign between them and the infidels."[50] As Affagart notes, Christians were not the only locals who made use of a corporeal mark: "[T]urks and Mores also each have on their foreheads or on their arms or hands certain characters or signs representing something from their faith just like Christians have a cross, or Jesus, or Maria."[51] These diverse people's tattoos and brands were known to early modern Christians as signs that could prove identity, as a story recounted by Franciscan Jean Boucher in his popular 1620 *Le Bouquet sacré ou le voyage de la terre sainte* suggests. He tells of a Venetian Consul in Cairo who, in 1611, used the baptismal brand to identify a boy he wished to take back with him to Venice as an Abyssian Christian rather than a Turk, so as not to be accused of enslaving a Muslim.[52] This tradition of body marking could be traced back to early Christianity, as Marc Lescarbot (ca. 1570–1641) underlines when discussing Amerindian practices he witnessed in New France: "And the first Christians, as they were walking under the banner of Jesus-Christ, took the same mark [the cross], which they imprinted in their hands, on their arms, so that they could recognize each other in times of persecution."[53] By the eighteenth century, the line linking long-standing eastern Christian tattooing and branding practices and the modern-day pilgrim tattoo was, in any case, well drawn, as the *Encyclopédie* (1751–1772) entry for *stigmates* attests:

> Procopius . . . remarks the ancient use among Christians, who made stigmata on their wrists and arms, that represented the cross or the monogram of J.C., a practice that still subsists among eastern Christians, and among those who have traveled to Jerusalem.[54]

Early modern pilgrims, familiar with these ancient and contemporary uses of the corporeal mark in the Middle East for religious identification, may have drawn inspiration from these traditions in authenticating their own identity as Holy Land pilgrims through marking.

As a distinctive mark worn upon the body to signal identity, the Holy Land tattoo also drew directly on European pilgrimage tradition as a new rendition on late medieval badges commonly worn by pilgrims on their hats and coats as they traveled the pilgrimage trail.[55] Stamped in inexpensive lead, pewter, tin, or brass and thus affordable to all, these mass-produced souvenir badges identified a pilgrim as having traveled to a given shrine.[56] A ca. 1508 engraving by Lucas van Leyden (ca. 1494–1533) portrays two resting pilgrims with badges on their hats: the scallop shell that denoted a pilgrim of Saint James at Santiago de Compostela, and an image of Christ's face known as the Veronica, or *vera icon*, that signified pilgrimage to Saint Peter's Basilica in Rome (see Figure 4.13).[57] Moreover, art historian Rembrant Duits notes that pilgrim badges "offered those who were otherwise condemned to a fairly colourless existence an opportunity to shape a more interesting identity for themselves," a desire that some Holy Land pilgrims who got tattoos may well have shared.[58] On a practical level, pilgrim badges clearly identified their bearers as pilgrims, affording them greater protection and hospitality from those they encountered along their path. Many travelers even invested their badges with talismanic properties, thinking them literally capable of warding off evil forces or bringing good fortune.[59] Some tattooed pilgrims may have seen their corporeal marks as performing similar apotropaic functions.

The practice of wearing identifying signs upon clothing was common among Jerusalem pilgrims as well. From at least the mid-sixteenth century, many wore the cross of the city embroidered upon the breast of their cloak, as does the well-prepared pilgrim portrayed at center at the base of the title page of De Vergoncy's 1615 *Pelerin Veritable* (see Figure 4.14).[60] In choosing to tattoo their bodies with this sign and other sacred iconography, then, pilgrims extended the well-established badge tradition, transferring the vestimentary symbols they typically wore onto to their very skin. More permanent than the badge or embroidery, tattoos similarly allowed them to authenticate their identity as pilgrims as they moved through foreign territory and served as proof of their journey once they returned home.

Tattoos as passports

As signs of identification, tattoos also resembled the stamped or sealed passports and letters of passage that helped ensure a traveler's safety along the pilgrimage road. As the engraving of the "true pilgrim," who travels with Prudence at his right side (see Figure 4.14), affirms, the dangers of the pilgrimage trail were many and only the well-prepared would avoid them: "The Pilgrim who travels is not wise, if he walks in any other company."[61] Pilgrim writers consistently highlight the potential perils of Holy Land travel in their narratives and stress the importance of carrying proper travel documents to guarantee personal safety. They encourage their fellow pilgrims to secure prior to departure letters of recommendation, letters of

Figure 4.13 Lucas van Leyden, *Resting Pilgrims* (ca. 1508). National Gallery of Art, Washington.

priesthood for the clergy among them, and passports—if possible, from the King himself—so as to ensure their safe journey from place to place.[62] Holy Land travelers also obtained official letters of passage from local rulers as they made their way along the pilgrimage trail, and some included copies of these vital documents in their published travel narratives. One such

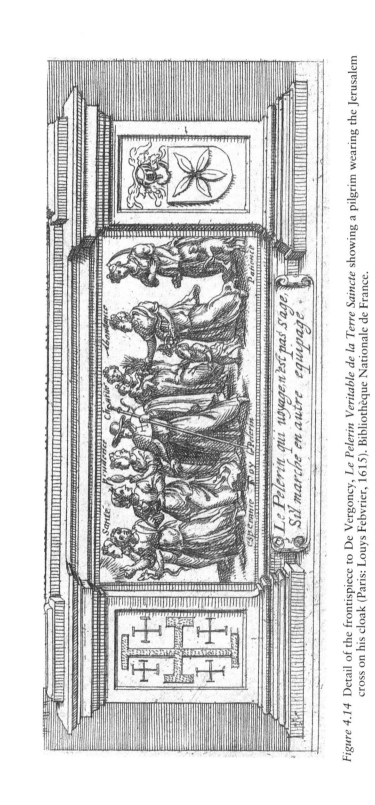

Figure 4.14 Detail of the frontispiece to De Vergoncy, *Le Pelerin Veritable de la Terre Saincte* showing a pilgrim wearing the Jerusalem cross on his cloak (Paris: Louys Febvrier, 1615). Bibliothèque Nationale de France.

passport, reproduced in the 1670 narrative of a group of French noblemen who traveled to the Levant in 1631, testifies to the resemblance in form and function between travel documents and the marks that pilgrims embossed on their skin. The authors preface their work with a reproduction and translation of the passport they obtained from the Turkish Sultan in Constantinople that prominently displays an engraving of the "Mark of the Ottoman family, through which in interlaced Arabic letters, is [represented] the name of the reigning Sultan" (see Figure 4.15).[63] The Ottoman Emperor's seal ensures the pilgrims' safety, the accompanying text commanding all who view it to "Honor the mark" of the royal family by allowing its bearers safe passage and hospitality.

Pilgrim accounts attest that tattoos, like the signed and sealed documents Holy Land travelers carefully carried upon them, functioned as safeguards during travel. Yet, unlike paper and ink texts, tattooed signs—permanently engraved upon the body—could not be lost or stolen along the way. Moreover, tattoos are portrayed as possessing a seemingly universal readability, which traveler-authors assert could serve a pilgrim well under threatening circumstances. Several pilgrims attest that the sacred signs upon their skin protected them from capture during their return trip, where episodes of blackmail, thievery, and violent attack were common. De Vergoncy writes:

> [T]he coat of arms and cross of Jerusalem . . . serve sometimes a great deal in moments of need, if by chance in passing through deserts and more removed places you fall into the hands of Turks, or of Arabs, who, without this mark that they recognize, will indubitably make the pilgrim a slave.[64]

Parisian Nicolas Bénard similarly testifies in 1621 that tattooing with crosses or the Jerusalem coat of arms "can serve those who go deeper into the deserts of Turkey and Arabia, because the Arabs, Turks and Mores, seeing this mark upon them do not keep them as slaves."[65]

De Vergoncy and Bénard's words echo those of Castela's earlier 1603 text, where the author emphasizes the importance of getting inked for protection, drawing his reader's attention to his discussion of tattooing with a marginal note highlighting its importance: "It is good to have oneself imprinted on the body with the arms of Jerusalem."[66] Personalizing his assertion, Castela advises future pilgrims that tattoos

> serve them as a safe-conduct (as I experienced) to cross through the deserts more easily and avoid capture. For this reason those who are forewarned of this have themselves marked by the inhabitants of Bethlehem with the sign of the cross.[67]

Those in the know—Castela's readers among them—should therefore submit themselves to the needle for their own safety. The author illustrates

PASSEPORT
DU GRAND TURC,
*Donné à Meßieurs Fermanel, Fauvel, Bau-
doüin, & de Stochove, traduit de la
langue Turquesque.*

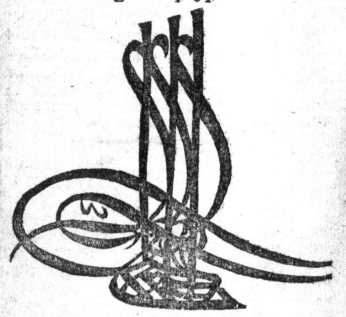

Marque de la famille Ottomane, dans
laquelle par lettres Arabiques entre-
laßées, est le nom de Sultan
regnant.

*Sultan Amurat fils de Sultan Achmet,
toûjours victorieux.*

ILLUSTRES & excellens Commandeurs refuge des triomphans, eminens, glorieux &

Figure 4.15 Reproduction and translation of a passport obtained from the Sultan in
Constantinople, bearing the Sultan's mark, in Gilles Fermanel, Robert
Fauvel, Baudouin de Launay, and Vincent Stochove, *Le Voyage d'Italie et
du Levant* (Rouen: Jacques Herault, 1670), following "Au Lecteur."
Bibliothèque Nationale de France.

his point with a dramatic mise-en-scène of his own experience. When his caravan runs into trouble on the way home with an army of attacking Arab thieves, Castela's pilgrim tattoo effectively saves his life. Having watched men fall all around him, and himself having been wounded in the hand by an arrow, Castela is brought before his attackers. But he has only to roll up his sleeve to prove his identity and escape capture:

> [T]hey called me over to them along with my guide, asking us what region or nation I was from, where I came from, and what my profession was. I began to stretch out my completely naked arm, upon which was imprinted the cross of Jerusalem, telling them as an answer that I was (*Iman Cassis Mesquin*), meaning a poor priest and Monk[.] [H]aving heard this, three of them came even closer to me to look more closely [to see] if I had the true marks of Jerusalem, and immediately after they had truly recognized them, explained in their language, the following two words, that are, *Mellie Cassis*, and touching me with their hands on the shoulder as a sign of freedom.[68]

Castela emphasizes the extraordinary authenticating power of the marks he wears: "immediately" upon having "truly recognized" the "true marks of Jerusalem" upon his skin, the Arab vandals let him go, albeit in exchange for a substantial ransom. The duly verified signs he wears not only apparently prove his identity beyond all doubt but gain him his freedom, indeed his very life.[69]

Signs of devotion

Whatever other reasons Europeans may have had for traveling to the Levant—diplomacy, trade, wanderlust, a taste for adventure—a sincere desire to gain physical proximity to the places where Christ and his entourage had lived and died strongly motivated those who made the long, costly, and potentially perilous journey. Each stop along the well-established itinerary led pilgrims in an intimate physical encounter with the places closely associated with Christ's life or those of his entourage. Pilgrims kissed Christ's birthplace, the alter upon which he was circumcised, the cave in which he nursed, the rock upon which he sat, the stone upon which his dead body was anointed, and the tomb in which he was buried. Many pilgrim writers use highly sensory language, borrowed from mystical vocabulary, to describe their experience of these sites. Boucher highlights, for example, the blissful encounter enjoyed by the pilgrim at Jesus's birthplace in Bethlehem:

> Those to whom God allows through his grace to kiss, see, and touch this holy Place will say marvelous things about it. Because they will confess that in kissing it, they seem to be sucking a sweet nectar, and smelling a precious salve. In seeing it they feel their imagination so

strongly moved that they seem to see in this place a Virgin holding a little baby to her chaste breast, whom she lovingly caresses. In short, the devout soul tastes here spiritual delights beyond words, so sweetly enticing and so strongly appealing, that a week seems like a day, a day like an hour, and an hour like a moment.[70]

As Boucher's description vividly suggests, all along the pilgrimage trial, pilgrims saw, touched, tasted, heard, and smelled their way toward a closer union with Christ. They literally followed in Christ's footsteps along the *Via dolorosa* in Jerusalem, meditating upon his corporeal suffering at each station. Pilgrims' quest for physical proximity to Christ surfaces as well in the multiple references they make to corporeal vestiges literally imprinted in stone, such as Christ's footprints left on the Mount of Olives at the moment of his ascension into heaven. Franciscan priest Jean-Jacques Rahier recounts his stop there in 1660:

[W]e went to the holy mount of olives where after having devoutly kissed the holy vestiges of the feet that our Savior imprinted there upon the rock as if upon wax the day he ascended into heaven . . . [we returned to Bethphage] where we visited several places sanctified by the corporeal presence of our Savior.[71]

By kissing, touching, and pressing themselves against the places that Christ's body and the body of his mother Mary had consecrated with their blood, sweat, milk, and tears, pilgrims made reliquaries of sorts of their own bodies.

Literally incorporating the holy sites where the pilgrim's body had been and embossing that intimate encounter with them permanently upon the flesh, tattooing extended the pilgrim's corporeal devotional experience.[72] For De Vergoncy, the act of getting marked, undertaken by the "most curious and devout" pilgrims, signaled the depth of a traveler's commitment to the pilgrimage experience.[73] Often casting the many trials they experienced during their travels as suffering undergone for Christ—an exercise in *imitatio Christi*—pilgrims may even have seen their submission to bodily wounding through tattooing as the logical culmination of this endeavor, their tattoos representing a sort of self-imposed stigmata that implied a certain degree of physical pain undergone for God. Like contemporary women religious who sought to express devotion and define their Christian identity through the inscription of holy names and signs upon their bodies, pilgrims too may have wished to wear a corporeal sign of their own spiritual commitment.[74] They thus interpreted Saint Paul literally—"From now on let no one cause me trouble, for I bear on my body the marks of Jesus" (*Galatians* 6:17)—as the sentiments Thomas Coryat expressed toward his Jerusalem tattoos suggest.[75] The bearer of a Jerusalem cross on his left wrist and a crucifix on his right, Coryat's feelings come to us secondhand through Edward Terry, who was with Coryat in India when he died and disapproved of his attitude toward his markings:

> This poor man would pride himself very much in beholding of those characters, and seeing them would often speak those words of St Paul, written to the Galations, Gal 6. 17 (though far besides the Apostles meaning) *I bear in my body the marks of Lord Jesus.*[76]

While Terry's is a unique testimonial, the ubiquitous Holy Land presence of the Franciscan order, whose founder, thirteenth-century Saint Francis of Assisi, famously bore Christ's bleeding wounds on his body, further supports this identification between tattoos and stigmata.[77] As Gabriel Brémond, who traveled to the Levant for the first time in 1645, explains, the five crosses that figured in both the Jerusalem seal and the coat of arms of the Franciscan custody symbolized the five wounds of the crucified Christ, most often presented in red on light cloth to reinforce this meaning: "As a sign of the Order, they wore (as they still do today) five red crosses in memory of the five wounds of our Savior."[78] Engraving the Jerusalem cross onto one's body in tattooing thus might be seen as a mimetic gesture, memorializing Christ's wounds through actual penetration of the flesh. Moreover, parallels between pilgrim tattoos received and Christ's wounds on the cross also seem likely given the usual calendar of Holy Land pilgrimage, as pilgrims typically received their stigmata at Eastertime, when Christ's crucifixion was commemorated.[79]

By reproducing on the traveler's skin the signs and architectural forms of the places the pilgrim visited, the tattoo also testified to the pilgrim's once physical presence in these spaces, as Lutheran theologian Lund affirms when presenting Stubbe's tattoos:

> It is still common today at the Holy Tomb, when Christians come to it, that many of them have several symbols pricked into their bodies, not out of heathen foolishness, but rather out of a particular devotion and as a sign that they have been there.[80]

Much like the meticulous descriptions and copious illustrations of each holy site characteristic of so many pilgrimage narratives, complete with precise legends and measurements made by the travelers with their own hands and feet, tattoos confirmed the material reality of the pilgrims' journey, lending authority to their intimate knowledge of the sacred geography and longevity to their otherwise fleeting passage through it.[81] As bodies on the move, or, in pilgrim Jean Doubdan's words, "people who only pass through," pilgrims sought to anchor and authenticate their experience in the materiality of their narrative and iconographic accounts but also in the materiality of their bodies.[82] The very spaces and sites that the pilgrim's own body had occupied or gazed upon during his time in the Holy Land took on new permanence through tattooing. Just as Bénard places himself kneeling before the Holy Sepulcher in an engraving produced for his 1621 narrative, enlarged quill in hand busy documenting his visit to the monument whose sites are shown to him by an angel (see Figure 4.16), so too did architecturally accurate tattoos commemorate the presence of the pilgrim within the shrine and his intimate knowledge of its particularities (see, for example, Stubbe and Gröben's Holy Sepulcher tattoos, Figures 4.3 and 4.7). Tattoos of the Stone of Unction recalled the spot the pilgrim reverently kissed upon arrival at Christ's tomb, those of Calvary recalled the crucifixion site and the cave below it where the pilgrim honored Adam's bones, and ascension tattoos included the footprints left by Christ on the Mount of Olives, as described by Rahier and visible at the top right of the engraving of Stubbe's arms (see Figure 4.3).

Particularly striking in this respect is the choice made by at least two pilgrims to imprint their bodies with actual maps of the spaces through which they had traveled. The unidentified portrait sitter who visited Bethlehem in the 1660s chose to tattoo his arm with the floor plan of the Chapel of the Nativity—the sensual experience of which Boucher described—thus preserving forever in corporeal form the space through which his own body had passed. The tattooed map represents in detail the steps the pilgrim followed down into the subterranean chapel, the star he gazed upon and embraced, and the altars he knelt at in prayer (see Figures 4.5, 4.11, and 4.12). Likewise, Gröben's choice to tattoo his arm with a labeled map of the stations of the *Via dolorosa*, the path that called on the pilgrim to imagine vividly each moment of Christ's suffering leading up to his crucifixion, commemorates his own body's movement along it and the devotional acts he performed in those locations (see Figure 4.9).[83] Through tattooing, pilgrims thus made their bodies living memorials to their physical and spiritual experience of traveling in the footsteps of Christ. Moreover, the images they imprinted on their skin offered enduring and infinitely portable mementos that the pilgrim eye could contemplate long after returning home to remember the experience of being there, an emphasis on the visual consistent with the Catholic Counter-Reformation valorization of the image as a privileged medium for meditation.

Marks of distinction

The importance of the pilgrim tattoo as a vector for expressing spiritual commitment, memorializing pilgrimage, and fashioning identity comes to the fore most spectacularly in the late seventeenth-century portraits and engravings that feature them. If tattooing made the pilgrim's body a memorial to the pilgrimage experience, visual representations of pilgrim tattoos in print and on canvass went one step further, extending the life of those icons beyond the ephemeral bodies of their bearers and preserving them for posterity. Gröben, Stubbe, and Lithgow's choice to commission engravings of their tattoos for

Figure 4.16 Nicolas Bénard at the Holy Sepulcher, *Le voyage de Hierusalem et autres lieux de la Terre sainte* (Paris: Denis Moreau, 1621), 185. Asia 9216.17*. Houghton Library, Harvard University.

inclusion in their published narratives testifies to the importance they accorded to their marking and their desire to make their exploit known beyond their more intimate circles. In choosing print as their medium, they opted to make their signs endlessly reproducible. Stubbe, whom Lund describes as a "silent religious man," chose to have his tattoos engraved in copper plates that he readily lent to Lund for further reproduction, first by Lund himself, then by his printer.[84] Lund recounts the transaction:

> I asked him if he wouldn't mind if both his arms were sketched. He said to me that he had them both in copper and wanted to send them to me, which he also did and which I received on the 18th of August the same year. . . . I immediately traced [them] and sent the copperplate back to him.[85]

Like Stubbe, Gröben had his flesh and blood engravings remade in copper for preservation and larger dissemination through the vehicle of print. He not only provided written descriptions of the design and execution of each of his tattoos in his narrative but, also like Stubbe, included legends with the engravings so that his readers and viewers could accurately interpret them. Lithgow similarly had his tattoos engraved for the 1640 edition of his text, where he too discussed the meaning of each of them to ensure their proper interpretation but also, perhaps more importantly, to draw attention to signs that glorified him as having traveled to distant and dangerous lands, a desire that his continental counterparts seem to have shared.[86]

The 1660s pilgrim portrait introduced above, one of two known surviving portraits of pilgrims displaying their tattoos, performs a similar function (see Figure 4.4).[87] As a genre, portraits celebrate an individual's past accomplishments but also look forward, validating the subject's identity for posterity. They are both "occasional," documenting a specific event—in this case the pilgrim's visit to the Holy Land—and enduring, here projecting the portrait sitter's chosen identity as a pilgrim and traveler into the future.[88] For members of the aristocracy and the bourgeoisie, portraiture represented a powerful medium for the construction and communication of identity, especially in the seventeenth century, when huge numbers of portraits were produced.[89] If returning pilgrims of the wealthy upper classes chose to commission portraits in which they proudly and prominently displayed their tattooed arms, purposefully pushing up their sleeves to feature them, it is, then, because their tattoos had extraordinary value for the fashioning of their identities, reinforcing not only their spiritual but also their worldly status.[90] They marked them as remarkable—as *hommes de marque*, worthy of consideration and distinction.[91] Model Christians, they were also courageous adventurers who had not settled for armchair pilgrimage but had made the long and difficult journey to the Holy Land "in corporeal presence," as Boucher distinguishes, rather than "in mind and thought" alone.[92] In this portrait, the pilgrim's tattoos identify him immediately as having traveled to foreign lands, a distinction reinforced by the ship that appears waiting in the background, the curtain drawn to show it, much as his tattoos are revealed by his pushed-up sleeves. The prominent visibility given by the painter to the undone buttonhole on the right sleeve further underlines the importance of the pilgrim's revelation of his Holy Land tattoos. The inclusion of a document that appears to be a certificate of induction into an honorary brotherhood, placed in parallel with the pilgrim's tattooed arms that hold and gesture toward it, further reinforces the importance of his marks themselves as honorary insignia (see Figures 4.4 and 4.17). Though the artist teases the viewer by obscuring the Latin text, it most likely signifies the pilgrim's induction into the Knights of the Order of Saint John, formerly known as the Hospitallers of Jerusalem.[93] The pilgrim's sober black robe and simple collar correspond to the secular costume worn for the ceremony of induction into that order.[94] First founded in Jerusalem around 1050 to establish hospitals for the care of pilgrims and closely associated with the Knights Templar, the Knights Hospitaller became a military order for the defense of the Holy Land as the Order of Malta, whose membership maintained close ties with the French navy, often serving in its ranks.[95] The red flags accented with white of the ship in the background, though roughly rendered, suggest the historical flag of Malta, and thus of the Knights—red with a white cross.[96] By the time of this pilgrim's induction in the seventeenth century, becoming a Knight of the Order of Saint John conferred honorific status as part of an elite Christian fighting force. The kings of France—notably Louis XIV—allowed and even encouraged their notables to join by granting them diplomatic posts and privileges.[97] According to Pierre de Lancre (1553–1631), the Knights of Saint John had traditionally been marked with a branded cross—"all those who are in the militia of Priest Jean, have a Cross lightly marked with a hot iron on their skin"—a mark of distinction that the pilgrim's tattoos may replace.[98] Moreover, given the close historical association between the Knights Templar and the Hospitallers of Jerusalem—many Templars were also Hospitallers or became so after the Templar's dissolution in 1312—the skull and crossbones that appear on the figure's right arm may be a reference back to this common Templar symbol signifying the Order's strong maritime presence, which would have appealed to a sea captain, a naval officer, or a frequent sea traveler.

While the definitive identification of the pilgrim's certificate remains elusive, the Jerusalem cross he and countless other pilgrims bore on their arms was unquestionably linked in the seventeenth century to another well-known chivalric order maintained by the Franciscans in Jerusalem, the Knights of the Holy Sepulcher. Though in theory an order reserved for aristocrats and members of the clergy, any relatively distinguished pilgrim—including captains, merchants, diplomats, and politicians—may have been invited to join.[99] Frenchmen were particularly prominent in the Order's ranks from the seventeenth through the early eighteenth centuries,

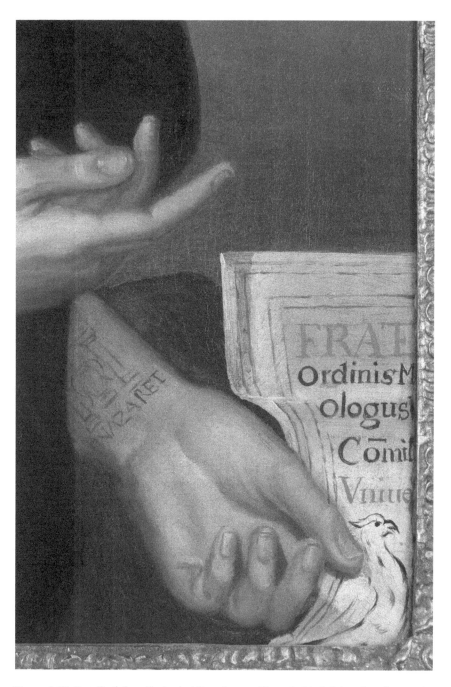

Figure 4.17 Detail of the pilgrim holding the certificate in his left hand and gesturing toward it with his right (ca. 1667). Private collection. Photograph by Andy Olenick, with the portrait owner's kind permission.

numbering first among Europeans, with over three times as many members as the next most numerous group, the Italians.[100] Since the Jerusalem cross served as the recognizable emblem of the Knights, into which many a pilgrim was inducted during his stay in the Holy Land, when used as a tattoo it explicitly referenced the honorary order.[101] Pilgrims saw their Jerusalem tattoos in accordance with heraldic tradition, referring to them as "a coat of arms," like those emblazoned upon clothing and other accouterments that communicated family descent and membership in prestigious organizations. Indeed, Gröben refers to the tattooed cross he bears on his arm as "the five crosses, the sign of the knights."[102] Many of the very same Knights of the Holy Sepulcher who, once inducted, wore a red Jerusalem cross embroidered upon the breast of their coats and as a medallion around their necks also wore the cross upon their arms as a tattoo.[103] Bénard, for example, first traveled to Bethlehem, where had his skin tattooed with the Jerusalem coat of arms, and then to Jerusalem itself, where he was inducted into the Order, receiving the privilege of bearing its emblem both upon his person and in his own family's coat of arms.[104] For those not fortunate enough to become Knights themselves, the tattooed Jerusalem cross may, then, have acted as a substitute, gleaning for its bearer a hint of the prestige attached to the Franciscan chivalric order.[105]

The well-traveled tattoo

Holy Land tattoos marked the European pilgrim's body as having journeyed elsewhere, walked on distant soil, and interacted with foreign peoples.[106] Rich with several sources and meanings, they were signs of their bearer's displacement, a permanent reminder of time spent beyond the normal frontiers, experiences, and constraints of everyday life. Moreover, these corporeal marks clearly had spiritual significance to pilgrims, as they memorialized their intimate devotional experience of the Holy Land, commemorating their bodies' passage through its landscapes and monuments and creating an infinitely portable and permanent iconography of this encounter upon their skin. At the same time, like the paper and ink passports that traveled with them, these highly legible signs also functioned on a practical level, as a means of identification, facilitating pilgrims' return home through potentially hostile territory. Once Holy Land pilgrims reintegrated their communities, like honorary insignia, their marks distinguished them among their peers as having made the arduous journey to Palestine, contributing to an enterprise of self-fashioning that brought them both spiritual and enduring social prestige.

The tattoo has long been associated in Western culture with distant lands and foreign cultures, an idea that continues to have currency today, even as the "tattoo renaissance" of the late twentieth and early twenty-first centuries has seen the proliferation and banalization of tattoos on the skin of an ever-wider population. Even adepts of movements like "Modern

Primitivism," born in the 1980s but still influential today, reinforce the stereotype that tattooing, at least at its origins, was something that Westerners did not do.[107] The many early modern European pilgrims, explorers, traders, and soldiers discussed in this chapter and the preceding chapter who wrote about and experimented with the art of tattooing, testify to the contrary. But while tattooing was not, as formerly assumed, an eighteenth-century import to the European continent, tattoos and travel were nonetheless intimately linked, as these chapters highlight. Like the tattoo itself that, inserted just under the skin, lies in a space in-between the body's interior and exterior, the traveler occupies a space in-between. This liminal space may offer new liberating and affirming possibilities of self-definition or it may require the assertion of identity for self-preservation. For the travelers who fill these pages, both the affirmation and refashioning of identity could be accomplished through corporeal marking.

As the juxtaposition of New and Old World tattooing in Chapters 3 and 4 makes clear, though the practice proliferated on both sides of the Atlantic, for early moderns, not all tattoos were considered of equal value. The corporeal signs that Amerindians wore continued to mark them as other, despite some early ethnographers' attempts to explain and naturalize them, and tattoos and body paint remain mainstays among stereotypes of Native American peoples in the popular Western imagination even today. While tattooing was practiced in both the North American and European contexts in the seventeenth and eighteenth centuries, Frenchmen who marked their bodies in New France with signs borrowed from Amerindian tradition did not enjoy the same general acceptance as did their tattooed pilgrim cousins, whose signs rarely departed from traditional Christian iconography and were made by Christian artisans. For early modern writers across Europe, pilgrim marking reaffirmed and embellished a traveler's preexisting European Christian identity, while New World marking of European skin generated new identities that called into question the very premises of the French colonial enterprise and its ability to inscribe the other into its social and cultural norm. Moreover, while Jerusalem pilgrims almost always returned to their native lands, bearing corporeal marks that were readily decipherable by European eyes, travelers to the Americas often did not. Instead many forged new lives for themselves on the North American continent, incorporating elements from both French and Amerindian cultures, a decision eloquently signaled by the hybridity of the symbols that marked their skin.

Yet, despite differences in their reception, what emerges as a constant in examining the tattoo on both American and European soil is the important role early moderns attributed to marks on skin for the expression of identity. For French colonists, tattoos provided a signifying system through which they could read the identities of the Amerindians they encountered, secure their own status and safety as they moved among native populations, and establish new identities for themselves as inhabitants of the North

American continent. Holy Land pilgrims too praised their tattoos as fool-proof signs that identified them as pilgrims and ensured their safety on the road home. Through their tattoos, they declared their newfound pilgrim identity, celebrated their religious commitment, and garnered prestige for themselves as accomplished travelers. Though the European use of tattooing in this period may surprise us today, its appeal as an expression of identity must be understood within the larger culture of marking that characterized early modern Europe. When the French encountered Amerindian tattooing practices, they found in them a method of identification that they recognized because it mirrored their own use of coats of arms, badges, and other honorific or defamatory emblems so commonly worn and displayed in early modern Europe for purposes of identification. These material signs by which people and things were recognized—*connus*, literally, "known"—served as their point of comparison when analyzing tattooing.[108] Indeed, both colonists' and pilgrims' tattoos were often corporeal versions of already existing vestimentary signs that indicated origin, social status, or distinction. These ubiquitous markers of identity made on cloth and metal were joined by the proliferation of commercial brands in early modern Europe, signs stamped on artisanal and agricultural products, books, and African captives sold as slaves to indicate their identity, provenance, and quality. Explorer Marc Lescarbot makes this link explicitly, describing Amerindian tattoos as marks "like those that our merchants imprint on their packages of merchandise" so as to identify them.[109] In a world where everyone and everything bore its distinctive mark, the display of such visible signs of belonging and distinction was not, in fact, at all foreign to European sensibilities, but highly familiar and full of meaning, participating in a system that they understood.

Notes

1 For references to the Holy Land tattoo in writings from New France see, for example, Gabriel Sagard-Théodat, *Le Grand voyage du pays des Hurons suivi du dictionnaire de la langue huronne* [1632], ed. Jack Warwick (Montréal: Presses de l'Université de Montréal, 1998), 229 and Sagard, *Histoire du Canada* (Paris: Claude Sonnius, 1636), 374. For further development regarding these references, see Chapter 3.

2 F. Thomas Noonan, *The Road to Jerusalem: Pilgrimage and Travel in the Age of Discovery* (Philadelphia, PA: University of Pennsylvania Press, 2007), 11.

3 Ibid. On the Protestant-Catholic polemic regarding pilgrimage, see: ibid., 84–100; Marie-Christine Gomez-Géraud, *Le Crépuscule du Grand Voyage. Les récits des pèlerins à Jérusalem (1458–1612)* (Paris: Honoré Champion, 1999), 61–189; and Robert Sauzet, "Contestations et renouveau du pèlerinage au début des Temps Modernes (XVIe-début XVIIe s.)" in *Les Chemins de Dieu. Histoire des pèlerinages chrétiens, des origines à nos jours*, ed. Jean Chélini and Henry Branthomme (Paris: Hachette, 1982), 235–58.

4 On the prominence of pilgrimage literature in the early modern period and the link between these narratives and New World exploration see Noonan, *The Road to Jerusalem* and Gomez-Géraud, *Le Crépuscule*, 15–25 and *Écrire le voyage au XVIe siècle en France* (Paris: Presses Universitaires de France, 2000). For literary analysis of French pilgrimage narratives, see Gomez-Géraud, *Le Crépuscule* and *Écrire le voyage*, Wes Williams, *Pilgrimage and Narrative in the French Renaissance. "The Undiscovered Country"* (Oxford: Clarendon Press, 1998), and Noonan, *The Road to Jerusalem*, 154–234.

5 The pilgrims discussed in this chapter are all men, as are all of the tattooed pilgrims identified to date. Women were few in number among Holy Land pilgrims. Jean-Pierre de Gennes cites the names of two of several rare women who made the pilgrimage to Jerusalem, Radegonde Guillier, from the diocese of Angers, and Alexie Bankes, the daughter of the English Supreme Court justice; *Les Chevaliers du Saint-Sepulcre de Jerusalem*, vol. 2, *Histoire de l'Ordre en France et Histoire de l'Ordre de 1847 à nos jours* (Versailles: Mémoires et Documents, 2004), 75–76 and 78. The *Navis Peregrinorum*, a register of all Jerusalem pilgrims from 1561 to 1695, records Guillier's arrival in Jerusalem on March 22, 1648, and Bankes's on February 4, 1679. For a modern print edition of the manuscript register, see Betrand Zimolong ed., *Navis Peregrinorum. Ein Pilgerverzeichnis aus Jerusalem von 1561 bis 1695: Mit Angaben über Pilger aus Deutschland, England, Frankreich, Italien und den Niederlanden, sowie aus anderen europäischen Ländern* (Köln: Verlag J. P. Bachem, 1938). On one woman pilgrim, see Marie-Christine Gomez-Géraud, "Pèlerinage au féminin: l'écriture confisquée. Le récit du voyage aux Lieux saints d'Hélène Chéron (1671)," in *Figures de femmes. Hommage à Jacqueline Ferreras*, ed. Thomas Gomez (Nanterre: Centre de Recherches ibériques et ibéro-américaines de l'Université de Paris-X, 2003), 159–70.

6 This chapter builds on the groundbreaking work of historian Mordechay Lewy, whose analyses have informed and enriched my own; "Jerusalem unter der Haut. Zur Geschichte der Jerusalemer Pilgertätowierung," trans. Esther Kontarsky, *Zeitschrift für Religions und Geistesgeschichte* 55.1 (2003): 1–39, first published in Hebrew under the English title "Towards a History of Jerusalem Tattoo Marks among Western Pilgrims," *Cathedra* 95 (2000): 37–66.

7 Most of the pilgrims discussed here—and all of the French—were tattooed by local Bethlehem Christians, who seem to have been known for their skill, for they even traveled to Jerusalem to offer their services. English traveler Thomas Coryat's tattoos were done in Jerusalem, as were Scotsman William Lithgow's,

though by the needle of "a Christian inhabiter of *Bethleem*" who worked for the Franciscans and came to the Holy Sepulcher to offer his services to Lithgow's party; William Lithgow, *The Totall Discourse, Of the rare Adventures, and painefull Peregrinations of long ninteene yeares Travailes from Scotland, to the most famous Kingdomes in Europe, Asia, and Affrica.* (London: J. Oakes, 1640), 285. This text is a later longer version of Lithgow's original travel narrative, *A Most Delectable, and True Discourse, of an admired and painefull peregrination in Europe, Asia, and Affricke* (London: Nicolas Okes, 1614). German pilgrim Otto Friedrich von der Gröben also had his work done by an artist from Bethlehem in Jerusalem; *Orientalische Reise-Beschreibung des brandenburgischen adelichen Pilgers Otto Friedrich von der Gröben* (Marlenwerder: S. Reinigem, 1694), 282. Nineteenth-century sources provide evidence for a similar devotional tattooing practice in Loreto, Italy, in that period, a tradition that Guido Guerzoni argues dates from the early modern period. See Guido Guerzoni, "*Notae divinae ex arte compunctae.* Prime impressioni sul tatuaggio devozionale in Italia (secoli XV-XIX)," *La Peau humaine. La pelle humana. The human skin,* special issue of *Micrologus. Natura, Scienze e Società Medievali* 13 (2005): 409–37 and "Devotional Tattoos in Early Modern Italy," special issue on *Wearing Images,* edited by Diane Brodart, *Espacio, Tiempo y Forma* 6 (2018): 119–36.

8 Jean Thévenot, *Relation d'un Voyage fait au Levant* (Paris: Louis Bilaine, 1664), engraving facing title page. Thévenot spent several years in Turkey, India, and the Middle East, visiting Palestine in 1658.

9 Thévenot, *Relation,* 403.

10 Maundrell, *A Journey,* 445.

11 Thévenot, *Relation,* 403–4. Bile was probably used in the ink mixture because of its properties as a fat dissolvent.

12 Ratge Stubbe mentions that an English count with whom he visited the tattoo parlor only had one design tattooed because he couldn't stand the pain; Johann Lund, *Die Alten Jüdishchen Heiligtümer* (Hamburg: Liebernickel, 1701), 732. Gröben suggests that the resulting inflammation and fever could even be fatal and should be avoided by "[a]ny man who has a weak constitution;" *Orientalische Reise-Beschreibung,* 286. All translations of Lund and Gröben's texts are by Bryn Savage. Only Henry Maundrell downplays the pain involved, writing that "[t]hese punctures they make with great quickness and dexterity, and with scarce any smart, seldom piercing so deep as to draw blood;" *A Journey from Aleppo to Jerusalem at Easter, A.D. 1697,* 2nd ed. ([Oxford: G. Delaune, 1703] Oxford: Jonah Bowyer, 1707), 446.

13 As Lewy underlines, the use of woodblocks sometimes resulted in the inversion of images on the pilgrims' arms, such as the crucified Jesus's head turning to his left rather than his right as was conventional in Christian iconography; Lewy, "Jerusalem unter der Haut," 28, 32, and 34. Lewy suggests that tattoo artists improved their accuracy over time thanks to contact with the European monks who would have known engraving techniques; ibid., 34. On the transfer error of a tattooed map of the *Via dolorosa* discussed below, see Robert Ousterhout, "Permanent Emphemera: The 'Honourable Stigmatisation' of Jerusalem Pilgrims" in *Between Jerusalem and Europe: Essays in Honour of Bianca Kühnel,* ed. Renana Bartal and Hanna Vorholt (Leiden and Boston: Brill, 2015), 94–109; 105–6.

14 Maundrell, *A Journey,* 445–46. My emphasis. Maundrell's *Journey* knew seven editions by 1749, was translated into French (1705 and 1706 editions), Dutch, and German, and figured in several compilations of travel accounts.

15 Edward Terry, *A Voyage to East-India* (London: J. Martin and J. Allestrye, 1655), 64–65.

16 Jane Caplan, ed., *Written on the Body: The Tattoo in European and American History* (Princeton, NJ: Princeton University Press, 2000), xxii. On the history and technique of pouncing, see Carmen Bambach Cappel, "Pouncing," *The Dictionary of Art*, ed. Jane Turner (New York: Grove's Dictionaries, 1996), vol. 25, 378–80 and Claude Boutet, *Traité de mignature, pour apprendre aisément à peindre sans maître* (Paris: C. Ballard, 1676), 2–3.

17 Gröben, *Orientalische Reise-Beschreibung*, 285–86. My emphasis. See also Terry's description, *A Voyage to East-India*, 64.

18 Lund, *Die Alten Jüdishchen Heiligtümer*, 732. Stubbe was originally from Hamburg but was a citizen of Itzeho, a small town north of Hamburg. On Stubbe, see also Lewy, "Jerusalem unter der Haut," 4.

19 Lithgow's tattoo is reproduced in his *The Totall Discourse*, 285. See also reprints in Lewy, "Jerusalem unter der Haut," 26, fig. 11 and Juliet Fleming, "The Renaissance Tattoo," in *Written on the Body*, ed. Caplan, 61–82, 80; Fleming's article first appeared in *Res: Anthropology and Aesthetics* 31 (1997): 34–52 and also appears in her *Graffiti and the Writing Arts of Early Modern England* (Philadelphia, PA: University of Pennsylvania Press, 2001), 79–112. All references here are to the Caplan edition.

20 Antoine Morison writes that pilgrims visiting the Holy Land purchase numerous devotional items that they have blessed at Christ's tomb and touch against several other holy places and then "send . . . to all parts of the Christian world, and even all the way to Canada, where they are received and kept with respect;" *Relation Historique d'un Voyage Nouvellement Fait au Mont de Sinaï et à Jerusalem* (Toul: A. Laurent, 1704), 297.

21 See, for example, Jesuit Michel Nau, *Voyage Nouveau de la Terre-Sainte* (Paris: J. Barbou, 1744), 396–97.

22 Henry Castela, *Le sainct voyage de Hierusalem et Mont Sinay* (Bordeaux and Paris: Laurens Sonnius, 1603), 274. See a similar description in the anonymously published *Le Pelerin Veritable de la Terre Saincte* (Paris: P. Louys Féburier, 1615), 358, attributed to the Sieur de Vergoncy. On the tourist trade see also Nicolas Bénard, *Le voyage de Hierusalem et autres lieux de la Terre sainte* (Paris: Denis Moreau, 1621), 122 and Jacques de Villamont, *Les Voyages du Seigneur de Villamont* (Paris: Claude de Montroeil et Jean Richer, 1600), 213.

23 Jean Doubdan, *Le Voyage de Terre-Sainte fait l'an 1652* (Paris: F. Clouzier, 1657), 151.

24 Lewy, "Jerusalem unter der Haut," 8 and esp. 12–14. Gröben's tattoo artist came to the monastery where he was staying in Jerusalem to offer his services; *Orientalische Reise-Beschreibung*, 282.

25 Lund, *Die Alten Jüdishchen Heiligtümer*, 732. Among French writers, none mention monks themselves as tattoo artists.

26 This method was still alive in the 1950s, as documented by John Carswell, who discovered a Jerusalem tattoo shop where the owner used woodblocks that had been handed down in his family for centuries. Carswell reproduces prints of the blocks, dating the earliest from the eighteenth century. Several of the designs are close or even exact replicas of pilgrim tattoos that appear in paintings and engravings of the seventeenth century. The Razzouk Tattoo shop still exists today. See Carswell, *Coptic Tattoo Designs* (Beirut: Faculty of Arts and Sciences, American University of Beirut, 1958). Gerzoni reproduces a similar set of wood tablets, which he dates to sixteenth-century Loreto, Italy; "Devotional Tattoos," 122–24 and 126.

27 George Sandys, *A Relation of a Journey Begun An.Dom. 1610* (London: W. Barrett, 1615), 56.

28 However, in the portrait discussed below, pilgrimage tattoos adorn the man's outer arm as well (see Figures 4.4 and 4.5) and De Vergoncy's *Pelerin Veritable* attests that tattoos were made on any part of the body, according to the customer's desires; 358. Castela is unique in reporting different tattoo locations for men and women, "that is to say for men on the neck of the arm, and for women on their cheeks or perhaps on the forehead or the stomach according to their will, because otherwise they are not obliged to take these marks;" *Le sainct voyage*, 274–75. It seems, however, unthinkable that Christian European women would have exposed their abdomens or faces to tattooing. Alteration of the human face was particularly problematic, as it was considered to be made in God's image. With the *Theodosian Code* of 438 emperor Constantine had famously outlawed the marking of convicts and slaves upon the face for this reason; Mark Gustafson, "The Tattoo in the Later Roman Empire and Beyond," in *Written on the Body*, ed. Caplan, 21, n. 12.

29 Lewy, "Jerusalem unter der Haut," 6.

30 Gomez-Géraud, *Le Crépuscule*, 14–15 and Lewy, "Jerusalem unter der Haut," 5–6.

31 Lithgow's tattoo is one exception, as the Jerusalem cross appears alone with, below it, Christ's name as a large "IHS" followed by "Jerusalem 1612." He writes that his entire party of eleven men received this specific design that was of "their own option and desire;" Lithgow, *The Totall Discourse*, 285. Coryat also bore the "Arms of *Jerusalem*, a *Cross Crossed*, or *Crosslets*" on his left wrist; Terry, *A Voyage to East-India*, 64. Emphasis in original.

32 Lund, *Die Alten Jüdishchen Heiligtümer*, 732. As Lewy points out, the tattooed arms pictured in this engraving have often been wrongly attributed to Gröben. On their proper identification by Otto Meinardus, see Lewy, "Jerusalem unter der Haut," 26–27.

33 While the portrait sitter's hair style appears more characteristic of the low countries than it does of France, his flamboyant gestures strongly resemble those of an unknown general painted ca. 1660 by French artist Louis Ferdinand Elle II (Paris 1648–1717), now held by the Musée de Beaux-Arts in Marseille. They may have been copied by a student in producing the pilgrim portrait, whose technique is more rudimentary than Elle's, but certainly French influenced; personal communication with Mark DeVitis, January 19, 2018. The portrait's composition, with the curtain drawn back to reveal ships in the background, also bears resemblance to portraits by Flemish artist Ferdinand Bol (Dordrecht 1616–Amsterdam 1680): a 1667 portrait of famous Dutch Admiral Michiel Adriaansz de Ruyter (1607–1676) and a 1669 portrait of the admiral's son, Michiel de Ruyter (1649–1683). It echoes as well the extensive portrait work of prominent Dutch painter Bartholomeus van der Helst (1613–1670), for example, the portrait of Captain Gideon de Wildt (1656), with ships in full sail in the background signaling his profession.

34 Regarding Louis XIV's regulation of pilgrimage, I refer the reader to Allison Stedman's work in progress, "Miraculous Journeys: Healing Pilgrimages and Individual Agency in the Age of Louis XIV," presented at the Society for Interdisciplinary French Seventeenth-Century Studies Annual Conference, Rutgers University, Nov. 5–7, 2015.

35 See also Lewy's detailed iconographical analyses of Stubbe, Gröben, Lithgow, and Ludoff's tattoos, "Jerusalem unter der Haut," 25–32.

36 Ibid., 28.

37 The crucifixion with Adam's bones below and the resurrection scene above the Church of the Holy Sepulcher also appear on the left arm of another tattooed portrait subject identified by Lewy as Heinrich Wilhelm Ludolf (1655–1712), a German expert in Slavic cultures and longtime diplomat in the service of England and Denmark, above the 1699 date of his voyage. Lewy reproduces the portrait in "Jerusalem unter der Haut," 33–34 and fig. 21, 33. See also the exhibition catalogue by Hendrik Budde and Mordechay Lewy, ed., *Von Halle nach Jerusalem: Halle, ein Zentrum der Palästinakunde im 18. und 19. Jarhundert* (Halle, Germany: Ministerium für Wissenschaft und Forschung des Landes Sachsen-Anhalt, 1994) and Lewy's article in that volume, "Die tätowierten Pilgerzeichen aus Jerusalem," 75–76.

38 Gröben, *Orientalische Reise-Beschreibung*, 282. Print reproductions of Gröben's tattoos reveal difficulties in translating corporeal signs to print. In the engraving of Gröben's crucifix tattoo (Figure. 4.6), the "N" in "INRI" is accidentally reversed. In the engraving of his Holy Sepulcher tattoo (Figure. 4.7), the final word may not reflect the actual inscription tattooed on the body. The printer chose to abbreviate "nostram" as "NRAM," using a standard printer's abbreviation mark of "~" over the R, for lack of space, just as he would have done to shorten a text on the printed page.

39 Gröben provides a detailed legend for the *Via dolorosa* map in his text (*Orientalische Reise-Beschreibung*, 283–84), transcribed and explained by Lewy, ibid., 29–31. The abbreviations indicate the following sites along the pilgrim's route: LF = Locus Flagellationis (Place of the Flagellation); DP = Domus Pilati (House of Pilate); DH = Domus Herodii (House of Herod); AP = Arcus Pilati (Ecce Homo Arch); LV = Labitur Virgo (Our Lady of the Spasm); CC = Cecidir Christus (Christ's First Fall); SC = Simon Cireneus (the place where Simon of Cyrene takes up the cross); DP = Damascena Porta (Gate of Damascus); DE = Domus Epulonis (House of the Rich Man); DL = Domus Lazari (House of the Poor Man); SV = Sancta Veronica (the place where Veronica wipes Christ's face with her veil); PI = Porta Iudicalis (Gate of Judgement); FI = Filii Ierusalem (the place where Christ spoke to the daughters of Jerusalem).

40 Terry, *A Voyage to East-India*, 64. Coryat served the eldest son of James I and published two wildly popular accounts of his extensive travels: *Coryats Crudities* (London: William Stansby, 1611) and *Coryats Crambe* (London: William Stansby, 1611). Emphasis in original.

41 Thévenot mentions the relative novelty of this destination in his *Relation*, 424.

42 Michel Nau, *Le Voyage de Galilée* (Paris: Michel Le Petit et Estienne Michallet, 1670), 162. See also the descriptions of the cave and pillars by 1668 Franciscan pilgrim Jacques Goujon, *Histoire et Voyage de la Terre Sainte* (Lyon: P. Compagnon et R. Taillander, 1671), 67 and Thévenot, who traveled to Nazareth in 1658, *Relation*, 424–25.

43 If this interpretation is correct, the expression of such Marian devotion—under Protestant attack in the period—would more likely find its place on the arm of a Catholic.

44 Bernardino Amico Da Gallipoli, *Trattato Delle Piante et Imagini De I Sacri Edificii Di Terrasanta* (Rome: Ex. Typographia Linguarum Externarum, 1609) in its facsimile edition with English translation, *Plans of the Sacred Edifices of the Holy Land*, ed. Fr. Bellarmino Bagatti O.F.M. and trans. Fr. Theophilus Bellorini O.F.M. and Fr. Eugene Hoade O.F.M. (Jerusalem: Franciscan Press, 1953), 56–60 and 64–66. Amico came to Palestine in 1593 and served as guardian of Bethlehem for six months in 1593 and as President of the Church of the Holy Sepulcher in 1596. He returned to Italy in 1598 after serving as chaplain in Cairo; Bagatti preface, ibid., 2–3.

45 For visual examples, see Ris-Paquot, *Dictionnaire encyclopédique des marques et monogrammes, chiffres, lettres initiales, signes figuratifs, etc., etc.*, 2 vols. (Paris: Henri Laurens, 1893; reed. New York: B. Franklin, 1964). See also Georges Auriol, *Le premier livre des cachets, marques et monogrammes* (Paris: Librairie centrale des beaux-arts, 1901). Though I have been unable to locate a catalogued monogram that corresponds exactly to the one on this pilgrim's arm, many resemble it closely. For collections of distinguishing marks on paper, which period representations of pilgrim tattoos also resemble, see Raymond Gaudriault, *Filigranes et autres caractéristiques des papiers fabriqués en France aux XVIIe et XVIIIe siècles* (Paris: CNRS, J. Telford, 1995) and Charles-Moïse Briquet, *Les Filigranes: Dictionnaire historique des marques du papier dès leur apparition vers 1282 jusqu'en 1600*, 4 vols. (facsimile rpt. of 1907 ed., Hildescheim and New York: G. Olms, 1977). On the importance of *marques* in the commercial realm, see Chapter 5.

46 Lithgow, *The Totall Discourse*, 285–86. On Lithgow's tattoos see Fleming, "The Renaissance Tattoo," 80–81 and Lewy, "Jerusalem unter der Haut," 26.

47 Lithgow, *The Totall Discourse*, 286.

48 Lithgow is one notable exception. He openly testifies to his patriotic desire to have King James's insignia emblazoned on his arm; ibid., 285–86. See also below the discussion of Coryat's spiritual-emotional attachment to his tattoos, which comes to us secondhand.

49 On criminal branding, see Chapter 5.

50 Greffin Affagart, *Relation de Terre Sainte (1533–1534)*, ed. J. Chavanon (Paris: Librairie Victor Lecoffre, 1902), 81. See also Lewy, "Jerusalem unter der Haut," 9–10. He discusses this use of branding as a literal interpretation of John the Baptist's announcement that he who followed him would baptize by fire. Affagart paints a far less favorable picture of body marking among another Christian sect, the Jacobites, whom he casts as heretical, in part for their use of body marking; Affagart, *Relation de la Terre Sainte*, 91.

51 Ibid., 81. See also: Lund, *Die Alten Jüdishchen Heiligtümer*, 732; Jean Boucher, *Le Bouquet sacré ou le voyage de la terre sainte* (Rouen: Jean B. Besogne, [1620] 1722), 599–600; Villamont, *Les Voyages*, fols. 182r-182v and 185v; Bénard, *Le voyage de Hierusalem*, 222–23; and Morison, *Relation Historique*, 300–9.

52 Boucher, *Le Bouquet sacré*, 599–600.

53 Marc Lescarbot, *Histoire de la Nouvelle-France* (Paris: Jean Millot, 1609), 723–24; qtd. here from Marie-Christine Pioffet's edition of book VI, chapter X of Lescarbot's work, "Description des mœurs souriquoises comparées à celles d'autres peuples," in *Voyages en Acadie (1604–1607) suivis de La Description des mœurs souriquoises comparées à celles d'autres peuples* (Québec: Presses de l'Université Laval, 2007), 320.

54 "Stigmates," Denis Diderot and Jean le Rond D'Alembert, ed., *Encyclopédie ou Dictionnaire Raisonné des Sciences, des Arts et des Métiers* (Paris: Briasson, David, Le Breton, and Durand, 1751–1772).

55 A.M. Koldeweij also makes the connection between pilgrim badges worn on clothing and signs on skin; "Lifting the Veil on Pilgrim Badges," trans. Ruth Koenig, in *Pilgrimage Explored*, ed. J. Stopford (Woodbridge, Suffolk, UK and Rochester, NY: York Medieval Press and The Boydell Press, 1999), 161–88; 161–63.

56 The use of badges was particularly widespread from the fourteenth through early sixteenth centuries, when the practice began to decline due to Protestant criticism; Rembrandt Duits, "Art, Class, and Wealth," in *Viewing Renaissance Art*, ed. Kim W. Woods, Carol M. Richardson, and Angeliki Lymberopoulou (New Haven, CT: Yale University Press, 2007), 27–28.

57 See also the 1664 engraving by Sébastien Le Clerc (1637–1714), presented in Chapter 1 (Figure 1.2). Another French example is by Jacques Callot, *Les Geueux* (1622 or 1623), whose figures wear the scallop shell; rpt. in Noonan, *The Road to Jerusalem*, fig. 14. Legend has it that a pious woman of Jerusalem was so moved by Christ's suffering as he carried his cross that she gave him her veil to wipe his face, which was therein miraculously impressed with his true resemblance. This "vera icon" or "true image" for which the woman was named Saint Veronica is kept at Saint Peter's Basilica in Rome.

58 Duits, "Art, Class, and Wealth," 27.

59 Ibid. See also Don C. Skemer, *Binding Words: Textual Amulets in the Middle Ages* (University Park, PA: The Pennsylvania State University Press, 2006), 68–69.

60 See also a 1571 engraving of Jerusalem pilgrims, one of whom wears the cross of Jerusalem on his left breast; Jean-Jacques Breuning de Buochenback, *Trois pèlerins de Jérusalem en 1571, avec à droite un chavalier du Saint-Sépulcre, gravure tirée de J.J. Breuning von Buochenbach* (N.p.: Erste Meerfahrt von Venedig auff Constantinopel, n.d. [1605]), 216. Rpt. in Lewy, "Jerusalem unter der Haut," 6, fig. 2 and Gennes, *Les Chevaliers*, vol. 1, 421, fig. 16.

61 "Le Pelerin qui voyage n'est pas Sage, S'il marche en autre equipage;" De Vergoncy, *Le Pelerin veritable*, title page.

62 See, for example: Loys Balourdet, *La Guide des chemins pour le Voyage de Hierusalem* (Chalons: C. Guyot, 1601), fols. 80r–80v; Henry Castela, *Le Guide et Adresse pour ceux qui veullent faire le S. Voyage de Hierusalem* (Paris: Laurens Sonnius, 1604), 54; Bénard, *Le voyage de Hierusalem*, 3–4; Félix Beaugrand, *Relation nouvelle et tres-fidelle du Voyage de la Terre Sainte* (Paris: Antoine Warin, 1700), 36–37. Passports began to develop from 1550–1650 and became obligatory in the seventeenth century. On the early history of the passport, see Valentin Groebner, *Who Are You? Identification, Deception, and Surveillance in Early Modern Europe*, trans. Mark Kyburz and John Peck (New York: Zone Books, 2007), esp. ch. 7, 171–221.

63 Gilles Fermanel, Robert Fauvel, Baudouin de Launay, and Vincent Stochove, *Le Voyage d'Italie et du Levant* (Rouen: Jacques Herault, 1670), n. pag.

64 De Vergoncy, *Le Pelerin Veritable*, 358.

65 Bénard, *Le voyage de Hierusalem*, 122.

66 Castela, *Le sainct voyage*, 274.

67 Ibid.

68 Ibid., 382–83. Emphasis in original.

69 In contrast, the testimony of Protestant pilgrim Fynes Moryson (1565–1630) suggests that bearing such an identifying mark could sometimes be hazardous. When the Catholics in their party get tattooed, Moryson and his brother make the excuse "that being to passe home through many Kingdomes, we durst not beare any such marke upon our bodies, whereby wee might bee knowne;" Fynes Moryson, *An itinerary*, 3 vols. (London: John Beale, 1617), vol. 1, 237.

70 Boucher, *Le Bouquet sacré*, 378. See also Amico's description, *Plans of the Sacred Edifices*, 64–66.

71 Letter by Jean-Jacques Rahier, rpt. in Jean Mauzaize, "Lettre inédite d'un Frère Mineur, gardien du couvent de Bethlem (1660)" in *Archivum franciscanum historicum* 74.1 (1981): [11] 255–56.

72 See also Ousterhout, "Permanent Emphemera," 96–97.

73 De Vergoncy, *Le Pelerin Veritable*, 358.

74 On stigmata and seventeenth-century women who marked their bodies as a devotional gesture, see Chapter 2. The only known official Church testimony interpreting tattooing as suffering for God is the centuries-earlier 787 A.D. report

of the Papal Legates to Northumbria, which affirmed that while the corporeal signs made by pagans should be considered demonic, those who suffered for God deserved praise: "Certainly if someone were willing to suffer the pain of dye for God, he would be handsomely rewarded;" Arthur West Haddan and William Stubbs, *Councils and Ecclesiastical Documents Relating to Great Britain and Ireland*, 3 vols. (Oxford: The Clarendon Press, 1964), vol. 3, 458.

75 The nature of Paul's marks (*stigmata* in Latin) has long been disputed. See Adnès, "Stigmates," col. 1212 and MacQuarrie, "Insular Celtic Tattooing," in *Written on the Body*, ed. Caplan, 35–36. Early modern theologians, both Catholic and Protestant, generally read Saint Paul's reference to his "stigmata" not as tattoos, brands, or divinely given wounds, but, as "scars . . . endured for the Gospel;" Augustin Calmet (1672–1757), *Commentaire Litteral Sur Tous Les Livres de l'Ancien et du Nouveau Testament*, 23 vols. (Paris: Pierre Emery, 1716), vol. 22, *Les Épitres de Saint Paul*, 79. See also Jean Calvin (1509–1564), *Commentaires de Jean Calvin sur le Nouveau Testament*, vol. 6, *Épîtres aux Galates, Éphésiens, Philippiens et Colossiens*, ed. Daniel Guex, Michel Réveillaud, and Roger Barilier (Aix-en-Provence: Éditions Kerygma, 1978), 131. For these writers, Paul's scars of physical suffering function to identify him as a servant of Christ, just as brands functioned in ancient times to identify slaves and soldiers; Calmet, *Commentaire Litteral*, vol. 22, 78–79 and Calvin, *Commentaires*, vol. 6, 131–32. See also Lescarbot, *Description des mœurs*, 320–21.

76 Terry, *A Voyage to East-India*, 65. On Terry's testimony and the reading of the pilgrim tattoo as stigmata, see also Fleming, "The Renaissance Tattoo," 79–80 and Lewy, "Jerusalem unter der Haut," 8–9.

77 On the early and medieval Christian history of tattooing see MacQuarrie, "Insular Celtic Tattooing," who underlines the dual associations of tattooing in the medieval period with both pagan tradition and Christ's wounds and Lewy, "Jerusalem unter der Haut," 2–5, who cites instances of crusader tattooing or branding. See also recent scholarly work presented at the "Nella Pelle/Into the Skin" conference held December 5–6, 2011, at the Pontificia Università Urbaniana in Vatican City and Pierre Adnès, "Stigmates," in *Dictionnaire de spiritualité ascétique et mystique, doctrine et histoire*, ed. Marcel Viller, F. Cavallera, and J. de Guibert, 17 vols. (Paris: G. Beauchesne, 1942–1995), vol. 14, 1211–43; 1212–13. Some popular tattoo histories discuss earlier instances of tattooing in the context of the crusades and medieval pilgrimage, but use loose chronologies and lack citation; see, for example, William Cruchet, *Tatouages et tatoués* (Paris: Tchou, 1976), 89–93.

78 Brémond's original French publication has been lost but appears in translation; Giuseppe Corvo, *Viaggi Fatti Nell'Egitto Superiore et Inferiore . . . Opera Del Signor Gabrielle Bremond Marsiliese* (Rome: Paolo Moneta, [1673] 1679), 31 [395 of entire work]. See also Villamont, *Les Voyages*, fols. 328v-329r.

79 Ousterhout, "Permanent Emphemera," 104.

80 Lund, *Die Alten Jüdishchen Heiligtümer*, 732.

81 On measuring with one's own body, see, for example, Boucher, *Le Bouquet sacré*, "Avertissement," n. pag. On the importance of measurement in pilgrimage, see Zur Shalev, "Christian Pilgrimage and Ritual Measurement in Jerusalem" (Berlin: Max Planck Institute for the History of Science, 2009). See also Ousterhout, "Permanent Emphemera," 96–97.

82 Doubdan, *Le Voyage de Terre-Sainte*, "Au lecteur," n. pag.

83 See also Ousterhout, "Permanent Emphemera," 105 and 108.

84 Lund, *Die Alten Jüdishchen Heiligtümer*, 732.

85 Ibid.

86 Fleming, "The Renaissance Tattoo," 80–81.
87 See also the portrait of Ludoff, rpt. in Lewy, "Jerusalem unter der Haut," 33, fig. 21.
88 Shearer West, *Portraiture* (Oxford: Oxford University Press, 2004), 43–44.
89 Ibid., 81–86.
90 I use Steven Greenblatt's term; *Renaissance Self-Fashioning: From More to Shakespeare* (Chicago and London: The University of Chicago Press, 1980).
91 "Marque," Antoine Furetière, *Dictionnaire universel* (La Haye and Rotterdam: Arnout & Reinier Leers, 1690).
92 Boucher, *Le Bouquet Sacré*, 7.
93 Similar mystery is maintained by the painter in his portrayal of the pilgrim's right arm, where he obscures the last digit of the date of pilgrimage as well as the first initial of the crowned monogram the sitter bears.
94 Pierre Marie Louis de Boisgelin de Kerdu, alias Caillot-Duval, *Ancient and Modern Malta: Containing a Full and Accurate Account of the Present State of the Islands of Malta and Goza, the History of the Knights of St. John of Jerusalem* (London: R. Phillips, 1805).
95 Paul Walden Bramford, "The Knights of Malta and the King of France, 1665–1700," *French Historical Studies* 3.4 (Autumn 1964): 429–53.
96 Cécile Bosman, personal communication, January 16, 2018.
97 Bramford, "The Knights of Malta," 429–30. The Knights of Saint John, though Catholic in origin, formed a Protestant branch at the Reformation and were active in seventeenth-century Holland and Germany as well as in predominantly Catholic countries, including France. The traveler could thus have belonged to the Order whatever his origin or confession. On the order, see Robert M. Clark, Jr., *The Evangelical Knights of Saint John: A History of the Bailiwick of Brandenburg of the Knightly Order of St. John of the Hospital at Jerusalem, Known as the Johanniter Order* (Dallas, TX: Robert M. Clark, Jr., 2003) and Guy Stair Sainty, *The Orders of Saint John: The History, Structure, Membership and Modern Role of the Five Hospitaller Orders of Saint John of Jerusalem* (New York: The American Society of the Most Venerable Order of the Hospital of Saint John in Jerusalem, 1991).
98 Pierre de Lancre, *Tableau de l'inconstance des mauvais anges et demons* (Paris: Jean Berjon, 1612), 183.
99 Thirteen merchant sea captains are listed on the Franciscan Order's rolls, all from Marseille, the French city from which pilgrims most often departed. Well-known political figures include President of the Parlement de Paris, François-Auguste de Thou, inducted in 1628, and Maréchaux de France, François de l'Hospital, inducted in 1654; Gennes, *Les Chevaliers*, vol. 2, 294. Moryson suggests that the Franciscans, in need of the money that was exchanged for the honor, took "anyone" in this period, though his testimony is of course colored by his distaste for Catholic practices: "I well knew that they had offered this honour (as they termed it) to a Plebean Frenchman our consort, and had heard, that the Friars used this art to get money from Pilgrimes, making no difference to whom they gave this title;" Moryson, *An itinerary*, vol. 1, 237.
100 Gennes, *Les Chevaliers*, vol. 1, 432–33.
101 The Order and its symbol receive contemporary treatment in *La Vraye et parfaite science des armoiries ou L'Indice Armorial du feu Maistre Louvan Geliot* (Paris: Jean Guignard le pere, Guillaume de Luynes, et Helie Josset, 1660), ed. Pierre Palliot, facsimile ed., 2 vols. (Paris: Édouard Rouveyre, 1895); vol. 2, 486–87. On the order, see Gennes's *Les Chevaliers*. Though temporarily

abolished with all chivalric orders by Louis XVI in 1791, the order continues to this day; ibid., vol. 2, 84.

102 Gröben, *Orientalische Reise-Beschreibung*, 285.

103 See also Lewy, "Jerusalem unter der Haut," 6–7. For visual examples of the embroidered cross, see the portraits of French Knights rpt. in Gennes, *Les chevaliers*, vol. 2.

104 Bénard, *Le voyage de Hierusalem*, 122. Bénard devotes significant portions of his text to discussion of the Order (176 ff.), recounting his own induction (ch. 28) and even reproducing the full articles of the Knights (196 ff.). The parchment attestation of membership also bore the official seal of the Jerusalem cross in red wax. See Nicolas de Hault's description in *Le Voyage de Hierusalem* (Rouen: Theodore Reinsart, 1601), 103. He reproduces the full text of his letters of induction (103–6) and recounts the ceremony of knighting in detail; 69–79. The use of the Jerusalem Cross in coats of arms is documented in H. de Gérin-Ricard, *La Croix de Jérusalem dans la numismatique, sur les sceaux et dans le blason* (Vannes: Lafolye Frères, 1905) and Émile Perrier, *La croix de Jérusalem dans le blason, étude héraldique et historique* (Valence: Valentinoise, 1905). Gennes reprints an engraving of the epitaph of Gilles Portes (†1634), Knight of the Holy Sepulcher of 1610, which prominently displays the cross of Jerusalem and the palm branches in several places on the gravestone; *Les Chevaliers*, vol. 2, 102, fig. 5. See also figs. 25 and 34.

105 The prevalence of Jerusalem tattoos even on the skin of non-pilgrims, such as those that adorned the bodies of European soldiers and servants in North America, none of whom had made the Holy Land pilgrimage, supports the prevalence of their use as symbolic capital, even as it questions their role as authoritative signs of completed pilgrimage. On colonists in New France who tattooed their bodies with iconography drawn from pilgrimage tradition, see Chapter 3. Craig Koslofsky's current research has brought to light advertisements for the retrieval of runaway servants that list the "Jerusalem Arms" among identifying corporeal marks; work in progress presented as "A Deep Surface? Taking Stock of the History of Skin in Early American Studies" at the 23rd Annual Conference of the Omohundro Institute of Early American History and Culture, Ann Arbor, MI, June 15–18 2017 and as "Tattooed Servants: The Jerusalem Arms in the Atlantic World" at the Renaissance Society of America Annual Conference, New Orleans, LA, March 22–24, 2018.

106 On the relationship between tattooing and nomadism, see also Dubé, *Tattootatoué*, 26 and 190.

107 On Modern Primitivism, see V. Vale and Andrea Juno, eds., *Modern Primitives: An Investigation of Contemporary Adornment and Ritual* (San Francisco, CA: RE/Search, 1989), Margo DeMello, *Bodies of Inscription: A Cultural History of the Modern Tattoo Community* (Durham, NC: Duke University Press, 2000), 174–84 and David Le Breton, "Anthropologie des marques corporelles," in *Signes du corps*, ed. Christine Falgayrettes-Leveau (Paris: Musée Dapper, 2004), 106–15, "La mythologie du primitivism;" full article 73–119.

108 See, for example, Joseph-François Lafitau, *Mœurs des sauvages amériquains comparées aux mœurs des premiers temps*, 2 vols. (Paris: Saugrain l'aîné and Charles Estienne Hochereau, 1724), vol. 2, 45 and Jean-François Benjamin Dumont de Montigny (1696–after 1753), *Mémoires historiques Contenant ce qui y est arrivé de plus mémorable depuis l'année 1687 jusqu'à présent* (Paris: J. B. Bauche, 1753), vol. 1, 185. For more examples, see Chapter 3.

109 Lescarbot, *Description des mœurs*, 320.

5   Stigma and state control
Branding the deviant body

But the body is also directly involved in a political field; power relations have an immediate hold upon it; they invest it, mark it, train it, torture it, force it to carry out tasks, to perform ceremonies, to emit signs.

—Michel Foucault, *Discipline and Punish*[1]

Shortly after the defeat of the Spanish at Leucate in 1637, an errant Spanish captain, Don Arnandes de Muranda, sought refuge in the city of Toulouse.[2] For a short time, he passed himself off as an Italian *operateur*, extracting teeth and performing other minor surgery, but soon found that he could not make a living at dentistry alone. So he turned to stealing vegetables from the marketplace on a regular basis with which he was said to have made "the most splendid feasts." Nicknamed "croca ravo," or "turnip eater," for his often repeated crime, he was finally brought before the court, where he was accused by vegetable sellers to have stolen from their stands and exposed as a counterfeiter of low-value coins, *doubles* and *sols*.[3] The court sentenced Don Arnandes to be publicly beaten and whipped at all the major intersections and squares of the city for the crime of stealing vegetables and to be branded with the fleur-de-lis on his shoulder for counterfeiting. Thus marked with the sign of the kingdom, he was forever banished from it, on pain of hanging if he returned. Local authorities carried out his sentence on September 6, 1638, "to the great detriment of his poor shoulders that were marked and gravely wounded."[4]

The print portrayal of Don Arnandes's punishment ridicules the condemned Spaniard in image and word (see Figure 5.1). He looks dejectedly over his shoulder at his spectators, his bare back exposed to the hot branding iron. His second *bourreau*, or executioner, above him on the cart, clutches the bundle of vegetables with which the accused has been, appropriately, beaten. Above the victim sits a magistrate on horseback, reading the text of the prisoner's sentence. His horse's head leans into the Spaniard's at the center of the image, encouraging comparison between beast and man. The engraver's unflattering rendering of the Spaniard's physiognomy reinforces this parallel, as does the act of branding, since

Figure 5.1 Spaniard receiving the whip and the fleur-de-lis, *Histoire veritable et facecieuse d'un Espaignol lequel à eu le fouet et la fleur de lis dans la Ville de Thoulouze pour avoir derobé des raves et roigné des doubles. Extraict d'une lettre escrite de ladite Ville de Thoulouze le 13. Septembre dernier* (1638). Bibliothèque Nationale de France.

livestock, including horses, were commonly branded during the period.[5] Jesting verses cast the convict as far more mournful for the lost vegetables than for his beaten and marked body:

> I do not regret that my shoulders are split
> From a thousand blows nor the fleur-de-lis,
> But to see lost on my back so many turnips
> In which I would indulge along with partridge.[6]

This seemingly banal disciplinary tale was made much of, no doubt, because of the ideal opportunity it provided for French wartime mockery of the Spanish. Labeled a "true and comical story," the case represented here may actually be fictitious, given the stereotypical depiction of the convict—complete with spurs, a long handlebar mustache, and radishes; French engravers of the period often caricatured Spaniards with root vegetables to mock their diets and portray them as raping the fertile land of France.[7] Nevertheless, fact or fiction, the judicial treatment inflicted upon Don Arnandes was indeed real and even common punishment in early modern France, for foreigners and Frenchmen alike. Branding with a hot iron punished minor infractions in France and its colonies, and, with modifications, throughout much of early modern Europe, from the mid-sixteenth century.[8] In France and the French Atlantic, the brand first took the shape of the fleur-de-lis to be joined later, especially after 1724, by brands made in the shape of letters corresponding to specific crimes or punishments.[9] A sentence of "fouet et flétrissure"—whipping and branding—commonly disciplined those found guilty of petty theft, fraud, or professional mendicancy. Lyonnais attorney Claude Le Brun de la Rochette's 1609 description of punishment for theft underlines both the prevalent use of the mark and its built-in degrees of severity:

> [I]n France, all thieves are punished according to the quality of their crime. This is to say: simple theft well and duly verified, with the whip, for the first time; for the second time, more beating, with the impression of a fleur-de-lis, which the executioner imprints with the hot iron on the shoulder of the thief. If they commit a subsequent third offence, they are hung and strangled. And of this sort there are ten thousand judgments delivered by Royal Justices and confirmed by the rulings of sovereign Courts.[10]

Branding also punished the more serious crimes of extortion, counterfeiting, and the smuggling of salt, tobacco, or painted fabrics. It had its place in the disciplinary hierarchy just below capital punishment, as Paris law professor Claude-Joseph de Ferrière (1680–1748) points out in his definition:

FLETRISSURE is the impression of the fleur-de-lis, or of some other mark that is made by the Executioner on the skin of the condemned criminal proven guilty of a crime that merits corporeal punishment, but does not absolutely merit death.[11]

In France and its North American colonies, the mark never stood alone in sentencing but was always paired with whipping, beating, exhibition in the iron collar or the stocks, banishment, or, increasingly during the personal reign of the Louis XIV, sentencing to service in the royal galleys.[12] In the French Antilles, article thirty-eight of the 1685 *Code Noir*, which enacted into law practices already in place since 1615, coupled the branding of fugitive slaves with further bodily mutilation. It prescribed that runaway slaves who evaded capture for a month be branded with the fleur-de-lis on the shoulder and have their ears cut off, and that fugitives at large a second month be hamstrung and branded on the other shoulder.[13]

As the text of the *Code Noir* testifies, when it came to branding, not all were treated equally. Fugitive African slaves, though branded with the fleur-de-lis like convicts in France, were also subject to far more horrific punishments of mutilation than were the white European-born slaves who populated the French galleys. Moreover, considered identical to livestock, enslaved Africans were not only marked as punishment but also systematically branded with a variety of signs to show provenance and ownership both before leaving Africa and upon their sale in the colonies.[14] French Dominican missionary Jean-Baptiste Labat (1663–1738) recounts in great detail the branding process by which captives were marked with their master's sign as practiced in Saint Domingue:

> The Inhabitants of Saint Domingue and Cow Island mark their *Negres* when they buy them. To do this they use a thin blade of silver, made so that it forms their monogram [*chiffre*], it is joined to a little handle, so that it can be held, and since these same monograms or letters could be encountered among several Inhabitants, they apply them in different places. Some above the stomach, others beneath it, some on the right, others on the left, some on the arms, others in other places. When one wants to stamp a *Negre*, you heat up the stamp, without letting it get red hot, rub the place where you want to apply it with a little soot or fat, and cover it with oiled or waxed paper, and apply the stamp to it as lightly as possible. The flesh swells immediately, and when the effect of the burn has passed, the mark stays imprinted on the skin, without it ever being possible to erase it. Because of this, a slave who had been sold and resold several times would appear in the end as covered with characters as the Egyptian obelisks.[15]

Marked with their slavers' and masters' distinctive signs, runaway slaves could thus be identified more easily in the case of recapture. How else,

Labat wonders, "could the Masters recognize those that belonged to them?" Such permanent marks, he writes, also hindered would-be thieves:

> It could even happen that people without conscience find fugitive *Negres* and take them for themselves, which isn't possible when they are marked, because their Master would recognize them and could easily prove that they belong to him, by showing the mark.[16]

Similar reflections regarding ease of identification characterized the theorization of the criminal brand in this period, as we will explore further below.

In France, though both female and male convicts were marked, women were not sentenced to the galleys for reasons of propriety but instead condemned to banishment or to the *Hôpital général* or a *maison de force* [workhouse]. They therefore sometimes received different marks than men did for similar crimes. Members of the French nobility avoided corporeal punishment as a rule, while the French lower classes who transgressed paid for their crime with a mark on their body rather than a stain on their reputation, as eighteenth-century Parlement de Paris lawyer and legal commentator, Pierre-François Muyart de Vouglans (1713–1791), explains: "In Crime, people from the lower classes [*les Vilains*] are more severely punished in body than are Noblemen. . . . And where the person from the lower class [*le Vilain*] would lose his life or a member of his body, the Nobleman would lose his honor and his standing in Court."[17] Paradoxically, then, an *homme marqué*—a marked man—could never be an *homme de marque*, a man of consideration and distinction.[18] The public branding of our Spanish nobleman, Don Arnandes de Muranda, thus debases him all the more.

The fleur-de-lis, as the emblem of the French monarchy dating back to the twelfth century, carried with it extraordinary symbolic capital, which Hyacinthe Rigaud's famous 1701 painting of Louis XIV in regalia, later engraved by Pierre Drevet, encapsulates (see Figure 5.2).[19] Fleurs-de-lis cover the King's body, scepter, and crown, as well as the furniture that surrounds him.[20] Stringent regulations circumscribed the use of the fleur-de-lis in seals, coats of arms, and decorative objects from the sixteenth through eighteenth centuries. The sign adorned the robes of royalty and the magistrates who carried out the monarch's justice—themselves extensions of the King's body—as well as the fixtures and fabrics that decorated the rooms in which they exercised their functions. Marking the convict's body with the fleur-de-lis thus operated a powerful symbolic transfer: the sign of sovereign power literally penetrated the King's subject, flesh replacing fabric as the convict's body became a site for the display of the royal emblem. A performative gesture that publicly reclaimed the deviant body for the King, public branding enacted an inclusionary exclusion on the criminal's body.[21] Even as it declared the offender's social marginalization and advertised his past guilt, the mark imprinted on his body was also a sign of

Figure 5.2 Louis XIV in regalia, Pierre Drevet (1712), after Hyacinthe Rigaud (1701).
Dallas Museum of Art, Junior League Print Fund (1949.63).

belonging, which designated the convict as the monarch's possession and recalled the King's authority over the bodies of all of his subjects.

This sign of ownership was far from benign. An extant fleur-de-lis branding iron of Acadian origin, probably made in France and sent for use in the colony, reifies the violent objectification of this inscription (see Figure 5.3).[22] Cast in bronze or gunmetal—an alloy of bronze, tin, and zinc—and made to be inserted into a longer handle, when heated and applied to the convict's back, its concave design would have left a clear imprint of the fleur-de-lis outline upon the skin.[23] This gesture of branding the body as a sign of possession, claiming the offender as the King's own, was all the more poignant for those actually enslaved. African slaves in Saint Domingue, branded as Labat described with their captors' and owners' distinguishing marks, and once again branded with the fleur-de-lis as punishment if caught at large, were considered quite literally property, marked "like one does Cattle and Horses."[24] In France, the *galérien* too became the King's

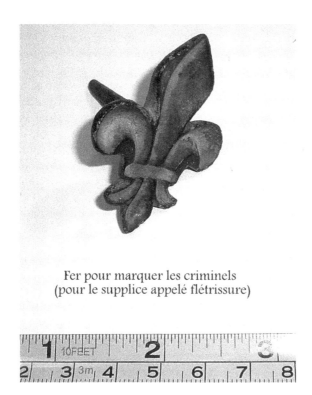

Fer pour marquer les criminels
(pour le supplice appelé flétrissure)

Figure 5.3 Extant fleur-de-lis branding iron (before 1755). Acadian Museum of the University of Moncton, New Brunswick, Canada. Photo courtesy of Ghislain Savoie and Bernard LeBlanc.

acquisition, a slave devoid of civil rights for the duration of his sentence in the royal galleys, which often lasted a lifetime.[25] As the Chancelier de Pontchartrain writes in 1700 to Baseau, royal prosecutor at the Presidial of Angoulême, about a prisoner destined for a life sentence in the galleys, "He is acquired by the king through this capital condemnation; he is a slave to his punishment."[26]

A sign of the times

Though today we associate branding with the inhumane and barbaric systems of corporeal punishment of a distant past, criminal branding was, in fact, a modern innovation, born and deployed in the courts of France and across Europe beginning in the mid-sixteenth century. Dictionary entries attest to the novelty and prevalence of branding in the early modern period, as old words took on new disciplinary meanings and new words were created to name what was a judicial novelty. Originally used primarily to describe a loss or alteration of beauty or vitality in a plant, and by extension, in the human face, the twelfth-century verb *fleistrir* and the thirteenth-century adjective, *fleistri*, began to carry an increasingly punitive signification in the sixteenth century. Randle Cotgrave's 1611 entry for *flaistri* in his *Dictionarie of the French and English Tongues* records this turn—"Marked, branded, burnt, as a rogue, in some apparent member, with an hot yron."[27] Cotgrave gives disciplinary meanings prominence in his definitions, placing them first: "Flaistrissure: f. a disgracefull brand, or mark;" "Fleurdeliser. To set a Flowerdeluce betweene the shoulders with a hot yron (the marke of a rogue);" "Fleurdelisé. Branded, or marked for a rogue, with the print of a Flowerdeluce, between his shoulders." The seventeenth-century appearance of the verb *fleurdeliser* for describing what was by then a common practice in France is particularly telling. By the end of the century, French dictionaries attest that a specific legal vocabulary for branding was well established. According to Antoine Furetière's 1690 *Dictionnaire universel*, "In Court language you say that a man is con-demned to be *flestri*, that is to say, to be marked on the shoulder with a fleur-de-lis applied with a hot iron." Similarly, the 1694 *Dictionnaire de l'Académie française* states that "in criminal terminology, we say of a man condemned to receive the fleur-de-lis, that he is condemned to be *flestri* on the shoulder with a fleur-de-lis."[28] Significantly, while they mention slave branding in ancient Rome and Greece, the dictionaries of the period omit any reference to the branding of the bodies of Africans in the context of the Atlantic slave trade, an erasure that speaks volumes regarding voluntary European blindness to the harsh realities of the slave system, even as the economies of the colonial powers began to depend on it.

While punishments that disfigured the body—the burning of the lips, brand-ing of cheeks, or removal of ears or hands—had been common throughout the Middle Ages and cruelly persisted in the French Antilles in the treatment of slaves, sentences involving bodily mutilation became increasingly rare in France for the punishment of noncapital crimes beginning in the sixteenth century.[29] As Alfred Soman asserts, the rapid abandonment of corporeal mutilation for petty crimes may represent the most remarkable transformation in early modern judicial procedure.[30] This shift suggests not only the emergence of a sensibility reflective of humanist ideals, albeit confined to white European bodies, but also a will on the part of authorities to repurpose the brand to suit the needs of a modernizing state apparatus. In intention at least, the brand—recast as an administrative sign—was no longer meant to stigmatize, but only to identify, if and when the convict committed another crime. With shame no longer the goal, rather than disfiguring the convict by placing the mark on readily visible parts of the body, the modern French system hid it under the clothes.

The judges who ordered marking—though undoubtedly not the convicts who underwent it—classified the brand as an secondary punishment, a *peine accessoire*, meant not as a punishment in and of itself but uniquely as a means to identify a repeat offender: "It was introduced so that those who had been subjected to one or the other of these punishments could be recognized by this mark."[31] Though jurists listed it among "afflictive" punishments because it harmed the body, they cast it as a purely administrative imprint, a memorandum so useful that the state was willing to invest in its relatively expensive execution, which only fees for capital punishment surpassed.[32] Like the printed registers of names and descriptions of ex-convicts that began to circulate from city to city in the seventeenth century in an effort to trace their movements, branding, at least in theory, allowed judicial authorities to track repeat offenders and to ensure their proper sentencing in the case of a new crime in a more efficient and permanent manner. As Muyart de Vouglans explains:

> [T]he particular motive that led to establishing the imposition of these marks, was to guarantee therein proof of the condemnation; so that in the case of subsequent offenses by the condemned, his Punishment could be augmented, and increased even to that of death.[33]

Louis XV himself underlined the brand's administrative purpose in an attempt to clarify his reasons for marking galley slaves. In letters of patent to the Parlement of Rouen, May 27, 1750, he describes the brand as a textual sign: "[The mark] should have been considered less as a punishment than as a sign [*une note*] that could serve to recognize those who, after having served their sentence in the galleys, would fall into new crimes."[34] In using the term "note," from the Latin *nota*, meaning "mark," the King invoked a word used foremost in the period to designate a textual sign made in books or documents, for purposes of recollection: "a mark that one puts in a certain place in a Book, or a written document, when there is something noteworthy, and that one wants to remember."[35] The brand therefore served as a permanent memorandum of an individual's past transgression, making the offender a vector through which state control could be implemented across time and space. In an age before computerized criminal records, photos, and fingerprinting, not to mention DNA registries or retinal scans, criminal branding transformed the body into the fleshy archive of an individual's passage through judicial hands. Moreover, because marking could be repeated for certain crimes upon second and sometimes even subsequent offenses, some convicts, like the slaves in Saint Domingue, carried not one but several brands on their backs. Their bodies could be read, then, to some extent, much as the text of a criminal record is today.

This system of recognition was not foolproof, however. Convicts were probably not always consistently marked, and marks made beyond French royal jurisdiction—where the fleur-de-lis was used exclusively until the end of the seventeenth century—varied in form and might be subject to mis-interpretation. Convicts also regularly attempted to cast the signs identified upon their skin as scars, rather than *marques de justice*. The archives of the Parlement of Paris include testimony in which convicts claimed that their apparent brand marks were due to accidents or disease.[36] However, jurists nonetheless express confidence in their new system. According to the 1588 testimony of Parisian lawyer Antoine Mornac (1554–1619), criminal brands were most often easily recognizable, at least to the authorities who pos-sessed the knowledge and experience to read them properly: "They wanted to say, undressing him, that a mark found on him was from a plague abscess he had had. Those who are knowledgeable said that it was a mark of justice."[37] Despite its flaws, the system represented an improvement on past practices, allowing judges to recognize repeat offenders and thus tailor their new sentence accordingly. The convict was marked so that he might be *marqué*—noticed, designated, known.

Early modern proponents of this "new and improved" judicial branding were careful to distinguish the practice and its purpose from that of earlier times.[38] In 1603, jurisconsult Louys Carondas Le Caron (ca. 1534–1613) notes that unlike the branding of the cheeks reported by his medieval predecessors, "[w]e no longer use the punishment of branding or marking on the face, but [brand] on the shoulder instead."[39] Legal commentators of the period emphasized the choice of a more hidden and less disfiguring placement of the brand on the shoulder as a sign of their humanity and modernity, as Ferrière later summarizes:

> In the past they branded on a visible place on the body, so that this mark served as a sign, both of the guilty person's crime and of the punishment that they had suffered as a result, so that he could never show himself without displaying his ignominy at the same time. But this rigor seemed too great . . . which made it so that today we only brand on the shoulder.[40]

In contrast to earlier mutilations of the face that condemned the convict to a life of hiding, the shoulder brand, as the anonymous author of the ca. 1640 *Recueil d'affaires criminelles* writes, "cannot be seen and indicates just as well that they have been touched by justice;" it served its administrative purpose without overly stigmatizing its bearer.[41] In choosing to brand in a more easily hidden location, the French also distinguished themselves from the English, who continued to mark the hand and face in some contexts even into the nineteenth century.[42] While Cotgrave's definition of *flaistrir* includes burning in the hand, ear, or forehead—practices common in his native England during this period—he consistently cites the distinctly French fleur-de-lis as imprinted on or between the shoulders.[43] Late seventeenth-century French dictionaries also specify that the brand is made the shoulder in their definitions, emphasizing this refinement upon which magistrates prided themselves.[44]

This idea that branding represented a kinder, gentler justice found itself reinforced in works of fiction as well. Anne-Marie-Louise d'Or-léans, duchesse de Montpensier (1627–1696), underlines the relative humanity of branding by including the practice in her *Royaume de la lune*, a parody of Cyrano de Bergerac's well-known *Histoire comique des états et empires de la lune* (1657).[45] Montpensier portrays a queen of the moon who, when doling out punishments, considers the possibility of branding criminals with an iron shaped in the form of a crescent representing her kingdom, the moon: "Next she decided to have the Crescent given to people who had not committed grave offences, like they imprint the fleur-de-lis on the shoulder of French pickpockets." However, branding does not prove harsh enough to satisfy her sadistic impulses: "[B]ut because this punishment did not thoroughly satisfy the spirit of cruelty that possessed her, she invented a whole new torment," deciding instead to hang offenders up on hooks by their noses.[46] Montpensier's transposition of branding to the lunar kingdom thus ironically supports the claim made by judicial authorities that branding was a relatively innocuous punishment, since it proved to be not cruel enough for her flamboyantly mad lunar queen.

It must be acknowledged, though, that despite judicial authorities' insistence on the shoulder mark as a more humane solution to the problem of tracking criminals, the ignominy still attached to branding was undeniable. Even on a purely linguistic level, the word *note*, so carefully chosen by the King in the letters of patent mentioned above, carried with it the idea of infamy, as a "[m]ark that degrades, or that is defamatory. *The accusation that was made against that man is a note in his life. That carries a certain note with it.*"[47] Decontextualized upon the body's surface, the mark dispossessed its bearer of the ability to reinvent himself, since the sign of authority imprinted on the skin imposed an interpretation over which he had no control. Despite the more hidden location of the mark, many branded convicts likely found themselves condemned to a life of constant suspicion and probable unemployability that may even have led for some to a permanent criminal existence. This problem was not lost on the brand's eighteenth-century opponents. As jurist Buterne laments through the use of bodily metaphor in his 1763 *Dictionnaire de législation*:

> No one can disagree that a marked Citizen is a lost member for Society, in relationship to which he degenerates more and more, his situation only rendering him more fit to bring harm to it, and to become the most determined and the most dangerous smuggler.[48]

Despite its potential to stigmatize its bearer, the hidden brand upon the convict's shoulders was, as we have seen, generally viewed as a more humane improvement upon earlier practices.[49] Moreover, it was consistently cast as a purely administrative imprint, a tool by which authorities sought to increase the efficiency and reliability of their judicial system and, more largely, to better control the ever-greater circulation of people across France. But gradual enlightenment represents only a small part of the story behind branding's invention and rise as a prominent practice in early modern France, encouraged and prized by magistrates who theorized the brand as a useful and legible textual sign. The development and proliferation of branding with a figurative mark—first with the fleur-de-lis and later with letters corresponding to the crime or the sentence—must be understood in relationship to the rise of print culture, defined not only as the proliferation of texts but also as the multiplication of techniques of impression on metal, cloth, coins and merchandise for purposes of identification, authentication, and control. Branding emerged as a judicial practice in a period that saw the increased circulation of people, texts, and goods, as well as greater efforts on the part of the state to control and regulate their movement and proliferation through marking. It participated in a world where the imprinted mark was gaining authority and proof value as an indicator of identity and origin. In a society enamored and imbued with the written and printed word as well as a host of other marking practices in the legal and commercial realms, branding was both a performance of power and a performance of the power of print. Rather than representing a bygone and backward punishment, criminal branding marked the birth of the modern state and became the hallmark of a modernizing judicial system. It was, indeed, a sign of the times.

Branding the body, imprinting the state

Bureaucracy loves paperwork, fetishizing the file over the real it represents for the fantasy of mastery it provides. The bureaucrats who inhabited early modern France were no exception. A late seventeenth-century engraving of the "Habit de procureur" by Nicolas de Larmessin appropriately represents the prosecutor's body covered in texts, highlighting the association between the legal profession and the abundance of the written and printed word upon which Old Regime justice so extensively relied (see Figure 5.4). The disciplinary world of early modern France was a realm where paper and punishment went hand in hand. Furetière's first examples for the verb *publier*—meaning in the seventeenth century "to make public," whether in print, writing, or speech—underline the importance of textual communication within the judicial context: "We *publish* Edicts and Declarations when we read them during Hearings, record them, have them placarded, printed, and read aloud in the streets."[50] From the multitude of handwritten minutes and judgments that obligatorily accompanied each step in a trial, to the writing and printing of placards declaring a convict's crime and sentence, to the lengthy detailed ordinances that regulated the paper upon which they could all be written, proper judicial practice demanded careful attention to the creation, control, and circulation of texts. A royal declaration of June 19, 1691 lays out in minute detail—down to the type of paper to be used for various proceedings, the size of margins, and the number of syllables allowed per line—the writing of judicial acts. Following an interminable list of all the documents to which the law applies, the declaration states that the former

> will be sent in Parchment in one unique volume, the pages of which will contain no more than 22 lines per page, 15 syllables per line. . . . That Judgments that contain more than 26 lines per page and 28 syllables per line will be made into Rolls and Sheets of Parchment, with Clerks being prohibited from folding them in four.[51]

Judicial authorities, too, constantly underlined the importance of proper procedure in regard to the creation and circulation of paper and ink trial documents that by law accompanied convicts as they were moved from place to place. Jurist Daniel Jousse (1704–1781), commenting a 1667 ordinance, emphasizes this point:

> If the Sentence handed down by the local Judge carries a condemnation of *corporeal punishment*, the galleys, *perpetual banishment,* or amende honorable, . . . *the Accused and his Trial documents shall be sent together, and safely in our Courts.* We prohibit Clerks from sending them separately, on pain of being barred from their duties, and paying a fine of five hundred *livres.*[52]

The need to reiterate such guidelines regularly and to threaten court workers with fines and firing suggests that clerks did not always follow established procedures consistently, creating the potential for frequent mistakes to be made. The introduction of branding responded in part to the

Figure 5.4 "Prosecutor's Costume," Nicolas de Larmessin (1695). Bibliothèque Nationale de France.

downfalls of a paper-and-ink-based system and the relative inefficiency of attempts at kingdom-wide compilation, printing, and circulation of lists that identified previously convicted persons. For early modern authorities, the body proved a more permanent, reliable medium than the written or printed text, compensating for the deficiencies inherent to a system that sought centralization but did not yet have the technological means to overcome the challenges of time and space.

The metaphor of body as text found reification in many judicial practices of the Old Regime, where bodies and texts participated intimately and often interchangeably in the spectacle of punishment. In sentences carried out in effigy, texts stood in for the bodies of the deceased, absent, or otherwise spared from actual execution.[53] Texts in turn were often treated like bodies, as seditious books underwent the same judicial spectacles, condemned to be "lacerated and burned at the Place de Grefe, by the Executioner of High Justice."[54] Disciplinary rituals made the body into text—"forc[ed] it . . . to emit signs"—the criminal's body itself in effect publishing—"making public"—his or her condemnation.[55] As Michel Foucault puts it in *Discipline and Punish*, "in him, on him, the sentence had to be legible for all"— and it became so through an elaborate ritual of gestures but also of texts: placards hung about the neck of the offender listing the crime, sentences read aloud repeatedly as the convict's body was transported from place to place, printed convictions displayed at the base of the scaffold or pillory and placed on the doors of courthouses and the condemned person's home.[56] The textual and visual representations of the Spaniard Don Arnandes's punishment with which this chapter began highlight the relationships between body and text inherent in the disciplinary rituals of the period (see Figure 5.1 and detail, Figure 5.5). As executioners parade the convict throughout the city, a magistrate reads the narrative of his crimes and condemnation aloud to spectators at each stop, even as the wounding prescribed by that text enacts the sentence upon his body in a performative inscription. A written placard stating his crime of counterfeiting coins hangs from his neck, labeling the spot on his back where the branding iron burns his flesh: "Marker of *sols* and clipper of *doubles*."[57]

Such placards, or *écritaux*, accompanied each sentence of branding. Wearing these texts contributed to the spectacle of degrading punishment in a society where honor and reputation were everything: "We normally attach two placards to them, one in front, the other behind, on which are written the crime that led to the condemnation."[58] Consistently printed in all capitals, probably to facilitate reading by the public and perhaps to make the executioner's task of copying it onto a placard easier, the text of the placard was personalized, containing the offender's name and specific crime. A certain Jean Dumont, for instance, convicted on September 2, 1724, of stealing fruit from the central market of Paris "was condemned to be attached in the Iron Collar at la Halle for three consecutive days, and to remain there from noon to two o'clock, having a Placard in front and

Figure 5.5 Detail of Spaniard receiving the whip and the fleur-de-lis, *Histoire veritable et facecieuse d'un Espaignol* (1638). Bibliothèque Nationale de France.

behind bearing these words: LA HALLE MARKET FRUIT THIEF." On the final day of his sentence, Dumont was "branded with a hot iron in the form of the letter V on the right shoulder" and banished from the city of Paris for three years. His sentence, signed by the crier and trumpeter, orders the text to be "read aloud and posted at la Halle and in all the usual Markets, Places, and Intersections" of the city and its surrounding areas.[59]

The August 28, 1760 case of Emmanuel-Jean de la Coste attests to a similar intimacy between criminal body and juridical text (see Figure

Figure 5.6 Emmanuel-Jean de la Coste in the iron collar, attached to the *carcan* (1760). Bibliothèque Nationale de France.

5.6). Originally a monk, De la Coste left his monastery and began fencing jewels and diamonds, swindling both merchants and private individuals. He then designed a fake lottery by fabricating counterfeit lottery tickets, coupons, lists, and advertisements for it that were all "falsely marked with a seal that he had had engraved for that particular purpose, representing the arms of [the] Seigneury of Gemont, and signed just as falsely with the imaginary name of *A. Broedebeq*, as Director of the aforementioned Lottery."[60] De la Coste apparently collected quite a sum of money, as well as wrote and published anonymous letters and defamatory libels accusing people of terrible deeds in both Paris and the provinces, though his sentence does not specify to what end. He was sentenced for these crimes on August 28, 1760 to exposure in the iron collar for three consecutive days from noon until two in the afternoon, first at the Place de Grève, then in the Carrefour de Bussy, and finally in the Place du Palais-Royal. There, he was branded on the right shoulder with the letters GAL and sent off to the royal galleys for life. As the engraving of the accused portrays, throughout his punishment, De la Coste wore placards "in front and behind" that declared him a "SWINDLER AND MAKER OF FALSE LOTTERY TICKETS AND DIFFAMATORY LIBELS."[61] The text of his sentence lies on the ground adjacent to a pan of burning coals, which heat the branding iron that will imprint him with the same letters that appear in that document—"GAL," stating his punishment, the royal galleys.[62] Indeed, the text of De la Coste's sentence not only accompanies but ultimately survives its corporeal twin, for the galleys meant civil death. Here the engraver clearly mocks the convict; his hat lies overturned at his feet to receive donations while a dog urinates on his leg. His accomplice in fraud, Louis Vanquetin, sentenced to witness De la Coste's punishment, sulks tied to the cart behind him, awaiting his own branding and nine years in the galleys, the state claiming his labor to pay back his violation of its mechanisms of control.

The close association between text and body practiced by Old Regime justice achieved its apotheosis in France when letters actually began to imprint the convict's skin. Though England had branded with letters since the sixteenth century, it was not until the early eighteenth century that their use became widespread in France, gradually replacing the iconic fleur-de-lis. The branding of a variety of characters into the flesh accompanied major legislation of March 4, 1724, but was already sanctioned for certain crimes prior to this date and came into use progressively.[63] By replacing the fleur-de-lis with crime-specific letters, authorities perhaps sought to lessen the interpretive ambiguity inherent in the figurative sign, fine-tuning their system of offender identification. *Voleurs* [thieves] were marked with a V or a W for recidivists; *mendians* [beggars] with an M; and *faux sauniers* [salt smugglers] with a G for *la gabelle*, the tax on salt. Those sentenced for various crimes to enslavement in the royal galleys— the case of the swindler De la Coste—most often received the infamous monogram, GAL. The Ordinance of 1786 concerning military personnel added the letters D for deserters and P for those who deserted on the eve or day of a battle. In 1802, the criminal court of the Département de la Seine punished a band of counterfeiters with the letter F, for *faussaire*.[64] A 1779 engraving of the branding of Marie Louise Nicolais, widow and accomplice of the infamous poisoner Antoine-François Derues, illustrates the common eighteenth-century use of letters to brand.[65] Before a crowd of onlookers, the iron imprints both her bared shoulder blades with the letter V prior to her incarceration in the Salpêtrière (see Figure 5.7).

Use of the fleur-de-lis continued as other crime-specific letters proliferated, with French magistrates occasionally encountering the marks of other countries and cities as well on the bodies of offenders. In England, the letter R indicated a robber, M a malefactor, B a blasphemer, S a runaway slave, SL a seditious libeler, V a vagrant or vagabond, and F a fray-maker—someone guilty of causing a disturbance in church. The same letter could thus, in certain cases, mean two different things depending on the place that the original marking had occurred; it had to be read in context. The cities of Amsterdam, Bern, and Brussels used image rather than text—an iron with three Andrew crosses, a cross, and an angel, respectively—reproducing emblems that figured in the coats of arms of those cities, marking the criminal with a sign of local authority. Similarly, the Ecclesiastical State in Rome branded with the arms of the Papacy, two keys crossed one on top of the other.[66]

Links between printing on paper and other materials and branding the criminal body were present at the most basic level in the language used to describe the act of branding: the convicted thief is subjected to "the *impression* of a fleur-de-lis, that the executioner *imprints* with the hot iron."[67] The vocabulary of branding also included the use of the terms "imprint," "character," "letter," and, as discussed above, "note," to describe the brand. Beyond the use of language borrowed from printing, the actual materials and methods of branding also had ties to the performance of print. Printing consisted of pressing a raised pattern, inked by rubbing with a leather ball, initially onto vellum or parchment—calf or sheep skin—and later onto paper, an act mimicked by branding human skin with a hot iron to create a similarly indelible mark. Branding irons themselves such as the GAL iron portrayed in the eighteenth-century rendering below were made in Roman font, here the letters curiously reversed so that they may be read by the viewer (see Figure 5.8). Judicial authorities' choice of Roman letters for the criminal brand, the by then dominant font style introduced in France in the sixteenth century by engraver and type founder Claude Garamond (1499–1561), underlined its distinct modernity.[68] It is also quite likely that later branding irons, with their raised Roman characters, were created by specialized type designers or at least produced in the same metal shops as punches and type. The professionals involved in the design and making of type were most often, not surprisingly, also engaged in other types of metalwork, as exemplified by Johann Gutenberg (ca.1397–1468), traditionally seen as the European inventor of printing, who

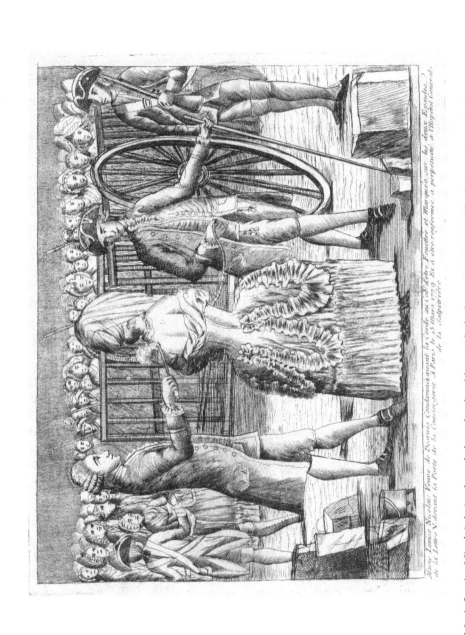

Figure 5.7 Marie Louise Nicolais being branded on the shoulders with the letter V (1779). Bibliothèque Nationale de France.

Figure 5.8 The branding iron of the *gallérien*, Musée de la Préfecture de Police, Paris (eighteenth century). Polymedia Meichtry and Bibliothèque Nationale de France.

was a goldsmith, as were many of the first-generation type founders.[69] Moreover, the branding iron had striking resemblances in its design to the strong metal *poinçon*, or punch, used to produce type as well as to mark a wide variety of commercial products with a distinctive sign. The technique used for the production of branding irons must have closely resembled that of casting the punch, the first stage in the process of creating type described by Lucien Febvre and Henri-Jean Martin in *The Coming of the Book*:

> For each letter or sign a punch must be made from hard metal at the end of which the letter is engraved in relief. The punch is used to strike a die in a softer metal which holds the intaglio (impression). Held in a mould, the die can then cast as many 'sorts' as desired, the letters being made from a metal which fuses at a low temperature, tin for instance or lead. The letters appear in relief as on the original punch.[70]

Given the material resemblances between the branding iron and the punch, it seems only fitting that the word *poinçon* itself, central to printing vocabulary, descends from the Latin *punctio*, a term for "pricking" or "puncture" that was originally used exclusively in medicine to describe the piercing of the flesh. Also used in the marking of print fabrics, coins, seals, silver, and gold, the *poinçon* thus had its roots in the penetration of the body.

Descriptions of the act of branding, much like those discussing improvements in print, emphasized qualities of permanence and clarity. Muyart de Vouglans emphasizes the brand's longevity:

> We content ourselves today to apply this Mark on the naked shoulders, the flesh of which the executioner first beats numb, so that the holes left by the hot iron fill with blood from the bruises, leaving traces *that can never be erased.*[71]

Blood, which assured nobles their rank, thus became the ink of social exclusion for the condemned criminal, rendering the traces of his punishment indelible. Guillaume-François Joly de Fleury (1675–1756), Procureur général du Parlement de Paris, touts the endurance of the mark made through another, more sophisticated, method in a 1724 letter to the directors of the *Hopitaux généraux* regarding the marking of the beggars entering their institutions. Though he models the chosen instrument on that used by surgeons for medical treatment, his description also resembles certain methods of early modern tattooing, where pigments were often rubbed into pricked incisions:

> To mark Beggars with the letter M [for *mendiant*, or beggar], you must have an instrument made expressly for this purpose and copied on the one used in surgery to scarify the place where cupping glasses are applied. This instrument resembles a little box in which are enclosed several lancet points that, all at once and in the blink of an eye are pushed by a spring, and make their impression on the skin without risking penetrating further than one should. This impression made, you throw pulverized canon powder onto these little wounds, that you light with a piece of burning paper, and immediately you cover the wound with a cloth wet with warm water infused with a third of alcohol.
>
> Through this method *the impression will be unremovable*, unless someone applies an acid to it that would completely remove the skin, but in this case, a mark would still be visible that would indicate that another had been erased.[72]

The permanence of the mark was thus increased with this "new and improved" method that inserted pigment under the skin, rendering all attempts to remove it useless, for erasure itself would leave its decipherable trace on the body. This change in method, however, also required a change in location, presumably to softer flesh: "The most suitable place for this mark is the outer and middle part of the arm, four ample finger widths above the elbow."[73]

Methods of marking the criminal body thus showed affinities not only with printmaking but also with many other impression, etching, and pouncing techniques used by a wide variety of artists and artisans. Seventeenth-century usage of the verb *fleurdeliser* and its participle, *fleurdelisé*, reinforces this link between the production of decorative objects through imprinting, pricking or incising, and that of marking the body. In addition to the punitive meanings cited above, Cotgrave lists decorative ones as well: "also, to flourish, beautify, sticke, set thicke, with Flowerdeluces," like the royal accessories, decor, and clothing that surrounds and adorns Louis XIV in Drevet's engraving (Figure 5.2). Similarly, the later *Dictionnaire de l'Académie française* includes "To cover with fleur-de-lis" as in "*Un baton fleurdelisé*" [a fleurdelised staff] alongside disciplinary meanings of the verb.[74] As these semantic crossovers between judicial and artisanal practice suggest, the branding of the body participated in a much wider culture of impression that proliferated in the early modern period through the burgeoning industry of print as well as in the artistic and commercial realms.

Marks of identification and control

Marking with the fleur-de-lis or other heraldic symbols did not serve decorative purposes alone in early modern France. Royalty, nobles, and wealthy bourgeois imprinted and engraved everything that belonged to their households—gates, doors, mantelpieces, carriages, furniture, silver, livestock, and barrels of wine, to name only a few—with the distinctive mark of their families, signaling their ownership and the respect demanded by their authority and lineage. Pierre Palliot's lengthy 1660 reedition of Louvan Geliot's 1635 *Vraye et parfaite science des armoiries*, which provides a detailed and comprehensive contemporary description of the period's coats of arms and the symbols of which they were composed, affirms the extraordinary role such signs of distinction played in the period.[75] Coats of arms and monograms—*chiffres*—allowed for ready identification of items as belonging to a particular family: "people engrave *chiffres* on seals, paint them on carriages, decorate furniture and tapestries with them, etc."[76] Imprinted signs also facilitated the eventual recognition of lost possessions in the case of theft: "Bourgeois have their mark put on their dishware, so that they can reclaim it, if it is stolen."[77] As noted above, brands upon the skin of runaway slaves in Saint Domingue performed a similar function.[78]

Marking extended not only to the identification of personal possessions but to the commercial realm as well. The same fleur-de-lis that marked the convict's body and identified him as the King's own also signified the legitimacy of coins and goods produced under royal authority. Satirist Charles Timoléon de Beauxoncles, sieur de Sigogne (ca. 1560–1611), exploits this parallel in verse, highlighting with irony the similarity between the criminal brand and the coat of arms to mock the destiny of a man repeatedly marked with the fleur-de-lis:

He was a great favorite of kings,
if what they say is true
that twice already he has received
the fleur-de-lis during his lifetime.
If he could, one day, merit
the third as compensation,
then, he could well brag
that he wears the arms of France.[79]

Sigogne's verses, though intended for humor, nonetheless underline the intimate link between the use of marks by both judicial and commercial authorities. The poet jokes that if marked three times, the man in question will wear the "Arms of France": three fleur-de-lis arranged as a triangle that marked not only the attributes and possessions of the royal family but also the French currency and all products manufactured under royal authority, as stamped on the reverse of this 1615 *double* (see Figure 5.9). The branding of bodies thus closely resembled the impression of countless French products with the seal of the King or the manufacturer, often done in identical fashion through branding packages with a hot iron, but also imprinted in wax or lead through stamping or engraving. A mid-seventeenth-century engraving by Corneille de Wael of galley slaves awaiting departure at a port juxtaposes marked bodies and marked merchandise (see Figure 5.10). The *galériens* on the left, their bodies compulsorily marked with the infamous GAL brand—though here, covered by clothing—sit on large bundles of goods to be shipped, each package bearing its own distinctive brand. Indeed, in the French Antilles, marked bodies and marked merchandise became one and the same, as enslaved Africans, bought

Figure 5.9 Obverse and reverse sides of a *double*, the reverse stamped with three fleurs-de-lis (1616). Private collection. Photograph by Dennis Griggs.

Figure 5.10 Galley slaves awaiting departure, Corneille de Wael (mid-seventeenth century). Bibliothèque Nationale de France.

and sold as goods, were branded with their owner's distinctive sign, just as were products of the plantation.

"A sign attesting to a control," the word *marque* entered commercial vocabulary in 1626 and only grew in prominence and semantic reach throughout the seventeenth century as such authoritative signs of identification multiplied.[80] The seventeenth century saw the proliferation of abundant new legislation regulating the creation and impression of *marques* on agricultural, mineral, metal, and paper products, which only intensified during the reign of Louis XIV and that of his Minister of Finances, Jean-Baptiste Colbert (1619–1683).[81] The modern French word *marque*, as used to designate the manufacturer of a product, and its English equivalent, "brand," issue directly from this period of increased central control.

Furetière defines *marque* as a "character that is imprinted by public authorities on many things, either for tax purposes, or for the police," for purposes of identifying the origin, producer, or owner of merchandise as it traveled the roads and seas.[82] "Every Merchant puts his *mark* on his merchandise," so that his products could be identified if stolen and appropriate taxes levied according to their origin and quality. Across commercial domains, new laws ordered that merchants and artisans declare or be assigned individual marks to designate their products, officially register them with the appropriate central authorities, and seek approval if they desired to change them, as Furetière underlines in his examples:

> A Coinsmith or an engraver, when they are received, are required to declare by an authentic document the *mark* that they would like to use, and it is registered with the *Cour des Monnaies* [Currency Court], and they cannot change it without permission. . . . Each Gold and Silver-smith or Tinsmith must have his punch, his unique *mark*, of which he must leave an imprint at the Police Clerk's office.[83]

Colbert himself maintained a register of all producers' marks that fell under royal jurisdiction, and marks performatively affirmed the control of the monarchy over all products whose manufacture and transport were the monopolies of the royal tax farms. Products often bore several marks; hallmarks punched on gold, silver, and tin objects indicated the item's producer or origin as well as the quality of the metal used, the taxes to be levied, and the fact that taxes had been paid.[84] The marking of products had become so common by the end of the century that dictionary definitions of *marque* and *marquer* ramble on. Yet all underline the mark's purposes of identification, recognition, authentication, and communication of authority or rights, as in this selection from the *Dictionnaire de l'Académie française*:

A *mark* is put on gold and silver tableware, either with the punch of the Master artisan who made it, or with the punch of the city or community, to indicate [*marquer*] its title and quality. The *mark* on currency is the image of the Prince, and of his authority, it is the *mark* that gives it value in commerce. Paper bears the *marks* of the paper mill where it was produced. You put *marks* on officially stamped paper, on barrels of wine in wine cellars, on carriages that go about the square, on playing cards, on fabrics, in order to preserve the rights that they may carry. . . . Merchants have distinctive *marks* to recognize their packages, to recognize their wood that they float. . . . Butchers have a *mark* to mark their livestock in the markets. . . . And in virtually all professions and privileges things are diversely *marked*.[85]

Such marks were central to the book trade. The distinctive figurative symbols printers placed on the books they produced were key to ensuring the value of their merchandise, as jurist Laurent Bouchel (1588–1629) underlines: "the marks of Printers are of great importance for the buzz about and the monetary value of their books, because the reputation of a good Printer is recognized by the mark."[86] Printers designed their individual marks, which ranged from simple designs and monograms to richly elaborate coats of arms and emblem-filled engravings. The title page of Nicolas Fontaine's 1691 *Dictionnaire Chrétien*, for example, displays printer Élie Josset's decorative mark based on the fleur-de-lis—his shop was to be found "à la Fleur de Lis d'or" [at the Golden Fleur-de-Lis]—including the motto, "Candor et Odor" [Brilliance and Fragrance], which enabled all the books produced on his press to be easily identified and helped protect his production rights (see Figure 5.11).[87] Like other commercial marks, printers' marks were subject to strict regulation. An edict of 1686, following on several earlier laws, declared that "[a]ll Booksellers and Printers will print and have books printed . . . with the name and the mark of the Printer that Printed it" and prohibited them "from imprinting the mark of any other bookseller or printer, on pain of be punished as counterfeiters."[88] Marks even took the form of badges worn like coats of arms by printers and their employees as identification. Beginning in 1653, traveling booksellers, or *colporteurs*, who roamed the countryside selling their merchandise, were required to wear a distinctive sign upon their bodies in the form of a "mark or copper badge on the front of their doublet, where Colporteur will be written."[89] The mark identified them as they traveled the roads of France, distinguishing them from vagabonds and validating their right to trade in books.

The ties between the criminal brand and the commercial mark become even more closely drawn when we consider that for many branded convicts, it was in fact their attempt to circumvent or hijack the very protocol of official marking that earned them the judicial mark. Counterfeiters—who forged false marks on books, paper, and coins—were subject to punishment by marking, as

LE
DICTIONNAIRE
CHRETIEN,

o ù

SUR DIFFERENS TABLEAUX DE LA NATURE;

L'ON APPREND PAR L'ECRITURE ET LES SAINTS PERES

A VOIR DIEU PEINT DANS TOUS SES OUVRAGES:

E T

A PASSER DES CHOSES VISIBLES AUX INVISIBLES.

Ouvrage tres utile aux Religieux & Religieufes , aux Perfonnes de pieté , aux Predicateurs & à tous ceux qui étudient ou qui ont à parler en public. *Par M. de Sacy Fontaine*

A PARIS;

Chez ELIE JOSSET, ruë faint Jacques , à la Fleur de Lis d'or.

M. DC. LXXXXI.

AVEC APPROBATION ET PRIVILEGE DV ROY.

Figure 5.11 Title page displaying the printer's mark, Nicolas Fontaine, *Dictionnaire Chrétien* (Paris: Elie Josset, 1691). Bibliothèque Nationale de France.

were smugglers of salt, tobacco, and fabrics, who sought to avoid state taxes and thus the receipt of the royal mark on commodities whose production and transport were monopolies of the royal tax farms. The sentence of the counterfeiting Spaniard with which this chapter began renders explicit the parallel between the impression of bodies and that of coins, underlining the links between the judicial practice of branding and his economic crime. Condemned for having cut *doubles* and marked *sols* with the fleur-de-lis, it was fitting, thought the author of the *Histoire véritable*, that Don Arnandes's punishment be that of receiving the mark himself:

> [H]e was moreover accused and convicted of having rather often sold rolls of slate fashioned to look like *doubles*, and of having clipped large numbers of them and marked many *sols* with a punch that was found among his tools of Tooth extractor. For these Crimes, Thefts and Larcenies was condemned as follows: *for having marked the sols with a fleur-de-lis to receive and wear forever in the same way the aforesaid fleur-de-lis marked and imprinted on his shoulder so that he could be recognized* [estre marqué] *by the hallmark of France.*[90]

So he who would illegitimately mark is marked "in the same way," as the author makes a point of emphasizing. The fleur-de-lis punch Don Arnandes used for marking coins, found among his belongings, led the convict to be marked in turn with a similar instrument. Over a century later, the swindler De la Coste met a similar fate because he too had defied state authority to become an expert forger and manipulator of marks. His crime of having produced fake lottery tickets that were stamped with a forged seal also earned him the brand, the letters GAL marking him forever as the King's possession. These men's very punishment, then, reminded the readers, viewers, and hearers of their condemnations that the right to mark—be it coins, silver, paper, books, fabrics, salt, or other commercial goods—belonged to the sovereign alone. As the text of the *Histoire véritable* affirms, using the language of commercial marking, those who would attempt to defy the state's exclusive right to mark find themselves imprinted with the "hallmark of France" and become forever identifiable as deviants by the sign of their condemnation.

On February 6, 1617, the Parlement of Paris issued a decree, proclaimed and posted throughout the city, to combat the mounting homicide, violence, and theft taking place under the cover of darkness:

> The aforementioned Court has ordered and orders all people who have the fleur-de-Lis, or any other mark of Judicial blame, and those who are banished from this city and its Suburbs to leave them, and to remove themselves within twenty-four hours after the publication of the present Decree, on pain of being hung and strangled, without any other form or figure of trial, other than the reading of the preceding decree against

them. And at the same time, all vagabonds, beggars, able-bodied and illegitimate persons will leave and remove themselves from the aforesaid city and its Suburbs, on pain of condemnation to the Galleys.[91]

Authorities called for patrols to walk the city, arresting anyone who disobeyed this order, setting up gallows in the squares, executing marked offenders, and enchaining the unmarked—but soon to be—for service in the royal galleys. This scene of the rounding up of the marked and the marginal from the early seventeenth century repeated itself again and again in the years that followed, attesting to the facility with which, once marked, a person's movements could be controlled. The registration of artisans, merchants, and commoners; the introduction of obligatory passports and letters of passage; and the required identification of individuals with cloth or metal insignia they wore upon their chests were all early modern methods of identifying and monitoring the circulation of persons of which branding was only one.[92] These policies and practices intensified during the 1670s and 1680s, when the French government undertook ever more extensive regulatory measures to track marginals, issuing numerous edicts and instituting policies to increase cooperation among municipalities. As historian Robin Briggs has noted, "At times the government's maxim appeared to be 'if it moves, regulate it.'"[93]

The branding of bodies and other forms of physical marking continued throughout the eighteenth century. For instance, 1749 legislation required that the "legitimate" native poor of Versailles wear copper badges signaling the parish to which they belonged and had to restrict their activities, so as to distinguish them from the vagabonds who were exhausting the city's charities. They were to wear, "for the Poor of the Notre Dame Parish, a round plaque marked with the letters ND and for those of the Saint Louis Parish, a plaque marked SL."[94] The text of the law reinforces the importance of the sign's visibility, specifying that it must be fastened "on the left side of their chest, in a highly visible place, and in a secure way, without their being allowed to wear them in another place, or only in their pockets."[95] Branding of the skin also long proved seductive because of its practicality and permanence. While, in contrast to the badges of the poor, the criminal brand was hidden under the clothing, it nonetheless provided ready and enduring confirmation of a person's past convictions. During the course of the eighteenth century, the judicial mark was subject to the same intense criticism that Enlightenment thinkers dealt all forms of corporeal punishment. However, though criminal branding was temporarily abolished by the Constituent Assembly in 1791—before its reestablishment by Napoléon in 1810—France did not definitively eliminate its use until 1832. Enslaved Africans in the French Antilles and *bagnards* leaving France for forced labor in French Guyana were the last to wear brands, the latter still bearing the mark of the galley slave, GAL—a vestige of earlier times.

Like all forms of corporeal punishment in the early modern period, judicial branding dramatized the power of the state over all members of the social body.[96] Yet the practice of branding the criminal body with the fleur-de-lis came closer than any other to literalizing what Michel Foucault and Michel de Certeau both described as the inscription of power on the body. As Certeau reminds us,

> [L]aw "takes hold of" bodies in order to make them its text. . . . [I]t transforms them into tables of the law, into living tableaux of rules and customs. . . . [T]he law constantly writes itself on bodies. It engraves itself on parchments made from the skin of its subjects. . . . It makes its book out of them.[97]

The use of corporeal marking to identify convicts attests to an early modern vision of the skin as a potent site for the impression of would-be unequivocal signs that, in the case of branding, rather than expressing individuality, perform instead subjection. Invested with remarkable credibility and endurance, the skin became, *à son corps défendant*, a vector of the authority whose marks could subsequently be read within the social body.

In its wide-reaching effort to monitor and control the circulation of both persons and products across its territory and beyond, the modernizing French state turned to marking of all kinds, creating what François Delpech has aptly termed "a great movement of signalization."[98] As this chapter has revealed, criminal branding must be understood as the symptom as well as the product of this newfound obsession for impression. The emergence and prominence of judicial branding from the mid-sixteenth through eighteenth centuries coincided with the blossoming of print and the rapid development and ever stricter regulation of commercial marking. Brands on paper, merchandise, and skin became the signs upon which the state depended in its attempt to identify and monitor the people and products under its authority. "Print culture," envisioned widely as a variety of practices of impression, produced a heretofore unknown readability of objects and persons and sought to ensure their identification across time and space.

But the proliferation of branding in the early modern period also inherently critiques the modernizing state's ability to maintain its hold over its subjects, for, in the words of Certeau, "[t]he law never stops needing an 'advance' of body, of corporeal capital, in order to make itself believed and practiced."[99] Unable to ensure control through paper alone, the state ultimately revealed its weakness through recourse to the corporeal. The use of branding thus signals the failure of French authorities to combat crime and to monitor the movement of people and goods effectively, despite the numerous new mechanisms of control at their disposal. In branding, the imprinted sign, so valorized for its stability and reach, exposes its limits when "paper is no longer enough for the law, and it is on the body that it writes itself."[100]

Notes

1 Michel Foucault, *Discipline and Punish: The Birth of the Prison*, trans. A. Sheridan (New York: Vintage Books, 1979), 25.

2 *Histoire veritable et facecieuse d'un Espaignol lequel à eu le fouet et la fleur de lis dans la Ville de Thoulouze pour avoir derobé des raves et roigné des doubles. Extraict d'une lettre escrite de ladite Ville de Thoulouze le 13. Septembre dernier* [1638], broadsheet, n. pag. The siege of Leucate (in Roussillon, Basque country), ended with the victory of the French over the Spanish on September 28, 1637. "Laucate," the spelling that appears in the text, is Occitan.

3 *Rave*, from the Provençal *rava*, was used in the seventeenth century to refer to a variety of root vegetables, including turnips, radishes, celeriac, and rutabaga; *Le Grand Robert de la langue française*, 2nd ed. (Paris: Le Robert, 1985). Antoine Furetière defines it as a "[s]weet and white root that one eats with salt, after having peeled it. There are three kinds of *rave*, long, flat, and round;" *Dictionnaire universel* (La Haye and Rotterdam: Arnout & Reinier Leers, 1690). In the hierarchy of seventeenth-century coinage, a *double* was worth two *deniers* and was among the lowest value coins. A *sol* was worth twelve *deniers*; "Monnaie," *Dictionnaire du français classique. XVIIe siècle*, eds. Jean Dubois, Renée Lagane, and Alain Lerond (Paris: Larousse, 1988).

4 *Histoire veritable.*

5 Horses and other livestock, like all goods and possessions, were branded or otherwise marked in seventeenth-century France to show ownership and origin. Definitions of *marquer* provided by Furetière's *Dictionnaire universel* and by the *Dictionnaire de l'Académie françoise* (Paris: La Veuve de Jean Baptiste Coignard, 1694) attest to the practice.

6 "Je ne regrette pas mes espaules fendues/De tant de mille coups ny de la fleur de lis,/Mais de voir sur mon dos tant de raves perdues/Dont je me traitterois ainsy que de perdris;" *Histoire veritable.*

7 Personal communication with Abby Zanger, May 9, 2003.

8 Alfred Soman dates the first rise in the use of branding by the Parlement of Paris to 1545 in "La Justice criminelle aux XVIe-XVIIe siècles: Le Parlement de Paris et les sièges subalternes," in *Sorcellerie et justice criminelle: Le Parlement de Paris (16e-18e siècles)* (Hampshire, UK and Brookfield, VT: Variorum, Ashgate, 1992), article VII, 37–38. Robert Munchembled dates its first use in Arras—then the capital of the Artois region—to 1552; *Le Temps des supplices: De l'obéissance sous les rois absolus. XVe-XVIIIe siècle* (Paris: Armand Colin, 1992), 138. Claude Le Brun de la Rochette includes branding in his early seventeenth-century comprehensive legal treatise, *Le Proces criminel* [1609] (Rouen: Pierre Calles, 1611), 51. It also appears in Cotgrave's French-English dictionary of that same year, suggesting it was already a prominent punishment by that time; "Flaistrir," "Flaistri," "Flaistrissure," "Fleurelisé," and "Fleurde-liser," Randle Cotgrave, *A Dictionarie of the French and English Tongues* ([London: A. Islip, 1611] Hildesheim: Georg Olms Verlag, 1970). Major French laws that prescribed branding included those regulating theft (March 4, 1724, which introduced crime-specific letters), contraband (February 22, 1667; May 1680; June 1722; August 1729), vagrancy and mendicancy (July 18, 1724; July 26, 1726; August 3, 1764), military personnel (July 1, 1786), and the treatment of slaves in the French Atlantic colonies (the 1685 *Code Noir*, the original legislation it promulgated dating from 1615). For more on the legislation and use of branding in the period, see: Jean-Marie Carabasse, *Histoire du droit pénal et de la justice criminelle*, 2nd ed. (Paris: Presses Universitaires de France, 2006), 364–65; Ann Kennedy and Véra Michel, "Les

Peines de Marque du XVIème siècle à nos jours," in *Les atteintes corporelles causées à la victime et imposées au condamné en France du XVIe siècle à nos jours. Actes des séminaires d'histoire du droit pénal, 1998–99, Strasbourg,* ed. Yves Jeanclos (Strasbourg: Université Robert Schuman, 1999): 113–40; Munchembled, *Le Temps des Supplices,* 138; Soman, "La Justice criminelle," 37–38; Marguerite Rateau, "La Récidive et sa preuve dans l'ancien droit français," *Revue internationale de criminologie et de police technique* 25.3 (July–September 1961): 168–77; and Marc Vigié, "La Flétrissure des forçats au XVIIIe siècle. Un exemple de justice emblématique," *Revue de science criminelle et de droit pénal comparé* 3 (July–September 1986): 809–17. See also Craig Koslofsky's work in progress, "Branding on the Face in England, 1600–1800," presented at the American Comparative Literature Association annual conference, Harvard University, Cambridge, MA, March 17–20, 2016. Eighteenth- and nineteenth-century collections and commentaries of Old Regime laws include: Buterne, *Dictionnaire de législation,* vol. 1 (Avignon: L. Chambeau, 1763); Daniel Jousse, *Traité de la justice criminelle de France,* 4 vols. (Paris: Debure père, 1771); Pierre-François Muyart de Vouglans, *Institutes au droit criminel* (Paris: Le Breton, 1757) and *Les loix criminelles de France* (Paris: Merigot, Crapart, Benoît Morin, 1780); Lerasle, "Flétrissure," *Encyclopédie méthodique. Jurisprudence,* vol. 4 (Paris: Panckoucke, 1784), 547–48; and François-André Isambert et al., eds., *Recueil général des anciennes lois françaises,* 30 vols. (Paris: Belin-Leprieur, 1825-30). All provide references to or transcriptions of laws that prescribed branding.

9 On branding in New France, see Jean-Pierre Hardy, *Chercher fortune en Nouvelle-France* (Montréal: Libre Expression, 2007), 141. England used letters as early as the sixteenth century, a practice exported to Canada and the New England colonies, while France preferred its iconic fleur-de-lis much longer. In England, the 1547 *Statute of Vagabonds* made branding with letters on the highly visible locations of the cheek or forehead. On England, see William Andrews, *Bygone Punishments* (London: William Andrews & Co., 1899), 138–42, Jean Kellaway, *The History of Torture and Execution* (New York: Lyons Press, 2000), 24–25, and Koslofsky, "Branding on the Face." For the later seventeenth- through eighteenth-century use of the brand in England, the proceedings of the Old Bailey, London's central criminal court, have been digitized and made easily accessible by Tim Hitchcock, Robert Shoemaker, Clive Emsley, Sharon Howard, Jamie McLaughlin, *et al., The Old Bailey Proceedings Online, 1674–1913,* version 7.0, March 24, 2012, www .oldbaileyonline.org. During this period in England, the letter brand was most often made on the inside of the thumb, though between 1699 and 1707, thieves were branded on the cheek, a practice that was soon abandoned because it made convicts unemployable; Emsley, Hitcock and Shoemaker, "Crime and Justice—Punishments at the Old Bailey," ibid., October 11, 2012. A search for branding as punishment between 1674 and 1799 turns up 3281 sentences, largely for theft in various forms, but also for bigamy, infanticide, and killing animals.

10 Le Brun de la Rochette, *Le Proces criminel,* 51. Punishment for theft could also vary in severity from these guidelines, even including death upon first offense, depending on the place the crime was committed. Theft in a royal house or a "place of justice" called for immediate hanging, because of the proximity of the crime to the body of the King or his authority; on these variations, see Carabasse, *Histoire du droit pénal,* 366–68.

11 Claude-Joseph de Ferrière, *Dictionnaire de droit et de pratique,* 2nd ed., 2 vols (Paris: Veuve Brunet, 1769), vol. 1, 610.

12 Jousse specifies that "[t]his punishment is almost always joined with that of the whip, or that of the galleys, and is almost never pronounced alone;" *Traité de la justice criminelle*, vol. 1, 57. On the rapid expansion of the *galères* during the period, see Nicole Castan and André Zysberg, "Galères et galériens en France à la fin du XVIIe siècle," *Criminal Justice History* 1 (1980): 49–115, Marc Vigié, *Les Galériens du Roi, 1661–1715* (Paris: Fayard, 1985), André Zysberg, *Les Galériens. Vies et destins de 60 000 forçats sur les galères de France, 1680–1748* (Paris: Le Seuil, 1987), and Nicole Castan and André Zysberg, *Histoire des galères, bagnes et prisons en France de l'Ancien Régime* (Paris: Privat, 2002).

13 *Le Code Noir* (Paris: Veuve Saugrain, 1685), 8. Given the value placed on the physical ability and health of the slave labor force, however, some question whether the more mutilating punishments were consistently enforced; Bernard Moitt, *Women and Slavery in the French Antilles, 1635–1848* (Bloomington, IN: Indiana University Press, 2001), 137.

14 On the branding of enslaved Africans see Katrina H.B. Keefer, "Marked by Fire: Brands, Slavery, and Identity," *Slavery & Abolition* (2019), DOI: 10.1080/0144039X.2019.1606521; Gabriel Debien, *Les Esclaves aux Antilles françaises* (Basse-Terre: Société d'Histoire de la Guadeloupe, 1974), 70; Orlando Patterson, *Slavery and Social Death: A Comparative Study* (Cambridge, MA and London: Harvard University Press, 1982), 58–59; Hugh Thomas, *The Slave Trade: The Story of the Atlantic Slave Trade: 1440–1870* (New York: Simon and Schuster, 1997), 396–97; and Michael Harrigan, *Frontiers of Servitude: Slavery in Narratives of the Early French Atlantic* (Manchester, UK: Manchester University Press, 2018), 259–61. The important issues raised by the branding of Africans in the context of the Atlantic slave trade merit full and separate treatment to do justice to their complexity and particularity. These lie beyond the scope of the current chapter, which focuses on criminal branding in France. Keefer has begun extensive research on the question. See her "Marked by Fire," which lays out her long-term project. Craig Koslofsky has begun important work on the importance of branding and so-called country marks for the identification of slaves in the colonies, as well as on the development of skin color itself as the ultimate marker of identity in this period. See his "Knowing Skin in Early Modern Europe, c. 1450–1750," *History Compass* 12/10 (2014): 794–806 and "A Deep Surface? Taking Stock of the History of Skin in Early American Studies," presented at the 23rd Annual Conference of the Omohundro Institute of Early American History and Culture, Ann Arbor, MI, June 15–17, 2017. On "country marks," see also Michael A. Gomez, *Exchanging our Country Marks: The Transformation of African Identities in the Colonial and Antebellum South* (Chapel Hill, NC: University of North Carolina Press, 1998).

15 Jean-Baptiste Labat, *Nouveau Voyage aux Isles de l'Amérique, contenant l'histoire naturelle de ces pays, l'origine, les mœurs, la religion et le gouvernement des habitans anciens et modernes*, 6 vols (Paris: Pierre-François Giffart, 1722), vol. 5, 255–56.

16 Ibid., 256. Labat insists, however, that branding for identification was not necessary in Martinique or Guadeloupe due to the smaller size and less severe terrain of those islands, where slaves were better known and hiding was more difficult; 256.

17 Muyart de Vouglans, *Les loix criminelles de France*, 64.

18 For *homme de marque*, see "marque," Furetière, *Dictionnaire universel*. See also Cotgrave's definition, *Dictionarie*.

19 For a seventeenth-century account of the significance of the fleur-de-lis, see its entry in *La Vraye et parfaite science des armoiries*, ed. Pierre Palliot, 2 vols. ([Paris: Jean Guignard le pere, Guillaume de Luynes, et Helie Josset, 1660] Fascimile reproduction, Paris: Édouard Rouveyre, 1895), vol. 1.

20 In the Middle Ages, the fleur-de-lis was even thought to be engraved by nature in the form of a birthmark on the bodies of royalty; Marc Bloch, *Les Rois thaumaturges. Étude sur le caractère surnaturel attribué à la puissance royale particulièrement en France et en Angleterre* (Paris: Armand Colin, [1924] 1961), 246–56 and 300–3.

21 Valentin Groebner makes a similar argument, linking branding and the religious understanding of the biblical mark of Cain (Genesis 4:15), which protects as much as it punishes, indicating "expiation and reintegration at the same time," a meaning we have not retained today; Valentin Groebner, *Who Are You? Identification, Deception, and Surveillance in Early Modern Europe*, trans. Mark Kyburz and John Peck (New York: Zone Books, 2007), 104.

22 Ghislain Savoie recently donated his collection of Acadian artifacts, including the branding iron, to the Acadian Museum of the University of Moncton (New Brunswick, Canada). This branding iron was first identified as such by Savoie and Jean-Pierre Hardy, former director of New France History and Archaeology at the Canadian Museum of Civilizations. It dates from sometime prior to the Great Expulsion of the Acadians by the British (1755–1764) and may be the only known specimen of its kind; personal communication with Ghislain Savoie, January 26, 2013.

23 This fleur-de-lis iron has a short square and tapered extension, which would have allowed it to fit snugly into a longer handle and kept it from turning in the handle; Ghislain Savoie, personal communication, January 29, 2013. This two-piece design, consistent with Labat's description of the iron used on slaves in Saint Domingue quoted above, many well have been conceived for easy export or transportation.

24 Labat, *Nouveaux voyages*, 256.

25 Vigié points out the particular status of the galley slave; "La flétrissure," 812. See also his *Les galériens du Roi*.

26 Georges Bernard Depping, *Correspondance administrative, sous le règne de Louis XIV*, 4 vols. (Paris: Imprimerie nationale, 1850-1855), vol. 2, 954–55.

27 Cotgrave, *Dictionarie*.

28 Furetière, *Dictionnaire universel* and *Dictionnaire de l'Académie françoise*. See also definitions for "flestrissure" and "fleur de lis."

29 Jean Bouteillier's late fourteenth-century *Somme Rural* attests to the late medieval practice of branding the face of convicted felons with the sign of the municipality in which the crime was committed. He writes that in certain localities, a convict must be "marked [*enseigné*] on the face," and is "to be put on the rack, and to be branded with the sign of the city heated red hot, on the cheek," though he cautions that it is offensive "to deface the face made in the resemblance of our savior's own image," an argument drawn from Constantine that later jurists will invoke in defense of branding on the shoulder (see note below); Jean Bouteillier, *Somme Rural*, ed. and augmented by Louys Carondas Le Caron (Paris: Barthelemy Macé, 1603); 871. Marking the face with letters and even whole words also had late medieval literary precedents, notably Dante's *Purgatorio*, indicating damnation or protection, a rewriting of the protective mark of Cain; Groebner, *Who Are You?*, 105, Stephen Greenblatt, *Hamlet in Purgatory* (Princeton, NJ: Princeton University Press, 2001), 83–84, and Robert Hollander, "The Letters on Dante's Brow," January 31, 2002, accessed November 1, 2012, www.princeton.edu/~dante/ebdsa/

bob013102.html. The mark on the forehead or cheeks was the first type of mutilation to disappear. The last case mentioning this punishment at the Parlement of Paris was in 1562. In the first half of the sixteenth century, under the reign of François Ier, *essorillement*, the removal of ears for theft, also disappeared; Soman, "La Justice criminelle," 37–38. Munchembled draws similar conclusions from manuscript sources for Arras, *Le Temps des supplices*, 138. On mutilations and their replacement by the mark, see also Carabasse, *Histoire du droit pénal*, 294–96. In the case of extreme blasphemy, mutilation of the lips or tongue continued to be prescribed, but only beginning with the sixth offense, and was relatively rarely practiced; Muyart de Vouglans, *Institutes au droit criminel*, 410. Mutilation was otherwise generally employed only as a prelude to execution, for example, the cutting off of a hand prior to hanging. However, separate laws governing military personnel reinstated mutilation in a December 4, 1684 ordinance, which punished deserters "to have their nose and their ears cut, to be marked with two fleurs-de-lis on their cheeks;" qtd. by Castan and Zysberg, "Galères et galériens," 75, my translation. Branding alone took the place of mutilation as punishment for military crimes in the latter part of the eighteenth century; Vigié, "La Flétrissure des forçats," 813. An October 31, 1684 ordinance declares that prostitutes who were found cavorting with soldiers stationed at Versailles would be punished with the removal of their noses. Carabasse notes, however, that these later declarations announcing mutilations were probably largely scare tactics and never actually executed; *Histoire du droit pénal*, 295.

30 Soman, "La justice criminelle," 37.
31 Jousse, *Traité de la justice criminelle*, vol. 1, 57–58.
32 Vigié raises this problem and lists jurisconsults who classified branding among "afflictive" punishments; "La Flétrissure des forçats," 814–15. On branding's place in the hierarchy of punishment, see also Andrews, *Law, Magistracy, and Crime*, vol. 1, 307–10. Regarding costs, in Navarre in 1643, an executioner earned 4 *écus* (12 *livres*) for "fustigation et marque au fer rouge d'un faux-monnayeur" and in 1744, the marking of "trois bohemians" in Besançon cost 73 *livres*; Georges d'Avenel, *Histoire économique de la propriété, des salaires, des denrées et de tous les prix en général. Depuis l'an 1200 jusqu'en l'an 1800*, 6 vols. (Paris: Imprimerie nationale/E. Leroux, 1894-1912), vol. 4, 39. Tariffs set on May 6, 1689, and confirmed by royal declaration September 18, 1749, set the price to "fustiger et flétrir" at 7 *livres* 10 *sols*; Idelette Ardouin-Weiss, *Les Exécuteurs des sentences criminelles en Touraine* (1636–1853) (Touraine: Collection Centre Généalogique de Touraine, 1983), 2–3.
33 Muyart de Vouglans, *Insitutes au droit criminel*, 64.
34 "Lettres patentes adressées au parlement de Rouen au sujet de la marque des condamnés aux galères," 27 mai 1750, *Archives nationales marine* AI LXXXV. Cited in Vigié, "La Flétrissure des forçats," 814.
35 "Note," Furetière, *Dictionnaire universel*. Another English translation for "remarquable" is, significantly, "striking," which recalls the metal punch hitting metal, or type hitting paper, as well as the violent gestures of discipline.
36 X^{2A} 964, February 22, 1602, Jean Hillier; and X^{2A} September 20, 1007, 1642, Edmé Gombault. Cited in Soman, "La Justice criminelle," 37–38 and n. 56.
37 X^{2B} April 2, 1099, 1588, speech by lawyer Mornac, qtd. by Soman, "La Justice criminelle," 38, n. 56. Accused witches made similar claims about the devil's marks found on their skin, attempting to pass them off as natural scars or birthmarks; see Chapter 1.

38 Furetière, in defining *stigmatiser*, denies any stigma attached to contemporary branding practices, choosing only examples from the ancient past or distant lands where facial branding occurs.

39 Le Caron makes this comment in his 1603 edition of Jean Bouteillier's late fourteenth-century *Somme rural*; Bouteillier, *Somme Rural*, 871. Jurists throughout the period compared the French initiative to that of the Emperor Constantine (ca. 274–337), the first purportedly Christian ruler who "prohibited judges from imprinting on the face any letter marking the crime committed by a convict, . . . so that . . . the face of man that is made in the image of celestial beauty, should not be dishonored;" Lerasle, "Flétrissure," 548. See also Ferrière, *Dictionnaire de droit*, vol. 1, 610. Bouteillier already refers to Constantine's stance in his late fourteenth-century work; *Somme Rural*, 871.

40 Ferrière, *Dictionnaire de droit*, vol. 1, 610. See also Lerasle, "Flétrissure," 548.

41 *Recueil d'affaires criminelles*, Bibliothèque municipale de Lille, Ms. 380, 57–59, qtd. by Munchembled, *Le Temps des supplices*, 138.

42 See Koslofsky's work in progress on "Branding on the Face in England, 1600–1800." 1789 marked the last sentence of branding in England, though, in the colonies, a D was marked on soldiers who deserted during the War of 1812 and it was not officially abolished until 1829. Branding on the face continued elsewhere in continental Europe as well. For example, Groebner cites Bernese legislation dating from 1571 that calls for beggars once expelled from the city and caught trespassing to be branded on the forehead with an iron cross; *Who Are You?*, 115, n. 51.

43 Cotgrave, *Dictionarie*: "Flaitrir." "To burn in the hand, or eare, to brand in the forehead, to marke for a rogue, with an hot yron;" see his definitions of "Fleurdeliser" and "Fleurdelisé" above.

44 See above and the following: "*Flestrissûre* . . . is also used to denote the mark of a hot iron, imprinted on a criminal's shoulder. They found two brand marks on his shoulders;" *fleur-de-lis* is "[t]he mark with which they brand pickpockets and other offenders in France with a hot iron, because at the end of this iron there is a fleur-de-lis imprinted. *He was condemned to receive whipping and the fleur-de-lis, they gave him whipping and the fleur-de-lis on the shoulder. He had the fleur-de-lis twice;*" *Dictionnaire de l'Académie françoise*. Emphasis in original.

45 Cyrano de Bergerac, *Histoire comique, . . . Contenant les Estats et Empires de la Lune* (Paris: 1657) and Anne-Marie-Louise d'Orléans, duchesse de Montpensier, *Histoire de Jeanne Lambert D'Herbigny, Marquise de Fouquesolles* (1653) (Elmar, NY: Scholars' Facsimiles & Reprints, 1999). I thank Juliette Cherbuliez for the Montpensier reference.

46 Montpensier, *Histoire de Jeanne Lambert D'Herbigny*, 170.

47 "Note," *Dictionnaire de l'Académie Françoise*. Emphasis in original. Gaston Cayrou's *Le Francais Classique. Lexique de la langue du dix-septième siècle* (Paris: Didier, 1948) provides the following etymological explanation: "It carries this derogatory meaning from the Latin nota, 'mark,' then, through a pejorative deviation, 'brand,' 'stain.'" The verb "noter" also often carries this nuance of dishonor.

48 Buterne, *Dictionnaire de législation*, vol. 1, 25. Since a marked convict could face execution for most crimes if arrested a second time, the recidivist was far more likely to resort to violent acts to avoid capture.

49 Pierre Adnès, "Stigmates," *Dictionnaire de spiritualité ascétique et mystique* (Beauchesne: Paris, 1990), col. 1211.

50 "Publier," Furetière, *Dictionnaire universel*.

51 *Déclaration du Roy portant reglement pour les ecritures qui doivent estre faites sur Papier et Parchemin Timbrez donné à Versailles le 19 Juin 1691.*

52 Daniel Jousse, *Nouveau commentaire sur l'ordonnance civile du mois d'Avril 1667*, 2nd ed., (Paris: Debure père, 1763), title 26, article 6, 468. Emphasis in original.

53 In sentences carried out in effigy, a *tableau* or *écriteau* that spelled out the convict's crime and sentence most often took the place of the criminal body at the pillory or *carcan*, or in another public place. Royal decrees of August 1670 and July 1749 stipulated the public display of a text (rather than an actual effigy of the offender) for all but death sentences; Muyart de Vouglans, *Les Lois criminelles*, 66–67 and Jousse, *Nouveau commentaire*, 361–62.

54 *Sentence du Chastelet de Paris, qui condamne deux écrits imprimés, intitulés, l'un: Mandement de Monseigneur l'évêque d'Orléans; et l'autre, Mandement de Monseigneur l'évêque d'Amiens, à être lacérés et brulés en la place de Grève, par l'exécuteur de la haute justice* (Paris: H. Guerin, 1756).

55 Foucault, *Discipline and Punish*, 25.

56 Ibid., 43.

57 "Marqueur de solz et roigneur de doubles;" *Histoire veritable.*

58 Jousse, *Traité de la justice criminelle*, vol. 1, 61. See Mowery on legal infamy, *Law Magistry and Crime*, 307–8.

59 *Arrest de la Cour de Parlement . . . Qui condamne JEAN DUMONT . . . Du deux Septembre 1727* (Paris: P. J. Mariette, Imprimeur de la Police).

60 *Jugement rendu . . . Qui condamna Emmanuel-Jean de la Coste . . . Du vingt-huit Août mil sept cens soixante* (H. L. Guerin and L. F. Delatour, Imprimeurs de la Police, 1760).

61 "EXCROC, ET FABRICATEUR D'UNE FAUSSE LOTERIE, ET DE LIBELES DIFFAMATOIRES."

62 The document reads: "Jugement rendu par le Lieutenant de Police qui condamna J. Emmanuel la Coste le 28 Aoust 1760. au Carcan pendant 3 jours [et] a la marque GAL" [Sentence pronounced by the Lieutenant of Police who condemned J. Emmanuel la Coste the 28th of August, 1760 to the iron collar for three days (and) to the mark GAL].

63 *Déclaration de mars 1724 sur les voleurs.* For example, in a crackdown on salt smugglers on July 5, 1704, Louis XIV declared that those violating the salt tax ordinance of 1680 would receive the mark of G, and a 1724 law on mendicancy discusses appropriate treatment of those already marked with the letter V, attesting to that mark's prior existence. Charles-Clément-François de L'Averdy, *Code penal* (Paris: Chez Desaint & Saillant, 1752), 319–20 and 133.

64 *Jugemens du Tribunal Criminel et Spécial du Département de la Seine, Séant au Palais de Justice, En date des 19 thermidor et 10 fructidor an 10.*

65 *Arrest de la Cour du Parlement, Qui condamne Marie-Louise Nicolais*, Du 9 Mars 1779 (Paris: chez P. G. Simon, Imprimeur du Parlement, 1779).

66 Munchembled also lists the "rat d'Arras" [the rat of Arras] as a brand used there beginning in the mid-sixteenth century, describing it as "the mark of a rat, . . . a sign of infamy founded on the play on words *A-rat!*," though it is unclear as to whether it took the shape of a rat or a rat's footprint; *Le Temps des supplices*, 96 and 138. The 1810 *Code pénal* included the letters TP for those condemned to *travaux forcés* in perpetuity, and T for those condemned for a limited time; Rateau, "La Récidive et sa preuve," 174–75. See also Vigié, "La Flétrissure des forçats," 810 and 813. On England, see Kellaway, *The History of Torture*, 24–25 and Andrews, *Bygone Punishments*, 138–42; on Amsterdam and Belgium, see Pieter Spierenburg, *The Spectacle of Suffering. Executions and the Evolution of Repression: From a Preindustrial Metropolis*

to the European Experience (Cambridge: Cambridge University Press, 1984), 70; on Bern, see Groebner, *Who Are You?*, 115, n. 51; on Rome, see Jousse, *Traité de la justice criminelle*, vol. 1, 58.

67 Le Brun de la Rochette, *Le Proces criminel*, 51. My emphasis.

68 Lucien Febvre and Henri-Jean Martin, *The Coming of the Book: The Impact of Printing, 1450–1800*, trans. David Gerard (London: NLB, 1971), 59.

69 Ibid., 48–49.

70 Ibid., 50.

71 Muyart de Vouglans, *Les loix criminelles*, 63–64. My emphasis.

72 B.N. Joly de Fleury, 1308, fol. 32. My emphasis. This printed letter followed the *Declaration du Roy, Contre les mendians et vagabonds* of July 18, 1724. An instrument of this nature, used for marking deserters with the letter D during the War of 1812, when Canada was under British rule, survives in the artifacts collection of Parks Canada in Québec City; personal communication with Ghislain Savoie, January 27, 2013. On tattooing, see Chapters 3 and 4.

73 B.N. Joly de Fleury, 1308, fol. 32.

74 Cotgrave, *Dictionarie* and "Lys," *Dictionnaire de l'Académie françoise*.

75 Palliot, ed., *Vraye et parfaite science des armoiries*.

76 "Chiffre," Furetière, *Dictionnaire universel*.

77 Ibid., "Marque."

78 Labat, *Nouveau Voyage*, 256. Qtd. above.

79 "Il estoit grand mignon des roys,/s'il est vray ce que l'on publie/qu'il a receu desja deux fois/la fleur de lys pendant sa vie./S'il pouvoit, un jour, meriter/la troisiesme pour recompense,/lors, il se pourroit bien venter/de porter les armes de France;" Sigogne, Regnier, Motin, Berhelot, Maynard, et al., *Le Cabinet Satyrique* [1618] (Paris: N.p., 1633), 699.

80 "Marque," *Le Grand Robert*.

81 See Isambert, *Recueil général*, for countless examples of ordinances and declarations regulating the commercial brand. Major legislation appeared in 1680, the same year laws were tightened regulating the salt trade and dictating branding for its smugglers: *Ordonnance du Louis XIV. Roy de France et de Navarre, Sur le fait des Entrées, Aydes, & autres droits . . . Juin 1680* (Paris: François Muguet, 1680), esp. 207–28.

82 "Marque," Furetière, *Dictionnaire universel*. Emphasis in original.

83 Ibid., The *Cour des Monnaies*, established in 1552, had jurisdiction over all civil and criminal law dealing with the making of coins as well as all use of gold and silver.

84 For examples of these marks, see E. Beuque and M. Frapsauce, *Dictionnaire des poinçons des maitres-orfèvres français du XIVe siècle à 1838* (Paris: F. De Nobele, 1964).

85 Ibid., "Marque" and "Marquer." Emphasis in original. I provide only a sample here. The *Dictionnaire de l'Académie françoise* definition of *marquer* similarly includes: "To mark sheep, horses. to mark dishware. to mark with a hot iron. to mark trees, to mark napkins, sheets. one marks the wine in cellars."

86 Laurent Bouchel, *La Bibliotheque ou Tresor du droit françois*, 3 vols., [1615] (Paris: Jean Girin et Barthelemy Riviere, 1671), vol. 2, 713. On the novel development of the printer's mark in the fifteenth century and for additional visual examples, see Febvre and Martin, *L'Apparition du livre*, 122–24 and *The Coming of the Book*, 83–86.

87 Nicolas Fontaine, *Le Dictionnaire chretien* (Paris: Chez Elie Josset, 1691), title page.

88 Jean de la Caille, *Histoire de l'imprimerie et de la librairie* [Paris: Jean de la Caille, 1689], facsimile ed. (Geneva: Slatkine Reprints, 1971), 9 and 12. La Caille reproduces the entire *Edit du Roy pour le reglement des imprimeurs et libraires de Paris; Registré en Parlement le 21 Aoust* 1686 (Paris, Denys Thierry, 1687). Legislation concerning booksellers' and printers' marks appeared for the first time in 1551.
89 La Caille, *Histoire de l'imprimerie*, 64.
90 *Histoire veritable.* My emphasis.
91 *Arrêt du Parlement de Paris expulsant de cette ville les gens marqués de la fleur de lys et autres bannis ainsi que les vagabonds et gens sans aveu. Du 2 juin 1617.*
92 See, for example, decrees of December 13, 1666; December 1, 1716; November 10, 1718; July 18, 1724; July 26, 1726; May 24, 1749; and August 3, 1764. See also Jacques Depauw, "Pauvres, pauvres mendiants, mendiants valides ou vagabonds? Les hésitations de la législation royale," *Revue d'histoire moderne et contemporaine* 21.3 (1974): 401–18. On the development of passports and other identifying documents, see Groebner, *Who Are You?* See the Introduction and Chapter 1 on the importance of signs worn on clothing.
93 Robin Briggs, *Early Modern France, 1560–1715*, 2nd ed. (Oxford and New York: Oxford University Press, 1998), 152.
94 *Ordonance du Roy, Contre les Vagabonds de Versailles*, May 24, 1749.
95 Ibid.
96 Foucault, *Discipline and Punish*. Paul Friedland's *Seeing Justice Done: The Age of Spectacular Capital Punishment in France* (Oxford: Oxford University Press, 2012), convincingly takes issue with the Foucauldian repressive thesis; for a summary of his argument, see 11–14. In the case of criminal branding with the fleur-de-lis, however, which was closely linked to other marking practices used to convey authority, Foucault's concept of the inscription of sovereign power on the body remains pertinent.
97 Michel de Certeau, *The Practice of Everyday Life*, trans. Steven F. Rendall (Berkeley: University of California Press, 1984), 139–40.
98 François Delpech, "La 'marque' des sorcières: logique(s) de la stigmatisation diabolique," in *Le Sabbat des sorciers. XVe-XVIIIe siècles*, ed. Nicole Jacques-Chaquin et Maxime Préaud (Grenoble: Jérôme Millon 1993), 368.
99 Michel de Certeau, "Des outils pour écrire le corps," *Traverses* 14–15 (1979), 12.
100 Certeau, "Des outils," 3.

Conclusion
Lasting impressions

"Everyone bears their fleur-de-lis."
—Nicolas Fontaine, *Dictionnaire chrétien* (1691)[1]

In his 1650 *Anthropometamorphosis*, English physician John Bulwer (1606–1656) accused the world's body modifiers of high treason, condemning "the mad and cruell Gallantry, foolish Bravery, ridiculous Beauty, filthy Finenesse, and loathsome Loveliness of most Nations fashioning and altering their Bodies from the mould intended by Nature."[2] Often considered the first work of comparative cultural anthropology, though with an openly moralizing bent, Bulwer's *Anthropometamorphosis* was, in his words,

> an *Enditement* framed against most of the nations under the Sun; whereby they are *arraigned* at the Tribunall of nature, as guilty of High-treason, in Abasing, Counterfeiting, Defacing, and Clipping her Coine, instampt with her Image and Superscription on the Body of Man.[3]

The offending peoples—or "Changlings," as Bulwer dubbed them—effectively sought to overwrite Nature's imprint on the human body or replace it with cheap imitations, temporarily or permanently altering its natural, divinely inspired "Humane Fabrick."[4] For Bulwer, the offending nations proved guilty of reworking the perfect body that was, as the biblical David whom he cites puts it, "curiously wrought in his Mothers womb as a piece of Embroidery or Needle-work."[5] Ironically, in quoting David, Bulwer chooses to describe Nature's work in the very terms he and his contemporaries commonly used to discuss man-made tattooing. But for Bulwer, Nature's handiwork, executed in the divine image, was not to be tampered with; doing so was to "question the wisdome of God," an act of blasphemy.

Bulwer's fascinating investigation of body modification traverses the globe, cataloguing a multiplicity of practices among the diverse peoples of the earth, including numerous methods of painting, tattooing, branding, and scarring the skin.[6] The frontispiece of the expanded and plentifully

Figure C.1 Frontispiece by Thomas Cross for the 2nd edition of John Bulwer's *Anthropometamorphosis* (London: William Hunt, 1653). H 57 16.53. Houghton Library, Harvard University.

illustrated 1653 edition of the *Anthropometamorphosis* portrays marked and otherwise altered representatives from around the world, standing before Nature to be judged for their bodily transgressions, elaborately pricked and painted Picts and Amerindians prominent among them (see Figure C.1).[7] Closer examination of the ostensibly global reach of Bulwer's critique, however, reveals a glaring absence. While his detailed examination of techniques for modifying the human form, organized by body part from head to toe, includes several "[n]ations that embroder their skins with Iron pens, and seare, race, pinke, cut, and pounce their Bodies," nowhere does he mention the tattooing, cutting, and branding taking place in his own time in Britain or on the European continent.[8] Though he discusses contemporary marking practices in the Americas—including those of the "Savages of *New France*"—and the world over, Bulwer turns a blind eye to marks on the skin of his contemporaries of which he could not help but be aware, namely pilgrim tattooing and judicial branding.[9] Moreover, if he acknowledges that "the penall lawes of some states, have indeed inflicted upon runnegate slaves and Malefactors, as notes of slavery and infamy, branded markes on the Forehead," Bulwer avoids, like his French contemporaries, any direct reference to contemporary state-sanctioned body marking as practiced in England's and France's criminal courts and upon the bodies of African captives brought to the Atlantic colonies.[10] He mentions body marking performed by the state only to underline what he sees as the absurdity of anyone choosing to mark their body of their own free will: "[B]ut for Men ingenious and free, to affect such stigmaticall characters, as notes of bravery, and Ensignes of Honour and Nobility, is a very strange and phantasticall prevarication."[11]

Bulwer's choice to elide contemporary European marking practices is all the more striking given the carefully orchestrated comparisons he makes between the body marking practices among foreign peoples and the vestimentary habits of the "English gallant" in the extensive critique of the excesses of current fashion that closes his treatise.[12] In his appendix, Bulwer, like Jacques Le Moyne de Morgues's paintings nearly a century earlier, provocatively arranges images side by side to underline the resemblances between, for instance, the slashed and pinked doublets of French and Englishmen—his example is French King François I's portrait—and the painted and cut torsos of Amerindians and other "barbarous Gallants who slash and carbonado their bodies" (see Figure C.2), or the paint and *mouche*-adorned faces of French and English ladies and the facial designs made by "barbarous Painter-stainers of *India*" (see Figures C.3 and C.4).[13] Strictly limiting his commentary to parallels between foreign skin and European fabric or cosmetics, Bulwer keeps any mention of permanent cutaneous marks at a safe geographical or historical distance, the product and problem of foreign lands, or an ancient custom of Europe's early peoples. In his campaign against all those who would use "audacious Art to forme and new shape themselves," Bulwer focuses his discussion of

Figure C.2 The fashion of "slashing, pinking, and cutting of our Doublets" compared
to cutting and pricking practices performed on the skin by other peoples,
John Bulwer, *Anthropometamorphosis* (London: William Hunt, 1653),
537. H 57 16.53. Houghton Library, Harvard University.

Europeans on their use of fashion alone to transform the body, directing his
wrath uniquely toward the vestimentary and cosmetic practices of his fellow
Englishmen and women, obscuring and protecting the skin beneath.[14]

Perhaps in part a product of Bulwer's legacy, signs on European skin have
historically been associated by Westerners with the foreign and seen as
products of commerce with a so-called savage, uncivilized other. By widening
the important, but limited, lens of the encounter phenomenon, this study has
joined other recent and ongoing scholarly work in expanding and deepening
our historical and cultural understanding of the mark on skin in Europe and its
colonies. The investigations of body marking in this book have revealed that in
the early modern period cutaneous signs were not restricted to the tattoos,
paint, or scarifications found on the skin of the Amerindian other or any
number of exoticized peoples described in the travel narratives of the time
and catalogued in Bulwer's treatise. Instead, as evidenced by Théophile Raynaud's *De Stigmatismo* (1647), marks on skin also played prominent roles in
the magical, religious, demonological, medical, and judicial arenas. As the
diverse contemporary practices, uses, meanings, and contexts of body marking

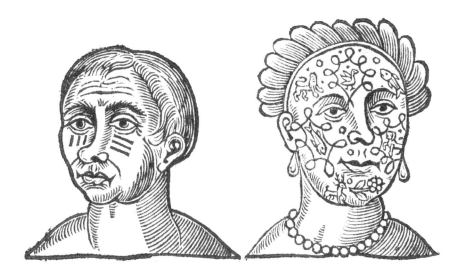

Figure C.3 Facial adornment practices of foreign peoples, compared in Bulwer's text to the European use of makeup, John Bulwer, *Anthropometamorphosis* (London: William Hunt, 1653), 534. H 57 16.53. Houghton Library, Harvard University.

Figure C.4 Women's fashion of wearing black patches, compared to "Indian" practices, the *mouche*-covered European woman at center, John Bulwer, *Anthropometamorphosis* (London: William Hunt, 1653), 535. H 57 16.53. Houghton Library, Harvard University.

examined in the five chapters of this book have shown, signing the body was both a common and multifaceted phenomenon in early modern Europe. Signs on skin—from the criminal brand to the pilgrim tattoo, from the devil's mark to divine stigmata, from the colonial tattoo to characters impressed by the planets—were well known to early modern Europeans and used by them to define, express, reinvent, and control identity.

This book has highlighted the familiarity with which early moderns greeted the appearance and use of corporeal signs and the connections they made between them. The post-possession legacy of Loudun prioress Jeanne des Anges's (1602–1665) signed hand, as reported by Parlement lawyer François Gayot de Pitaval (1673–1743) in his monumental collection of *Causes célèbres et intéressantes*, provides a final illustration of the ease with which writers of this period understood and navigated between the diverse cutaneous signs that filled their imaginary and their daily lives. In his treatment of the Loudun possession, Gayot de Pitaval recounts that, despite the official minutes and authoritative testimony that defended the supernatural origin of the names the prioress bore on her body, "the skeptics said that art had produced these characters."[15] The many alternative etiologies that Jeanne des Anges's contemporary critics offer for her marks testify to their knowledge of or even firsthand experience with the wide variety of man-made body marking techniques that proliferated in early modern Europe and the Atlantic colonies. For Gayot de Pitaval, the prioress's markings resemble the Amerindian tattoo on the bodies of French colonists he has read about in published relations, though, he jokes, they were less well executed by her demon than by the native inhabitants of New France:

> I saw in a relation about Louisiana, that the French, following the example of the Savages, traced on their skin figures of diverse colors, of men, of animals. Here is how they did it. They first drew these figures on their skin, then they pricked all the lines of the drawing with a needle, and put colors that infiltrated through these little holes, tracing a permanent figure. If Balaam had attended the school of the Savages, he would have better succeeded and would not have formed characters that faded on the hand of the Superior, and that they were obligated to renew.[16]

Similarly, scholar Gilles Ménage (1613–1692) recognizes in the prioress's cutaneous signs the tattoos he has seen on the arms of pilgrims returning from Jerusalem: "these words were in fact engraved, but lightly and in the way that those Crosses and Crucifixes that you see on the arms of Pilgrims to the Holy Land are engraved."[17] François Hédelin, Abbé d'Aubignac (1604–1676), writing in 1637, links her inscriptions to a body marking technique he saw performed at court by a skilled female alchemist:

> [I] met an ingenious young woman knowledgeable in many secrets, because she had long practiced the philosopher's stone, who had taught

herself (because she never wanted to say how she came to know it) that by pricking the skin of a man with a very sharp iron, deep enough to make the blood come out, but not so deep as to cause it to flow and stream out, and then by letting the drops of blood that had come out of each of the pricks, which were close to each other, marks remain in whatever form that one wants to make them in pricking the skin, and that they last seven or fourteen days. She wore on her arm letters that were shown to Monseigneur the Cardinal and Madame Aisguillon and to many trustworthy people. I saw and examined them; they resembled completely the characters that are on the Ursuline superior's hand, without the least imaginable bit of difference.[18]

Abbé d'Aubignac cites as well an alternative method that, he has on good faith, would produce a time-delayed impression: "some curious naturalists told me that with certain strong liquids you write on the human skin what you want without anything appearing, except a little later."[19] Jeanne des Anges's signatures might also be compared, he writes, to cutaneous marks made for love, for "we well know that in Malta lovers imprint out of gallantry the name of their mistresses on their skin and that they never fade."[20] Queen Anne of Austria's ladies in waiting bring this last comparison closer to home. Pitaval reports that, passing by Loudun, curiosity took them to the Ursuline convent's grille to see the characters imprinted on Jeanne des Anges's hand. Upon viewing them, they remarked, "*Well, . . . is that all it is? all our lovers, without any magic other than that of love, wear our names written with the same method on their arms.*"[21] The women's allusion to lovers embossing their skin with the names of their mistresses only underscores the banality and ubiquitous nature of body marking in the period, confirming the relatively ordinary status of an early modern European tattoo once thought extraordinary.[22]

With notable exceptions, studies of body marking in the sixteenth through eighteenth centuries have examined various types of marks on skin—the devil's mark, divine stigmata, scarifications, tattoos, criminal brands, birthmarks, moles—in isolation from each other. As the contemporary readings of Jeanne des Anges's hand and examples throughout this book have illustrated, such an approach runs counter to the way in which early moderns themselves thought about the corporeal mark. When theorizing signs worn on the body, they rarely conceived of one type of marking as independent from another. The brand on the most hardened criminal was not unrelated to the stigmata of the holiest saint, the tattoos made on the arms of the most devout pilgrims were not so different from those engraved on the skin of rebellious colonists by their Amerindian hosts. When Bordeaux judge Pierre De Lancre (1553–1631) describes the devil's mark on witches, he finds points of comparison with the mark of baptism, the cut of circumcision, the stigmata of saints, birthmarks on infants, and brands on slaves.[23] Similarly, when cross-Atlantic traveler Marc Lescarbot (ca. 1570–1641) describes

Amerindian tattooing, he refers his reader back to a vast tradition of corporeal marking on the European continent, from branding, to stigmata, to the pilgrim tattoo.[24] As early modern writers interpreted and theorized the marking practices they witnessed or even invented, they drew parallels between the forms and functions of a diversity of cutaneous signs. While remaining conscious of the specificities inherent in each marking practice investigated here, this study has followed suit and endeavored to bring these relationships to light.

The analyses undertaken here do not, however, suggest a single overarching conclusion about how cutaneous signs were conceived, witnessed, and practiced in France or Europe during the long period from the mid-sixteenth through mid-eighteenth centuries. Such a conclusion would necessarily over-simplify the complexities inherent in the varied discourses, uses, and reso-nances of the different types of early modern body marking. Each chapter of this book has examined a distinct corpus that raises questions and suggests its own context-specific conclusions. Nonetheless, despite these specificities, cer-tain threads have woven themselves through the pages of this book that merit brief exploration here. I offer them in response to the question that has lingered persistently throughout work on this project: Why did signs on skin occupy a place of such importance in early modern European culture?

First, the extraordinary proliferation of corporeal marks in the early modern period seems, at least in part, to be the product of a desire for visible and enduring signs of truth in a time of profound upheaval and uncertainty, when new ideas and realities contested traditional systems of belief. The Protestant Reformation put the institutional and doctrinal foundations of Christian identity and belief into question. Violence and insecurity dominated the lives of the French during the Wars of Religion and their long and uncertain aftermath. Catholic reform, though initially slowed by the religious wars and the country's enduring hostility to the dictates of Rome, encouraged religious revival and introduced major changes in institutional structures. Dramatic transformations were underway in French society, with the expansion of new technologies such as print, a shifting system of political and cultural alle-giances, and the development of new economic relationships. Exposure to foreign peoples and cultural practices through voyages of exploration, coloni-zation, and tourism widened European perspectives and questioned societal norms. Intellectuals attempted to reckon with a vast body of knowledge newly available from Greek, Roman, and Arabic traditions, which ignited intense debates. A fast-developing scientific discourse offered novel explanations of the natural world that put into question former ways of seeing human beings and their relationship to the universe. With the advent of anatomy, new visions of the human body itself challenged established knowledge, traditional world-views, and societal taboos. In a time when past beliefs, identities, and systems of knowledge proved unstable or unreliable, early moderns increasingly sought indisputable signs of identification, authority, and belonging in the materiality and relative permanence of the cutaneous sign. No longer securely marked by the traditional authoritative discourses of the past, they looked to the body, seen as a stable signifier, to express identity, profess belief, affirm truth, and assert authority.

While the increased reliance on and investment in the corporeal mark was undoubtedly fueled by anxiety over the unraveling of past certainties, it was also distinctly a sign of modernity. The devil's mark, demons' cutaneous signs of departure, the pilgrim tattoo, the colonial tattoo, and the judicial brand all came into existence and proliferated in the early modern period. Steadily gaining in influence, scientific disciplines privileged empirical verification and objectivity, grounding their conclusions in the authority of material signs. This valuing of verifiable markers of truth was echoed in the evolving judicial system, where material evidence began to take on paramount importance in the assignment of guilt or innocence. Signs on skin, locatable and invested with proof value, became key elements in sentencing and trials, as doctors entered the judicial arena as invited experts to examine bodies and to provide testimony. The advent and rise in the late sixteenth century of the devil's mark on the accused witch's body testifies eloquently to this development. The need for a material sign of proof upon the skin was made manifest in the Loudun and Louviers possession cases of the 1630s and 1640s as well, where a new hybrid cutaneous sign emerged to verify a demon's departure from the body. The permanence—or at least relative endurance—and visibility—even when invisible, as was often the case of the devil's mark—of corporeal marks placed them high in the hierarchy as signs of truth. Both the advent of the Holy Land pilgrim tattoo in the final years of the sixteenth century and the institution of branding during this same period for those convicted of noncapital crimes responded to a similar desire for material, verifiable signs.

At the same time, other marks, like the stigmata of women religious or the plentiful apotropaic signs early moderns wore against their skin or drew upon their bodies, represented extensions and revisions of medieval marking traditions. Even those cutaneous signs that were novel in the sixteenth and seventeenth centuries were elaborated and understood in terms of a common heritage of both Judeo-Christian and Greco-Roman traditions. Early marking practices contributed to the development of the early modern pilgrim tattoo and the state branding of accused criminals and slaves. The newly invented devil's mark on witches and demon's cutaneous signs of departure were deeply informed by biblical sources and medieval stigmatic tradition, even as they drew on burgeoning forensic science. Signs on skin in this period seem to hover, then, between a worldview heavily influenced by ancient, religious, magical, and astrological practice and belief, and a modern collective imaginary born of empiricism, centralization, and imperialism.

Modernization meant movement. The heightened value of the cutaneous sign in this period can be intimately tied to the response on the part of the state to the ever-greater circulation of texts, people, and goods. Royal and local authorities created new systems of identification and verification to better monitor these movements and maintain control over them. The sixteenth century saw the increased prominence of the signature on official documents as an authenticating sign. Thought of more as a seal or stamp than as a product of writing, this ink-on-paper sign found its homologue in similar marks on skin. The devil's mark on the witch's body, for instance, mirrored his signature made in blood upon their written pact. The corporeal mark also had close ties with the advent of the passport and the increased enforcement of its use in the period. The signed and sealed passport—a kind of paper double for the body it authenticated—became increasingly mandatory for establishing identity and monitoring people's movements across France and beyond. Not only did passports themselves carry an official mark and record their bearer's distinguishing bodily marks, but corporeal signs sometimes even stood in for official papers, as both pilgrims and convicts experienced. Pilgrim accounts testify that displaying the Jerusalem tattoo authenticated the traveler's identity and protected him from capture during the dangerous journey home. Here, the corporeal sign superseded in legibility and reliability its more easily lost or stolen paper cousin. If signs made on the body resembled those made on paper they also offered, at least in theory, a more permanent solution to the failures of the written or printed text. This was clearly the case in the judicial system's recourse to corporeal branding for the monitoring of criminals, which made convicts easily identifiable to court authorities if they later fell once more into the hands of justice. Indeed, criminal brands mirrored those placed on the commercial goods that also traveled the roads, controlling their production and circulation. From printers' devices on books, to artisans' impressions on silver, to producers' brands on bags of grain—all referred to as *marques*— brands became widespread and obligatory in this period characterized by the increased centralization of commerce under royal control. The corporeal mark was not, then, a throwback to less enlightened times but was instead closely linked to other mechanisms of control being developed by the modern state.

As examples cited throughout the pages of this book suggest, the increased importance of corporeal marking in early modern Europe must also be linked to the invention and profusion of the new techniques and technologies that characterized print culture, in its largest sense. Materials and methods for making cutaneous signs closely resembled those of marking paper, leather, and metal, and they shared a common vocabulary. The nouns "impression," "imprint," "engraving," "stamp," and "punch" and their corresponding verbs —many of which came into existence in the sixteenth and early seventeenth centuries—were just as common in the print shop as they were in descriptions of scarring, tattooing, branding, and stigmata, both divine and diabolical. As we have seen, writers' descriptions of corporeal marking consistently compare it to the techniques of impression and engraving so prevalent in the increasingly print-filled world they inhabited. Indeed, many of the tools of the print trade— from wood blocks, to the punch, to the engraver's burin—were also used in creating corporeal marks. This study has brought to the fore the ways in which writing on, imprinting, stamping, or otherwise marking paper, metal, and other materials interacted dynamically with practices of corporeal marking in this print-saturated time. A certain intimacy between bodies and texts traverses the practices examined here, with texts accompanying the body, bound to it, and issuing forth from its orifices, printing or writing finding their support sometimes on paper, sometimes on skin. The close connections between bodies, paper, and parchment made by early moderns in the ways they thought about and executed corporeal marking of many kinds suggest not only a vision of the human body as a potent bearer of text but also a deep preoccupation with the problems and potentialities of paper and print.

Finally, body marking was intimately linked to identity in the early modern period. Those writing about marks on skin cast them plainly as signs of identity not unlike the widespread vestimentary and commercial marks of the time that served purposes of distinction, identification, and authentication. The badges worn on hats or clothing, the coats of arms that decorated the possessions of nobles and their servants' uniforms, the insignia that hung outside of workshops and were impressed upon the products they produced all constituted a larger marking culture of which the corporeal mark was a part. As the close relationship between the pilgrim tattoo and the passport as well as the resemblances between insignia on clothing and cutaneous signs suggest, marks on skin served as distinctive signs to identify early moderns—pilgrims, convicts, witches, saints, soldiers, lovers. If quack healers such as the *Pauliani* and the *Saludadores* used signs on skin to bolster their authority and thus convince potential patrons to buy their remedies, it is because the cutaneous mark carried authority, affirming its bearer's identity as a descendent of Saint Paul or Saint Catherine who was endowed with special powers.

Steeped in the European marking traditions of their own times and well versed in those of Antiquity—notably the marking of prisoners, slaves, and soldiers—as they ventured outside of Europe, French travelers clearly saw the marks they encountered on the skin of Coptic Christians in Palestine and the native peoples of the Americas as signs of identity, interpreting them as such in their narratives. In Europe and the Atlantic colonies, the advent of marks such as the criminal brand or the devil's mark, as well as the branding of slaves, placed confidence in the cutaneous sign as way of defining identity and making it material. The judicial brand came into use for the express purpose of designating offenders and fugitives across time and space, just as the devil's mark on witches, an inversion of the baptismal sign, identified them as Satan's own.

Marks on skin played important roles in the ways in which early moderns envisioned their individual, social, and cultural identities and negotiated their relationships with power, both secular and supernatural. Pilgrims, colonists, and women religious all sought to rewrite their identities or social status through the use of corporeal signs. Through tattooing, pilgrims engaged in an enterprise of self-fashioning; some even displayed their Holy Land marks for posterity in engravings and portraits. New France colonists adopted Amerindian tattooing methods to inscribe sets of heterogeneous signs upon their skin that reflected their new hybrid identities as French inhabitants of North America. Through corporeal inscription, Jeanne de Chantal (1572–1641) guaranteed her future as a spouse of Christ and founder of a new religious order, rather than find herself pushed into a second secular marriage. Inspired by her model, Jeanne des Anges successfully recast her identity from that of demonically possessed woman to that of admired spiritual counselor and aspiring saint by negotiating a new set of bodily inscriptions to replace those originally promised by her demons. Marks on skin thus served as powerful signs of distinction, creating visibilities and projecting a message about the marked body, a body that was always meant to be read, whether for better—signaling sanctity, devotion, status, belonging—or for worse—stigmatizing the sinner, the criminal, the slave, the savage, the outsider.

The myriad of interrelated histories, methods, and meanings of corporeal marking that proliferated in early modern Europe and the Atlantic colonies have, to be sure, left lasting impressions on our perceptions and practices surrounding the sign on skin today. Of these, the investment early moderns made in cutaneous marks as signifiers of identity resonates perhaps most poignantly with our twenty-first-century sensibilities. Though they have never been absent from human experience, in recent decades, tattooing and other body marking practices have become mainstream in Europe and North America.[25] Already in the late 1990s, tattoo studios were among the top six growth businesses in the United States, their number having increased exponentially from the 1960s.[26] The tattoo has taken its place in popular culture and media, on the skins of celebrity icons, and in advertising. Tattooing finds particular favor with Millennials, with nearly four in ten sporting at least one tattoo, according to a 2010 report by the Pew Research Center.[27] The remarkable enthusiasm for body marking today begs the question as to what may lie behind the dramatic rise and increasingly widespread interest in the corporeal sign as a means of registering, communicating, and shaping identity. Might, as one 2006 study concludes, the current recourse to the bodily canvas as a means of self-expression and self-determination be a symptom of a search for stability, even for proof of personal identity, within a world characterized by the erosion of national identities, the decline of institutionalized religion, and the redefinition of the family?[28] If so, we may share with our early modern ancestors, across centuries and vastly different cultural contexts, a desire to anchor identity in the skin and thus to assert it on our own terms. Indeed, while Bulwer's 1650 work condemned body modification as unnatural, even monstrous, its appearance also signaled an important change in the way he and his contemporaries thought about how the body was written, one that still resonates today.[29] No longer were bodies uniquely passive recipients of impression as they had often been characterized by many earlier Renaissance thinkers. Bulwer's work, for all its moralizing, effectively recast human beings as active agents in their own corporeal inscription, who—like our twenty-first-century "changling" selves—made deliberate choices about the ways in which their bodies should be written and, ultimately, about how they wished to be read.

Notes

1 Nicolas Fontaine, *Dictionnaire chrétien* (Paris: Elie Josset, 1691), 98.
2 John Bulwer, *Anthropometamorphosis: Man Transform'd: Or, The Artificiall Changling, Historically presented* [1650], 2nd ed. (London: William Hunt, 1653), title page.
3 Ibid., "Epistle Dedicatory," n. pag. Emphasis in original.
4 Ibid., title page. Bulwer's choice of term recalled Andreas Vesalius's (1514–1664) famous 1543 celebration of the human anatomy, *De humani corporis fabrica* (Basel: Joannis Oporini, 1543).
5 Bulwer, *Anthropometamorphosis*, "Introduction," n. pag., from Psalm 139, verse 15. Bulwer or his printer mistakenly cite Psalm 39.
6 Bulwer, *Anthropometamorphosis*, esp. 107, 163–66, 547–52, 286–87, 455–66. In contrast to Théophile Raynaud's (1583–1663) contemporaneous treatise on stigmata, Bulwer does not limit his study to marks upon the skin but discusses numerous techniques for reshaping various body parts. Distinct from Raynaud, he concentrates on processes linked to ornamentation and aesthetics and does not examine medical or supernatural markings of any kind, whereas demonic and divine stigmata make up the bulk of the theologian's work; Théophile Raynaud, *De stigmatismo, sacro et profano, divino, humano, daemoniaco* [1647], 2nd ed. (Lyon: Antoine Cellier, 1654). On Bulwer's attention to fashion, see Joel Konrad, "'Barbarous Gallants': Fashion, Morality, and the Marked Body in English Culture, 1590–1660," *Fashion Theory* 15.1 (2011): 29–48.
7 See Bulwer's "The intent of the Frontispiece unfolded," n. pag. On his text's publication history, see William E. Burns, "The King's Two Monstrous Bodies: John Bulwer and the English Revolution," in *Wonders, Marvels, and Monsters in Early Modern Culture*, ed. Peter G. Platt (Newark, DE: University of Delaware Press, 1999), 201, n. 34 and H.J. Norman, "John Bulwer and His *Anthropometamorphosis*" in *Science, Medicine, and History: Essays in Honour of Charles Singer*, ed. Edgard Underwood, 2 vols. (London: Oxford University Press, 1953), vol. 2, 82–99. On Bulwer's work, see also Margaret Hodgen, *Early Anthropology in the Sixteenth and Seventeenth Centuries* (Philadelphia, PA: University of Pennsylvania Press, 1964), 128–29 and Elizabeth Stephens, "Queer Monsters: Technologies of Self-Transformation in Bulwer's *Anthropometamorphosis* and Braidotti's *Meamorphoses*," in *Somatechnics: Queering the Technologisation of Bodies*, ed. Nikki Sullivan and Samantha Murray (Farnam, UK and Burlington, VT: Ashgate, 2009), 171–86. It remains uncertain if the *Anthropometamorphosis* was known in France during the period, though given its multiple editions and its critique of French fashion imports, it is highly likely. Marin Mersenne (1588–1648) was aware of Bulwer's earlier *Philocopus* (1648), on gestural language for the deaf—but died prior to the *Anthropometamorphosis*'s publication; Jeffery Wollock, "John Bulwer (1606–1656) and Some British and French Contemporaries," *Historiographia Linguistica* 40.3 (2013): 331–75, esp. 339–43.
8 Bulwer, *Anthropometamorphosis*, index. Similarly, the anonymous *Wonder of Wonders: or, a Metamorphosis of Fair Faces voluntarily transformed into foul visages: or, an Invective against Black-spotted Faces* (London: J.G. for Richard Royston, 1662) discusses the marking customs of ancient peoples but does not mention contemporary practices beyond makeup and *mouches*; Jennipher A. Rosecrans, "Wearing the Universe," in *Written on the Body: The Tattoo in European and American History*, ed. Jane Caplan (Princeton, NJ: Princeton University Press, 2000), 46-60.
9 Bulwer, *Anthropometamorphosis*, 79. Emphasis in original.
10 Ibid., 83–84.
11 Ibid., 84.

12 See Bulwer's "Appendix, Exhibiting the Pedigree of the English Gallant" in *Anthropometamorphosis*, 529–59. For examples of permanent and temporary body marking and painting compared to English fashion, see esp. 533–38, 541, and, in the main treatise, 261–63, 286–87. For Bulwer's treatment of the Picts, see 464–66. On the treatment of the Pict in Bulwer and contemporaries, see Joel Konrad, "'Curiously and Most Exquisitely Painted:' Body Marking in British Thought and Experience, 1580–1800," Doctoral dissertation, McMaster University (Canada), 2011, 87–134.

13 Emphasis in the original. Both fashions were French imports. On visual parallels made between Europeans and Amerindians by Jacques Le Moyne de Morgues, see Juliet Fleming, "The Renaissance Tattoo," in *Written on the Body*, ed. Caplan, 61–82; 71–72. Fleming's article first appeared in *Res: Anthropology and Aesthetics* 31 (1997): 34–52 and also appears in her *Graffiti and the Writing Arts of Early Modern England* (Philadelphia, PA: University of Pennsylvania Press, 2001), 79–112. On *mouches*, see Bulwer 261–63 and 534–35, Jaberg, "The Birthmark," 332–38, and Claire Goldstein, "*Mouches Volantes*: The Enigma of Paste-On Beauty Marks in 17th-Century France" (unpublished manuscript, last modified May 2019), Microsoft Word file. These "black patches" were artificial moles made from fabric in various figurative shapes, worn upon the face to hide blemishes or to make the complexion appear whiter. A *mouche*-covered woman stands in profile at the bottom left of the frontispiece (see Figure C.1).

14 Bulwer, *Anthropometamorphosis*, "Introduction," n. pag.

15 François Gayot de Pitaval, *Causes célèbres et intéressantes, avec les jugemens qui les ont décidées*, 20 vols. (Paris: Theodore Legras et al., 1734–1748), vol. 2, 520.

16 Ibid., 520–21.

17 *Menagiana ou Les Bons mots et remarques critiques, Historiques morales & d'érudition, de Monsieur Menage* [1693/94], 4 vols. (Paris: Florentin Delaulne, 1715), vol. 4, 48; for his full discussion of the Loudun case, see 37–49. Also qtd. in Pitaval, *Causes célèbres*, vol. 2, 533.

18 François Hédelin, abbé d'Aubignac, *Relation de M. Hédelin, Abbé d'Aubignac, touchant les possédés de Loudun au mois de septembre 1637*, rpt. in Robert Mandrou, *Possession et sorcellerie au XVIIe siècle. Textes inédits* (Paris: Fayard, 1979), 144–94; 153–54. On alchemical inscriptions made on the body, see Rosecrans, "Wearing the Universe."

19 Abbé d'Aubignac, *Relation*, 153–54.

20 Ibid., 153.

21 Pitaval, *Causes célèbres*, vol. 2, 533. Emphasis in original.

22 Honoré d'Urfé's (1567–1625) best-selling novel, *L'Astrée* (1607–1627), includes the intercalated tale of Palinice, Sileine, and Amilcar where one of the rival lovers proves his enduring devotion through allowing Palinice to tattoo her monogram on his arm; Honoré d'Urfé, *L'Astrée*, 5 vols. (Geneva: Slatkine Reprints, 1966), vol. 4, bk. 9, 539–40.

23 Pierre de Lancre, *Tableau de l'inconstance des mauvais anges et démons* (Paris: Jean Berjon, 1612), "De la marque des Sorciers," Discours II, 181–84 and 190–91.

24 Marc Lescarbot, *Voyages en Acadie (1604–1607) suivis de La Description des mœurs souriquoises comparées à celles d'autres peuples*, ed. Marie-Christine Pioffet (Québec: Presses de l'Université Laval, 2007), 320–21.

25 Social scientists have documented this phenomenon. See, for example: Clinton Sanders, *Customizing the Body: The Art and Culture of Tattooing* (Philadelphia, PA: Temple University Press, 1989, rev. ed. 2008); David Le Breton, *Signes d'identité. Tatouages, piercings et autres marques corporelles* (Paris: Métailié, 2002) and "Anthropologie des marques corporelles," in *Signes du corps*, ed. Christiane Falgayrettes-Leveau (Paris: Musée Dapper, 2004), 73–119; Terrence

Turner, "The Social Skin," in *Not Work Alone: A Cross-Cultural View of Activities Superfluous to Survival*, ed. Jeremy Cherfas and Robert Lewin (London: Temple Smith, 1980), 112–40, rpt. in the *Journal of Ethnographic Theory* 2.2 (2012): 486–504; Margo DeMello, *Bodies of Inscription: A Cultural History of the Modern Tattoo Community* (Durham, NC: Duke University Press, 2000); and Victoria Pitts, *In the Flesh: The Cultural Politics of Body Modification* (New York: Palgrave Macmillan, 2003). Arnold Rubin was the first to describe a twentieth-century "tattoo renaissance" in *Marks of Civilization: Artistic Transformations of the Human Body* (Los Angeles: Museum of Cultural History, University of California, 1988).

26 Anne M. Velliquette, Jeff B. Murray, and Deborah J. Evers, "Inscribing the Personal Myth: The Role of Tattoos in Identification," *Research in Consumer Behavior* 10 (2006): 35–70; 36.

27 As of 2010, in the United States, of the 38% of Millennials who have a tattoo, half have two to five tattoos, and 18% have six or more. 32% of Gen Xers also have at least one tattoo, compared to 15% among Baby Boomers; Paul Taylor and Scott Keeter, eds., *Millennials: Confident. Connected. Open to Change. A Portrait of Generation Next* (Washington, D.C.: Pew Research Center, 2010), 57–58.

28 Velliquette et al., "Inscribing the Personal Myth" and Chris Weller, "The Identity Crisis Under the Ink," *The Atlantic*, November 25, 2014.

29 Stephens, "Queer Monsters," 173.

Bibliography

Primary Sources

Abbeville, Claude d'. *Histoire de la Mission des Pères Capucins en l'Isle de Maragnan et terres circonvoysines ou est traicte des singularitez admirables & des Meurs merveilleuses des Indiens habitans de ce pais Avec les missives et advis qui ont este envoyez de nouveau.* Paris: François Huby, 1614. Facsimile reproduction, Austria: Akademische Druck- und Verlagsanstalt Graz, 1963.

"Abregé de la Vie & des Vertus, de feuë Nôtre-trés honnorée Sœur Margueritte Angelique Cadeau, Decedée dans ce Monastere de la Visitation Sainte Marie de Blois, le 22. Mars 1717. âgée de 83. ans, Professe de 66." In *Circulaires des Religieuses de la Visitation de Ste-Marie*, vol. 24. Blois, 1717.

"Abregé de la vie et des vertus de nôtre tres honorée Sœur & ancienne Mere Anne Angelique Loppin décedée en ce Monastére de la Visitation Ste. Marie de Beaune le 17. May 1707." In *Circulaires des Religieuses de la Visitation de Ste-Marie*, vol. 21. Beaune, 1707.

Affagart, Greffin. *Relation de Terre Sainte (1533–1534).* Edited by J. Chavanon. Paris: Librairie Victor Lecoffre, 1902.

Agrippa of Nettesheim, Henry Cornelius. *Les Œuvres magiques de Henri-Corneille Agrippa, latin et français, avec des Secrets occultes.* Liège: N.p., 1788.

Agrippa of Nettesheim, Henry Cornelius. *Three Books of Occult Philosophy.* Edited by Donald Tyson. Translated by James Freake. Woodbury, MN: Llewellyn Publications, 2006.

Alacoque, Marguerite-Marie. *Vie et Œuvres de Sainte Marguerite-Marie Alacoque.* Edited by François-Léon Gauthey. 3 vols. Paris: Ancienne Librairie Poussielgue, 1920.

Amico da Gallipoli, Bernardino. *Trattato Delle Piante et Imagini De I Sacri Edificii Di Terrasanta Disegnate In Gierusalemme Secondo le regole della prospettiva, & vera misura della lor grandezza.* Rome: Ex. Typographia Linguarum Externarum, 1609. Facsimile edition. *Plans of the Sacred Edifices of the Holy Land.* Edited by Fr. Bellarmino Bagatti O.F.M. Translated by Fr. Theophilus Bellorini O.F.M., and Fr. Eugene Hoade O.F.M. Jerusalem: Franciscan Press, 1953.

Amico da Gallipoli, Bernardino. *Trattato delle piante e imagini de' sacri edifizi di Terra Santa disegnate in Ierusalemme.* Florence: P. Cecconcelli, 1620.

Arrest de la Cour de Parlement, Confirmatif de la Sentence Rendue par Monsieur le Lieutenant Criminel; Qui condamne Jean Dumont à estre attaché au Carcan à la Halle pendant trois jours de Marché consecutifs, & le troiéme desdits jours estre foüetté & fletri de la lettre V. & en trois ans de Bannissement, pour avoir volé du

Fruit sur le Carreau de la Halle. Du deux Septembre 1727. Paris: P.J. Mariette, Imprimeur de la Police.

Arrest de la Cour du Parlement, Qui condamne Marie-Louise Nicolais, veuve d'Antoine-François Derues, à être, ayant la corde au col, battue & fustigée nue de verges, & flétrie d'un fer chaud en forme de la lettre V, sur les deux épaules, par l'Exécuteur de la Haute-Justice, au devant de la porte des prisons de la Conciergerie du Palais; ce fait, menée & conduite en la Maison de force de l'Hôpital Général de la Salpêtriere, pour y être détenue & renfermée à perpétuité, pour avoir méchamment & sciemment pratiqué différentes manœuvres & faussetés à l'effet de s'emparer, de concert avec Antoine-François Derues son mar, de la Terre de Vuisson-Soef, sans bourse délier; & en outre véhémentement suspecte d'avoir participé aux autres crimes commis par ledit Derues. Extrait des registres du Parlement. Du 9 Mars 1779. Paris: P.G. Simon, Imprimeur du Parlement, 1779.

Arrêt du Parlement de Paris expulsant de cette ville les gens marqués de la fleur de lys et autres bannis ainsi que les vagabonds et gens sans aveu. June 2, 1617.

Aubignac, François Hédelin, Abbé d'. Aubignac, François Hédelin. *Relation de M. Hédelin, Abbé d'Aubignac, touchant les possédés de Loudun au mois de septembre 1637.* Reprinted in *Possession et sorcellerie au XVIIe siècle. Textes inédits,* edited by Robert Mandrou, 144–94. Paris: Fayard, 1979.

Aubigné, Agrippa d'. *Histoire universelle du Sieur D'Aubigné.* 3 vols. Maille: Jean Moussat, 1620.

Aubin, Nicolas. *Histoire des diables de Loudun.* Amsterdam: Abraham Wolfgang, 1694.

Augustine. *Trois Sermons de S. Augustin, non moins doctes que utiles en ce temps. Les deux premiers traictent du nom & devoir du Chrestien, & l'autre est la necessité de payer les dimes. Ausquels il est enseigné que ceux qui adherent aux magies, sorceleries, superstitions & infestations diaboliques, pour neant sont Chrestiens & abusent de leur foy.* Translated by M. René Benoist. Paris: Jean Poupy, 1579.

Averdy, Charles-Clément-François de l'. *Code penal, ou Recueil des principales ordonnances, edits et declarations, sur les crimes & délits. Première partie. Précis des loix ou des dispositions des ordonnances, edits & déclarations.* Paris: Chez Desaint & Saillant, 1752.

Balourdet, Loys. *La Guide des chemins pour le Voyage de Hierusalem, et autres Villes & lieux de la Terre Sainte. Avec la description de plusieurs villes & forteresses, & de leurs antiques et modernes singularitez: De la mer, de sa cruauté, & de la Hierarchie Nautique: De la croyance, ceremonies, mœurs, & façons de vivre des Turcs, Arabes, & autres infidels, & de la valleur & changement de leurs monnoyes. Plus la remarque des Saincts lieux ou le Sauveur du monde a faict des miracles: Et des ceremonies qu'observent les nations Crestiennes qui gardent le S. Sepulchre.* Chalons: C. Guyot, 1601.

Bavant, Magdelaine. *Histoire de Magdelaine Bavant, Religieuse du Monastere de Saint-Loüis de Louviers, avec sa Confession generale & testamentaire, où elle declare les abominations, impietez et sacrileges qu'elle a pratiqué & veu pratiquer, tant dans ledit Monastere qu'au Sabat, & les personnes qu'elle y a remarquées.* Edited by Charles Desmarets. Paris: J. Le Gentil, 1652.

Bavant, Magdelaine. *Récit de l'histoire de sœur Magdelaine Bavent, Religieuse du monastère de Saint-Louis de Louviers, atteinte et convaincue du crime de magie, et ce qu'elle a dit au Parlement de Rouen touchant les abominations qu'elle a vu pratiquer au sabat et ailleurs: avec sa confession générale et testamentaire qu'elle a faite dans sa prison.* Rouen: Deshays, 1878.

Bavant, Magdelaine. *Histoire de Magdelaine Bavent*. In *Les Possédées de Louviers. Histoire de Magdelaine Bavent d'après les documents de l'époque*, Edited by Roger Dubos, 14–99. Mondeville: Charles Corlet, 1990.

Beaugrand, Félix. *Relation nouvelle et tres-fidelle du Voyage de la Terre Sainte, Dans laquelle se voit tout ce qu'il y a de remarquable, tant par Mer que par Terre, depuis le départ de Marseille jusqu'au retour de ce saint Voyage*. Paris: Antoine Warin, 1700.

Beaumarchais, Pierre Augustin Caron de. *La Folle Journée ou le Mariage de Figaro*. 1785. Paris: Garnier, 1985.

Belot, Jean. *Instruction Familiere et tres facile pour apprendre les sciences de chiromance et physiognomie. Dans laquelle est enseigné le plus parfaict des secrets de la Memoire Artificielle, dites l'Art bref de Raymond Lulle, Grandement necessaire tant à ceux qui font Profession de Prescher, Haranguer, Plaider que pourceux qui font grand commerce de marchandise. Plus un Discours Astrologique & Description Geographique & Topographique du Comette qui apparust sur nostre Hermisphere, L'Année derniere 1618. Avec les predictions d'iceluy, dont les evenements en seront formidables*. Paris: Nicolas Rousset and Nicolas Bourdin, 1619.

Belot, Jean. *Œuvres de M. Jean Belot Curé de Milmonts, Professeur aux sciences divines et celestes. Contenant la chiromence; Physionomie, L'Art de Memoire de Raymond Lulli; Traité des Divinations, Augures & Songes; les Sciences Steganographiques, Paulines, Armadrilles & Lullistes; Art de doctement Prescher & Haranguer, &c*. Rouen: Jacques Cailloüé, 1640; Rouen: Jean Berthelin, 1669.

Bénard, Nicolas. *Le voyage de Hierusalem et autres lieux de la Terre sainte*. Paris: Denis Moreau, 1621.

Bergerac, Cyrano de. *Histoire comique, . . . Contenant les Estats et Empires de la Lune*. Paris: 1657.

Bertet de la Clue Sabran, Jean-François. *A Voyage to Dauphin Island in 1720: The Journal of Bertet de la Clue*. Edited and translated by Francis Escoffier and Jay Higginbotham. Mobile, AL: Museum of the City of Mobile, 1974.

Binsfeld, Peter. *Tractatus de confessionibus maleficorum & Sagarum an et quanta fides iis adhibenda sit?* Trier: Heinrich Bock, 1589.

Binsfeld, Peter. *Tractat von Bekanntnuß der Zauberer und Hexen*. Munich: Adam Berg, 1591.

Binsfeld, Peter. *La Theologie des pasteurs et autres prestres ayans charge des Ames: Et de la Doctrine necessaire à ceux qui desirent estre admis aux Ordres sacrez. Oeuvre tres utile à tous les Ecclesiastiques qui se veulent acquitter dignement de leurs charches: Et mesmes aux personnes seculieres, pour leur instruction & consolation*. 1594. Translated by Philippe Bermyer. Rouen: Louys du Mesnil, 1640.

Blondel, Jacques. *The strength of imagination in pregnant women examin'd and the opinion that marks and deformities in children arise from thence, demonstrated to be a vulgar error*. London: J. Peele, 1727.

Blondel, Jacques. *Dissertation physique sur la Force de l'imagination Des Femmes enceintes sur le Fetus*. Translated by Albert Brun. Leiden: Gilbert Langerak and Theodore Luct, 1737.

Boaistuau, Pierre. *Histoires Prodigieuses Les Plus Mémorables qui Ayent Esté Observées Depuis La Nativité de Jesus-Christ, jusques à nostre siecle: Extraictes de plusieurs fameux autheurs Grecz & Latins, sacrez & prophanes*. Paris: Vincent Sertenas, Jean Longis, and Robert Le Mangnier, 1560.

Bodin, Jean. *Six livres de la République*. Paris: Jacques du Puys, 1576.

Bodin, Jean. *De la démonomanie des sorciers*. Paris: Jacques du Puys, 1580.

Boguet, Henry. *Discours execrable des sorciers. Ensemble leurs Procez, faits depuis deux ans en çà, en divers endroicts de la France. Avec une instruction pour un Juge, en faict de Sorcelerie.* 1602. 2nd ed. Paris: Denis Binet, 1603.

Boguet, Henry. *Discours execrable des sorciers.* 1602. Edited by Nicole Jacques-Chaquin and Philippe Huvet. Paris: Le Sycomore, 1980.

Boissard, Jean-Jacques. *De Divinatione et magicis præstigiis.* Oppenheim: Hieronymus Galler, 1611.

Bonnefons, Joseph-Charles. *Voyage au Canada fait depuis l'an 1751 jusqu'en l'an 1761.* Edited by Claude Manceron. Paris: Aubier Montaigne, 1978.

Bossu, Bernard. *Nouveaux Voyages aux Indes Occidentales; Contenant une Relation des differens Peuples qui habitent les environs du grand Fleuve Saint-Louis, appellé vulgairement le Mississipi; leur Religion; leur gouvernement; leurs mœurs; leurs guerres & leur commerce.* 2nd ed. Paris: Le Jay, 1768.

Bossu, Bernard. *Jean-Bernard Bossu's Travels in the Interior of North America, 1751–1762.* Edited and translated by Seymour Feiler. Norman, OK: University of Oklahoma Press, 1962.

Bouchel, Laurent. *La Bibliotheque ou Tresor du droit françois, ou sont traitées les matieres civiles, criminelles, et beneficiales, Tant Reglées par les Ordonnances & Coustumes de France, Que Decidées par Arrests des Cours Souveraines; Sommairement Extraites des plus celebres Jurisconsultes & Practiciens François, & conferées en plusieurs endroits avec les Loys, & Coustumes des Nations Estrangeres.* 1615. 3 vols. Paris: Jean Girin et Barthelemy Riviere, 1671.

Boucher, Jean. *Le Bouquet sacré ou le voyage de la terre sainte; Composé des Roses du Calvaire, des Lys de Bethléem, & des Hiacinthes d'Olivet.* 1620. Rouen: Jean B. Besogne, 1722.

Bougainville, Louis-Antoine conte de. *Voyage autour du monde, par la frégate du Roi La Boudeuse, et la flûte L'Étoile; en 1766, 1767, 1768 & 1769.* Paris: Saillant & Nyon, 1771.

Bourneville, Désiré Magloire. *La Possession de Jeanne Fery, religieuse professe du couvent des sœurs noires de la ville de Mons.* 1584. Paris: Adrien Delahaye and Émile Lecrosnier, 1886.

Bouteillier, Jean. *Somme Rural ou Le Grand Coustumier General de Pratique Civil et Canon. Reveu, Corrigé sur l'Exemplaire Manuscript, illustré de Commentaires & Annotations, enrichies de plusieurs Ordonnances Royaux, Arrests des Cours Souveraines, Singulieres Antiquitez & Notables Decisions du droict Romain, & autres observations.* Edited and augmented by Louys Carondas Le Caron. Paris: Barthelemy Macé, 1603.

Boutet, Claude. *Traité de mignature, pour apprendre aisément à peindre sans maître.* Paris: C. Ballard, 1676.

Bouvet. *Les Manieres admirables pour découvrir toutes sortes de crimes et sortileges. Avec l'instruction solide pour bien juger un procez criminel. Ensemble l'espece des Crimes, & la punition d'iceux, suivant les loix, ordonnances, canons, & arrests.* Paris: Jean de la Caille, 1659.

Bouyer, Marc and Jean-Paul Duviols, eds. *Le Théâtre du Nouveau Monde. Les Grands Voyages de Théodore de Bry.* Paris: Gallimard, 1992.

Bressani, Francesco Gioseppe. *Breve relatione d'aucune missioni de PP. della Compagnia di Giesù nella Nuova Francia.* Macerata: Agosino Grisel, 1653.

Bry, Theodor de and Thomas Harriot. *Admiranda narratio, fida tamen, de commodis et incolorum ritibus Virginiae.* Frankfurt: Johann Wechel, 1590.

Bry, Theodor de, Thomas Harriot and Le Moyne de Morgues. *Brevis narratio eorum quae in Florida Americae provicia Gallis acciderunt.* Frankfurt: Johann Wechel, 1591.

Bulwer, John. *Anthropometamorphosis: Man Transform'd: Or, The Artificiall Changling, Historically presented, In the mad and cruell Gallantry, foolish Bravery, ridiculous Beauty, filthy Finenesse, and loathsome Loveliness of most Nations fashioning and altering their Bodies from the mould intended by Nature; With Figures of those Transfigurations. To which artificiall and affected Deformations are added, all the Native and Nationall Monstrosities that have appeared to disfigure the Humane Fabrick. With a Vindication of the Regular Beauty and Honesty of Nature. And an Appendix of the Pedigree of the English Gallant.* 1650. 2nd ed. London: William Hunt, 1653.

Buterne. *Dictionnaire de législation, de jurisprudence et de finances sur toutes les fermes-unis de France.* Avignon: L. Chambeau, 1763.

Caille, Jean de la. *Histoire de l'imprimerie et de la librairie, Où l'on voit son origine & son progrés, jusqu'en 1689. Divisee en deux livres.* Paris: Jean de la Caille, 1689. Facsimile edition. Geneva: Slatkine Reprints, 1971.

Calmet, Augustin. *Commentaire Litteral Sur Tous Les Livres de l'Ancien et du Nouveau Testament.* 23 vols. Paris: Pierre Emery, 1716.

Calvin, Jean. *Épîtres aux Galates, Éphésiens, Philippiens et Colossiens.* Vol. 6 of *Commentaires de Jean Calvin sur le Nouveau Testament.* 7 vols. Edited by Daniel Guex, Michel Réveillaud, and Roger Barilier. Aix-en-Provence: Éditions Kerygma, 1978.

Cambounet de la Mothe, Jeanne de. *Journal des Illustres Religieuses de l'Ordre de Sainte Ursule, Avec Leurs Maximes & Pratiques Spirtuelles. Tiré des Chroniques de l'Ordre & autres Memoires de leurs Vies. Composé par une Religieuse du même Ordre, au Monastére de Bourg en Bresse. Divisé en Quatre Parties.* 4 vols. Bourg en Bresse: Joseph Ravous, 1684–1690.

Campeau, Lucien ed. *Monumenta Novae Franciae.* 9 vols. Rome: Monumenta Historica Societatis Jesu, 1967–2003.

Cardan, Jérôme [Gerolamo Cardano]. *La Metoposcopie.* Translated by C.M. de Lavrendiere. Paris: Thomas Jolly, 1658.

Cartier, Jacques. *Relations.* Edited by Michel Bideaux. Montréal: Presses de l'Université de Montréal, 1986.

Castela, Henry. *Le sainct voyage de Hierusalem et Mont Sinay, faict en l'an du grand Jubilé, 1600. Avec plusieurs figures tant des Saincts lieux que des Eglises, & des choses plus remarquables.* Bordeaux and Paris: Laurens Sonnius, 1603.

Castela, Henry. *Le Guide et Adresse pour ceux qui veullent faire le S. Voyage de Hierusalem.* Paris: Laurens Sonnius, 1604.

Ceriziers, René de. *Les heureux commencemens de la France chrestienne sous l'apôtre de nos roys S. Rémy.* Reims: François Bernard, 1633.

Charlevoix, Pierre François Xavier. *Histoire et description générale de la Nouvelle France, avec le Journal historique d'un voyage fait par ordre du roi dans l'Amérique septentrionale.* 1722. 3 vols. Paris: Nyon fils, 1744.

Cocles, Bartolommeo della Rocca. *Chyromantie ac Physionomie Anatasis cum approbatione Magistri Alexandri de Achillinis.* Bologna: Joannem Antonium, 1504.

Cocles, Bartolommeo della Rocca. *Le compendion & brief enseignement de physiognomie & chiromancie.* Paris: Pierre Regnault, 1546.

Le Code Noir, ou Edit du Roy, Servant de Reglement Pour le Gouvernement et l'Administration de Justice & la Police des Isles Françoises de l'Amerique, et pour la Discipline et le Commerce des Negres et Esclaves dans ledit Pays. Donné à Versailles au mois de Mars 1685. Paris: Le Veuve Saugrain, 1685.

Codex Canadenis, Library and Archives Canada, Accessed June 15, 2017, www.collectionscanada.gc.ca/codex/index-e.html.

Cook, James. *Relation d'un voyage fait autour du monde, Dans les années 1769, 1770 & 1771.* Paris: Nyon & Merigot, 1772–1776.

Cook, James. *Voyage dans l'hémisphère austral, et autour du monde, fait sur les vaisseaux de roi, L'Aventure, & La Résolution, en 1772, 1773, 1774 & 1775, . . . traduit de l'Anglois.* 6 vols. Paris: Hotel de Thou, 1778.

Corvo, Giuseppe. *Viaggi Fatti Nell'Egitto Superiore et Inferiore: Nel Monte Sinay, e Luoghi Piu Cospicui Di quella Regione: in Gerusalemme, guidea, Galilea, Sammaria, Palestina, Fenicia, Monte Libano, & altre Provincie di Siria: Quello Della Meka, E Del Sepolcro Di Mahometto Con Esatte, Ecuriose Osservationi Intorno i Costumi, Leggi, Riti, & Habiti de'Turchi, degli Arabi, et Nationi convicine. Opera Del Signor Gabrielle Bremond Marsiliese Da lui scritta in Francese, e fatta tradurre in Italiano.* 1673. Rome: Paolo Moneta, 1679.

Coryat, Thomas. *Coryats Crudities. Hastily gobled up in Five Moneth's Travells in France, Savoy, Italy, Rhetia commonly called the Grisons country, Helvetia alias Switzerland, some parts of high Germany and the Netherlands. Newly digested in the hungry aire of Odcombe in the county of Somerset, and now dispersed to the nourishment of the travelling members of this kingdome.* London: William Stansby, 1611.

Coryat, Thomas. *Coryats Crambe, or his Coleworte twice Sodden and now served in with other macaronicke dishes, as the second course to his Crudities.* London: William Stansby, 1611.

Cotgrave, Randle. *A Dictionarie of the French and English Tongues.* London: A. Islip, 1611. Hildesheim: Georg Olms Verlag, 1970.

Creux, François du. *Historia Canadensis.* Paris: Sébastien Cramoisy, 1664.

Creux, François du. *The History of Canada or New France.* 2 vols. Edited by James B. Conacher. Translated by Percy J. Robinson. Toronto: The Champlain Society, 1951.

Cureau de la Chambre, Marin. *L'art de connaître les hommes.* 2nd ed. Paris: J.D. Allin, 1653.

Daneau, Lambert. *Les Sorciers. Dialogue tres-utile et necessaire pour ce temps: Auquel ce qui se dispute aujourdhui des Sorciers & Eriges, est traité bien amplement, & resolu.* Geneva: Jacques Bourgeois, 1574.

Declamation contre l'erreur detestable des maleficiers sorciers, Magiciens, Devins, Enchanteurs, Nicromanciens, leurs suppotz, & semblables &c. Aux Francoys. N.p.: N.p., n.d. [1578].

Déclaration de mars 1724 sur les voleurs.

Declaration du Roy, Contre les mendians et vagabonds. July 18, 1724.

Déclaration du Roy portant reglement pour les ecritures qui doivent estre faites sur Papier et Parchemin Timbrez donné à Versailles le 19 Juin 1691.

Delrio, Martin Antoine. *Disquisitionum magicarum libri sex.* Louvain: Gerard Rivius, 1599–1600.

Delrio, Martin Antoine. *Les Controverses et Recherches Magiques . . . Divisees en Six Livres, Ausquels sont exactement et doctement confutees les Sciences Curieuses, les*

Vanitez, et Superstitions de toute la Magie. Avecques la Maniere de Proceder en Iustice contre les Magiciens et Sorciers, accommodee à l'instruction des Confesseurs. Oeuvre Utile et Necessaire à tous Theologiens, Juris consultes, Medecins, et Philosophes. Edited and translated by André Du Chesne Tourangeau. Paris: Regnauld Chaudière, 1611.

Delrio, Martin Antoine. *Investigations into Magic.* Edited and translated by Peter G. Maxwell-Stuart. Manchester, UK: Manchester University Press, 2000.

La Demonomanie de Lo[u]dun, qui montre la veritable possession des religieuses ursulines, et autres seculières, 2nd ed. La Flèche: George Griveau, 1634.

Denis, Jean Ferdinand, ed. *Une fête brésilienne célébrée à Rouen en 1550, suivie d'un fragment du XVIe siècle roulant sur la théogonie des anciens peuples du Brésil, et des poésies en langue tupique de Christovam Valente.* Paris: J. Techener, 1850.

Dictionnaire de l'Académie françoise. Paris: Jean-Baptiste Coignard, 1694.

Dictionnaire de l'Académie françoise. 5th ed. Paris: J.J. Smits, 1798.

Dictionnaire de l'Académie françoise. 6th ed. Paris: Firmin Didot Frères, 1835.

Diderot, Denis and Jean le Rond D'Alembert, eds. *Encyclopédie ou Dictionnaire Raisonné des Sciences, des Arts et des Métiers.* Paris: Briasson, David, Le Breton, and Durand, 1751–1772.

Dièreville, Dière de. *Relation du Voyage du Port Royal de l'Acadie, ou de la Nouvelle France, Dans laquelle on voit un Détail des divers mouvemens de la Mer dans une Traversée de long cours; la Description du Païs, les Occupations des François qui y sont établis, les Manieres des differentes Nations Sauvages, leurs Superstitions & leurs Chasses; avec une Dissertation exacte sur le Castor.* Rouen: Jean-Baptiste Besongne, 1708.

Doubdan, Jean. *Le Voyage de Terre-Sainte fait l'an 1652.* Paris: F. Clouzier, 1657.

Dumont de Montigny, Jean-François Benjamin. *Mémoires historiques Contenant ce qui y est arrivé de plus mémorable depuis l'année 1687 jusqu'à présent; avec l'établissement de la Colonie Françoise Religion des Sauvages qui l'habitent; leurs mœurs & leurs coutumes, &c.* Paris: J.B. Bauche, 1753.

Dumont de Montigny, Jean-François Benjamin. *Regards sur le monde atlantique, 1715–1747.* Edited by Carla Zecher, Gordon M. Sayre, and Shannon Lee Dawdy. Sillery, Québec: Septentrion, 2008.

Dumont de Montigny, Jean-François Benjamin. *The Memoir of Lieutenant Dumont, 1715–1747: A Sojourner in the French Atlantic.* Edited by Gordon M. Sayre and Carla Zecher. Translated by Gordon M. Sayre. Chapel Hill, NC: University of North Carolina Press for the Omohundro Institute of Early American History and Culture, 2012.

Duncan, Marc. *Discours sur la possession des religieuses ursulines de Lodun.* N.p.: N.p., 1634.

L'Edit du Roy pour le reglement des imprimeurs et libraires de Paris; Registré en Parlement le 21 Aoust 1686. Avec les Autoritez des anciennes Ordonnances, Statuts, Arrests & Reglemens. Paris: Denys Thierry, 1687.

L'entrée de Henri II à Rouen, 1550: A Facsimile with an Introduction by Margaret M. McGowan. Amsterdam: Theatrum Orbis Terrum and New York: Johnson Reprint Corporation, 1970.

Esprit du Bosroger. *La Pieté Affligée ou Discours Historique et Theologique de la Possession des Religieuses dittes de Saincte Elizabeth de Louviers.* Rouen: Jean Le Boulenger, 1652.

Estienne, Robert. *Dictionnaire Latinogallicum*. London: Carolum Stephanum, 1552.

Fermanel, Gilles, Robert Fauvel, Baudouin de Launay, and Vincent Stochove. *Le Voyage d'Italie et du Levant* . . . *Contenant la description des Royaumes, Provinces, Gouvernemens, Villes, Bourgs, Villages, Eglises, Palais, Mosquées, Edifices, anciens & modernes; Vies, mœurs, actions tant des Italiens, que des Turcs, Juifs, Grecs, Arabes, Armeniens, Mores, Negres, & autres Nations qui habitent dans l'Italie, Turquie, Terre Sainte, Egypte, & autres lieux de tout le païs du Levant*. Rouen: Jacques Herault, 1670.

Ferrière, Claude-Joseph de. *Dictionnaire de droit et de pratique, contenant l'explication des termes de droit, d'Ordonnances, de Coutumes & de Pratique*. 2nd ed. 2 vols. Paris: Veuve Brunet, 1769.

Ferville, le sieur D.F.D.L. de. *La méchanceté des femmes*. Paris: Pierre Rocolet, 1618.

Fery, Jeanne. [Memoir]. In *Discours admirable et veritable, des choses advenues en la ville de Mons en Hainaut, à l'endroit d'une religieuse possessee, et depuis delivree*, 90–129. Douay: Jean Bogart, 1586.

Fontaine, Jacques. *Discours des marques des sorciers et de la reelle possession que le diable prend sur le corps des hommes*. Paris: Denis Langlois, 1611.

Fontaine, Nicolas. *Le Dictionnaire chretien, ou sur differens tableaux de la nature, l'on apprend par l'ecriture et les saints peres a voir Dieu peint dans tous ses ouvrages: et a passer des choses visibles aux invisibles. Ouvrage tres utile aux Religieux & Religieuses, aux Personnes de pieté, aux Predicateurs & à tous ceux qui étudient ou qui ont à parler en public*. Paris: Elie Josset, 1691.

Furetière, Antoine. *Dictionnaire universel, Contenant generalement tous les Mots François, tant vieux que modernes, & les Termes de toutes les Sciences et des Arts*. 3 vols. La Haye and Rotterdam: Arnout & Reinier Leers, 1690.

Gayot de Pitaval, François. *Causes célèbres et intéressantes, avec les jugemens qui les ont décidées, Recueillis par M***, Avocat au Parlement*. 20 vols. Paris: Theodore Legras, followed by Durand and J. de Nully, 1734–1748.

Geliot, Louvan. *La Vraye et parfaite science des armoiries ou L'Indice Armorial du feu Maistre Louvan Geliot. Advocat au Parlement de Borgogne. Apprenant, et expliquant sommairement les Mots & Figures dont on se sert au Blason des Armoiries, & l'origine d'icelles. Augmenté de nombre de termes, et enrichy de grande multitude d'exemples des Armes des familles tant Françoises qu'estrangeres, des Institutions des Ordres & de leurs Colliers, des marques des Dignités & Charges, des ornemens des Escus, de l'Office des Roys, des Herauds, & des Poursuivans d'Armes, & autres curiosités despendantes des Armoiries*. Paris: Jean Guignard le pere, Guillaume de Luynes, et Helie Josset, 1660. Facsimile of the 1660 edition, edited by Pierre Palliot. 2 vols. Paris: Édouard Rouveyre, 1895.

Giraudet, Gabriel. *Discours du Voyage d'Outre Mer au S. Supuchre de Jerusalem, & autres lieux de la terre Saincte. Et du mont de Sinay, qui est és deserts d'Arabie, où Dieu donna la Loy à Moyse*. Rouen: David Ferrand, 1637.

La Gloire de S. Joseph, Victorieux des principaux Demons de la Possession des Ursulines de Lodun. Paris: Sébastien Huré, 1636.

La Gloire de S. Ursule, divisee en deux parties. La premiere contient l'Histoire & Martyre des onze mills Vierges, avec quelques considerations là dessus. La deuxième est un abregé de la vie d'aucunes filles de S. Ursule, signalées en sainteté. Valentiennes: Jean Boucher, 1656.

Goujon, Jacques. *Histoire et Voyage de la Terre Sainte*. Lyon: P. Compagnon et R. Taillander, 1671.

Grand, Pierre. *Sur la nécessité d'abolir la marque ou flétrissure.* In his *Pétitions sur de graves intérêts à la Chambre des députés, présentées au nom de l'auteur.* Paris: Chez Delaforest, 1828. 15–28.

Gröben, Otto Friedrich von der. *Orientalische Reise-Beschreibung des brandenbur-gischen adelichen Pilgers Otto Friedrich von der Gröben: Nebst der brandenbur-gischen Schifffahrt nach Guinea, und der Verrichtung zu Morea, unter ihrem Titel.* Marlenwerder: S. Reinigem, 1694.

Guazzo, Francesco Maria. *Compendium Maleficarum.* Milan: Apud Haeredes August. Tradati, 1608; Milan: Ex Collegij Ambrosiani Typographia, 1626.

Guazzo, Francesco Maria. *Compendium Maleficarum.* 1608. Edited by Montague Sum-mers. Translated by E.A. Ashwin. Secaucus, NJ: University Books, 1974.

Guyon, Jeanne Marie Bouvier de La Motte. *Vie par elle-même.* Edited by B. Sahler. Paris: Dervy-Livre, 1983.

Harriot, Thomas. *A Briefe and True Report of the New Found Land of Virginia.* London: R. Robinson, 1585; Frankfurt: Theodor de Bry, 1690.

Harriot, Thomas. *A Briefe and True Report of the New Found Land of Virginia. The Complete 1590 Edition with the 28 Engravings by Theodor de Bry After the Drawings of John White and Other Illustrations.* Facsimile edition by Paul Hulton. New York: Dover Publications, 1972.

Hault, Nicolas de. *Le Voyage de Hierusalem Fait l'an mil cinq cens quatre vingts treize. Contenant l'ordre, despense, & remarques notables en iceluy.* Rouen: Theo-dore Reinsart, 1601.

Hawkesworth, John. *An Account of the Voyages Undertaken by the Order of His Present Majesty for Making Discoveries in the Southern Hemisphere, and Suces-sively Performed by Commodore Byron, Captain Wallis, Captain Carteret, and Captain Cook, in the Dophin, the Swallow, and the Endeavour, Drawn up from the Journals which Were Kept by the Several Commanders, and from the Papers of Joseph Bankes, Esq.* 3 vols. London: A. Strahan and T. Cadell, 1773.

Histoire veritable et facecieuse d'un Espaignol lequel à eu le fouet et la fleur de lis dans la Ville de Thoulouze pour avoir derobé des raves et roigné des doubles. Extraict d'une lettre escrite de ladite Ville de Thoulouze le 13. Septembre dernier. N.p.: N.p., n.d. [1638].

Hitchcock, Tim, Robert Shoemaker, Clive Emsley, Sharon Howard, Jamie McLaugh-lin, et al. *The Old Bailey Proceedings Online, 1674–1913*, version 7.0, Accessed March 24, 2012, www.oldbaileyonline.org.

Hulton, Paul. *The Work of Jacques Le Moyne de Morgues, a Huguenot Artist in France, Florida, and England.* 2 vols. London: British Museum Publications, 1977.

Hulton, Paul. *America 1585: The Complete Drawings of John White.* Chapel Hill: University of North Carolina Press; London: British Museum Publications, 1984.

Institoris, Heinrich and Jakob Sprenger. *The Maleficarum of Heinrich Kramer and James Sprenger.* 1486. Edited and translated by Montague Summers. London: Pushkin Press, 1971.

Institoris, Heinrich and Jakob Sprenger. *Le Marteau des Sorcières.* Translated by Amand Danet. Grenoble: Jérôme Millon, 1990.

Isambert, François-André et al., eds. *Recueil général des anciennes lois françaises, depuis l'an 420 jusqu'à la révolution de 1789.* 30 vols. Paris: Belin-Leprieur, 1825–1830.

Jeanne des Anges. *Autobiographie d'une hystérique possédée, d'après le manuscrit inédit de la Bibliothèque de Tours, annoté.* Paris: Aux Bureaux du Progès médical,

1866. Edited by Gabriel Legué and Gilles de la Tourette. Reprinted as *Autobiographie (1644)*. Grenoble: Jérôme Millon, 1990.

Jousse, Daniel. *Nouveau commentaire sur l'ordonnance civile du mois d'Avril 1667*. 2nd ed. Paris: Debure père, 1763.

Jousse, Daniel. *Traité de la justice criminelle de France*. 4 vols. Paris: Debure père, 1771.

Joutel, Henri. *Relation de Henri Joutel*. 1684–1688, first published in 1713. In Vol. 3 of *Mémoires et Documents pour servir à l'histoire des origines françaises des pays d'outre-mer. Découvertes et Etablissements des Français dans l'Ouest et dans le Sud de l'Amérique Septentrionale (1614–1754)*, edited by Pierre Margry. 6 vols. Paris: Maisonneuve et Cie, 1879–1888.

Jouvency, Joseph. *Canadicae missionis relatio ab anno 1611 usque ad annum 1613, cum statu eiusdem missionis annis 1703 et 1710*. Rome: Georgii Plachi, 1710.

Jugemens du Tribunal Criminel et Spécial du Département de la Seine, Séant au Palais de Justice, En date des 19 thermidor et 10 fructidor an 10.

Jugement de messeigneurs les archevêques, évesques, docteurs de Sorbonne, et autres sçavans, députés par le roy, sur la prétendüe possession des filles d'Auxonne. Chalon-sur-Saône: Philippe Tan, 1662.

Jugement rendu par Monsieur Le Lieutenant Général de Police, Et Messieurs Les Officiers et Gens tenant le Siege Présidial du Chastelet de Paris, Commissaires du Roi en cette partie: Qui condmane Emmanuel-Jean de la Coste au Carcan pendant trois jours, & aux Galeres à perpétuité; Louis Vanquetin à assister à l'exécution, & aux Galeres pour neuf ans. Du vingt-huit Août mil sept cens soixante. Paris: H.L. Guerin and L.F. Delatour, Imprimeurs de la Police, 1760.

Kalm, Pehr. *Peter Kalm's Travels in North America. The English Version of 1770*. Edited by Adolph B. Benson. 2 vols. New York: Dover Publications, 1964.

Labat, Jean-Baptiste. *Nouveau Voyage aux Isles de l'Amérique, contenant l'histoire naturelle de ces pays, l'origine, les mœurs, la religion et le gouvernement des habitans anciens et modernes*. 6 vols. Paris: Pierre-François Giffart, 1722.

Lafitau, Joseph-François. *Mœurs des sauvages amériquains comparées aux mœurs des premiers temps*. 2 vols. Paris: Saugrain l'aîné and Charles Estienne Hochereau, 1724.

Lalement, Louis. *Mémoire sur la manière de juger les sorciers*. 1671. Reprinted in *Possession et sorcellerie au XVIIe siècle. Textes inédits*. Edited by Robert Mandrou, 223–30. Paris: Fayard, 1979.

Lancre, Pierre de. *Tableau de l'inconstance des mauvais anges et demons, ou il est amplement traicté des Sorciers et de la Sorcellerie. Livre tres-utile et necessaire, non seulement aux Juges, mais à tous ceux qui vivent soubs les loix Chrestiennes*. Paris: Jean Berjon, 1612; Paris: Nicolas Buon, 1613.

Lancre, Pierre de. *L'incrédulité et mescréance du sortilège plainement convaincue, où il est amplement et curieusement traicté de la vérité ou Illusion du Sortilège, de la Fascination, de l'Attouchement, du Scopelisme, de la Divination, de la Ligature ou Liaison Magique, des Apparitions: Et d'une infinté d'autres rares & nouveaux subjects*. Paris: Nicolas Buon, 1622.

Laudonniere, René. *L'Histoire Notable de la Floride située es Indes Occidentales, contenant les trois voyages faits en icelle par certains Capitaines & Pilotes François, descrits par le Capitaine Laudonniere, qui y a commandé l'espace d'un an trois voys: à laquelle a esté adjousté un quatriesme voyage fait par le Capitaine Gourgues*. Edited by M. Basanier. Paris: Guillaume Auvray, 1586.

Le Brun de la Rochette, Claude. *Le procès civil et criminel, divisé en cinq livres: Contenant en tables abregees la Methodique liaison du Droict et de la Practique*

Judiciaire. A Monsieur Seve, Sieur de Montilly, Conseiller du Roy en la Seneschaucee et Siege Presidial de Lyon. 1609. Rouen: Pierre Calles, 1611.

Leclercq, Chrestien. *Nouvelle Relation de la Gaspesie, qui contient Les Mœurs & la Religion des Sauvages Gaspesiens Porte-Croix, adorateurs du Soleil, & d'autres Peuples de l'Amerique Septentrionale, dite le Canada.* Paris: Amable Auroy, 1691. Edited by Réal Ouellet. Montréal: Presses de l'Université de Montréal, 1999.

Le Jeune, Paul. *Brieve relation du voyage de la Nouvelle France, Fait au mois d'Avril dernier par le P. Paul le Jeune de la Compagnie de Jesus.* Paris: Sébastien Cramoisy, 1632.

Le Jeune, Paul. *Relation de ce qui s'est passé en La Nouvelle-France.* 1634. In *Monumenta Novae Franciae*, edited by Lucien Campeau. 9 vols. Vol. 2, 531–740. Rome: Monumenta Historica Societatis Jesu, 1967–2003.

Le Loyer, Pierre. *Quatre livres des spectres ou apparitions et visions d'esprits, anges et demons, se monstrans sensiblement aux hommes.* Angers: Georges Nepveu, 1586; Paris: Gabriel Buon, 1586.

Le Loyer, Pierre. *Discours de spectres; ou Visions et apparitions d'esprits, comme anges, demons, et ames, se monstrans visibles aux hommes, où sont rapportez les arguments et raisons de ceux qui revocquent en doute ce qui se dit sur ce subject, & autres qui en approchent, comme les voix, & sons prodigieux, Signes, Ecstases & songes admirables, & encore les Histoires des des Apparitions, & semblables prodiges advenus en chasque siecle, prinses des meilleurs autheurs; & puis finalement les moyens de discerner les bons & mauvais Esprits, ensemble les remedes & exorcismes pour chasser & conjurer les Demons.* 1605, revised and expanded from *Quatre livres des spectres.* 1586. 2nd ed. Paris: Nicolas Buon, 1608.

Lerasle, M. "Flétrissure." In *Encyclopédie méthodique.* Vol. 4, *Jurisprudence*, 547–48. Paris: Panckoucke, 1784.

Le Roy Bacqueville de La Potherie, Claude-Charles. *Histoire de l'Amerique septentrionale. Qui contient L'Histoire des Iroquois, leurs Mœurs, leurs Maximes, leurs Coûtumes, leur Gouvernement, leurs Interêts avec les Anglois leurs Alliez, tous les mouvemens de guerre depuis 1689. jusqu'en 1701. leurs Négociations, leurs Ambassades pour la Paix generale avec les François, & les peuples Alliez de la Nouvelle France.* Paris: Jean-Luc Nion and François Didot, 1722.

Léry, Jean de. *Histoire d'un voyage fait en la terre du Bresil, autrement dite Amerique. Contentant la navigation, & choses remarquables, veuës sur la mer par l'aucteur: le comportement de Villegagnon, en ce pais la. Les meurs & façons de viure estranges des sauuages ameriquains: auec vn colloque de leur langage. Ensemble la description de plusieurs animaux, arbres, herbes, & autres choses singulieres, & du tout inconuës par deça.* La Rochelle: Antoine Chuppin, 1578.

Lescarbot, Marc. *Histoire de la Nouvelle-France. Contenant les navigations, découvertes, & habitations faites par les François és Indes occidentals & Nouvelle-France, par commission de nos Roys tres-chrétiens, & les diverses fortunes d'iceux en l'execution de ces choses, depuis cent ans jusques à hui. En quoy est comprise l'histoire morale, naturelle, & geographique des provinces cy décrites.* Paris: Jean Millot, 1609.

Lescarbot, Marc. *Voyages en Acadie (1604–1607) suivis de La Description des mœurs souriquoises comparées à celles d'autres peuples.* Edited by Marie-Christine Pioffet. Québec: Presses de l'Université Laval, 2007.

Lithgow, William. *A Most Delectable, and True Discourse, of an admired and painefull peregrination from Scotland, to the most famous Kindomes in Europe, Asia and Affricke.* London: Nicolas Okes, 1614.

Lithgow, William. *The Totall Discourse, Of the rare Adventures, and painefull Peregrinations of long ninteene yeares Travailes from Scotland, to the most famous Kingdomes in Europe, Asia, and Affrica.* London: J. Oakes, 1640.

L.S.D.L.L. *La femme généreuse qui montre que son sexe est plus noble, meilleur politique, plus vaillants, plus savants, plus vertueux et plus econome que celui des hommes.* Paris: François Piot, 1643.

Lund, Johann. *Die Alten Jüdishchen Heiligtümer, Gottes-dienste und Gewohnheiten.* Hamburg: Liebernickel, 1701.

Malebranche, Nicolas de. *De la recherche de la vérité, où l'on traite de la nature de l'esprit de l'homme, et de l'usage qu'il en doit faire pour éviter l'erreur des sciences,* 1674–1675. Edited by Geneviève Rodis-Lewis. Paris: J. Vrin, 1945.

Marsecot, Michel. *Discours véritable sur le fait de Marthe Brossier, de Romorantin, prétendue démoniaque.* Paris: Mamert Patisson, 1599.

Marescot, Pierre. *Traité des marques des Possedez et la preuve de la veritable possession des Religieuses de Louviers.* Rouen: Claude Osmont, 1644.

Massé, Pierre. *De L'Imposture et Tromperie des diables.* Paris: Jean Poupy, 1579.

Maundrell, Henry. *A Journey from Aleppo to Jerusalem at Easter, A.D. 1697.* Oxford: G. Delaune, 1703; 2nd ed. Oxford: Jonah Bowyer, 1707.

Maupas du Tour, Henry de. *La Vie de la Venerable Mere Jeanne Francoise Fremiot, Fondatrice, Premiere Mere & Religieuse de l'Ordre de la Visitation de Sainte Marie.* 1644. Paris: Simeon Piget, 1672.

Ménage, Gilles. *Menagiana ou Les Bons mots et remarques critiques, Historiques morales & d'érudition, de Monsieur Menage, Recueillies par ses Amis.* 4 vols. Paris: Florentin Delaulne, 1715.

Ménardaye, P.-J.-Baptiste de la. *Examen et discussion critique de l'histoire des diables de Loudun, de la possession des religieuses ursulines et de la condamnation d'Urbain Grandier.* Paris: Debure l'aîné, 1747.

Mercuriale, Girolamo. *De morbis cutaneis et omnibus corporis humani excementis tractatus.* Venice: Meietos, 1572.

Michaëlis, Sébastien. *Histoire admirable de la possession et conversion d'une penitente, Seduite par un Magicien, la faisant Sorciere & Princesse des Sorciers au païs de Provence, conduite à la Scte Baume pour y estre exorcizee l'an M.DC.X. au mois de Novembre, soubs l'authorité du R.P.F. Sebastien Michaëlis, Prieur du Convent Royal de la Scte Magdaleine à S. Maximin & dudict lieu de la Ste Baume. Commis par luy aux exorcismes & recueil des actes de François Domptius docteur en theologie en l'Université de Louvain, Flamant de nation, residant au susdit Convent de S. Maximin, soubs la discipline reguliere, et reformation de l'Ordre de Freres Prescheurs: le tout fidelement recueilly, et tres-bien verifié.* 1613. 3rd ed. Paris: Charles Chastellain, 1614.

Montaigne, Michel Eyquem de. *Les Essais.* 1580. Edited by P. Villey and Verdun L. Saunier. Paris: Presses Universitaires de France, 1965.

Montcalm, Louis-Joseph de Saint-Véran de. *Journal du Marquis de Montcalm durant ses campagnes en Canada de 1756 à 1760.* Vol. 7 of *Collection des manuscrits du maréchal de Lévis.* Edited by Henri-Raymond Casgrain. 12 vols. Montréal: C.O. Beauchemin & fils, 1895.

Montpensier, Anne-Marie-Louise d'Orléans duchesse de. *Histoire de Jeanne Lambert D'Herbigny, Marquise de Fouquesolles*. 1653. Elmar, NY: Scholars' Facsimiles & Reprints, 1999.

Morison, Antoine. *Relation Historique d'un Voyage Nouvellement Fait au Mont de Sinaï et à Jerusalem. On trouvera dans cette relation un détail exacte de ce que l'autheur a vû de plus remarquable en Italie, en Egipte & en Arabie. Dans les principales provinces de la Terre-sainte. Sur les côtes de Syrie & en Phœnicie. Dans les Isles de la Méditerranée & de l'Archipel. Dans l'Asie mineure & dans la Thrace, sur les côtes de Negrepont du territoire d'Athénes, de la Morée & de la Barbarie. On y verra aussi en abregé l'origine, l'etendue, la puissance & le gouvernement politique de l'Empire Othoman; avec une idée juste de la religion, du génie, des mœurs & des coûtumes des Turcs.* Toul: A. Laurent, 1704.

Moryson, Fynes. *An itinerary written by Fynes Moryson first in the Latin tongue and then translated by him into English: Containing his ten yeeres travell through the twelve dominions of Germany, Bohmerland, Sweitzerland, Netherland, Denmarke, Poland, Italy, Turky, France, England, Scotland, and Ireland.* 3 vols. in 1. London: John Beale, 1617.

Ms. Fr. 7618–7619. *Recueil de pieces originales du procès d'Urbain Grandier et des Ursulines de Loudun.* 1630–1638.

Muyart de Vouglans, Pierre-François. *Institutes au droit criminel, ou Principes généraux sur ces matières, suivant le droit civil, canonique, et la jurisprudence du royaume; Avec un Traité particulier des crimes.* Paris: Le Breton, 1757.

Muyart de Vouglans, Pierre-François. *Les loix criminelles de France, dans leur ordre naturel.* Paris: Merigot, Crapart, Benoît Morin, 1780.

Nau, Michel. *Voyage Nouveau de la Terre-Sainte, Enrichi de plusieurs remarques particulieres qui servent à l'intelligence de la Sainte Ecriture. Et De Diverses Réflexions Chrétiennes qui instruisent les Ames dévotes dans la connoissance & l'amour de J. C.* Paris: J. Barbou, 1744.

Nau, Michel. *Le Voyage de Galilée.* Paris: Michel Le Petit et Estienne Michallet, 1670.

Navis peregrinorum, continens nomina, cognomna et nationes peregrinorum omnium, qui invisandi gratia sacrosancta Loca Redemptoris nostri Jesu Christi praesentia decorata, pedibus calcata, lachrymis perfusa sudore conspersa, sanguine consecrata, operum ac miraculorum insignium illustrata huc accesserunt; necnon annos, menses et dies, quibus in hanc Santam Civitatem pervenerunt. Ab. adm. R.P. fr. Paulo a Lauda Ordinis Minorum Strictoris Observentiae, Provinciae Seraphicae, in partibus Orientis Apostolico comm.rio Terrae Sanctae custode ac Sacri Montis Sion guardiano ad praestabiliorem rationem retituta. Anno Domini MDCXXXIII. Appears in modern edition as *Navis Peregrinorum. Ein Pilgerverzeichnis aus Jerusalem von 1561 bis 1695: Mit Angaben über Pilger aus Deutschland, England, Frankreich, Italien und den Niederlanden, sowie aus anderen europäischen Ländern.* Edited by Betrand Zimolong. Köln: Verlag J.P. Bachem, 1938.

Nicolas, Augustin. *Si la torture est un moyen seur a verifier les crimes secrets; Dissertation morale et juridique, Par laquelle il est amplement traitté des Abus qui se commettent par tout en l'Instruction des Procés Ciminels, & particulierement en la recherche du Sortilege. Ouvrage necessaire à tous Juges, tant Souverains que Subalternes, & à tous Avocats consultans & patrocinans.* Amsterdam: Abraham Wolfgang, 1682.

Nicot, Jean. *Le Thresor de la langue francoyse, tant ancienne que moderne.* Paris: David Douceur, 1606.

Ordonnance du Louis XIV. Roy de France et de Navarre, Sur le fait des Entrées, Aydes, & autres droits. Donnée à Fontainebleau au mois de Juin 1680. Paris: François Muguet, 1680.

Ordonance du Roy, Contre les Vagabonds de Versailles. May 24, 1749.

Ostermann, Peter. *Commentarius juridicus ad L. Stigmata C. de Fabricensibus. . . . In quo de variis speciebus Signaturarum . . . imprimis vero Antichristi et de illorum quae sagis inusta deprehenduntur . . . hinc derivata* origine. Cologne: Petrus Metternich, 1629.

Paré, Ambroise. *Œuvres complètes d'Ambroise Paré.* Edited by Joseph-François Malgaigne. 3 vols. Paris: J.-B. Baillière, 1840–1841.

Paré, Ambroise. *Des monstres et prodiges.* 1573. Edited by Jean Céard. Geneva: Droz, 1971.

Pauw, Cornelius de. *Recherches philosophiques sur les Américains ou Mémoires intéressants, pour servir à l'histoire de l'espèce humaine.* Berlin: G.J. Decker, 1768–1769.

Polidoro, Valerio, Girolamo Menghi, Zaccaria Visconti, Pietro Antonio Stampa, and Maximilien de Eynatten. *Thesaurus Exorcismorum atque coniurationum terribilum, potentissimorum, efficissimorum, cum practica probatissima: quibus spiritus maligni daemones maleficiaque omnia de corporibus humanis obsessis, tanquam flagellis, fustibusque fugantur, expelluntur, doctrinis refertissimus at[que] uberrimus.* 1608. Cologne: Laar Zezner, 1626.

Pommereu, Marie de. *Les chroniques de l'Ordre des Ursulines.* 2 vols. Paris: J. Henault, 1673.

Pomponazzi, Pietro. *De naturalium effectuum causis, sive de incantationibus.* 1556. Edited and translated by Henri Busson as *Les Causes des merveilles de la nature ou Les Enchantements.* Paris: Les Éditions Rieder, 1930.

Porta, Giambattista della. *De Humana Physiognomonia.* Vici Aequensis: Cacchius, 1586.

Porta, Giambattista della. *La Physiognomie humaine.* Rouen: J. et D. Berthelin, 1655.

Quillet, Claude. *La Callipédie, ou La Maniere d'avoir de beaux enfans.* 1665, 1st Latin ed. Translated by J.M. Caillau. Paris: Durand and Pissot, 1749.

Rahier, Jean-Jacques. Letter. In Jean Mauzaize, "Lettre inédite d'un Frère Mineur [Jean-Jacques Rahier], gardien du couvent de Bethlem (1660)." *Archivum franciscanum historicum* 74.1 (1981): 245–64.

Raulin, Hippolyte. *Panégyre orthodoxe mystérieux et prophétique sur l'antiquité, dignité, noblesse, splendeur des fleurs de lys.* Paris: F. Jacquin, 1626.

Raynaud, Théophile. *De stigmatismo, sacro et profano, divino, humano, daemoniaco.* 1647. 2nd ed. Lyon: Antoine Cellier, 1654.

Raynaud, Théophile. *Theophili Raynaudi Societatis Jesu theologi opera omnia: tam hactenus inedita, quam alias excusa, longo authoris labore aucta et emendata.* Edited by Jean Bertet. Lyons: Horace Boissat, Georges Réméus and Camille de Neufville, 1665.

Recit veritable de ce qui s'est passé à Loudun. Contre Maistre Urbain Grandier, Prestre Curé de l'Eglise de S. Pierre de Loudun. Paris: Pierre Targa, 1634.

Relation de la Sortie du Demon Balam du corps de la Mere Prieure, des Urselines de Loudun. Paris: Jean Martin, 1635.

Rémy, Nicolas. *Demonolatriæ libri tres.* Lyon: Vincentii, 1595.

Rémy, Nicolas. *Demonolatry.* Edited by Montague Summers. Translated by E.A. Ashwin. Secaucus, NJ: University Books, 1974.

Representation et Sommaire des Signes Miraculeux qui ont esté faicts à la gloire de Dieu et de son Eglise, en la sortie des sept Demons qui possedoient le Corps de la Mere Prieure des Religieuses Ursulines de Loudun. Rouen: David Ferrand, n. d. [1637].

Richelet, Pierre. *Le Nouveau dictionnaire François.* Lyon: Jean-Baptiste Girin, 1719.

Sagard-Théodat, Gabriel. *Histoire du Canada et Voyages que les Freres Mineurs Recollects y ont faicts pour la conversion des Infidelles. Divisez en Quatre Livres, Où est amplement traicté des choses principales arrivées dans le pays depuis l'an 1615 jusques à la prise qui en a esté faicte par les Anglois. Des biens & commoditez qu'on en peut esperer. Des mœurs, ceremonies, creance, loix & coustumes merveilleuses de ses habitans. De la conversion & baptesme de plusieurs, & des moyens necessaires pour les amener à la cognoissance de Dieu. L'entretien ordinaire de nos Mariniers, & autres particularitez qui se remarquent en la suite de l'histoire.* Paris: Claude Sonnius, 1636.

Sagard-Théodat, Gabriel. *Le Grand voyage du pays des Hurons suivi du dictionnaire de la langue huronne.* 1632. Edited by Jack Warwick. Montréal: Presses de l'Université de Montréal, 1998.

Sales, François de. *Œuvres de saint François de Sales.* Edited by André Ravier and Roger Devos. Paris: Gallimard, La Pléiade, 1969.

Sandys, George. *A Relation of a journey begun An. Dom. 1610. Foure Books Containing a Description of the Turkish Empire of Aegypt, of the Holy Land, of the Remote Parts of Italy and Ilands Adjoyning.* London: W. Barrett, 1615.

Saunders, Richard. *Physiognomonie and Chiromancie, Metoposcopie, The Symmetrical Proportions and Signal Moles of the Body, Fully and accurately explained; with their Natural Predictive Significations both to Men and Women.* London: Nathaniel Brook, 1653; 2nd ed. 1671.

Scot, Reginald. *The Discoverie of Witchcraft.* London: W. Brome, 1584.

Scot, Reginald. *The Discoverie of Witchcraft.* Edited by Montague Summers. New York: Dover Publications, 1972.

Sentence du Chastelet de Paris, qui condamne deux écrits imprimés, intitulés, l'un: Mandement de Monseigneur l'évêque d'Orléans; et l'autre, Mandement de Monseigneur l'évêque d'Amiens, à être lacérés et brulés en la place de Grève, par l'exécuteur de la haute justice. Paris: H. Guerin, 1756.

Sigogne, Charles Timoléon de Beauxoncles sieur de, Regnier, Motin, Berhelot, Maynard, et al. *Le Cabinet Satyrique, ou Recueil Parfaict des vers picquans & gaillards de ce temps. Tiré des secrets Cabinets des Sieurs de Sygognes, Regnier, Motin, Berhelot, Maynard, & autres des plus signalez Poëtes de ce Siecle.* 1618. Paris: N.p., 1633.

Sinistrari, Ludovico Maria. *De la Démonialité et des animaux incubes et succubes où l'on prouve qu'il existe sur terre des créatures raisonnables autres que l'homme, ayant comme lui un corps et une âme, naissant et mourant comme lui, rachetées par N.-S. Jésus-Christ et capables de salut ou de damnation.* 1699. Edited by Xavier Carrère and Isabelle Hersant. Translated by Isidore Lisieux. Toulouse: Éditions Ombres, 1998.

Spee, Friedrich. *Cautio Criminalis, or a Book on Witch Trials.* 1631. Translated by Marcus Hellyer. Charlottesville and London: University of Virginia Press, 2003.

Surin, Jean-Joseph. *Lettre Escrite A Monseigneur L'Evesque de Poitiers par un des Peres Jesuistes qui exorcisent à Loudun.* Paris: Jean Martin, 1635.

Surin, Jean-Joseph. *Histoire abrégée de la possession des Ursulines de Loudun, et des peines du Père Surin.* Paris: Bureau de l'Association Catholique du Sacré-Cœur, 1828.

Surin, Jean-Joseph. *Correspondance.* Edited by Michel de Certeau. Paris: Desclée De Brouwer, 1966.

Surin, Jean-Joseph. *Triomphe de l'amour divin sur les puissances de l'enfer et Science expérimentale des choses de l'autre vie (1653–1660).* Grenoble: Jérôme Millon, 1990.

Terry, Edward. *A Voyage to East-India. Wherein some things are taken notice of in our passage thither, but many more in our abode there, within that rich and most spacious empire of the Great Mogol. Mix't with some parallel observations and inferences upon the storie, to profit as well as delight the reader.* London: J. Martin and J. Allestrye, 1655.

Thévenot, Jean. *Relation d'un Voyage fait au Levant. Dans laquelle il est curieusement traité des Estats sujets au Grand Seigneur, des Mœurs, Religions, Forces, Gouvernemens, Politiques, Langues, & coustumes des Habitans de ce grand Empire. Et des signularitez particulieres de l'Archipel, Constantinople, Terre-Sainte, Egypte, Pyramides, Mumies, Deserts d'Arabie, la Meque. Et de plusieurs autres lieux de l'Asie & de l'Affrique, remarquées depuis peu, & non encore décrites jusqu'a present. Outre les choses memorables arrivées au dernier Siege de Bagdat, les Ceremonies faites aux receptions des Ambassadeurs du Mogol: Et l'entretien de l'Autheur avec celuy du Pretejan, où il est parlé des sources du Nil.* Paris: Louis Bilaine, 1664.

Thiers, Jean-Baptiste. *Traité des superstitions selon l'écriture sainte, les decrets des conciles, et les sentimens des saints peres, et des theologiens.* Paris: Antoine Dezallier, 1679.

Thwaites, Reuben Gold, ed. *The Jesuit Relations and Allied Documents: Travels and Explorations of the Jesuit Missionaries in New France, 1610–1791.* 73 vols. Cleveland: Burrows Brothers, 1896–1901.

Tonti, Henri de. *Relation de la Louisianne ou Mississipi. Ecrite à une Dame, par un Officier de Marine,* in *Relations de la Louisiane, et du fleuve Mississipi. Où l'on voit l'état de ce grand Païs & les avantages qu'il peut produire &c.* Amsterdam: Jean Frederic Bernard, 1720.

Turner, Daniel. *De morbis cutaneis. A Treatise of diseases incident to the skin.* London: R. Bonwicke et al., 1714.

Turner, Daniel. *The Force of the Mother's Imagination Upon Her Foetus in Utero, Still farther considered: In the Way of a Reply to Dr. Blondel's last Book.* London: J. Walthoe et al., 1730.

Turner, Daniel. *Traité des maladies de la peau en general; Avec un court Appendix sur l'efficacité des Topiques dans les Maladies internes, & leur maniére d'agir sur le Corps humain.* Paris: Jacques Barois, 1743.

Urfé, Honoré d'. *L'Astrée.* 1607–1627. 5 vols. Geneva: Slatkine Reprints, 1966.

Vair, Leonard. *Trois livres des charmes, sorcelages, ou enchantemens. Esquels toutes les especes, & causes des Charmes sont methodiquement descrites, & doctement expliquees selon l'opinion tant des Philosophes que des Theologiens; avec les vrais contrepoisons pour rabattre les impostures & illusions des Dæmons: & par mesme moyen les vaines bourdes qu'on met en avant touchant les causes de la puissance des sorceleries y sont clairement refutees.* Translated by Julian Baudon. Paris: Nicolas Chesneau, 1583.

Van Eynatten, Maximillian. *Manuale exorcismorum.* Antwerp: Plantiniana B. Moreti, 1626.

Van Eynatten, Maximillian. *Manuale exorcismorum/Manuel d'exorcismes.* Paris: Édition Communication Prestige, 1995.

Vergoncy, de. *Le Pelerin Veritable de la Terre Saincte, Auquel Soubs Le Discours figuré de la Ierusalem Antique et Moderne de la Palestine est enseigné le chemin de la Céleste*. Paris: P. Louys Féburier, 1615.

Vesalius, Andreas. *De humani corporis fabrica libri septem*. Basel: Joannis Oporini, 1543.

Villamont, Jacques de. *Les Voyages du Seigneur de Villamont, Chevalier de l'Ordre de Hierusalem*. Paris: Claude de Montroeil et Jean Richer, 1600.

Voet, Gijsbert. *Selectarum disputationum ex priori parte theologiae decimae, pars prior, de natura & operationibus daemonum*. Utrecht: Aegidius Roman, 1638.

Weyer, Johann. *De Præstigiis dæmonum et incantationibus ac venificiis*. Basel: Joannes Oporinus, 1563.

Weyer, Johann. *Cinq Livres de l'Imposture et Tromperie des Diables: Des enchantements et sorcelleries*. Translated by Jacques Grévin. Paris: Jacques Dupuys, 1567.

Weyer, Johann. *Histoires, disputes et discours des illusions et impostures des diables, des magiciens infâmes, sorcières et empoisonneurs: des ensorcelés et des démoniaques, et de la guérison d'iceux: item de la punition que méritent les magiciens, les empoisonneurs et les sorcières. Le tout comprins en Six Livres (augmentez de moitié en ceste dernière édition)*. Geneva: Jacques Chovet, 1579.

Weyer, Johann. *De praestigiis daemonum*. 1563. 6th edition of 1583 edited by George Mora and Benjamin Kohl. Translated by John Shea as *Witches, Devils, and Doctors in the Renaissance*. Binghamton, NY: Medieval and Renaissance Texts and Studies, 1991.

Wonder of Wonders: or, a Metamorphosis of Fair Faces voluntarily transformed into foul visages: or, an Invective against Black-spotted Faces: By a Well-willer to modest Matrons and Virgins. London: J.G. for Richard Royston, 1662.

Yvelin, Pierre. *Examen de la possession des religieuses de Louviers*. Paris: N.p., 1643.

Yvelin, Pierre. *Apologie pour l'autheur de L'Examen de la possession des religieuses de Louviers, à Messieurs L'Emperière et Magnart Medecins à Roüen*. Rouen and Paris: N.p., 1643.

Secondary Sources

Adnès, Pierre. "Stigmates." In *Dictionnaire de spiritualité ascétique et mystique*, edited by Marcel Viller, F. Cavallera, and J. de Guibert. 17 vols. Paris: G. Beauchesne, 1932–95. Vol. 14, 1211–43.

Albert, Jean-Pierre. "Hagio-graphiques. L'écriture qui sanctifie." *Terrain* 24 (March 1995): 75–82.

Albert, Jean-Pierre. *Le sang et le Ciel. Les saintes mystiques dans le monde chrétien*. Paris: Aubier, 1997.

Amann, E. "Stigmatisation." In *Dictionnaire de théologie catholique*, edited by A. Vacant, E. Mangenot, and E. Amann. Vol. 14, 2616–24. Paris: Librairie Letouzey et Ané, 1941.

Anderson, Bonnie S. and Judith P. Zinsser. *A History of Their Own: Women in Europe from Prehistory to the Present*. Oxford: Oxford University Press, 1999.

Andrews, William. *Bygone Punishments*. London: William Andrews & Co., 1899.

Ankarloo, Bengt, Stuart Clark, and William Monter. *Witchcraft and Magic in Europe: The Period of the Witch Trials*. Philadelphia, PA: University of Pennsylvania Press, 2002.

Antolini, Paola. *Au-delà de la rivière. Les cagots: histoire d'une exclusion*. Paris: Éditions Nathan, 1989.

Anzieu, Didier. *The Skin Ego: A Psychoanalytic Approach to the Self*. Translated by Chris Turner. New Haven, CT: Yale University Press, 1989. Originally published in French, 1985.

Ardouin-Weiss, Idelette. *Les Exécuteurs des sentences criminelles en Touraine 1636–1853*. Touraine: Collection Centre Généalogique de Touraine, 1983.

Auriol, Georges. *Le premier livre des cachets, marques et monogrammes*. Paris: Librairie centrale des beaux-arts, 1901.

Avenel, Georges d'. *Histoire économique de la propriété, des salaires, des denrées et de tous les prix en général. Depuis l'an 1200 jusqu'en l'an 1800*. 6 vols. Paris: Imprimerie nationale/E. Leroux, 1894–1912.

Backus, Irena. *Le Miracle de Laon. Le Déraisonnable, le raisonnable, l'apocalyptique et le politique dans les récits du miracle de Laon (1566–1578)*. Paris: Librairie Philosophique Jean Vrin, 1994.

Balvay, Arnaud. "Tattooing and Its Role in French-Native American Relations." *French Colonial History* 9 (2008): 1–14.

Baschwitz, Kurt. *Procès de sorcellerie: histoire d'une psychose collective*. Paris: Arthaud, 1973.

Benthien, Claudia. *Skin: On the Cultural Border Between Self and Other*. Translated by Thomas Dunlap. New York: Columbia University Press, 2002. Originally published in German, 1999.

Berchon, Ernest. *Discours sur les origines et le but du tatouage*. Bordeaux: G. Gounouilhou, 1886.

Bergamo, Mino. *Jeanne des Anges. Autobiographia. Il punto di vista dell'indemoniata*. Venice: Marsilio Editori, 1986.

Bériac, Françoise. *Histoire des lépreux au Moyen-Age. Une société d'exclus*. Paris: Imago, 1980.

Bériac, Françoise. *Des lépreux aux cagots. Recherche sur les sociétés marginales en Aquitaine medieval*. Bordeaux: Fédération historique du Sud-Ouest, 1990.

Beuque, E., and M. Frapsauce. *Dictionnaire des poinçons des maitres-orfèvres français du XIVe siècle à 1838*. Paris: F. De Nobele, 1964.

Bilinkoff, Jodi. *The Avila of Saint Teresa: Religious Reform in a Sixteenth-Century City*. Ithaca, NY: Cornell University Press, 1989.

Biller, Peter, et al. *Black Skin the Middle Ages/La Peau noire au Moyen Âge*. Sismel-Edizioni del Galluzzo, 2014.

Bloch, Marc. *Les Rois thaumaturges. Étude sur le caractère surnaturel attribué à la puissance royale particulièrement en France et en Angleterre*. Paris: Armand Colin, 1961. First published 1924 by Strasbourg Librairie Istra.

Boisgelin de Kerdu, Pierre Marie Louis de, alias Caillot-Duval. *Ancient and Modern Malta: Containing a Full and Accurate Account of the Present State of the Islands of Malta and Goza, the History of the Knights of St. John of Jerusalem, Also a Narrative of the Events Which Attended the Capture of These Islands by the French, and Their Conquest by the English: and an Appendix, Containing Authentic State Papers and Other Documents*. London: R. Phillips, 1805.

Bowman, Frank. "From History to Hysteria: Nineteenth-Century Discourse on Loudun." In *French Romanticism: Intertextual and Interdisciplinary Readings*, 106–21. Baltimore, MD: Johns Hopkins University Press, 1990.

Bramford, Paul Walden. "The Knights of Malta and the King of France, 1665–1700." *French Historical Studies* 3.4 (Autumn 1964): 429–53.

Brazeau, Brian. *Writing a New France, 1604–1632: Empire and Early Modern French Identity*. Farnam, UK and Burlington, VT: Ashgate, 2009.

Briggs, Robin. *Early Modern France, 1560–1715*. 2nd ed. Oxford and New York: Oxford University Press, 1998.

Briquet, Charles-Moïse. *Les Filigranes: Dictionnaire historique des marques du papier dès leur apparition vers 1282 jusqu'en 1600*. 4 vols. Facsimile of 1907 edition. Hildescheim and New York: G. Olms, 1977.

Bruno, C. *Tatoués, qui êtes vous . . . ?* Brussels: Éditions de Feynerolles, 1970.

Bryson, Scott. "La Chair devenue parole: Aliénation et raison d'État dans la possession de Loudun." In *Le Labyrinthe de Versailles. Parcours critiques de Molière à La Fontaine. À la mémoire d'Alvin Eustis*, edited by Alvin Eustis and Martine Debaisieux, 133–55. Amsterdam and Atlanta: Rodopi, 1998.

Budde, Hendrik and Mordechay Lewy, eds. *Von Halle nach Jerusalem: Halle, ein Zentrum der Palästinakunde im 18. und 19. Jarhundert*. Halle, Germany: Ministerium für Wissenschaft und Forschung des Landes Sachsen-Anhalt, 1994.

Bullough, Vern and Bonnie. *An Illustrated Social History of Prostitution*. New York: Crown Publishers, 1978.

Burns, William E. "The King's Two Monstrous Bodies: John Bulwer and the English Revolution." In *Wonders, Marvels, and Monsters in Early Modern Culture*, edited by Peter G. Platt, 187–202. Newark, DE: University of Delaware Press, 1999.

Bynum, Carolyn Walker. *Jesus as Mother: Studies in the Spirituality of the High Middle Ages*. Berkeley, CA: University of California Press, 1982.

Bynum, Carolyn Walker. *Holy Feast and Holy Fast: The Religious Significance of Food to Medieval Women*. Berkeley, CA: University of California Press, 1987.

Bynum, Carolyn Walker. *Fragmentation and Redemption: Essays on Gender and the Human Body in Medieval Religion*. New York: Zone Books, 1992.

Caciola, Nancy. *Discerning Spirits: Divine and Demonic Possession in the Middle Ages*. Ithaca, NY: Cornell University Press, 2003.

Campbell, Mary B. "The Illustrated Travel Book and the Birth of Ethnography: Part I of De Bry's *America*." In *The Work of Dissimilitude: Essays from the Sixth Citadel Conference on Medieval and Renaissance Literature*, edited by David G. Allen and Robert A. White, 177–95. Newark, DE: University of Delaware Press, 1992.

Caplan, Jane, ed. *Written on the Body: The Tattoo in European and American History*. Princeton, NJ: Princeton University Press, 2000.

Cappel, Carmen Bambach. "Pouncing." In *The Dictionary of Art*, edited by Jane Turner. Vol. 25, 378–80. New York: Grove's Dictionaries, 1996.

Carabasse, Jean-Marie. *Histoire du droit pénal et de la justice criminelle*. 2nd ed. Paris: Presses Universitaires de France, 2006.

Carmona, Michel. *Les Diables à Loudun. Sorcellerie et politique sous Richelieu*. Paris: Fayard, 1988.

Carswell, John. *Coptic Tattoo Designs*. Beirut: Faculty of Arts and Sciences, American University of Beirut, 1958.

Caruchet, William. *Tatouages et tatoués*. Paris: Tchou, 1976.

Castan, Nicole and André Zysberg. "Galères et galériens en France à la fin du XVIIe siècle." *Criminal Justice History* 1 (1980): 49–115.

Castan, Nicole and André Zysberg. *Histoire des galères, bagnes et prisons en France de l'Ancien Régime*. Paris: Privat, 2002.

Catechism of the Catholic Church. Vatican City: Libreria Editrice Vaticana, 1993. Accessed June 27, 2012. www.vatican.va/archive/ENG0015/_INDEX.HTM.

Cavallera, Ferdinand. "L'autobiographie de Jeanne des Anges d'après des documents inédits" (1928). Rpt. in *Autobiographie (1644)* by Jeanne des Anges, 291–300. Grenoble: Jérôme Millon, 1990.

Cayrou, Gaston. *Le Francais Classique. Lexique de la langue du dix-septième siècle.* Paris: Didier, 1948.

Céard, Jean. *La nature et les prodiges. L'insolite au XVIe siècle en France.* Geneva: Droz, 1977.

Certeau, Michel de. "Des outils pour écrire le corps." *Traverses* 14–15 (1979), 3–14.

Certeau, Michel de. *The Practice of Everyday Life.* Translated by Steven F. Rendall. Berkeley, CA: University of California Press, 1984.

Certeau, Michel de. "Jeanne des Anges." In Jeanne des Anges, *Autobiographie d'une hystérique possédée, d'après le manuscrit inédit de la Bibliothèque de Tours, annoté,* edited by Gabriel Legué and Gilles de la Tourette, reprinted as *Autobiographie (1644)*, 301–44. Grenoble: Jérôme Millon, 1990.

Certeau, Michel de. *La Possession de Loudun.* Paris: Gallimard/Julliard, 1990.

Charcot, Jean-Martin and Paul Richer. *Les démoniaques dans l'art.* Paris: Adrien Delahaye and Émile Lecrosnier; Paris: Macula, 1984.

Clark, Jr., Robert M. *The Evangelical Knights of Saint John: A History of the Bailiwick of Brandenburg of the Knightly Order of St. John of the Hospital at Jerusalem, Known as the Johanniter Order.* Dallas, TX: Robert M. Clark, Jr., 2003.

Clark, Stuart. *Thinking with Demons: The Idea of Witchcraft in Early Modern Europe.* Oxford and New York: Oxford University Press, 1997.

Closson, Marianne. "Avaler le pacte, être possédée." In *Écritures du corps. Nouvelles perspectives*, edited by Pierre Zoberman, Anne Tomiche, and William J. Spurlin, 174–88. Paris: Classiques Garnier, 2013.

Collin de Plancy, Jacques-Albin-Simon. *Dictionnaire infernal, ou Bibliothèque universel, Sur les Etres, les Personnages, les Livres, les Faits et les Choses qui tiennent aux apparitions, à la magie, au commerce de l'enfer, aux divinations, aux sciences secrètes, aux grimoires, aux prodiges, aux erreurs et aux préjugés, aux traditions et aux contes populaires, aux superstitions diverses, et généralement à toutes les croyances merveilleuses, surprenantes, mystérieuses et surnaturelles.* 1818. 2nd ed. Paris: P. Mongie aîné, 1825.

Connor, Steven. *The Book of Skin.* London: Reaktion Books, 2004.

Courcelles, Dominique de, ed. *Stigmates. Les Cahiers de l'Herne* 75. Paris: Éditions de l'Herne, 2001.

Courtine, Jean-Jacques and Claudine Haroche. *Histoire du visage. Exprimer et taire ses émotions (du XVIe siècle au début du XIXe siècle).* Paris: Payot et Rivages, 1988.

Crouzet, Denis. "A Woman and the Devil: Possession and Exorcism in Sixteenth-Century France." In *Changing Identities in Early Modern France*, edited by Michael Wolfe, 191–215. Durham, NC: Duke University Press, 1997.

Cruchet, William. *Tatouages et tatoués.* Paris: Tchou, 1976.

Cuénin, Micheline. "Fausse et vraie mystique: Signes de reconnaissance, d'après la *Correspondance* de Jeanne de Chantal." In *Les Signes de Dieu aux XVIe et XVIIe siècles*, edited by Geneviève Demerson and Bernard Dompnier, 177–87. Clermont-Ferrand: Faculté des Lettres et Sciences humaines de l'Université Blaise-Pascal, 1993.

Dardy, Claudine. "L'identité-papier." *Les Cahiers de médiologie* 4 (1997), 224.

Darr, Orna Alyagon. "The Devil's Mark: A Socio-Cultural Analysis of Physical Evidence." *Continuity and Change* 24.2 (August 2009): 361–87.

Dauge-Roth, Katherine. "Médiations, figures et expériences de l'autre vie: Jean-Joseph Surin à la rencontre du démoniaque." In *L'autre au dix-septième siècle*, edited by Ralph Heyndels and Barbara Woshinsky, 375–84. Tübingen: Gunter Narr, 1999.

Dauge-Roth, Katherine. "Ventriloquism and the Voice of Authority: Nuns, Demons, and Exorcists in Early Seventeenth-Century France." In *Early Modern Convent Voices: The World and the Cloister*, edited by Thomas M. Carr, Jr., 75–112. *EMF: Studies in Early Modern France* 11, (2005).

Dauge-Roth, Katherine. "Textual Performance: Imprinting the Criminal Body." In *Intersections*, edited by Faith Beasley and Kathryn Wine, 126–42. *Bibio-17*. Tübingen: Gunter Narr, 2005.

Dauge-Roth, Katherine. "Marquage du corps et modernité: La flétrissure des condamnés aux XVIIe et XVIIIe siècles en France." In *Écritures du corps. Nouvelles perspectives*, edited by Pierre Zoberman, Anne Tomiche, and William J. Spurlin, 17–30. Paris: Classiques Garnier, 2013.

Dauge-Roth, Katherine. "*Prêt à porter*: Textual Amulets, Popular Belief and Defining Superstition in Sixteenth and Seventeenth-Century France." Special issue on *Wearing Images*, edited by Diane Brodart, *Espacio, Tiempo y Forma* 6 (2018): 84–114.

Davis, Natalie Zemon. *The Return of Martin Guerre*. Cambridge, MA: Harvard University Press, 1983.

Debien, Gabriel. *Les Esclaves aux Antilles françaises*. Basse-Terre: Société d'Histoire de la Guadeloupe, 1974.

Delcambre, Étienne. *Le concept de la sorcellerie dans le duché de Lorraine au XVIe et au XVIIe siècle*. 2 vols. Nancy: Société d'archéologie lorraine, 1948.

Delcambre, Étienne and Jean Lhermitte. *Un cas énigmatique de possession diabolique en Lorraine au XVIIe siècle: Élizabeth de Ranfaing, l'énergumène de Nancy*. Nancy: Société d'Archéologie Lorraine, 1956.

Delpech, François. "Les Marques de naissance: Physiognomonie, signature magique et charisme souverain." In *Le Corps dans la société espagnole des XVIe et XVIIe siècles*, edited by Augustin Redondo, 27–49. Paris: Publications de la Sorbonne, 1990.

Delpech, François. "La 'marque' des sorcières: logique(s) de la stigmatisation diabolique." In *Le Sabbat des sorciers. XVe-XVIIIe siècles*, edited by Nicole Jacques-Chaquin and Maxime Préaud, 347–68. Grenoble: Jérôme Millon, 1993.

DeMello, Margo. *Bodies of Inscription: A Cultural History of the Modern Tattoo Community*. Durham, NC: Duke University Press, 2000.

Demonet, Marie-Luce. "'Si les signes vous fâchent . . . ': Natural Inference and the Science of Signs in the Renaissance." Translated by Nancy Virtue. *South Central Review* 6 (1989): 76–99.

Demonet, Marie-Luce. "Les marques insensibles, ou les nuages de la certitude." *Littératures Classiques* 25 (Fall 1995): 97–134.

Depauw, Jacques. "Pauvres, pauvres mendiants, mendiants valides ou vagabonds? Les hésitations de la législation royale." *Revue d'histoire moderne et contemporaine* 21 (3) (1974): 401–18.

Depping, Georges Bernard. *Correspondance administrative, sous le règne de Louis XIV, entre le cabinet du roi, les secrétaires d'État, le chancelier de France et les intendants et gouverneurs de province*. 4 vols. Paris: Imprimerie nationale, 1850–1855.

Dickason, Olive Patricia. *The Myth of the Savage and the Beginnings of French Colonialism in the Americas.* Alberta: The University of Alberta Press, 1984.

Dickason, Olive Patricia and David T. McNab. *Canada's First Nations: A History of Founding Peoples from Earliest Times.* 4th edition. Oxford: Oxford University Press, 2008.

Didi-Huberman, Georges. *Invention de l'hystérie. Charcot et l'Iconographie photographique de la Salpêtrière.* Paris: Macula, 1982.

Dubé, Philippe. *Tattoo-tatoué. Histoire, techniques, motifs du tatouage en Amérique française, de la colonisation à nos jours.* Montréal: Jean Basile, 1980.

Dubois, Jean, Renée Lagane, and Alain Lerond, eds. *Dictionnaire du français classique. XVIIe siècle.* Paris: Larousse, 1988.

Duits, Rembrandt. "Art, Class, and Wealth." In *Viewing Renaissance Art*, edited by Kim W. Woods, Carol M. Richardson, and Angeliki Lymberopoulou, 21–56. New Haven, CT: Yale University Press, 2007.

Fabre, Michel. *Le mystère des cagots, race maudite des Pyrénées.* Pau: M.C.T., 1987.

Falgayrettes-Leveau, Christiane. *Signes du corps.* Paris: Musée Dapper, 2004.

Faudemay, Alain. *Le Clair et l'obscur à l'âge classique.* Geneva: Slatkine, 2001.

Febvre, Lucien and Henri-Jean Martin. *The Coming of the Book: The Impact of Printing, 1450–1800.* Translated by David Gerard. London: NLB, 1971.

Ferber, Sarah. "The Demonic Possession of Marthe Brossier, France 1598–1600." In *No Gods Except Me: Orthodoxy and Religious Practice in Europe, 1200–1600*, edited by Charles Zika, 59–83. Melbourne: University of Melbourne Press, 1991.

Ferber, Sarah. *Demonic Possession and Exorcism in Early Modern France.* London and New York: Routledge, 2004.

Fishman, Laura. "Claude d'Abbeville and the Tupinamba: Problems and Goals of French Missionary Work in Early Seventeenth-Century Brazil." *Church History* 58.1 (March 1989): 20–35.

Fleming, Juliet. "The Renaissance Tattoo." *Res: Anthropology and Aesthetics* 31 (1997): 34–52.

Fleming, Juliet. "The Renaissance Tattoo." In *Written on the Body: The Tattoo in European and American History*, edited by Jane Caplan, 61–82. Princeton, NJ: Princeton University Press, 2000.

Fleming, Juliet. *Graffiti and the Writing Arts of Early Modern England.* Philadelphia, PA: University of Pennsylvania Press, 2001.

Foucault, Michel. *Discipline and Punish: The Birth of the Prison.* Translated by A. Sheridan. New York: Vintage Books, 1979.

Fraenkel, Béatrice. *La Signature, genèse d'un signe.* Paris: Gallimard, 1992.

Friedland, Paul. *Seeing Justice Done: The Age of Spectacular Capital Punishment in France.* Oxford: Oxford University Press, 2012.

Friedman, Anna Felicity. *Tattooed Transculturites: Western Expatriates Among Amerindian and Pacific Islander Societies, 1500–1900.* PhD dissertation, University of Chicago, 2012.

Friedman, Anna Felicity. "Tattoohistorian.com." https://tattoohistorian.com.

Gagnon, François-Marc. "'Ils se peignent le visage . . .': Réaction européenne à un usage indien au XVIe et au début du XVIIe siècles." *Revue d'histoire de l'Amérique française* 30(3) (1976): 363–81.

Gagnon, François-Marc. *Premiers peintres de la Nouvelle-France.* 2 vols. Québec: Ministère des affaires culturelles, 1976.

Gagnon, François-Marc and Denise Petel. *Hommes effarables et bestes sauvaiges. Images du Nouveau-Monde d'après les voyages de Jacques Cartier.* Montreal: Boréal, 1986.

Gagnon, François-Marc and Denise Petel. *The Codex Canadensis and the Writings of Louis Nicolas. The Natural History of the New World, Histoire naturelle des Indes occidentales.* Montréal: McGill–Queens University Press, 2011.

Garnier, Samuel. *Barbe buvée, en religion sœur Sainte-Colombe et la prétendue possession des ursulines d'Auxonne (1658–1663). Étude historique et médicale d'après les manuscrits de la Bibiothèque nationale et des Archives de l'ancienne province de Bourgogne.* Paris: Aux Bureaux du Progrès Médical, Félix Alcan, 1895.

Garnot, Benoit. *Le Diable au couvent. Les Possédées d'Auxonne (1658–1663).* Paris: Imago, 1995.

Gaskill, Malcolm. *Witchfinders: A Seventeenth-Century English Tragedy.* Cambridge, MA: Harvard University Press, 2005.

Gaudio, Michael. *Engraving the Savage: The New World and Techniques of Civilization.* Minneapolis, MN: University of Minnesota Press, 2008.

Gaudriault, Raymond. *Filigranes et autres caractéristiques des papiers fabriqués en France aux XVIIe et XVIIIe siècles.* Paris: CNRS, J. Telford, 1995.

Gay, Kathlyn and Christine Whittington. *Body Marks: Tattooing, Piercing, and Scarification.* Hong Kong: The Millbrook Press, 2002.

Gélis, Jacques. *History of Childbirth: Fertility, Pregnancy and Birth in Early Modern Europe.* Translated by Rosemary Morris. Boston: Northeastern University Press, 1991.

Gell, Alfred. *Wrapping in Images: Tattooing in Polynesia.* Oxford: Clarendon Press, 1993.

Gennes, Jean-Pierre de. *Les Chevaliers du Saint-Sépulcre de Jérusalem. Essai critique.* 2 vols. Versailles: Mémoire & Documents, 2004.

Gentilcore, David. *Healers and Healing in Early Modern Italy.* Manchester and New York: Manchester University Press, 1998.

Gérin-Ricard, H. de. *La Croix de Jérusalem dans la numismatique, sur les sceaux et dans le blazon.* Vannes: Lafolye Frères, 1905.

Gimaret, Antoinette. *"L'Autobiographie de Jeanne des Anges (1644): histoire d'une âme ou réécriture d'une affaire de possession ?"* In *Les femmes témoins de l'histoire*, edited by Armel Dubois-Nayt and Claire Gheeraert-Graffeuille, 22–49. *Études Épistémè* 19 (2011).

Gimaret, Antoinette. *Extraordinaire et ordinaire des Croix. Les représentations du corps souffrant, 1580–1650.* Paris: Honoré Champion, 2011.

Giroud, Jean. *De la rouelle à l'étoile. La présence des Juifs à Cavaillon.* Cavaillon: Imprimerie Rimbaud, 2010.

Golden, Richard M., ed. *The Encyclopedia of Witchcraft: The Western Tradition.* 4 vols. Santa Barbara, CA: ABC-Clio, 2006.

Goldsmith, Elizabeth C. "Public Sanctity and Private Writing: The Autobiography of Jeanne des Anges." In *Publishing Women's Life Stories in France, 1647–1720: From Voice to Print*, 42–70. Aldershot, UK and Burlington, VT: Ashgate, 2001.

Goldstein, Claire. *"Mouches Volantes*: The Enigma of Paste-On Beauty Marks in 17th-Century France." Unpublished manuscript, last modified May 2019. Microsoft Word file.

Gomez, Michael A. *Exchanging our Country Marks: The Transformation of African Identities in the Colonial and Antebellum South.* Chapel Hill, NC: University of North Carolina Press, 1998.

Gomez-Géraud, Marie-Christine. *Le Crépuscule du Grand Voyage. Les récits des pèlerins à Jérusalem (1458–1612)*. Paris: Honoré Champion, 1999.

Gomez-Géraud, Marie-Christine. *Écrire le voyage au XVIe siècle en France*. Paris: Presses Universitaires de France, 2000.

Gomez-Géraud, Marie-Christine. "Pèlerinage au féminin: l'écriture confisquée. Le récit du voyage aux Lieux saints d'Hélène Chéron (1671)." In *Figures de femmes. Hommage à Jacqueline Ferreras*, edited by Thomas Gomez, 159–70. Nanterre: Centre de Recherches ibériques et ibéro-américaines de l'Université de Paris-X, 2003.

Goodman, Dena. *The Republic of Letters: A Cultural History of the French Enlightenment*. Ithaca and London: Cornell University Press, 1994.

Le Grand Robert. Dictionnaire alphabétique et anologique de la langue française. 9 vols, 2nd ed. Paris: Le Robert, 1985.

Greenberg, Mitchell. "Passion Play: Jeanne des Anges, Devils, Hysteria and the Incorporation of the Classical Subject." In *Subjectivity and Subjugation in Seventeenth-Century Drama and Prose: The Family Romance of French Classicism*. Cambridge: Cambridge University Press, 1992. 65–86.

Greenblatt, Stephen. *Renaissance Self-Fashioning: From More to Shakespeare*. Chicago and London: The University of Chicago Press, 1980.

Greenblatt, Stephen. *Marvelous Possessions: The Wonder of the New World*. Oxford: Clarendon Press, 1992.

Greenblatt, Stephen. "Mutilation and Meaning." In *The Body in Parts: Fantasies of Corporeality in Early Modern Europe*, edited by David Hillman and Carla Mazzio, 221–41. London and New York: Routledge, 1997.

Greenblatt, Stephen. Foreword to *The Possession at Loudun* by Michel de Certeau. Translated by Michael B. Smith. Chicago: The University of Chicago Press, 2000.

Greenblatt, Stephen. *Hamlet in Purgatory*. Princeton, NJ: Princeton University Press, 2001.

Groebner, Valentin. *Who Are You? Identification, Deception, and Surveillance in Early Modern Europe*. Translated by Mark Kyburz and John Peck. New York: Zone Books, 2007.

Guerzoni, Guido. "*Notae divinae ex arte compuntae*. Prime impressioni sul tatuaggio devozionale in Italia (secoli XV-XIX)." *La Peau humaine. La pelle humana. The human skin*, special issue of *Micrologus. Natura, Scienze e Società Medievali* 13 (2005): 409–37.

Guerzoni, Guido. "Devotional Tattoos in Early Modern Italy." Special issue on *Wearing Images*, edited by Diane Brodart, *Espacio, Tiempo y Forma* 6 (2018): 119–36.

Gustafson, Mark. "The Tattoo in the Later Roman Empire and Beyond." In *Written on the Body: The Tattoo in European and American History*, edited by Jane Caplan, 17–30. Princeton, NJ: Princeton University Press, 2000.

Haddan, Arthur West and William Stubbs. *Councils and Ecclesiastical Documents Relating to Great Britain and Ireland*. 3 vols. Oxford: The Clarendon Press, 1964.

Hamburger, Jeffrey F. *Nuns as Artists: The Visual Culture of a Medieval Convent*. Berkeley, CA: University of California Press, 1997.

Hardy, Jean-Pierre. *Chercher fortune en Nouvelle-France*. Montréal: Libre Expression, 2007.

Harrigan, Michael. *Frontiers of Servitude: Slavery in Narratives of the Early French Atlantic*. Manchester, UK: Manchester University Press, 2018.

Harvard, Gilles. *Empire et métissages: Indiens et Français dans le Pays d'en Haut, 1660–1715*. Sillery, QC: Les éditions du Septentrion, 2003.

Harvard, Gilles. "Virilité et 'ensauvagement': Le corps du coureur de bois (XVIIe et XVIIIe s.)." *Amériques métisses, Clio: Histoire, femmes, société* 27 (2008): 57–74.

Hennepe, Mieneke te. "Of the Fisherman's Net and Skin Pores. Reframing Conceptions of the Skin in Medicine, 1572–1714." In *Blood, Sweat and Tears: The Changing Concepts of Physiology from Antiquity into Early Modern Europe*, edited by Manfred Horstmanshoff, Helen King, and Claus Zittel, 523–48. Leiden: Brill, 2012.

Hitchcock, Tim, Robert Shoemaker, and Clive Emsley. "Crime and Justice—Punishments at the Old Bailey." *Old Bailey Proceedings Online*, version 7.0, October 11, 2012. www.oldbaileyonline.org.

Hodgen, Margaret. *Early Anthropology in the Sixteenth and Seventeenth Centuries*. Philadelphia, PA: University of Pennsylvania Press, 1964.

Höfer, Bernadette. *Psychosomatic Disorders in Seventeenth-Century French Literature*. Farnam, UK: Ashgate, 2009.

Hollander, Robert. "The Letters on Dante's Brow." January 31 2002. Accessed November 1, 2012. www.princeton.edu/~dante/ebdsa/bob013102.html.

Hotton, Hélène. *Les marques du diable et les signes de l'Autre: rhétorique du dire démonologique à la fin de la Renaissance*, Doctoral thesis, Université de Montréal, 2011.

Houdard, Sophie. *Les Sciences du diable. Quatre discours sur la sorcellerie (XVe-XVIIe siècle)*. Paris: Les Éditions du Cerf, 1992.

Houdard, Sophie. "De l'exorcisme à la communication spirituelle: le sujet et ses demons." *Littératures Classiques* 25 (1995): 187–99.

Houdard, Sophie. "Des fausses saintes aux spirituelles à la mode; les signes suspects de la mystique." *Dix-septième siècle* 50.3 (1998): 417–32.

Hsia, Ronnie Po-chia. *The World of Catholic Renewal, 1540–1770*. Cambridge: Cambridge University Press, 1998.

Huet, Marie-Hélène. *Monstrous Imagination*. Cambridge, MA: Harvard University Press, 1993.

Hughes, Diane. "Distinguishing Signs: Ear-Rings, Jews and Franciscan Rhetoric in the Italian Renaissance City." *Past and Present* 112 (August 1986): 3–59.

Huxley, Aldous. *The Devils of Loudun*. New York: Harper, 1952.

Imbert-Gourbeyre, Antoine. *Les Stigmatisées*. Paris: Palmé, 1873.

Imbert-Gourbeyre, Antoine. *La Stigmatisation*. Clermont-Ferrand: L. Bellet, 1894.

Jaberg, Karl. "The Birthmark in Folk Belief, Language, Literature, and Fashion." *Romance Philology* 10.4 (1957): 307–42.

Jablonski, Nina. *Skin: A Natural History*. Berkeley, CA: University of California Press, 2006.

Jablonski, Nina. *Living Color: The Biological and Social Meaning of Skin Color*. Berkeley, CA: University of California Press, 2012.

Jacques-Chaquin, Nicole. Introduction to *Discours exécrable des sorciers*, by Henry Boguet. Edited by Nicole Jacques-Chaquin and Philippe Huvet. Paris: Le Sycomore, 1980.

Jacques-Chaquin, Nicole, and Maxime Préaud, eds. *Le sabbat des sorciers en Europe, XVe-XVIIIe siècles*. Grenoble: Jérôme Millon, 1993.

Jacquin, Philippe. *Les Indiens Blancs. Français et Indiens en Amérique du Nord (XVIe-XVIIIe siècle).* Paris: Payot, 1987.

Jaenen, Cornelius J. "Problems of Assimilation in New France, 1603–1645." *French Historical Studies* 4.3 (Spring 1966): 265–89.

Jaenen, Cornelius J. *Friend and Foe: Aspects of French-Amerindian Cultural Contact in the Sixteeenth and Seventeenth Centuries.* Ontario: McClelland and Steward Limited, 1976.

Jones, Ann Rosalind and Peter Stallybrass. *Renaissance Clothing and the Materials of Memory.* Cambridge: Cambridge University Press, 2000.

Jones, C.P. "Stigma and Tattoo." In *Written on the Body: The Tattoo in European and American History*, edited by Jane Caplan, 1–16. Princeton, NJ: Princeton University Press, 2000.

Keefer, Katrina H.B. "Marked by Fire: Brands, Slavery, and Identity." *Slavery & Abolition* (2019). DOI: 10.1080/0144039X.2019.1606521.

Kellaway, Jean. *The History of Torture and Execution.* New York: Lyons Press, 2000.

Kennedy, Ann and Véra Michel. "Les Peines de Marque du XVIème siècle à nos jours." In *Les atteintes corporelles causées à la victime et imposées au condamné en France du XVIe siècle à nos jours. Actes des séminaires d'histoire du droit pénal, 1998–99, Strasbourg*, edited by Yves Jeanclos, 113–40. Strasbourg: Université Robert Schuman, 1999.

Koldeweij, A.M. "Lifting the Veil on Pilgrim Badges." Translated by Ruth Koenig. In *Pilgrimage Explored*, edited by J. Stopford, 161–88. Woodbridge, Suffolk, UK and Rochester, NY: York Medieval Press and The Boydell Press, 1999.

Konrad, Joel. "'Curiously and Most Exquisitely Painted:' Body Marking in British Thought and Experience, 1580–1800." Doctoral dissertation, McMaster University (Canada), 2011.

Konrad, Joel. "'Barbarous Gallants': Fashion, Morality, and the Marked Body in English Culture, 1590–1660." *Fashion Theory* 15.1 (2011): 29–48.

Koslofsky, Craig. "Knowing Skin in Early Modern Europe, c. 1450–1750." *History Compass* 12/10 (2014): 794–806.

Koslofsky, Craig. "Branding on the Face in England, 1600–1800." Paper presented at the American Comparative Literature Association Annual Conference, Harvard University, Cambridge, MA, March 17–20, 2016.

Koslofsky, Craig. "A Deep Surface? Taking Stock of the History of Skin in Early American Studies." Paper presented at the 23rd Annual Conference of the Omohundro Institute of Early American History and Culture, Ann Arbor, MI, June 15–18, 2017.

Koslofsky, Craig. "Tattooed Servants: The Jerusalem Arms in the Atlantic World." Paper presented at the Renaissance Society of America Annual Conference, New Orleans, LA, March 22–24, 2018.

Kruta, Venceslas. *Les Celtes. Histoire et dictionnaire. Des origines à la romanisation et au Christianisme.* Paris: Robert Laffont, 2000.

La Tourette, Gilles de. *Traité clinique et thérapeutique de l'hystérie d'après l'enseignement de la Salpêtrière.* Paris: E. Plon, Nourrit et Cie, 1891.

Lavenia, Vincinzo. "Witch's Mark." In *The Encyclopedia of Witchcraft: The Western Tradition*, edited by Richard M. Golden. 4 vols. Vol. 4, 1220–21. Santa Barbara, CA: ABC-Clio, 2006.

Lea, Henry Charles. *Materials Toward a History of Witchcraft.* Edited by Arthur C. Howland, 3 vols. New York and London: Thomas Yoseloff, 1957.

Le Breton, David. *Signes d'identité. Tatouages, piercings et autres marques corporelles.* Paris: Métailié, 2002.

Le Breton, David. "Anthropologie des marques corporelles." In *Signes du corps*, edited by Christiane Falgayrettes-Leveau, 73–119. Paris: Musée Dapper, 2004.

Le Brun, Jacques. "L'institution et le corps, lieux de mémoire, d'après les biographies spirituelles féminines du XVIIe siècle." *Corps écrit* 11 (1984): 111–21.

Le Brun, Jacques. "*Cancer serpit.* Recherches sur la représentations du cancer dans les biographies spirituelles féminines du XVIIe siècle." *Sciences Sociales et Santé* 2.2 (June 1984): 9–31.

Le Brun, Jacques. "À corps perdu. Les biographies spirituelles féminines du XVIIe siècle." In *Corps des dieux. Le temps de la réflexion*, edited by Charles Malamoud and Jean-Pierre Vernant, 389–408. Paris: Gallimard, 1986.

Le Brun, Jacques. "Mutations de la notion de martyre au XVIIe siècle d'après les biographies spirituelles féminines." In *Sainteté et martyr dans les religions du livre*, edited by Jacques Marx, 77–96. Brussels: Université de Bruxelles, 1989.

Le Brun, Jacques. "Les biographies spirituelles françaises du XVIIème siècle: Écriture féminine? Écriture mystique?" In *Esperienza religiosa e scritture femminili tra medioevo ed età moderna*, edited by Marilena Modica Vasta, 135–51. Palermo: Bonanno, 1992.

Le Brun, Jacques. "Les discours de la stigmatisation au XVIIe siècle." In *Stigmates*, edited by Dominique de Courcelles, *Les Cahiers de l'Herne* 75, 103–18. Paris: Éditions de l'Herne, 2001.

Levack, Brian P. *The Witch-Hunt in Early Modern Europe.* London and New York: Longman, 1988.

Lewy, Mordechay. "Jerusalem unter der Haut. Zur Geschichte der Jerusalemer Pilgertätowierung." Translated by Esther Kontarsky. *Zeitschrift für Religions und Geistesgeschichte* 55.1 (2003): 1–39. First published in Hebrew under the English title "Towards a History of Jerusalem Tattoo Marks Among Western Pilgrims." *Cathedra* 95 (2000): 37–66.

Littré, Émile. *Dictionnaire de la langue française.* 2nd ed. Paris: Hachette, 1872–1877.

Lorédan, Jean. *Un grand procès de sorcellerie au XVIIe siècle. L'abbé Gaufridy et Madeleine de Demandolx (1600–1670) d'après les documents inédits.* Paris: Perrin et Cie, 1912.

Machielsen, Jan. *Martin Delrio: Demonology and Scholarship in the Counter-Reformation.* Oxford: Oxford University Press, 2015.

Maclean, Ian. *Woman Triumphant: Feminism in French Literature, 1610–1652.* Oxford: Oxford University Press, 1977.

MacQuarrie, Charles W. "Insular Celtic Tattooing: History, Myth and Metaphor." In *Written on the Body: The Tattoo in European and American History*, edited by Jane Caplan, 32–45. Princeton, NJ: Princeton University Press, 2000.

Maertens, Jean-Thierry. *Ritologiques I. Le Dessein sur la peau. Essai d'anthropologie des inscriptions tégumentaires.* Paris: Aubier Montaine, 1978.

Malcolmson, Christina. *Studies of Skin Color in the Early Royal Society: Boyle, Cavendish, Swift.* Burlington, VT: Ashgate, 2002.

Malquoiri Fondi, Giovanna. "De l'irrationnel diabolique au surnaturel angélique: *l'Autobiographie* de Jeanne des Anges." *Littératures Classiques* 25 (1995): 201–11.

Mandrou, Robert. *Magistrats et sorciers en France au XVIIe siècle. Une analyse de psychologie historique.* Paris: Éditions du Seuil, 1980.

Maxwell-Stuart, Peter G. *Witch Hunters: Professional Prickers, Unwitchers & Witch Finders of the Renaissance*. Gloucestershire, UK: Tempus Publishing Ltd., 2003.

Melzer, Sara E. "The Underside of France's Civilizing Mission: Assimilationist Politics in 'New France.'" *Biblio 17* 131 (2001): 151–64.

Melzer, Sara E. "L'Histoire oubliée de la colonisation française: Universaliser la francité." *Dalhousie French Studies* 65 (Winter 2003): 33–44.

Melzer, Sara E. "Une 'Seconde France'? Re-penser le paradigme 'classique' à partir de l'histoire oubliée de la colonisation française." In *La littérature, le XVIIe siècle et nous: dialogue transatlantique*, edited by Hélène Merlin-Kajman. Paris: Presses Sorbonne Nouvelle, 2008, 75–85.

Melzer, Sara E. *Colonizer or Colonized: The Hidden Stories of Early Modern French Culture*. Philadelphia, PA: University of Pennsylvania Press, 2012.

Melzer, Sara E. "'Volontary Subjection': France's Theory of Colonization/Culture in the Seventeenth Century." In *Structures of Feeling in Seventeenth-Century Cultural Expression*, 2nd ed., edited by Susan McClary, 93–116. Toronto: University of Toronto Press, 2013.

Métraux, Alfred and Jacques Lafaye. Introduction to the facsimile edition of *Histoire de la Mission des Pères Capucins en l'Isle de Maragnan* by Claude d'Abbeville. Paris: François Huby, 1614. Austria: Akademische Druck- und Verlagsanstalt Graz, 1963.

Michael, Robert. *A History of Catholic Antisemitism: The Dark Side of the Church*. New York: Palgrave Macmillan, 2008.

Michelet, Jules. *La Sorcière* [1862]. Paris: Garnier-Flammarion, 1966.

Miller, Charlotte Rose. "The Witch's Familiar in Sixteenth-Century England." *Melbourne Historical Journal* 38 (2010): 113–30.

Miller, Sarah E. "Bringing up Demons." *Diacritics* 18(1) (Spring 1988): 2–17.

Monter, William. *Witchcraft in France and Switzerland: The Borderlands During the Reformation*. Ithaca and London: Cornell University Press, 1976.

Monter, William. "Devil's Mark." In *The Encyclopedia of Witchcraft: The Western Tradition*, edited by Richard M. Golden. 4 vols. Vol. 1, 275–77. Santa Barbara, CA: ABC-Clio, 2006.

Munchembled, Robert. *La Sorcière au village (XVe-XVIIIe siècle)*. Paris: Gallimard-Julliard, 1979.

Munchembled, Robert. *Le Temps des supplices: De l'obéissance sous les rois absolus. XVe-XVIIIe siècle*. Paris: Armand Colin, 1992.

Munchembled, Robert. *A History of the Devil from the Middle Ages to the Present*. Translated by Jean Birrell. Cambridge, UK: Polity Press, 2003.

Murphy, Gwénael. "La dévotion corporelle dans les couvents de femmes (XVIIe-XIXe siècles)." In *La Blessure corporelle. Violences et souffrances, symboles et représentations*, edited by Pierre Cordier and Sébastien Jahan, 63–76. *Les Cahiers du Gerhico* 4 (2003).

"My Skin." Curated by Mieneke te Hennepe. Boerhaave Museum, the National Museum of the History of Science and Medicine. Leiden, Netherlands, 2007.

"Nella Pelle/Into the Skin: First International Conference on the Identity, Symbolism, and History of Permanent Body Marks." Conference held December 5–6, 2011. Pontificia Università Urbaniana, Vatican City.

Noonan, F. Thomas. *The Road to Jerusalem: Pilgrimage and Travel in the Age of Discovery*. Philadelphia, PA: University of Pennsylvania Press, 2007.

Norman, H.J. "John Bulwer and His *Anthropometamorphosis.*" In *Science, Medicine, and History: Essays in Honour of Charles Singer*, edited by Edgard Underwood. 2 vols. Vol. 2, 82–99. London: Oxford University Press, 1953.

Nyffenegger, Nicole and Katrin Rupp, eds. *Writing on Skin in the Age of Chaucer.* Berlin: De Gruyter, 2018.

Odahl, Charles Maston. *Constantine and the Christian Empire.* London and New York: Routledge, 2004.

Odle, Mairin. "Pownced, Pricked, or Paynted: Tattooing and Indigenous Literacies." Conference presentation. American Comparative Literature Association, Harvard University, March 20, 2016.

Oettermann, Stephan. *Zeichen auf der Haut. Die Geschichte der Tätowierung in Europa.* Frankfurt am Main: Syndikat, 1979.

Ostorero, Martine. *"Fôlatrer avec les démons." Sabbat et chasse aux sorciers à Vevey (1448).* Lausanne: Université de Lausanne, 1996.

Ostorero, Martine. "Les Marques du diable sur le corps des sorcières (XIVe-XVIIe siècles)." *Micrologus. Natura, Scienze e Società Medievali* 13 (2005): 359–88. Special issue on *La Peau humaine. La pelle umana. The Human Skin.*

Ousterhout, Robert. "Permanent Emphemera: The 'Honourable Stigmatisation' of Jerusalem Pilgrims." In *Between Jerusalem and Europe: Essays in Honour of Bianca Kühnel*, edited by Renana Bartal and Hanna Vorholt, 94–109. Leiden and Boston: Brill, 2015.

Oxford English Dictionary. 20 vols, 2nd ed. Oxford: Oxford University Press, 1989. Online edition: www.oed.com/.

Paige, Nicholas. "Je, L'Autre et la possession; ou pourquoi l'autobiographie démoniaque n'a jamais constitué un genre." In *L'autre au dix-septième siècle*, edited by Ralph Heyndels and Barbara Woshinsky, 385–92. Tübingen: Gunter Narr, 1999.

Paige, Nicholas. *Being Interior: Autobiography and the Contradictions of Modernity in Seventeenth-Century France.* Philadelphia, PA: University of Pennsylvania Press, 2001.

Paresys, Isabelle. "Corps, apparences vestimentaires et identités en France à la Renaissance." *Apparence(s)* 4 (2012). Accessed July 26, 2013. http://apparences. revues.org/1229.

Paris, Gaston. "Le cycle de la gageure." Edited by J. Bédier. *Romania* 32 (1903): 481–551.

Park, Katharine. "The Criminal and the Saintly Body: Autopsy and Dissection in Renaissance Italy." *Renaissance Quarterly* 47.1 (Spring 1994): 1–33.

Park, Katharine. "Country Medicine in the City Marketplace: Snakehandlers As Itinerant Healers." *Renaissance Studies* 15.2 (2001): 104–20.

Park, Katharine. "Holy Autopsies: Saintly Bodies and Medical Expertise, 1300–1600." In *The Body in Early Modern Italy*, edited by Julia L. Hairston and Walter Stephens, 61–73. Baltimore, MD: The Johns Hopkins University Press, 2010.

Patterson, Orlando. *Slavery and Social Death: A Comparative Study.* Cambridge, MA and London: Harvard University Press, 1982.

Pearl, Jonathan L. *The Crime of Crimes: Demonology and Politics in France, 1560–1620.* Waterloo, ON: Wilfrid Laurier University Press, 1999.

La Peau humaine. La pelle humana. The human skin. Special issue of *Micrologus. Natura, Scienze e Società Medievali* 13 (2005).

Pellegrin, Nicole. "L'écriture des stigmates. (XVIe-XVIIIe siècles)." In *La Blessure corporelle. Violences et souffrances, symboles et représentations*, edited by Pierre Cordier and Sébastien Jahan. *Les Cahiers du Gerhico* 4 (2003): 41–62.

Pellegrin, Nicole "Fleurs saintes. L'écriture des stigmates (XVIe-XVIIIe siècles)." In *Femmes en fleurs, femmes en corps. Sang, Santé, Sexualités du Moyen Âge aux Lumières*, edited by Cathy McClive and Nicole Pellegrin, 101–22. Saint-Étienne: Publications de l'Université de Saint-Étienne, 2010.

Penderecki, Krzysztof. *The Devils of Loudun: Opera in Three Acts.* Mainz: B. Schott's Söhne, 1969.

Perrier, Émile. *La croix de Jérusalem dans le blason, étude héraldique et historique.* Valence: Valentinoise, 1905.

Pfister, Christian. *L'énergumène de Nancy, Élizabeth de Ranfaing et le couvent du Refuge.* Nancy: Berger-Levrault, 1901.

Phillips, Edward. "Théophile Raynaud." *The Catholic Encyclopedia.* Vol. 12. New York: Robert Appleton Company, 1911. Accessed July 30, 2012. www.new advent.org/cathen/12672c.htm.

Pierrat, Jérôme and Éric Guillon. *Les hommes illustrés. Le tatouage des origines à nos jours.* Clichy: Larivière, 2000.

Pihlajamäki, Heikki. "Swimming the Witch, Pricking for the Devil's Mark: Ordeals in the Early Modern Witchcraft Trials." *Journal of Legal History* 21.2 (April 2000): 35–58.

Pitts, Victoria. *In the Flesh: The Cultural Politics of Body Modification.* New York: Palgrave Macmillan, 2003.

Poutrin, Isabelle. "Les Stigmatisées et les clercs: Interprétation et répression d'un signe–Espagne, XVIIe siècle." In *Les Signes de Dieu aux XVIe et XVIIe siècles*, edited by Geneviève Demerson and Bernard Dompnier, 189–99. Clermont-Ferrand: Faculté des Lettres et Sciences humaines de l'Université Blaise-Pascal, 1993.

Rateau, Marguerite. "La Récidive et sa preuve dans l'ancien droit français." *Revue internationale de criminologie et de police technique* 25.3 (July–September 1961): 168–77.

Regnard, Paul. *Sorcellerie, magnétisme, morphinisme, délire des grandeurs. Les Maladies épidémiques de l'esprit.* Paris: E. Plon, Nourrit et Cie, 1887.

Rey, Alain. *Dictionnaire historique de la langue française.* Paris: Le Robert, 1992.

Richter, Daniel K. *Facing East from Indian Country: A Native History of Early America.* Cambridge, MA: Harvard University Press, 2003.

Ris-Paquot. *Dictionnaire encyclopédique des marques et monogrammes, chiffres, lettres initiales, signes figuratifs, etc., etc.* 2 vols. Paris: Henri Laurens, 1893; reedited New York: B. Franklin, 1964.

Robert, Ulysee. *Les signes d'infamie au Moyen Âge: Juifs, Sarrasins, hérétiques, lépreux, Cagots et filles publiques.* Paris: Honoré Champion, 1891.

Robins, Rossell Hope, eds. *The Encyclopedia of Witchcraft and Demonology.* New York: Crown Publishers, 1959.

Roper, Lyndal. *Oedipus and the Devil: Witchcraft, Sexuality and Religion in Early Modern Europe.* London: Routledge, 1994.

Rosecrans, Jennifer Allen. "Wearing the Universe: Symbolic Markings in Early Modern England." In *Written on the Body: The Tattoo in European and American History*, edited by Jane Caplan, 46–60. Princeton, NJ: Princeton University Press, 2000.

Rubin, Arnold. *Marks of Civilization: Artistic Transformations of the Human Body.* Los Angeles: Museum of Cultural History, University of California, 1988.

Russell, Ken. *The Devils.* New York: Warner Brothers, 1971.

Sainty, Guy Stair. *The Orders of Saint John: The History, Structure, Membership and Modern Role of the Five Hospitaller Orders of Saint John of Jerusalem.* New York:

The American Society of the Most Venerable Order of the Hospital of Saint John in Jerusalem, 1991.

Sanders, Clinton. *Customizing the Body: The Art and Culture of Tattooing*. Philadelphia, PA: Temple University Press, 1989.

Sauzet, Robert. "Contestations et renouveau du pèlerinage au début des Temps Modernes (XVIe-début XVIIe s.)." In *Les Chemins de Dieu. Histoire des pèlerinages chrétiens, des origines à nos jours*, edited by Jean Chélini and Henry Branthomme, 235–58. Paris: Hachette, 1982.

Sawday, Jonathan. *The Body Emblazoned: Dissection and the Human Body in Renaissance Culture*. London and New York: Routledge, 1995.

Sayre, Gorden M. *Les Sauvages Américains: Representations of Native Americans in French and English Colonial Literature*. Chapel Hill and London: The University of North Carolina Press, 1997.

Sayre, Gorden M. and Carla Zecher. "A French Soldier in Louisiana: The Memoir of Dumont de Montigny." *French Review* 80(6) (2007): 1265–77.

Scutt, Ronald W.B., and Christopher Gotch. *Skin Deep: The Mystery of Tattooing*. London: P. Davies, 1974.

Seignolle, Claude. *Les Évangiles du diable*. Paris: Robert Laffont, 1998.

"Les signes du corps." Musée Dapper. Paris. September 23, 2004–April 3, 2005.

Shalev, Zur. *Christian Pilgrimage and Ritual Measurement in Jerusalem*. Berlin: Max Planck Institute for the History of Science, 2009.

Siraisi, Nancy G. *Medieval and Early Renaissance Medicine. An Introduction to Knowledge and Practice*. Chicago: University of Chicago Press, 1990.

Skemer, Don C. *Binding Words: Textual Amulets in the Middle Ages*. University Park, PA: Pennsylvania State University Press, 2006.

"Skin." Curated by Javier Moscoso. Wellcome Collection. London. June 10–September 26, 2010.

"Skin/Peau." Musée de la Main, Fondation Claude Verdun. Lausanne, Switzerland. June 16, 2011–April 29, 2012.

Sluhovsky, Moche. "A Divine Apparition or Demonic Possession? Female Agency and Church Authority in Sixteenth-Century France." *Sixteenth Century Journal* 27.4 (1996): 1039–55.

Sluhovsky, Moche. "The Devil in the Convent." *American Historical Review* 107.5 (2002): 1379–411.

Sluhovsky, Moche. *"Believe Not Every Spirit": Possession, Mysticism, and Discernment of Spirits in Early Modern Catholicism*. Chicago: University of Chicago Press, 2007.

Soman, Alfred. *Sorcellerie et justice criminelle: Le Parlement de Paris (16e-18e siècles)*. Hampshire, UK and Brookfield, VT: Variorum, Ashgate, 1992.

Soman, Alfred. "Le sabbat des sorciers." In *Le Sabbat des sorciers. XVe-XVIIIe siècles*, edited by Nicole Jacques-Chaquin and Maxime Préaud, 85–99. Grenoble: Jérôme Millon 1993.

Spierenburg, Pieter. *The Spectacle of Suffering. Executions and the Evolution of Repression: From a Preindustrial Metropolis to the European Experience*. Cambridge: Cambridge University Press, 1984.

Stedman, Allison. "Miraculous Journeys: Healing Pilgrimages and Individual Agency in the Age of Louis XIV." Conference presentation. Society for Interdisciplinary French Seventeenth-Century Studies Annual Conference, Rutgers University, November 5–7, 2015.

Stephens, Elizabeth. "Queer Monsters: Technologies of Self-Transformation in Bulwer's *Anthropometamorphosis* and Braidiotti's *Meamorphoses*." In *Somatechnics: Queering the Technologisation of Bodies*, edited by Nikki Sullivan and Samantha Murray, 171–186. Farnam, UK and Burlington, VT: Ashgate, 2009.

Summers, Montague. *The History of Witchcraft and Demonology*. New York: Alfred A. Knopf, 1926.

Summers, Montague. *The Physical Phenomena of Mysticism, with Especial Reference to the Stigmata, Divine and Diabolic*. London and New York: Rider, 1950.

"Tatoueurs, tatoués." Musée du Quai Branly. Paris. May 6, 2014–October 18, 2015.

Taylor, Paul and Scott Keeter, eds. *Millennials: Confident. Connected. Open to Change. A Portrait of Generation Next*. Washington, D.C.: Pew Research Center, 2010.

Thomas, Hugh. *The Slave Trade: The Story of the Atlantic Slave Trade: 1440–1870*. New York: Simon and Schuster, 1997.

Thorndike, Lynn. *A History of Magic and Experimental Science*. 8 vols. New York: Macmillan, 1923–1958.

Thurston, Herbert. *The Physical Phenomena of Mysticism*. London: J.H. Crehan, 1952.

Trépanier, Hélène. "Entre amour-propre et anéantissement: le "je" des autobiographies mystiques féminines." In *La femme au XVIIe siècle*, edited by Richard G. Hodgson, 301–13. Tübingen: Gunter Narr, 2002.

True, Micah. *Masters and Students: Jesuit Mission Ethnography in Seventeenth-Century New France*. Montréal and Kingston: McGill-Queen's University Press, 2015.

Turner, Terrence. "The Social Skin." In *Not Work Alone: A Cross-Cultural View of Activities Superfluous to Survival*, edited by Jeremy Cherfas and Robert Lewin, 112–40. London: Temple Smith, 1980. Rpt. in the *Journal of Ethnographic Theory* 2.2 (2012): 486–504.

Vale, V., and Andrea Juno, eds. *Modern Primitives: An Investigation of Contemporary Adornment and Ritual*. San Francisco, CA: RE/Search, 1989.

Vauchez, André. *Sainthood in the Later Middle Ages*. Translated by Jean Birrell. Cambridge: Cambridge University Press, 1997.

Velliquette, Anne M., Jeff B. Murray, and Deborah J. Evers. "Inscribing the Personal Myth: The Role of Tattoos in Identification." *Research in Consumer Behavior* 10 (2006): 35–70.

Verciani, Laura. *Le Moi et ses diables. Autobiographie spirituelle et récit de possession au XVIIe siècle*. Paris: Honoré Champion, 2001.

Vermeylen, Alphonse. *Sainte Thérèse en France au XVIIe siècle, 1600–1660*. Louvain: Publications Universitaires de Louvain, 1958.

Vidal, Daniel. *Critique de la Raison Mystique. Benoît de Canfield: Possession et dépossession au XVIIe siècle*. Grenoble: Jérôme Millon 1990.

Vigié, Marc. *Les Galériens du Roi, 1661–1715*. Paris: Fayard, 1985.

Vigié, Marc. "La Flétrissure des forçats au XVIIIe siècle. Un exemple de justice emblématique." *Revue de science criminelle et de droit pénal comparé* 3 (July–September 1986): 809–17.

Villeneuve, Roland. *La mystérieuse affaire Grandier. Le Diable à Loudun*. Paris: Payot, 1980.

Walker, Anita M., and Edmund H. Dickerman. "'A Woman Under the Influence': A Case of Alleged Possession in Sixteenth-Century France." *Sixteenth Century Journal* 22.3 (1991): 535–54.

Walker, Anita M., and Edmund H. Dickerman. "The Haunted Girl: Possession, Witchcraft and Healing in Sixteenth-Century Louviers." *Proceedings of the Annual Meeting of the Western Society for French History* 23 (1996): 207–18.

Walker, Anita M., and Edmund H. Dickerman. "A Notorious Woman: Possession, Witchcraft and Sexuality in Seventeenth-Century Provence." *Historical Reflections/ Réflexions Historiques* 27.1 (2001): 1–26.

Walker, D.P. *Spiritual and Demonic Magic: From Ficino to Campanella.* Notre Dame, IN: University of Notre Dame Press, 1975.

Walker, D.P. *Unclean Spirits: Possession and Exorcism in France and England in the Late Sixteenth and Early Seventeenth Centuries.* London: Scholar Press, 1981.

Waterworth, James, ed., and translated by *The Council of Trent. The Canons and Decrees of the Sacred and Oecumenical Council of Trent.* London: C. Dolman, 1848.

Weber, Alison. *Teresa of Avila and the Rhetoric of Femininity.* Princeton, NJ: Princeton University Press, 1990.

Weber, Alison. "Between Ecstasy and Exorcism: Religious Negotiation in Sixteenth-Century Spain." *Journal of Medieval and Renaissance Studies* 23.2 (Spring 1993): 221–34.

Weber, Alison. "Demonizing Ecstasy: Alonso de la Fuente and the Alumbrados of Extremadura." In *The Mystical Gesture: Essays on Medieval and Early Modern Spiritual Culture in Honor of Mary C. Gilles,* edited by Robert Boenig, 147–65. Aldershot, UK and Burlington, VT: Ashgate, 2000.

Weber, Alison. "Spiritual Administration: Gender and Discernment in the Carmelite Reform." *Sixteenth Century Journal* 31.1 (2000): 123–46.

Weber, Henri. "L'Exorcisme à la fin du XVIe siècle, instrument de la Contre Réforme et spectacle baroque." *Nouvelle revue du seizième siècle* 1 (1983): 79–101.

Weller, Chris. "The Identity Crisis Under the Ink." *The Atlantic,* November 25, 2014.

West, Shearer. *Portraiture.* Oxford: Oxford University Press, 2004.

Whiting, John. *The Devils, A Play.* New York: Hill and Wang, 1961.

Wilkin, Rebecca M. "Feminizing the Imagination in France, 1563–1678." PhD dissertation, The University of Michigan, 2000.

Wilkin, Rebecca M. "Essaying the Mechanical Hypothesis: Descartes, La Forge, and Malebranche on the Formation of Birthmarks." *Observation and Experiment in Seventeenth-Century Anatomy, Early Science and Medicine* 13.6 (2008): 533–67.

Wilkin, Rebecca M. *Women, Imagination and the Search for Truth in Early Modern France.* Aldershot, UK and Burlington, VT: Ashgate, 2008.

Williams, Wes. *Pilgrimage and Narrative in the French Renaissance. "The Undiscovered Country."* Oxford: Clarendon Press, 1998.

Wilson, Philip K. *"Out of Sight, Out of Mind?" The Daniel Turner-James Blondel Debate over Maternal Impressions.* Baltimore, MD: Johns Hopkins, 1987.

Wilson, Philip K. *Surgery, Skin and Syphilis: Daniel Turner's London (1667–1741).* Amsterdam and Atlanta: Rodopi, 1999.

Wintroub, Michael. *A Savage Mirror: Power, Identity, and Knowledge in Early Modern France.* Stanford, CA: Stanford University Press, 2006.

Wittig, Monique, "The Mark of Gender." In *The Straight Mind and Other Essays,* 76–89. Boston: Beacon Press, 1992.

Wollock, Jeffery. "John Bulwer (1606–1656) and Some British and French Contemporaries." *Historiographia Linguistica* 40.3 (2013): 331–75.

Zika, Charles. *Exorcising Our Demons: Magic, Witchcraft and Visual Culture in Early Modern Europe*. Leiden and Boston: Brill, 2003.

Zysberg, André. *Les Galériens. Vies et destins de 60 000 forçats sur les galères de France, 1680–1748*. Paris: Le Seuil, 1987.

Index